The Wrecking Crew of '33

12/17/10

To Bob,

Thank you so much for your support.

From one big baseball fan to another, I hope you enjoy the story of the 1933 Senators.

Sincerely,

Gary A. Sarnoff

The Wrecking Crew of '33

The Washington Senators'
Last Pennant

GARY A. SARNOFF

McFarland & Company, Inc., Publishers
Jefferson, North Carolina, and London

Unless otherwise noted, all photographs are from the National Baseball Hall of Fame and Museum, Cooperstown, New York.

LIBRARY OF CONGRESS CATALOGUING-IN-PUBLICATION DATA

Sarnoff, Gary A.
    The Wrecking Crew of '33 : the Washington Senators' last pennant / Gary A. Sarnoff.
        p.   cm.
    Includes bibliographical references and index.

    ISBN 978-0-7864-4291-1
    softcover : 50# alkaline paper ∞

    1. Washington Senators (Baseball team : 1886–1960)— History.
    2. Baseball players— United States— History.   I. Title.
    GV875.W3S27   2009
    796.357'640975309043 — dc22   2009024872

British Library cataloguing data are available

On the cover: Team photograph of the 1933 Washington Senators

Manufactured in the United States of America

McFarland & Company, Inc., Publishers
    Box 611, Jefferson, North Carolina 28640
    www.mcfarlandpub.com

To my parents—
for their love, their support—
and for taking me to baseball games

ACKNOWLEDGMENTS

Like any other author I needed support, and I am thankful to have had the support from so many who helped make this book become a reality, beginning with my good friend Hank Thomas, who wrote a biography about his grandfather titled *Walter Johnson: Baseball's Big Train*. We met for the first time during the fall of 2004, and we have been friends ever since. It was Hank's book, and his knowledge of the Washington Senators, that helped inspire me to write my book.

Baseball author and historian Doug Feldmann, who has written several baseball books, including *September Streak, El Birdos*, and *Dizzy and the Gashouse Gang*, was very supportive in sharing his writing and baseball knowledge.

I am thankful I had Mike Kopf as my copy editor, and his hustle and hard work made a big difference.

Jim Hartley, Washington baseball author and historian, is the most enthusiastic Washington baseball fan I know. It is always fun to talk about baseball and the Washington Senators with Jim.

Ms. Carolyn Thomas, the daughter of Walter Johnson, took the time to give me an interview. It was truly an honor to meet the daughter of the Big Train, and to hear her memories about her dad and the Senators.

Mr. Stevey Myer, the son of Buddy Myer, was nice enough to give me two interviews. I am still thrilled over having the opportunity to talk with the son of my favorite ballplayer from yesteryear.

I had a nice conversation with Mr. Tom Cronin, the oldest son of Joe and Mildred Cronin. Likewise, I enjoyed speaking with Mr. Legg, the executive director of the Alabama Sports Hall of Fame, who knew Ben Chapman after his baseball career, and remembers him as a devoted husband who was likeable and very easy to get along with.

I am also appreciative to have had the support of George Michael (*Sports Machine*), who was prompt in responding to my questions, and from Mike Sowell, who wrote my favorite baseball book, *The Pitch That Killed*. Mr. Sowell was very helpful in explaining his experience when writing his first book.

I was very excited to hear from former Washington Senators All-Star Buddy

Lewis, who sent me a very nice letter about his memories of the players from the 1933 Senators.

I would like to give a special thank you to Mr. Cecil Jordan, and the friendly community of Ellisville, Mississippi. Mr. Jordan knew Buddy Myer and took care of his two bird dogs, Joe and Snow, when Myer was away during the baseball season.

Michael Fellman, historian and Civil War author, who wrote *The Making of Robert E. Lee, Inside War,* and *Citizen Sherman,* kept my spirits up by sharing his writing experiences, and kept reminding me to keep on working.

It was a pleasure to talk with Doug Williams, author of *So Many Summer Fields,* who was nice enough to share his research with me.

Murella Powell, Biloxi, Mississippi, historian, and the staff at the Biloxi Public Library, were very helpful in assisting me with my research during my visit to the Mississippi Gulf Coast. And I also want to acknowledge Susan Blakely of the Laurel-Jones, Mississippi, Library for her help.

Likewise I want to thank the staff at the Cedar Rapids, Iowa, History Center, the staff at the Library of Congress, and the Martin Luther King Library in Washington, D.C., for their support.

I had the pleasure of working with reference librarian Claudette Burke and the rest of the staff, who were all very responsive to my questions and requests.

I would also like to recognize three members of SABR (Society for American Baseball Research): Maxwell Kates, Roger Erickson, and Dave Zeman. Whenever I needed an answer concerning statistics or record holders, these were the gentlemen I turned to.

TABLE OF CONTENTS

1933 WASHINGTON SENATORS ROSTER

Number	Player	POS	B-T	HT	WT	Age	Season*
1	Buddy Myer	2B	L-R	5' 10½	162	29	9
2	Joe Kuhel	1B	L-L	6'	180	26	4
3	Heinie Manush	LF	L-L	6' 2	200	31	11
4	Joe Cronin	SS-MGR	R-R	5' 11	180	26	8
5	Goose Goslin	RF	L-R	5' 11½	185	32	13

1933: *Top row:* Sewell, c; Berg, c; White Hill, p; Prim, p; Schulte, of; Manush, of; McColl, p; Bluege, if; Kuhel, if; Crowder, p; Boken, if. *Middle row:* Russell, p; Thomas, p; Chapman, p; Travis, if; Burke, p; Kerr, if; Weaver, p; Myer, if. *Bottom row:* Rice, of; Stewart, p; Goslin, of; Schacht, coach; Griffith, president; Cronin, if manager; Harris, if; Bolton, c; Altrock, c. *Bat boy:* Mahoney.

1

Number	Player	POS	B-T	HT	WT	Age	Season*
6	Fred Schulte	CF	R-R	6'2	180	32	7
7	Ossie Bluege	3B	R-R	5'11	160	32	12
8	Luke Sewell	C	R-R	5'9	160	32	13
9	Cliff Bolton	C	L-R	5'9	160	26	2
10	Moe Berg	C	R-R	6'	170	31	9
11	Earl Whitehill	P	L-L	5'9	169	34	10
12	General Crowder	P	L-R	5'10	170	34	8
14	Lefty Stewart	P	R-L	6'	170	32	8
15	Tommy Thomas	P	R-R	5'10	175	33	8
16	Monte Weaver	P	L-R	6'	170	26	3
17	Jack Russell	P	R-R	6'1	178	27	8
18	Bobby Burke	P	L-L	6'2	150	26	7
19	Bill McAfee	P	R-R	6'2	186	25	4
22	Sam Rice	CF	L-R	5'9	150	43	19
23	John Kerr	INF	R-R	5'8	158	34	7
24	Dave Harris	RF	R-R	5'11	190	32	6
25	Bob Boken	INF	R-R	6'2	165	25	1
26 & 31	Cecil Travis	3B	L-R	6'1	185	19	1
27	Nick Altorck	Coach				56	
28	Al Schacht	Coach				40	
0	Jimmy Mahorney	Batboy				15	
19	Ed Chapman	P	S-R	6'1	185	27	1
20	Ed Linke	P	R-R	5'10	180	21	1
21	Bud Thomas	P	R-R	6'1	178	22	2
26	John Campbell	P	R-R	6'1	184	25	1
26	Alex McColl	P	B-R	6'1	178	39	1

*Seasons in majors including 1933

Prologue:
Nats Win Flag by
Nosing Out Browns, 2–1

When Joe Cronin arrived at the Washington baseball club's office at Griffith Stadium on the morning of September 22, he was on top of the world. Today was his day, the day after a 2–1 victory over the Browns had clinched the 1933 American League pennant.

He was greeted by stacks of telegrams, sent from all corners of the country, from fans who extended their congratulations, and best wishes for the World Series. There was a telegram sent by the American League President, and many from club executives and managers around the American League. These appeared in the local newspapers:

> Heartiest congratulations to you and all members of your team on winning the American League Nineteen Hundred Thirty-Three championship pennant. The splendid achievement in your first year as manager is outstanding and we are all proud of you. I know the Senators will be successful in the big series, and will bring home the honors for the American League.—Will Harridge, American League President
>
> Congratulations. You are a great boy, Joe. Will be pulling for you on October 3 [first game of the World Series].—Connie Mack, Philadelphia Athletics manager
>
> Congratulations on clinching the Pennant. The American League certainly has a typical representative for the series.—Tom Yawkey, owner of the Boston Red Sox

The Biloxi, Mississippi, Chamber of Commerce sent their best wishes. The small city along the Gulf Coast was the spring training site for the Washington Senators, and their citizens viewed the Nats as their hometown team.

> When the news arrived, the city celebrated.—George Stannus, president of the Biloxi Chamber of Commerce

The New York Yankees, who had been bitter rivals of Washington throughout the season, showed good sportsmanship by sending Cronin their best wishes.

Congratulations, Joe. I will be pulling hard for you in the World Series.— Joe McCarthy, New York Yankees manager

Keep the World Series in San Francisco.— Frank Crosetti, shortstop of the New York Yankees, who was a rookie for the World Series Champion Yankees in 1932. Like Cronin, he was from San Francisco.

With the pennant now wrapped up, the focus of the Washington sportswriters and baseball fans was on the New York Giants, the National League pennant winners, and the start of the World Series, which was less than two weeks away. Later that day a group of sportswriters stopped by to speak with Cronin.

"Are you going to beat the Giants, Joe?" someone asked.

"Did I say that?" replied Cronin. "I'm not making any rash predictions."

Cronin did not have much else to say about the World Series. Not on this day. For now he wanted to enjoy the moment of winning the American League pennant.

1

SPRING TRAINING

"When Clark Griffith hired Joe Cronin as the youngest manager in baseball, his critics (and there were plenty of them) referred to his actions as a 'noble experiment.'"

— Shirley Povich

The community of Biloxi, Mississippi, was hard at work preparing their city for the arrival of the Washington baseball club, which was heading to the small city on the Gulf Coast for spring training. At Biloxi Stadium the ground crew began to lay out the infield, while another crew started to assemble the bleachers. In the locker room Washington's veteran trainer Mike Martin and his assistant "Bobo" Baxter unpacked trunks filled with equipment, uniforms, and medical supplies, and began to organize the lockers and their trainer's area. At the recently renovated Hotel Biloxi the chambermaids dusted, and made sure each room had clean sheets and towels. In the dining room the chef went over the final details with his staff of cooks and waitresses.

After the workday ended, and the sun began to set behind the Biloxi Stadium grandstand, the city became quiet. At Hotel Biloxi the lobby was silent until the familiar radio voice of Ed Wynn was heard coming from behind the door of one of the guest rooms. Inside the room the hotel guest sat up in bed as he pondered managing his baseball team through the 1933 season. He was too deep in thought to comprehend Wynn and his NBC radio show, *Texaco Fire Chief*.

"The Big Show," he said as he leaned up, twisted around, punched his pillow, and laid back. After thinking for another moment he declared, "The ball club makes the manager."

Seated in a chair across the room was Shirley Povich, a twenty-seven-year-old sports editor and columnist for the *Washington Post*, who wasn't sure he agreed. Didn't tough managers like Bucky Harris and John McGraw mold the character of their championship ball clubs? He tried to explain. "But look here, Joe. I thought a manager had to be kind of tough with the boys."

The manager with the 1933 Washington Senators didn't agree. He intended not to be a dictatorial type manager. In his mind the players knew they had a chance to win the pennant, and it was up to them to take it.

Twenty-six-year-old Joe Cronin, the best shortstop in baseball, was about to begin a new chapter in his life as the manager of the Washington Senators. Manager at the age of twenty-six? Fans, players, and writers questioned his hiring. They believed he would fail, and expected the strain of player-manager to be the demise of his great playing career. Who would take such a chance to hire him to manage? The answer was Clark Griffith, the sixty-three-year-old majority owner of the Washington ball club.

Clark Griffith, known around baseball as the "Old Fox," a nickname bestowed upon him years before by an umpire for his resourcefulness, wasn't afraid to take chances when selecting a manager, and he had taken a big risk nine years earlier when he hired his twenty-seven-year-old second baseman Bucky Harris to manage. The press had had a field day with his decision, labeling it "Griffith's Folly," but nobody laughed after the season, when Washington won the American League pennant and the World Series. A year later they repeated as American League champions.

The Senators remained contenders after their brief dominance, but two of baseball's greatest dynasties prevented them from winning another pennant. The New York Yankees won three consecutive pennants from 1926 to 1928, followed by three consecutive for the Philadelphia Athletics. In 1932 the Yankees reclaimed the pennant by winning 107 games, then swept the Chicago Cubs in the World Series, and the American League appeared to be in the midst of another dynasty.

After a losing record in 1928, Griffith replaced Harris with Washington's greatest ballplayer, Walter Johnson. It was believed Johnson would be too nice to be a successful manager, but the former pitching great proved he could keep the discipline and manage a winner, and the Senators won over ninety games under his leadership for three consecutive seasons, 1930–1932.

After the 1932 season Griffith made a tough decision and dismissed Johnson. He admired the great pitcher, and had the utmost respect for him as a person, but believed he lacked something in his character to manage a pennant winner, and decided to return to the "Boy Manager" theme with Joe Cronin.

In Cronin, Griffith saw a leader, and an excellent student of the game, who was eager to learn. He liked the way Cronin took control on the field by firing up his teammates. He made several trips to the mound to talk to his pitchers. He would ask Al Simmons or Lou Gehrig what kind of pitch they hit as they stood on second base. Off the field he would talk with Athletics manager Connie Mack and ask him questions about the game, and would speak with pitcher Lefty Grove about certain hitters around the league. This was the kind of man Griffith wanted to lead his team.

Before leaving for Biloxi, Griffith met with a group of reporters who questioned his managerial decision. The Old Fox leaned back in his chair, put his hands behind his head, and smiled as he puffed on a cigar. He took his cigar out of his mouth to explain to his guests that he wanted Cronin to take the job, but also assured him that it wouldn't be easy, and even suggested he might consider waiting a few years. He assured the reporters that he knew what he was doing in offering Cronin the job, and Cronin knew what he was doing when he accepted it. And he made it clear that the job of leading wouldn't affect his playing.

A few minutes later the meeting adjourned, and as the visitors headed to the door, the last sportswriter in line turned around and took a parting shot at Griffith. "Joe's going to make a few errors and is going to fail at bat at times, but for heaven's sake, don't blame it on his managerial duties."

Not everyone predicted failure for Cronin. Many backed Griffith's choice, including Connie Mack. "I have no doubt Joe Cronin will prove successful as the new manager of the Washington club," said the seventy-year-old manager. "I have watched him play shortstop ever since he broke in with Clark Griffith. Not only is he a great infielder and hitter but also possesses the quality of an inspirational leader. I do not agree with persons who say Cronin will lose some of his efficiency because of his arduous duties as manager. He is broad-shouldered enough to stand the strain without showing ill effects."

American League umpire Roy Van Graflan, who officiated Washington's exhibition games each spring, also approved. While in Biloxi in 1932, Van Graflan told Griffith that Cronin was the likeliest managerial timber in the Majors. "Joe is an outstanding student," Van Graflan said upon hearing about Cronin's hiring. "He always asks for a rule interpretation when a call he does not agree on is made."

Joe Cronin grew impatient as he waited for his players to arrive for the first practice, scheduled for 10 A.M. on February 22. Nine members of the Senators were also restless after the engine broke from the train taking them to Biloxi, and caused the locomotive to come to a halt in the middle of Alabama. As mechanics worked for several hours to reattach the engine, the players stared out the windows at the red mud and cotton plants, and wondered how much longer. After what seemed like an eternity, the engine was reattached; the train moved on and finally arrived in Biloxi, where the players were greeted by the locals, who stood shoulder to shoulder on the station's platform. Biloxi Mayor John J. Kennedy, a huge baseball fan who took an active interest in the Senators, was present to make sure the ballplayers were guided through the crowd and to their waiting cars, which took them to Hotel Biloxi with an escort from the Mississippi State Police.

The happiest ballplayer in Biloxi was outfielder Goose Goslin, who was excited to be back with the Senators, the team he had started his major league career with twelve years earlier. The Washington baseball fans idolized Goslin, and were thrilled when informed back in December that Griffith had traded to bring him back home.

Hotel Biloxi, seen here in a postcard, served as the Washington baseball club's head-quarters from 1930 to 1935 (courtesy of the Biloxi Public Library).

After seven excellent seasons in Washington, Goslin's batting numbers plunged in 1929, mostly due to a falling-out with manager Walter Johnson, and in 1930 his statistics continued to decline. Midway through the 1930 season the fans were shocked when their hero was traded to the Browns, and they expressed their disapproval by booing Heinie Manush, one of the players acquired in the trade, and who replaced the idol in left field.

Goslin was missed and often referenced after a Senators loss. In 1931, as the fans walked down the crowded ramp at Griffith Stadium after Washington lost their opener to the Athletics in extra innings, one fan said, "We ought to get Goslin back," and another fan nodded, believing the outcome would have been different if Goslin were around. Griffith must've agreed because he attempted to get Goose back after the '31 season, but the outfielder balked, saying he wouldn't play for Walter Johnson. When Johnson was dismissed after the 1932 season, Goslin anticipated a trade to the Senators and began to check on train schedules to Washington.

When Goslin arrived in Biloxi he asked to see Griffith, and he was informed the Old Fox was ill with lumbago after playing thirty-six holes of golf the day before. He went directly to the club president's room where he found him in bed. "What's the matter, Pop?" a concerned Goslin asked.

"Nothing now, Goose. The sight of you is a tonic," Griffith replied, and broke into a smile.

Two days later Goslin put on a show at the team's first batting session by belting several long drives. Standing behind the batting cage was a now healthy Griffith. "It looks natural to see Goslin back in a Senators uniform," he said. "He didn't look natural in any other."

"Sure I'm happy to be back," said Goslin. "Washington was my entrance into the Majors. It was the scene of my greatest baseball success. St. Louis was a small city, and the folks there treated me right, but you know 'home' is the place where you are happiest after all."

Joining a team expected to contend for the 1933 American League pennant made the other newcomers almost as happy as Goslin. Their new surroundings made them feel like they were born again with a second chance to their careers.

"For nine years I have been with a losing club. I now find myself in new surroundings with a club that has been up there the last few years," said Earl Whitehill, a lefty pitcher, whom the Senators obtained from Detroit. "I'm glad to get with Washington. It'll be great to be with a ball-hitting club for a change."

"To be with a winning club for a change will be a treat after six years in Boston," said pitcher Jack Russell. "They did everything possible for me there, but something was missing."

"I expect to have a better year than I did with the Browns," said pitcher Lefty Stewart, who came to Washington in the same trade with Goslin. "A tighter defense, and hitters like Cronin, Goslin, and Manush, and the rest of the boys ought to give me more runs to work with."

Another addition to the pitching staff was a cocky twenty-one-year-old Chicagoan named Ed Linke, who had had quite a year in 1932 while pitching for Davenport of the Missouri Valley League. In 240 innings he struck out 232 batters, and with numbers like that, Cronin and Senators trainer Mike Martin expected him to be a menacing sight of over six feet and built like Walter Johnson. To their surprise the rookie was only 5'10" and built like Fatty Fothergill. Linke weighed in at 220 pounds, forty pounds over his playing weight. Cronin handed him a rubber jacket and told him to wear it at all times while on the field.

Linke wasn't sure where he'd play in 1933, with the Senators or with the Senators farm team in Chattanooga. "I hope I could stay with the team long enough to make the trip to Philadelphia," he said. "I know a girl there and I could get some home cooking."

Luke Sewell was Washington's new catcher, acquired in a trade with the Indians back in January. He arrived in excellent spirits and told his new teammates the one about the photographer and the bowling team. Shirley Povich was more amused by the catcher's Alabama accent than his punch line and joked about Sewell's drawl being thick enough to make mud pies. After a week of practices Sewell liked what he saw. "It should have everything. For the first time in a long time Washington will have the batting power it always needed, with fellows like Goslin, Manush, Cronin."

When Washington made their trade with the Browns for Goslin and Stewart, Griffith and Cronin realized this gave them an unbalanced lineup of five left-handed and three right-handed batters. To balance their lineup they made a trade they didn't want to make, but felt they had no choice. They parted with Sam West, who was the best defensive center fielder in the American League. West could cover ground, had a strong throwing arm, and was a good hitter, but he batted from the left side. Therefore Griffith and Cronin added to the trade by swapping center fielders with St. Louis, and got Fred Schulte, a right-handed batter.

"I always did like to play center field in Washington. Plenty of room to field," said Schulte, who believed this was the career break he needed. When he came to the Browns in 1927, he was projected as baseball's next super outfielder, and he began to believe it. He hit .347 in 1926 while playing with the Milwaukee Brewers of the American Association, and the Browns paid $75,000 for him, plus sent the Brewers three players to increase his value to $100,000. In his rookie season he lived up to his press clippings by hitting .317, and earned the praise of the St. Louis fans, but his maiden season ended when he broke a collarbone after colliding with the outfield wall. A year later he collided with teammate Heinie Manush while chasing a fly ball, resulting in another injury and a few cracked teeth.

Schulte bounced back from his injuries and continued to play well by batting over .300 two more times, and twice scoring over one hundred runs, but this didn't fulfill the fans' expectations, since they were looking for another Ty Cobb or Tris Speaker. "I felt a responsibility every time I stepped up to the plate, every time I went after a fly. I overdid it on myself."

Motivated by his new surroundings, Schulte, known to be a hard worker, turned things up a notch. "I never saw Schulte work so hard," said Lefty Stewart, who had been his teammate since the outfielder broke into the Major Leagues.

There were several rookies in Biloxi hoping to earn a spot on Washington's roster. The most promising was Cecil Travis, a nineteen-year-old natural hitter. In 1932, while playing third base for the Chattanooga Lookouts championship team, he hit .362, knocking out thirty-six doubles and nineteen triples. During his first turn in batting practice he hit baseballs far into the Biloxi Stadium outfield. "Did you bat fourth last year?" asked one of the veterans who was impressed by his hitting display.

"No, seventh," answered Travis. "Seventh?" He was serious.

There was talk about Travis batting seventh for Washington and taking over at third base for twelve-year veteran Ossie Bluege. "No one is going to oust me this season," Bluege insisted when asked about losing his starting position. Bluege was an average hitter, but a great defensive player, the best at his position in the American League. "Better than Brooks Robinson," Luke Sewell insisted years later.

Defensively Travis had the tools—a strong throwing arm, a quick release, and good fielding against bunts. He had a few fielding flaws, however, one being his throwing form. Cronin worked with him, correcting his throwing style by showing him the proper way to throw the ball to first base. "I've been throwing the wrong way for two years and that's the first time anyone ever pointed that out to me," Travis said.

By the end of spring training, Travis knew he was destined for another season in Chattanooga and he was OK with that. "I'll be up here someday, anyhow."

Another promising rookie was infielder Bob Boken, who his new teammates called "Frankenstein" because of his square jaw, big feet, and 6'2" frame. The Senators had purchased him for $12,000 from Kansas City of the American Association, where he hit .280 and drove in 113 runs in 1932. He was a handy player to have because he could play all the infield positions, and he was destined to stick with Washington for the season. Joe Engel, Washington's one-man scouting staff, wrote in his report that Boken was another Cronin. Maybe he saw another Cronin because he had a similar lantern jaw, something Griffith found humorous, and each time he looked at Boken's chin he would crack up over how much it reminded him of Cronin's.

Cliff Bolton was a twenty-six-year-old catcher destined to make the Washington roster. In 1931 he played for Washington and spent nearly the entire season watching from the dugout. He did get into twenty-three games, made eleven hits in forty-three at bats for a .256 batting average. In 1930 and 1932, while playing for Chattanooga, he chewed up Southern Association pitching, batting .380 and .338. Cronin knew he had a good hitter in Bolton and wanted him around for pinch-hitting purposes.

Second baseman Buddy Myer called from his home in Ellisville, Mississippi, and left word he was leaving for Biloxi. He was expected to arrive the next day, six days before the mandatory date. It was a full week before he appeared, and his teammates joshed him by concluding he drove through the state of Mississippi in first gear. Although it took him longer than expected to arrive, he was on time and worked hard as usual to ready himself for the season.

Myer was a streaky player who was one of the best second basemen in the league when he was on. When he was in a slump it was hard to believe he was the same player. He was known to be a good hitter, but since he'd hit .313 in 1928 his average had dropped each season, and in 1932 he batted a disappointing .279. For Myer to hit this low, twenty points below his current lifetime batting average, was unacceptable.

What would it take for Myer to break out and become the player the Senators knew he was? Cronin believed he could find an answer and started by building up his confidence. At a Biloxi Chamber of Commerce banquet he introduced him as the best second baseman in the American League. This was a first for Myer.

Joe Kuhel, Washington's twenty-six-year-old first baseman, would move into the starting lineup now since Washington's long-time first baseman and fan favorite Joe Judge was sold to the Brooklyn Dodgers. Ever since Kuhel joined the Senators during the 1930 season, he had been tabbed as Washington's first baseman of the future. In 1931 he unexpectedly started when Judge became ill, and in 1932 he started during the second half of the season after Judge sustained an injury. He played well enough to convince Washington's management he was now their first baseman of the present. Cronin was most enthused about Kuhel and expected a big year from him. While talking to the press in Biloxi he suddenly changed the subject to Kuhel: "Incidentally, watch out for Joe Kuhel this year. With Joe Judge removed as a continual mental hazard Kuhel ought to come along strongly."

All but two players were in Biloxi. One was holding out for more money, while the other's whereabouts were unknown. It was known that Moe Berg had gone to Japan along with Lefty O'Doul and Ted Lyons to teach the game of baseball to the natives, but since then he hadn't been heard from. The player holding out was Heinie Manush, but he soon came to terms with Griffith, and the sweet-swinging outfielder arrived in Biloxi in time to practice and play the entire exhibition season. When he arrived he made a loud entrance and gave his teammates a slap on the back. Griffith cringed when he felt Manush strike his bad back, but didn't seem to mind. He was happy to see his best hitter.

Cronin received a message at the front desk from Berg's dad, who notified him his son had arrived in New York and was heading to Biloxi. Soon the scholarly catcher was present and became the center of attention with his stories about Japan. Each evening the Senators would gather in the lobby and listen to Berg.

"In Japan, 45,000 kids play the game, and they are coming along in great style," Berg told his fascinated teammates. "They are great defensive players, and quick throwers, and they thrive off the applause of the crowd.... A pinch hitter bows to the catcher, umpire, and pitcher. And when the batter is hit by a pitch he bows to the pitcher."

"Baseball has become their national pasttime," Berg continued. "Children play day and night — under the street lamps of Tokyo, or in front of well-lit store windows. There are many sandlot teams and business-sponsored teams. They draw 40,000 to 70,000 a game. College baseball is their Big Leagues. Their talent is equivalent to our class A Baseball."

Berg spoke about the culture, and mentioned how they eat with chopsticks. "Just think — chopsticks," a rookie whispered to another rookie. His teammates requested a demonstration, and someone ran outside, found two sticks, came back to the lobby, and handed them to Berg. He attempted to pick up an object with the sticks, and his teammates laughed when he was unable to do it.

Spring training had an entirely new look compared to previous ones. The

Mildred Robertson (left) and Violet Linda Whitehill enjoy a boat ride in Biloxi in the spring of 1933. At the time Miss Robertson was dating Joe Cronin. Mrs. Whitehill, a model in her younger days, claimed to be the young girl we know today on the box of Sun-Maid Raisins.

Biloxi Daily Herald reported Cronin had his players working hard and injected a college-like spirit into them. Luke Sewell, who claimed this team was better than any other he had been with, believed the team was putting extra effort into their workouts because they liked Cronin. "And then again the old sap of ambition starts to run up and down your muscles with greater speed when you see a pennant hanging over you."

"You know, I'm a ballplayer first, manager second, and the boys know how I feel about it," said Cronin, who was called "Jo-Jo" by his players. "I can't tell you how much I appreciate the wonderful spirit they are showing in training, and the fine straightforward manner in which they deal with me."

Each spring the Senators had a family squabble, and this one involved the manager and his right-hand man, coach Al Schacht. Griffith rented an old rusted Ford for the coaches and trainers to use, and one night Cronin planned on using it to take out his girlfriend Mildred Robertson, who was Clark Griffith's niece. He was forced to change his plans when Schacht took it for his date. When Schacht returned to the hotel at one o'clock in the morning he received a word of warning. "You better stay away from Cronin. He's sore as hell," the night clerk told him.

"How come?" asked Schacht.

"He wanted to take Mildred out, and when he found out you had the car and said you would be back at ten, he waited for you. He quit waiting at midnight. He's steaming."

At the morning meeting the next day Cronin told his team he waited up after the midnight curfew for Schacht and some of the others, and warned he would fine anyone who didn't make curfew. "And that goes for coaches too," he said while looking at Schacht.

Schacht didn't appreciate being singled out before the entire team, and when the meeting adjourned he decided to give the manager a piece of his mind. After each meeting Cronin would ask Schacht for his feedback, but this time received it before asking. "You always ask what kind of speech you made. I want to tell you right quick that this one was the lousiest one you ever made." Cronin glared at Schacht, and Schacht glared right back at him. Then the two smiled. Schacht laughed and Cronin gave him a playful punch.

The Biloxi community was excited over hosting six Senators exhibition games, including two against the Cleveland Indians. Mayor Kennedy declared a half-holiday for the day of the first Indians game, and Biloxi celebrated. The day was filled with festivities, starting with Nick Altrock, Washington's comical coach, leading a parade through the streets with the Biloxi High School Band following. The game drew over 2,000 people, who were disappointed after watching the Senators fall to the Indians 8–5. Late in the game Cronin made a costly error, leaving a Biloxi sportswriter questioning if the role as manager would distract him in the field.

The following day heavy rains soaked the field, and the game was called

Biloxi Stadium was the spring training home of the Washington Senators from 1930 to 1935. The tents on the field are for the encampment of the Minnesota National Guard during a special exercise in 1939. Where the stadium once stood is now the grounds of Keesler Air Force Base (courtesy of the Keesler Air Force base).

after Cronin and Indians manager Roger Peckinpaugh agreed not to play and risk player injury. Biloxi baseball fans hoped they would reconsider when the sun broke through, but the Indians had already left town. Cronin took advantage of the sunshine by calling for a team practice where he put his players through an intense workout.

The people of Biloxi wished the Senators good luck as they departed to continue the rest of the exhibition season in other cities. One of those cities was Atlanta, where Griffith and another businessman, who at that time called Atlanta's federal prison his home, were creating a great human-interest story by planning a ball game featuring players from the Senators and the Atlanta Crackers versus a team of inmates. The other businessman, Al Capone, would get a cut of the gate receipts, but the game never happened due to lack of interest among the inmates.

While in Atlanta, Nick Altrock, Heinie Manush, and a few others toured the penitentiary. During their journey they passed through the working area and spotted inmate number 40886. Capone looked up, noticed he was being watched, and didn't approve. He expressed his dissatisfaction by glaring at his observers. Altrock gave him a salute, and Capone acknowledged the group of ballplayers with a smile.

The sportswriters picked the Yankees as the overwhelming choice to repeat as American League champions. Washington was predicted to finish second. No one believed Griffith's off-season transactions mattered, but felt Connie Mack's Athletics, who finished in second place in 1932, wouldn't be as good due to his sale of three everyday players to the White Sox, including outfielder Al Simmons, who drove in 151 runs and scored 144 in 1932. Mack claimed the economic conditions motivated him to sell Simmons, along with third baseman Jimmie Dykes and center fielder Mule Haas, but Mack believed his A's would contend with last year's MVP first baseman Jimmie Foxx and catcher Mickey Cochrane in his lineup, and with the best pitcher in the league in Lefty Grove. Mack also insisted he had quality replacements for the three departed with Pinky Higgins, an excellent player in the Pacific Coast League in 1932, at third base. "Indian" Bob Johnson, another highly rated rookie, would replace Simmons in left field. Doc Cramer, who batted .336 for the A's in 1932, would start in center field.

Picked for fourth were the Cleveland Indians, a talented team coming off four consecutive winning seasons under manager Roger Peckinpaugh, who claimed this year's team was his best since becoming the team's manager in 1928. Cleveland had one of the best pitching staffs with Wes Farrell, who had won over twenty games in each of the last four seasons, and Clint Brown, Mel Harder, Willis Hudlin, and Oral Hildebrand. The Tribe's hitting attack was led by outfielder Earl Averill, who had hit thirty-two home runs in each of the last two seasons, and was a constant thorn in the sides of Washington pitchers.

The Detroit Tigers, managed by Bucky Harris—the former Boy Wonder Manager for the Senators, who didn't enjoy the same success in Detroit as he had in Washington—were picked for fifth. The Tigers had yet to finish in the first division in the four years Harris managed, and he was believed to be on his way out after the 1932 season, but instead received a two-year contract. Twenty-six-year-old Tommy Bridges, who won all five of his decisions over Washington in 1932, including a one-hit shutout, was an up-and-coming star, and Fred Marberry, whom Washington traded to Detroit for Whitehill, would be a welcome addition to the pitching staff. Second baseman Charlie Gehringer was Detroit's best hitter, and this season he would be joined by a powerful rookie named Hank Greenberg, who won the 1932 Texas League MVP award while leading Beaumont to the league championship.

Picked for sixth place were the White Sox, a team that had lost 102 games in 1932, but with the addition of Al Simmons, Jimmy Dykes, and Mule Haas, they were expected to dramatically improve.

The Browns and Red Sox were expected to finish at the bottom of the league, but Browns manager Bill Killifer disagreed, feeling the three-players-for-three-players trade with Washington made his team better by giving them a balance of youth and experience. From Washington the Browns received left-handed pitcher Lloyd Brown, and outfielders Sam West and Carl Reynolds.

The Boston Red Sox had been a dying franchise since their famous sale of Babe Ruth in 1920, and in 1932 the franchise died. Their final record of 43–111 had people saying this was baseball's worst team ever. Hope was on the way, however, with a new owner in a thirty-year-old businessman from New York named Tom Yawkey, who was committed to making the Red Sox a winner, and started by hiring Eddie Collins as his general manager. Collins, who was one of baseball's greatest second basemen, was remembered as a clever ballplayer, and was highly respected for his knowledge of the game. With Yawkey's fortune, and with Collins's smarts, everyone around baseball knew the Red Sox would be revived.

All members of the Senators, from Griffith to Cronin, down to the last reserve, agreed they would not settle for second place. "The Yankees can't be any better than in 1932. We can," Griffith insisted. "That is our one slant that seems to be overlooked. Spirit is something also overlooked and this team is the most spirited team Washington has ever had — more than the 1924 club."

Joe Cronin also spoke out about the overlooked factors. "If we could get a break with the Yankees [in the 1932 season series] without effective left-handed pitching against their wrong-sided power hitters last season, I see no reason why we cannot get a good margin over New York this year with men like Stewart and Whitehill to shoot southpaw slants at Combs, Ruth, Gehrig, and Dickey."

Throughout their careers both Whitehill and Stewart were tough on the Washington batters. Whitehill's curve ball, the best in the American League, snapped like a whip, and each time he faced the Senators he would whiplash the Washington batters with that curve ball. His mastery over them drove manager Walter Johnson up a wall. After a loss in 1931 Johnson, sick and tired of his team's fear of Whitehill, lectured his team. "In the first three innings I was watching closely, and Whitehill didn't have a thing, but you let his reputation for almost always beating us scare you."

Scared of Whitehill was exactly what Washington was and Buddy Myer admitted it, but not necessarily because of just his "reputation" for beating Washington. "Boy, am I glad I don't have to bat against Whitehill this year. His curves used to scare me to death."

With both Whitehill and Stewart now with Washington, the Senators would not have to face them, and hoped the left-handed duo would dominate the Yankees the way they used to dominate the Senators. But the two were not as successful against the Yankees. In 1932 Stewart lost four of his five decisions to New York, while Whitehill lost all of his decisions to the Yankees. "Those scores were close enough for me to have taken the Yanks if I had punch behind me at bat or in the field," said Stewart.

Whitehill knew Cronin intended to match him against Lefty Gomez, the flame throwing lefthander for the Yankees, who had won twenty-four games in 1932, and he welcomed the challenge. "I could beat Gomez any time we meet," he assured the sportswriters.

Joining Stewart and Whitehill in the pitching rotation would be Washington's two twenty-game winners from 1932. General Crowder led the American League with twenty-six wins, and finished the season by winning his last fifteen decisions. Monte Weaver won twenty-two games in his rookie season.

For a spot starter Cronin had the luxury of choosing from Jack Russell, Ed Linke, Bill McAfee, who had won five of six decisions after joining the Senators late in the 1932 season, Bobby Burke, who had hurled a no-hitter in 1931, or Tommy Thomas, who was obtained during the 1932 season and pitched well, but was victimized by lack of run support.

The Yankees were aware the Senators were tabbed as their chief competition, but figured they would handle them with ease. "Our club won 107 games last season," Yankees manager Joe McCarthy noted. "And any team that can do that one year can safely be expected to approach the record the following season, if it doesn't equal it."

Babe Ruth and Lou Gehrig insisted Washington wouldn't be as good as in 1932, and believed they would miss pitchers Lloyd Brown and Fred Marberry. Gehrig also claimed the job of player-manager "would ruin a swell shortstop." "Playing managers like Bucky Harris come along only once in a generation," Gehrig added. "Cronin is not the same type of player."

Philadelphia pitcher George Earnshaw and Al Simmons went against the morals of society and predicted the Yankees to win the pennant. It was considered disloyal back then to predict any team but your own to win. Simmons, who had no love for the Senators or their fans, said "those Yankees should be twenty-five games in front of the field by the last half of July. Who's going to stop them? Washington won't do it."

"If that isn't rank disloyalty then Benedict Arnold led the thirteen colonies to victory in the Revolutionary War," responded Clark Griffith. "I wouldn't want a player like that on my team."

Public enemy number one among the Washington baseball fans since the tail end of the 1930 season was Simmons. His mouth, and the fact he continuously hurt the Senators with his clutch hitting, earned him the ranking, but he lost it in 1932 to the entire Yankees team, Bill Dickey in particular, who slugged a Washington outfielder following a collision. After that incident the respect the Senators and Yankees had for one another turned to hatred, and their bitter rivalry was intensified when the Senators took eleven of the twenty-two games with New York in 1932 to prove they were the one team in baseball who didn't fear them.

No doubt players from both teams circled the dates of the twenty-two Senators-Yankees games on their 1933 schedules. Their first meeting would be in Washington on April twenty-third.

2

THE OLD FOX, THE BIG TRAIN, AND THE WASHINGTON SENATORS (NATIONALS)

"What an old fox you are."
— Umpire Joe Cantillon to pitcher Clark Griffith

In 1912 baseball changed forever in Washington, D.C. when Clark Griffith arrived in the nation's capital to manage the Senators. The group of businessmen who made up the ownership of the Senators believed Griffith to be the man who could change the fortunes of their troubled ball club, and to convince him to accept the job, they offered him an option to buy into the team's ownership. Intrigued by the offer, Griffith accepted the job, and to raise the funds to buy into the team, he mortgaged his ranch in Montana for $27,000, enough for ten percent of the team's ownership.

Managing Washington wouldn't be an easy task. Since the founding of the American League in 1901, the Senators had yet to have a winning season, even with the luxury of having baseball's best pitcher, Walter Johnson. During the first eleven American League seasons the Senators finished last four times, lost over one hundred games three times, and earned the title of baseball's most notable losers. Their losing reputation extended beyond baseball to the vaudeville stage, where a punch line used to describe the city of Washington was "First in War, First in Peace, and Last in the American League."

Washington's losing baseball tradition went back to the 1890s when they played in the National League. The team had the misfortune of being owned by the Wagner Brothers, who constantly sold off the team's best players, assuring the Senators of losing seasons and a place near the bottom of the standings.

In 1903 and 1904 the American League Senators finished last, losing 113 games in 1904. The problem was believed to be the name "Senators," which served as a reminder of the Wagners, so to differentiate and change their luck, the team's name was changed to "Nationals" before the 1905 season. The "Washington Nationals" was the actual team name, but they would never rid themselves of the name Senators, and the team would always be called by either name.

Griffith was determined to change the team's reputation and began in spring training by going back to the fundamentals. The ballplayers went through a spring training like they had never experienced, with Griffith drilling them and re-drilling them, and by evening the players were too exhausted to think about enjoying the nightlife or sneaking out after curfew. The only thing they wanted to do was sleep, and this helped Griffith keep the discipline in his camp.

Clark Calvin Griffith was forty-two years old when he came to Washington in the spring of 1912. He was born in a log cabin on November 20, 1869, in Vernon County, Missouri, the fifth child of Isaiah and Sarah Griffith. Isaiah supported his family by hunting and trapping game until his life came to a tragic end when he was accidentally shot while deer hunting by a seventeen-year-old neighbor. Clark was only three years old when he lost his dad.

With the help of her children Sarah Griffith was able to make ends meet, and as soon as Clark was old enough he pitched in by earning money after learning how to become a trapper and saddling up the horses for the cowboys who passed through the county. One time he saddled the horse for a cowboy by the name of Jesse James, not realizing it until the famous outlaw had ridden.

When Clark wasn't working he played baseball with the other boys around the county. Most of their games took place by the county's hanging tree, and each day Griffith would take a peek to see if he recognized any of the condemned.

Money was scarce and the boys played their games with homemade baseballs, but once they were able to combine their savings for ten cents, enough to buy a baseball from an older lad. The first time someone batted the ball it went flat, and the boys spent the rest of the day looking for the dishonest vendor. They were unable to find him until the following morning when they saw him ... swinging from the hanging tree. Griffith enjoyed telling this story, claiming it was his "first honesty lesson in baseball."

Clark was often ill during his childhood, including a bout with malaria. Sarah was advised that she could help her son regain his health by moving him out of the region, and she choose the town of Bloomington, Illinois, a place she had relatives. Once there, Griffith regained his health, and soon he was back to playing baseball. He earned a reputation around Bloomington as a good pitcher, and one day he caught the eye of the manager of the local team, who signed him to a contract. The manager's name was Jesse Fell, who would never be as well known as his grandson Adlai Stevenson, who went on to be a two-time nominee for the Democratic Party for president.

In 1888, after becoming Bloomington's best pitcher, Griffith was offered a contract by Milwaukee of the Western League. In 1891 he was with the St. Louis Browns of the American Association, considered a major league at that time, then moved on to Oakland after the American Association went under. While in Oakland he led a successful revolt against team ownership for back pay.

Toward the end of the 1893 season Griffith broke into the National League with the Chicago Colts (now known as the Cubs), and one year later he began a streak of six consecutive seasons of over twenty victories. He didn't have an overpowering fastball, or an outstanding breaking ball, but he was brilliant at studying and learning each batter in the league and pitching to their weaknesses. Best of all, he was a master of doctoring up the baseball — a legal tactic in those days. Griffith would cut the baseball with his cleats, rub dirt on it, or do whatever it took to make his pitches approach the batter with an assortment of crazy twists and curves. "Amos Rusie was faster. Any one pitcher could beat Griffith in some sort of twirling. But for brains, cunning, and ability to mix them up, Griff was the best," sportswriter Hugh Fullerton wrote.

Once Griffith was pitching against the Phillies, a team with two of the greatest hitters in baseball history, Ed Delahanty and Nap Lajoie. In the ninth inning Griffith was one out away from a win, had a one-run lead, but there were two runners on base, and due up were Delahanty and Lajoie. Griffith had no idea how he was going to pitch to these guys in this situation. He decided to not pitch to Delahanty and intentionally walked him to load the bases. As Lajoie stepped up to the plate Griffith asked himself, "What are you going to do? Pray or something?" Then an idea came to him.

Recalling how he had pitched the previous winter in the indoor baseball league, where the pitchers threw underhand, he thought he could distract Lajoie by using the same style. Sure enough, his first pitch was popped into the air and the ball was caught to end the game. As Griffith walked off the field, home plate umpire Joe Cantillon, impressed by Griffith's strategy, said, "What an old fox you are." The nickname "the Old Fox" stuck with Griffith for the rest of his playing days, throughout his managing career, and as a baseball executive.

Washington baseball fans became fed up with watching losing teams, and with the Wagners, who would treat the ballplayers as if they were stocks by selling them once they reached stardom. Disheartened and frustrated, the fans elected to stay away from the ballpark, and this cost Washington its team. After the 1899 season the National League decided to contract from twelve to eight teams, eliminating the four teams with the lowest attendance. Along with Washington the cities of Baltimore, Cleveland, and Louisville lost their baseball teams.

The National League's decision to contract opened the door for a second major league to emerge, and a man by the name of Ban Johnson, who at the time served as president of the Western League, took notice. Ban Johnson was a big man who weighed nearly three hundred pounds, had big ideas, and always put his energy and enthusiasm behind his ideas to make them become reality.

His energy and enthusiasm made the Western League into the strongest minor league ever, and now he was about to put his next idea into act — making the Western League into the next major league. To help him he had the loyalty and support of his good friend Charles Comiskey, a former baseball star who managed the St. Paul team of the Western League.

The Western League was made up of teams in the Midwest, and to compete with the National League, Johnson intended to expand his league into the East. He took advantage of the National League's decision to abandon Baltimore and Washington, and put teams in those cities to join his new teams in Philadelphia and Boston to become his league's four teams in the East. In the Midwest the teams would be in Cleveland, Detroit, Chicago, and Milwaukee (which would relocate after one season and become the St. Louis Browns). And the name "Western League" was changed to "American League."

Important for the survival of the American League was to have players who were established stars, and the only place to find these stars was in the National League. To get these stars to jump ship, Johnson and Comiskey knew they needed a recruiter, someone who had the confidence and respect of the National League players. The person they had in mind was Clark Griffith, who, in addition to pitching for Chicago, served on the board of the Protective Association of Professional Players, an organization that filed grievances with the National League owners. Griffith wasn't happy with the direction of the National League and believed it was in such disarray it was ruining baseball. He noticed attendance was getting smaller, and wasn't surprised when the league decided to contract. His decision to leave the National League and join Johnson and Comiskey wasn't difficult.

In 1900 Griffith began his recruiting trip, confident enough to promise Johnson and Comiskey he could deliver forty players to them. He fell one short of his promise, but convinced stars Jimmy Collins, Nap Lajoie, Joe McGinnity, and Cy Young to make the change. The one star he could not convince was Honus Wagner. For his efforts Griffith was rewarded with the managing position of Comiskey's new ball club, the Chicago White Sox. With his pitching career still active, he won twenty-four games for the White Sox, who won the American League pennant in its inaugural season of 1901.

Ban Johnson wanted a team in New York City, but wasn't sure which of the teams to transfer. In 1903 he made the decision to move the team with the league's lowest attendance, the Baltimore Orioles, who became the New York Highlanders. Later they would change their name to the New York Yankees. The Highlanders had to be good in order to compete with the other two teams in New York City, the Giants and the Dodgers of the National League. To help them get recognition from the New York sportswriters, Wee Willie Keeler and Jack Chesbro, well-known stars of the National League, were both lured and added to the Highlanders roster. And to be sure the team would be in good hands, Griffith was assigned to manage the Highlanders.

In 1904 Jack Chesbro was magnificent, winning an all-time record of forty-one games for New York, who came within 1½ games of winning the pennant. In 1906 Griffith once again had the Highlanders in contention, but fell short by three games, finishing second to the White Sox. During the 1908 season, with the Highlanders slipping in the standings, Griffith was released as their manager. With the two leagues now on good terms, he returned to the National League and worked the rest of the season as a scout for the Reds, then became their manager for the next three seasons before coming to Washington.

The Senators didn't get off to a very good start in 1912, and by the end of May they were in their familiar place near the bottom of the American League standings. Then suddenly all the hard work and drills during spring training, and the new spirit Griffith injected into the team, took shape. On Memorial Day the Senators won the second game of a double-header in Boston, then headed to the Midwest to play fifteen games in four different cities, and won all fifteen. With a sixteen-game winning streak, they returned home to play the Athletics and won. The streak ended at seventeen games, but put the Nationals in contention for the first time in team history.

Washington remained in contention through the summer, mostly due to the fact they had Walter Johnson, who was now entering his prime at the age of twenty-four. He had won twenty-five games in each of the two previous seasons, and in 1910 he struck out 313 batters while posting a league-best ERA of 1.35. During the second half of the 1912 season Johnson put together a sixteen-game winning streak, breaking Jack Chesbro's American League record of fourteen consecutive wins, and had his sights set on Rube Marquard's major league record of nineteen.

When Griffith arrived in Washington he had no idea what he was getting in Walter Johnson. He had gotten a glimpse of him when he managed the Highlanders and knew Johnson had a lot of speed, but he had not seen enough of him to know he was destined for greatness. From 1908 through 1911, when Griffith was in the National League, he heard a lot about Johnson's reputation, but said he had to see him with his own eyes to believe "he was the pitcher the American League said he was."

Johnson's winning streak came to a controversial end in late August, when he entered a tie game as a relief pitcher with two runners on base and gave up a hit that scored both runners. The scoring rules of the day made Johnson the losing pitcher, even though the responsibility for the two base runners belonged to the previous pitcher. An outcry from baseball fans throughout the country followed, with unhappy fans writing to the American League office and requesting that Johnson not be charged for the loss, but American League president Ban Johnson backed up the ruling of the official scorer. The fans continued to complain until Walter Johnson put an end to the issue by telling the sportswriters he was personally responsible for the loss.

In September a pitcher for the Red Sox, Smokey Joe Wood, was threatening to top Johnson's winning streak. He had won thirteen games in a row, and would be going for his fourteenth straight against Washington, who came into Fenway Park to face Wood and the Red Sox on September 6. Smokey Joe knew it wouldn't be easy to equal Johnson's string of sixteen, especially since he would have the challenge of pitching against Johnson, who would be tougher than usual with the incentive to defend his record. Wood won the game, 1–0.

Fifty years later Wood recalled the game when interviewed by baseball writer Lawrence Ritter, who used the interview for his book *The Glory of Their Times*. "Well, I may have won the game 1–0, but don't let that fool you. In my opinion the greatest pitcher who ever lived was Walter Johnson. If he'd ever had a good ball behind him what records he would have set!"

Wood won his next two decisions to equal Johnson's record, but he wouldn't surpass it. He lost his next decision on September 20. Johnson finished the 1912 season with thirty-three wins, second to Wood's thirty-four, but once again led the league ERA at 1.39, and with 303 strikeouts.

Washington finished a very successful season in second place with ninety-one wins and finished fourteen games behind the first-place Red Sox, but finished a game ahead of the powerful Philadelphia Athletics, who had won the World Series the two previous seasons. No one could've imagined that outcome before the season started. A name change and the presence of Walter Johnson couldn't make the Senators contenders, but the Old Fox did.

In 1913 Woodrow Wilson threw out the ceremonial first ball on opening day to continue a young Washington baseball tradition dating back to 1910, when President William Howard Taft attended the season's opener and threw out the first ball. The president missed the 1911 season, but Griffith invited Taft to return for opening day in 1912.

After President Wilson made his toss, Walter Johnson took the mound and gave up a run in the first inning, but didn't allow another in Washington's 2–1 win over New York. Johnson would not allow a run for the next forty-eight innings to set a record of fifty-six consecutive scoreless innings, a record that would stand for fifty-five seasons. One day in Boston, with the streak still intact, Johnson allowed a second-inning single before retiring twenty-six batters in a row. In the bottom of the eleventh, a Boston batter singled to center field, and when the ball skidded through the legs of the usually dependable Clyde Milan, the batter made it all the way to third base. A moment later the runner crossed home plate to snap Johnson's amazing streak and give him a heartbreaking 1–0 loss.

For Johnson it was another tough 1–0 loss in his career. He had pitched 10⅓ innings, allowed only two hits, and struck out ten batters while not allowing a single walk. Most remarkably, he threw seventeen consecutive strikes at one point during the contest. As usual, Johnson handled the loss with class, calmly answering the sportswriters' questions, and when asked about Milan's misplay, he responded by saying the outfielder didn't do that often.

The 1913 season was another successful year for Griffith and the Senators, who won ninety games—good enough for another second-place finish. As for Johnson, he won a career-high thirty-six games against only seven losses, pitching eleven shutouts while posting a record low earned run average of 1.14, another record that would stand for fifty-five seasons.

In 1914 a new major league emerged, known as the Federal League, and they took the American League recipe for success by raiding the rosters of the two leagues. They were able to get pitchers Eddie Plank, Chief Bender, and Three-Finger Brown to sign, and while Ty Cobb and Tris Speaker were thinking things over, Walter Johnson was approached. He admired the Federal League for its courage and enthusiasm enough to fix his signature to a contract that would pay him a salary of $16,000 a year, and he also received a signing bonus for another $10,000. When Griffith heard the news, he hit the roof. He threatened Johnson with a lawsuit for breach of contract, but Johnson ignored the threat. When the 1914 season ended, he intended to join the new league and his new team, the Chicago Whales.

Following the 1914 season, Johnson returned to his farm in Kansas with his wife, Hazel, and his family. One night a visitor came by, a fellow Kansan, Fred Clarke, who currently was outfielder-manager for the Pittsburgh Pirates. Clarke got right down to business. He didn't make any threats or say anything about an obligation to a contract. Instead he spoke about the people of Washington, D.C., and how much their hero, Walter Johnson, meant to them.

Clarke's words hit Johnson like a ton of bricks. The pitching star became teary-eyed when Clarke said good night, and this was enough to make him reconsider. A few days later he drove up to Kansas City with Hazel to meet with a much calmer Clark Griffith, who promised to raise the pitcher's salary from $12,500 to $16,000, and in return Johnson gave his word to remain in Washington. There was a problem, however—his brother had already spent the $10,000 signing bonus that Walter had given him to buy a garage, and the bonus would have to be returned to the Federal League.

Griffith gasped at the thought of $10,000, a lot of money in 1915, and it was money neither he nor the nearly bankrupt Senators ownership had. He needed to come up with it right away or lose his pitcher to the Federal League. He went to Ban Johnson for help, but the American League president refused his request. He went to Johnson a second time, reminding him that Walter Johnson would be the Federal League's top gate attraction, but the American League president wouldn't budge.

They didn't call Griffith the Old Fox for nothing, and he went to his former boss, Charles Comiskey, to explain the consequences for his ticket sales if Walter Johnson was pitching for the Chicago Whales. Comiskey had just paid Connie Mack $50,000 for his star second baseman Eddie Collins, and Comiskey also would have to pay Collins's high-priced contract of $15,000. If the Chicago baseball fans were bypassing his ballpark for the chance to see Walter Johnson, then how could he make back the money he spent for Collins and pay the star's salary? Comiskey gave Griffith the $10,000 he needed and Johnson remained in Washington.

There was one important detail still remaining, and that was to make sure Johnson would show up for spring training, and until that actually happened, Griffith and the Senators couldn't rest. To add to the tension, the train Johnson was on was delayed by bad weather, and as Griffith waited impatiently for the train to finally arrive, a Washington sportswriter made reference to "the Big Train" bringing Johnson to spring training, and one of baseball's best-known nicknames was created.

As time moved on the Big Train continued to add to his legend by piling up the victories and the strikeouts, but each season the Senators slipped in the standings, with the exception of 1918 when they managed to finish in third place. In 1919 and 1920 Washington finished in the second division and began to remind people of the pre–1912 Senators.

In 1920 Johnson pitched a no-hitter against the Red Sox, the only one of his career, and this appeared to be the great pitcher's last hurrah. For the first time in his career he developed a sore arm, and later in the season suffered a leg injury, hampering his effectiveness. Johnson finished the season with a losing record for the first time since his rookie season in 1907.

By now Griffith had an opportunity to buy out the current Senators ownership, and in order to do this he needed a business partner. In 1919 Connie Mack introduced him to a Philadelphia businessman by the name of William Richardson, who supported Griffith by putting up the money for forty-eight percent of the ball club, while Griffith borrowed the money from the Metropolitan National Bank to purchase fifty-two percent. Now as the team's president and majority owner, Griffith stepped down as manager and concentrated on his new career of running the day-to-day operations of his ball club.

Two years later Griffith entered another new chapter in his life, this one as the guardian of two children. He and wife, Addie, would never have children of their own, but in 1922 two of Addie's sister's children, Calvin and Thelma, moved in with the Griffiths. No one ever knew why, but it was decided after Addie went to Montreal to visit her sister. Calvin was to be the only one of the seven children to make the move, but after he threw a tantrum it was decided his sister Thelma would join him. Addie arrived back in Washington with Calvin and Thelma and went directly to Griffith Stadium during a ball game, where the two children met their Uncle Clark for the first time.

Back in Montreal, Calvin and Thelma had lived in a poor household. Their father was rarely at home, and when he was present Calvin often was slapped around, until it got to the point where he began to hide when he heard his dad enter their home. In Washington, it was a whole new life for the kids, who now had their own bedrooms, wore clean clothes every day, and had a home with two loving adults. A year after arriving, Calvin went to work for the Senators, starting as the team's batboy. Later he would join the team in their pregame workouts as the batting practice catcher, then pitched batting practice, and would work his way through the front office in preparation to take over the team someday.

A few years later, after Addie's brother-in-law died, the other five children, and Addie's sister, would join the Griffiths in Washington. The oldest child of the family, Mildred, was dating Joe Cronin in 1933.

After retiring as manager, Griffith promoted his long-time shortstop, George McBride, to the position of manager. Washington had a winning record in 1921, but after the season McBride decided he liked coaching more than managing and stepped down. Clyde Milan, another long-time Washington player, took over in 1922, but was too easygoing and the Senators finished with a losing record. In 1923 Donie Bush was hired to manage, but Griffith and Bush didn't see eye-to-eye, and at the end of the year, with the Nats finishing with another losing season, Bush was fired.

In 1924 Griffith made a decision to hire Bucky Harris, his twenty-seven-year-old second baseman, who had never managed, and had only four full seasons of major league experience. His decision was laughed at and tabbed "Griffith's Folly," but Griffith's so-called folly proved to be a brilliant decision when the Nationals won the American League pennant.

Walter Johnson reported for spring training in Tampa in 1924 and felt great after a winter of walking over hills while hunting. He felt even better when he realized the knot under his right armpit had completely healed. That knot had developed a few years before, and prevented him from throwing his blazing fastball with the usual velocity. With his arm at full strength Johnson had one of his best seasons ever in 1924, leading the American League in strikeouts, shutouts, ERA, and in wins with twenty-three. Late in the season he was voted the American League's Most Valuable Player for the first time in his career.

The difference for the Senators and Johnson in 1924 was the supporting cast. First baseman Joe Judge, left fielder Goose Goslin, and right fielder Sam Rice supplied the hitting punch, while Bucky Harris, a fierce competitor, led the way with his strong leadership, clutch hitting, good fielding, and overall aggressive style of play. Smooth fielding shortstop Roger Peckinpaugh served as an inspiration while being the glue of one of the best infields in baseball. Third baseman Ossie Bluege was an excellent defensive player, as was catcher Muddy Ruel, who did a great job in handling the pitching staff. Rookie center fielder Earl McNeely rounded out the starting lineup, and hit .330 after joining the Nats in mid-season. Joining Johnson to help lead the Senators to the best team ERA in the league were lefties Tom Zachary and George Mogridge, and hard-throwing right-hander Fred Marberry, who was baseball's first relief specialist.

Going into the World Series, the Senators were underdogs to the more experienced New York Giants, who had won their fourth consecutive National

League pennant. Fans believed the Nationals were not strong enough to take the Giants, but figured Walter Johnson would get to live his lifelong dream of pitching a win in a World Series game. That didn't happen, however, as Johnson lost both his starts. In game one, he pitched a great game, but lost a tough 4–3 decision in twelve innings. Johnson pitched all twelve innings and threw 164 pitches. Worn out from his outing in game one, he didn't have the usual zip on his fastballs in game five and lost, 6–2.

The Senators hung in there and remained tough throughout the series. With their backs against the wall in game six by being a loss away from elimination, they rose to the occasion and eked out a 2–1 victory to force a seventh game that would be played in Washington.

In game seven Washington scored two runs in the bottom of the eighth to tie the score at 3–3, and with the crowd knowing a pinch hitter had been used for the pitcher during the two-run rally, there came a chant of "We want Johnson! We want Johnson!" And out of the dugout came the Big Train, who headed for the mound with another chance to live his lifetime dream.

October 10, 1924, after Earl McNeeley's single scored Muddy Ruel in Game Seven of the World Series, Washington erupted into a celebration that topped the one on Armistice Day in 1918.

Johnson would work out of a jam in the ninth inning, and again in the tenth. He pitched through the eleventh inning, and the twelfth. In the bottom of the twelfth, with the game still tied at 3–3, and with the Griffith Stadium crowd on the brink of exhaustion, there was one out, no runners on base, when catcher Muddy Ruel hit a pop-up over home plate. The crowd let out a groan, thinking this would be the second out. New York's veteran catcher, Hank Gowdy, didn't think of this as another routine play, such as he had made through out his fourteen-year career. Instead he thought about the game's circumstances, and as he camped under the pop-up he showed his anxiety by vigorously shuffling his feet. Then he made a mental mistake when he dropped his mask onto his path to the ball, instead of throwing it far off to either side. The result was he stepped into it, stumbled, almost fell to a knee as he reached for the ball with his glove hand, and flat-out missed the catch. After the ball hit the ground in foul territory with a "plop" the crowd let out a sigh of relief.

Given a second chance, Ruel hit one down the left field line and made it to second base with a double. Johnson followed by hitting a hard grounder to New York's shortstop, Travis Jackson, who booted the ball for an error. Ruel held at second base, and up came rookie Earl McNeeley.

McNeeley hit a ground ball, heading directly for the third baseman, Freddy Lindstrom, with all the looks of an inning-ending double play. Then the ball mysteriously took a high hop after it apparently struck a pebble. Lindstrom made a high leap in desperation, with his glove hand extended upward, but the ball sailed over him and into the outfield. Ruel headed for third base and saw third base coach Al Schacht violently waving his arm in a circular motion, the signal for him to round third base and attempt to score. Ruel rounded third and proceeded to cross home plate with the winning run to make Washington the World Champions, and best of all Walter Johnson the winning pitcher.

The instant Ruel crossed home plate, Washington, D.C., erupted in its biggest celebration since the Great War ended six years earlier. The crowd at Griffith Stadium stormed the field while the Senators ran to the safety of their clubhouse to celebrate.

After partaking in part of the team's clubhouse celebration, Griffith went back upstairs to his office to get Thelma, who wept in silence as she sat alone in her uncle's office. He grabbed his niece's hand and led her out of his office, then was spotted from below by several fans that cheered at the sight of the Old Fox, shouting out "Speech.... Speech."

"I'm too happy to speak right now," Griffith told the happy crowd. "But it ended the way I wanted it to, with Walter Johnson winning."

3

JOE CRONIN

"Keep swinging, Joe, it looks like the tide of base hits is turning your way."

— *The Kansas City Star*, pulling for Joe Cronin

Jeremiah Cronin considered himself a lucky man, even after he lost everything he owned when the Great Earthquake devastated the city of San Francisco on the morning of April 18, 1906. His children, his wife, Mary, who was pregnant with the couple's third child, and the rest of his family, all were safe following the earthquake and the wide range of fires caused by the tremor.

One piece of furniture, a rocking chair, was all that remained from the Cronins' residence, and along with their one piece of property, they moved into the basement of the small home of Jeremiah's sister, located on Twenty-Ninth Street in the Mission district. It was not a very comfortable situation, but it was at least a place to live, and that was more than most of the earthquake victims had.

Six months later, while the Cronins' were still living in the basement, Mary gave birth to her third child, a boy, who had the same square chin as Jeremiah, and the same sparkling blue eyes as Mary. The name given to their newborn was Joseph Edward.

Shortly after the birth of his third child, Jeremiah found work and he saved enough to buy a house on Persia Street, located in the Excelsior district. Mary and the children also worked to help make ends meet, and when old enough, Joseph contributed to the family income, earning money by delivering newspapers and running errands for whoever needed his help.

When young Joseph wasn't working he was either in school, or participating in sports offered by the playground system of San Francisco. The city had a wonderful playground system for children, and there were playgrounds everywhere, including one within half a mile of the Cronins' residence.

Joe Cronin loved sports, and he excelled on the playground, especially in the game he loved — baseball. He had a dream to play for his favorite team, the

San Francisco Seals. There was no doubt in his mind he would be there some-day, then go on to the major leagues, and he wasn't bashful predicting it to his friends.

Since the Cronins needed every cent, Joe never had a cent to buy a ticket for a Seals game. But he was fortunate when the Seals' owner, Charlie Graham, gave two tickets to every school in the city for every Friday home game. The teachers at Cleveland School, who adored Cronin for his cooperation and good manners, knew how much he loved baseball, and to reward him for his good behavior, they gave him the tickets.

At Rec Park, the home of the Seals, Cronin would focus on the shortstops since that was his position on the playgrounds. While he admired the short-stops, his favorite player was third baseman Willie Kamm, who played with the Seals for four seasons before being purchased by the White Sox.

On the day of any of his baseball games on the playground, Cronin would be the first to arrive, and as he waited for the other boys, he would watch Miss Stella Harris, the director of the Excelsior Playground, prepare the field by push-ing a heavy roller over the infield. Miss Harris noticed Cronin was always the first boy to arrive and was aware of his big blue eyes watching her as she worked.

"How would you like to help me, Joe?" she asked one day.

"What do you want me to do?" replied Cronin.

"Well, you can push one side of the roller while I push the other," Miss Harris said. "I can use a boy with big muscles. I'll give you two cents."

It was hard work for a nine-year-old boy, but Cronin did his best, and soon he was hired as a regular assistant by the playground system.

Miss Harris appreciated his hard work, and she rewarded him a few years later when she purchased a pair of sneakers for Cronin.

"What are these for?" Cronin asked.

"You can't wear old sneakers for the tournament," replied Miss Harris, "you'll trip over them. So I want you to wear these. Maybe they'll bring you good luck."

Cronin was as good in tennis as he was in baseball, and at the age of four-teen he won the San Francisco Junior Tennis Championship. Also at age four-teen he entered Mission High School, and in the spring he was the varsity's starting shortstop for a talented team. The lineup included Wally Berger, who would someday play on the National League All-Star Team; Benny Lom, who went on to be a three-time All-American for the University of California foot-ball team; and Jack Shelly, who wouldn't go on to stardom in athletics, but would make a career as a congressman.

During Cronin's sophomore year Mission High burned down in the spring and classes were called off for the rest of the year, which was fine with Cronin because it gave him more time to play baseball. The following fall the recon-struction was not completed and classes were moved to a Protestant church, which did not make his Catholic parents happy. Mary withdrew her son from classes and sent him to a Christian Brothers high school known as Sacred Heart. This was OK with Joe since he had friends there, many of whom were close friends from his games on the baseball diamond.

At Sacred Heart, Cronin played on the school's soccer and basketball teams, and of course, the baseball team, and he still participated in tennis. With his busy schedule of going to school, studying, and athletics, he still found the time to work and contribute to the family income.

In the spring of 1924 the Sacred Heart Fighting Irish had a great baseball team with Cronin, one of the best prep players in the city, as captain. A teammate of his, Dutch Gloistein, was recognized as one of the best pitchers in California, and with Cronin and Gloistein, the Fighting Irish went undefeated and kept winning through the city playoffs to advance to the championship game. But during the playoffs, Sacred Heart suffered a serious setback when Cronin sprained an ankle and was lost for the championship game against the Wildcats of St. Ignatius High. The Wildcats had a great pitcher named Bud Demeyer, and without Cronin's bat, beating Demeyer and the Wildcats would be tough.

On May 31, fifteen hundred spectators packed Ewing Field, including Jeremiah and Mary Cronin, to witness the city championship. Joe Cronin, who was on crutches, watched the game from the dugout in frustration as Demeyer mowed down his teammates. By the end of the top half of the ninth inning, the St. Ignatius star pitcher had not allowed a single hit. Fortunately for Sacred Heart, Dutch Gloistein was also at his best, and when he retired the Wildcats in the bottom of the ninth, he had not allowed a run while giving up just two hits.

The game moved to extra innings and in the top of the tenth Cronin's teammate, Jim Roddy, got the first hit off Demeyer, a double. With a player in scoring position, and the city championship on the line, Cronin got the call to pinch-hit. He put down his crutches, grabbed a bat, and hobbled to the batter's box for the biggest at bat of his youth.

Demeyer made his pitch, Cronin swung and connected, and the Sacred Heart crowd cheered as the ball fell into the outfield for a hit. Cronin winced in pain as he limped to first base, as Jim Roddy rounded third base and easily made it home for the game's first run. Cronin hobbled back to the dugout as a pinch runner came in. His proud parents, and the rest of the crowd, applauded his brave effort, and his teammates patted him to death after he reached the dugout.

Inspired by their captain's courage, the Fighting Irish rallied for four more runs, and then took the field to finish off the Wildcats in the bottom of the tenth. The Wildcats, however, weren't going down without a fight, and they rallied for two runs. But they fell short, and the Sacred Heart Fighting Irish capped an undefeated season with a 5–2 win to become the City Champions of San Francisco.

After graduation Cronin was offered a basketball-baseball scholarship to

St. Mary's College, but since his family needed him to work, he had to decline the offer, and went to work as an alternate instructor on the playgrounds. He also earned money by playing baseball every Sunday in the semipro league of Napa Valley. Sundays were long days for Cronin with a long journey to the games, starting with a ride on a street car to the Bay after attending Mass at 6:00 A.M., then a trip on a ferry, followed by a train ride to get to the ball-park.

For playing semipro baseball Cronin was offered $7.50 per game, but declined since he knew what others were making, and he negotiated his payment to $12.50. The extra money was worth it to the team since Cronin excelled, and at the end of the summer he was paid a visit by Pittsburgh Pirates scout Joe Devine, who took time off from scouting in San Francisco. He had been looking over a Seals outfielder named Paul Waner. Cronin's favorite team, the Seals, were also interested in him and offered a contract, but the Pirates were the major leagues, and he accepted Devine's offer. For signing he received a

The Sacred Heart infield in 1924, the year the Fighting Irish went undefeated and won the San Francisco city championship: left to right, Amarosa (third base), Joe Cronin (shortstop), Jim Roddy (second base) and Homer (first base).

$200 bonus, which he gave to his family to help pay off the mortgage on their home.

The following spring, at the age of eighteen, Cronin reported to the Pirates for spring training. Knowing he needed seasoning, he wasn't surprised when he was assigned to play the 1925 season in Johnstown, Pennsylvania, of the Mid-Atlantic League. Cronin played well, hitting .313 in ninety-nine games, as he and his teammates won the second half of the season with a 39–19 record, then went on to win the playoffs for the league championship.

The Pirates, who won the National League Pennant, felt they had a great prospect in Cronin, and after the Mid-Atlantic League playoffs they invited the young shortstop to join the team in Pittsburgh for the World Series. Cronin was not eligible to play, but was allowed to sit in the dugout during the series. Pittsburgh's opponent was the Senators, and Cronin had no way of knowing he was cheering against the team he would soon play for, and manage someday. Something else he couldn't have imagined was he would be dating the pretty young lady by the name of Mildred, who was seated in a box seat next to her uncle, Clark Griffith.

In the Series, the defending World Champion Senators won three of the first four games and appeared to be heading for another world championship. At the time no team in the twenty-two-year history of the World Series had ever come back to win after being down three games to one. But the Pirates managed to pull it off to become baseball's world champions.

The following season Cronin was on the Pirates' roster when the season began, but only left the bench to pinch run in the late innings for catcher Earl Smith. On April 29 he appeared in his first major league game, and the following day crossed home plate for his first major league run. A week later he was sent to the minor leagues again, this time to New Haven. He played well, hitting .320, while scoring sixty-one runs in sixty-six games, and helped make New Haven a contender as they battled Providence for the league title.

Cronin wouldn't be around for the conclusion, however. In mid–August the Pirates, who were in a battle for the National League pennant, once again wanted him on their roster. The day he joined the Pirates he sat on the bench feeling too timid to join his teammates on the field during their pre-game practice. Bill McKechnie, the Pirates' manager, wasn't happy when he saw Cronin sitting alone while the others were on the field, practicing.

"Say, who is this kid with the do or die look on his face?" McKechnie asked one of his coaches. "Get this kid to work," he ordered.

The Pirates' manager liked what the saw in Cronin, and he found a place for him in the Pirates' starting lineup at second base, putting him in the number-seven spot in the batting order. He had enough confidence in the nineteen-year-old to start him on September fourth, in a crucial double-header at Wrigley Field. The Cubs won both ends of the twin bill, with Cubs slugger Hack Wilson going three for five in the first game with a home run. Cronin played well, handling all of his fielding chances while getting a pair of hits. Four days later he showed flashes of talent by going three for five in the nightcap of a double-header against the Reds while again handling all of his fielding chances.

McKechnie felt he had a ballplayer in Cronin, who hit .265 in thirty-eight games during his rookie season, and Cronin looked forward to playing more in 1927. But McKechnie wouldn't manage the Pirates in '27 due to personal differences with the team's vice president, Fred Clarke. The new manager was Donie Bush, the same Donie Bush whom Clark Griffith fired after the 1923 season.

Bush didn't see anything in Cronin, and if he could have gotten rid of him, he would have. Fred Clarke still believed he had a good prospect, and he insisted on keeping him. He couldn't send Cronin back to the minors since the Pirates had already assigned him to play in Johnstown and New Haven. The rule of the day was if a team sent a player to the minors for a third time they would have to part with the ballplayer and any team was free to sign him. Clarke wasn't ready to part with Cronin.

The way Bush saw it he had to keep Cronin, but didn't have to play him, and he never played him. For the entire season Cronin got into only twelve games, and it would have been fewer had there not been an emergency. It happened on June 29 in St. Louis, with the first-place Pirates holding a one-game lead over the Cardinals. Glenn Wright, the talented twenty-six-year-old short-stop for the Pirates, was at bat. Cardinals pitcher Vic Keen accidentally misdirected his fastball, and the ball struck the star behind his ear. Wright fell to the ground like he had been shot and was out like a light. Keen sprinted towards the plate, fearful the worst had occurred, his face expressing panic. The players and spectators also panicked and several spectators screamed — two of them were so frightened they fainted. Players from both teams emptied out of the dugouts and ran towards home plate to attend to the injured ballplayer.

Wright regained consciousness while his teammates were carrying him to the clubhouse, where a physician examined him and said he was not seriously injured. He was taken to St. John's Hospital for precautionary reasons, and would remain there for the next few days. When Wright was discharged from the hospital he headed back to Pittsburgh by train with teammate Lee Meadows, who was sent with him to be sure he made it home safely. When their train reached Dennison, Ohio, it collided with a freight train. The two ballplayers and the other passengers were shaken up, but OK. They transferred to a different train and got home without any other problems.

With Wright out of action, Bush called on a replacement, and it wasn't Cronin. Hal Rhyne, a former San Francisco Seals infielder who was in his second season in the majors, got the call, and he didn't do very well. In his second start Rhyne made two errors in Pittsburgh's 10–9 loss, and when the Pirates returned home to play the Reds, Bush turned to Cronin.

To this point in the season, Cronin had played in only five games, four of them as a late inning substitution at second base, and one game as a pinch hitter. Cronin responded by belting out three hits in five at bats in the first game of a double-header. The next day he went three for five again, and helped the Pirates come from a 5–1 deficit and win 7–6.

The series with the Reds moved to Cincinnati, with Cronin in the lineup for the third consecutive day. The Pirates led in the sixth inning and appeared to be on their way to another win until disaster struck. Cronin lost his composure in the field and made three throwing errors in one inning on three consecutive ground balls. The Reds capitalized and rallied for a big inning to take the lead. In the dugout Donie Bush was seething as he watched his first baseman leap high three times attempting to catch Cronin's errant throws, and in the top of the seventh the Pirates manager humiliated him by removing him from the game for a pinch-hitter. A day later sixty thousand came to Forbes Field to watch the Pirates and Cardinals battle in a morning and afternoon game. Rhyne played shortstop in both games and went three for eight on the day as the Pirates won both ends of the double-header, and were on their way to the National League pennant.

Cronin was out of the picture, and for all practical purposes, he was done with the Pirates. He would start in one more game — the day after the Pirates won the pennant, when all the reserves started so the regulars could rest for the coming World Series against the Yankees. Not trusting Cronin as a shortstop, Bush put him at first base. In the World Series, Cronin never left the dugout and watched his teammates get swept in four straight games.

When spring training started in 1928, Cronin had plenty of competition for the last infield spot on the Pirates' roster. Hal Rhyne was gone, but there were two promising youngsters in camp, and another infielder who was added during the spring. Among the utility infielders, Bush was highest on twenty-year-old Dick Bartell. "This kid, Bartell, is a cinch to land a big league job before many summers pass," Bush told the press. As for Cronin, it was known he wouldn't be a Pirate much longer. He got a chance to stay around and play when Bartell went out of action with a bruised knee, and he made the best of his chance by helping the reserves win four straight games over the regulars in the Pirates inter-squad games. Manager Donie Bush, however, reiterated to the press that he was not impressed with Cronin.

A few days later Cronin hit a home run against the San Francisco Seals in what turned out to be his last at bat for the Pirates. Bartell rejoined the team the following day, and that evening Cronin received word he was going back to the minor leagues. This was Cronin's third trip to the minors, and it meant he was no longer under contract with the Pirates. Pittsburgh elected to send him to the Kansas City Blues of the American Association, a minor league team the Pirates were close to, so maybe someday the Pirates would pay the Blues to get Cronin back.

Cronin arrived in Kansas City on a cold day and reported to his new manager, Dutch Zwilling, a former catcher for Kansas City who had played in the major leagues for Chicago's three major league teams, the Cubs, the White Sox, and the Whales of the Federal League. George Muehlebach owned the Blues and usually put a strong team on the field. Because his teams were good, the people of Kansas City often came out to Muehlebach Stadium in large numbers. The support of the fans of Kansas City won the only award the fans could earn in baseball, the Hickory Cup, given each year to the team in the American Association with the best opening day attendance. In 1928 Kansas City would once again win the prize with an opening day crowd of 14,150.

With the temperature in the low forties, and after a long train ride from California, the last thing anyone would want to do was practice. But Cronin was determined to make it back to the Big Show, and after he was fitted with a uniform with a big number "17" on the back, he joined his new teammates on the field. A sportswriter from the *Kansas City Star* watched him and was impressed. He liked the way the Californian handled himself in the field, and he liked his range. After practice Cronin told the writer he would rather be in the minors and play every day rather than wear a major league uniform and watch the games from the dugout.

A few days later the Chicago Cubs were at Muehlebach Stadium to take on the Blues in an exhibition game on a very cold and windy day. Five hundred brave fans attended the game. "Five hundred fans who should have their heads examined," according to the *Chicago Tribune*. Midway through the game Cronin came off the bench and replaced the Blues shortstop, Topper Rigney, who was the starting shortstop the year before with Washington for a short time. Cronin went hitless in his two at bats, but won the praises of Cubs Manager Joe McCarthy. "Cronin will prove to be one of the fielding sensations of the American Association. If he can hit he will be worth a lot of money," McCarthy told Muehlebach.

"But could he hit?" questioned the *Kansas City Star*, claiming Cronin needed a lot of batting practice. The next day he showed maybe he could hit when he tagged Cubs pitcher Pat Malone for a triple.

Cronin continued to work after the season started, often remaining on the field after practices or a game to take additional fielding practice. He always could find someone willing to hit ground balls to him. "He looks like real class the way he gobbles up grounders, getting to them all directions they are hit. And he throws well. He's a hustler," the *Kansas City Star* reported.

Joining Cronin as a newcomer to the Blues was a promising twenty-one-year-old first baseman purchased from Lincoln, Nebraska, of the Western League, named of Joe Kuhel. Kuhel was acquired to fill the shoes of Joe Hauser, who went to the Athletics after having a great 1927 season in Kansas City. Hauser was most of the reason the Blues had contended the year before, but without him the Blues were expected to sink in the standings.

Kansas City got off to an 11–5 start, with Joe Kuhel leading the way with his batting, and his good work began to make the Kansas City fans forget about Joe Hauser. In one game the young first baseman showed lots of potential by smacking out five hits, scoring four runs, driving home three runs, and stealing three bases. When asked about the pitching in the American Association, he said he found it easier than that of the lower level Western League.

The news about Kuhel quickly spread, and the Cubs sent a scout to look him over. The scout the Cubs sent was Joe Cantillon, the former umpire who had given Griffith his nickname years earlier. (He had played a huge role in Washington baseball history in 1907 while serving as the Senators manager, when he sent someone to scout and sign a semipro pitcher in Idaho named Walter Johnson.) "Kuhel looks like a good find to me. He knows how to handle himself and I think he can hit," Cantillion told the *Kansas City Star*. He informed the Cubs about Kuhel, saying he was the goods and recommending they purchase his contract. Kuhel, however, came down with influenza and wound up in a hospital in St. Joseph for several days. The Cubs called off the deal.

There was another scout in the crowd who watched Kuhel, and that was Joe Engel, Washington's one-man scouting team. Engel watched several games, then left town without signing a player, or even saying a word to Muehlebach. It was reported he did not see anything worthwhile — but he would be back.

With Kuhel out, Zwilling adjusted his infield by moving his third baseman to first base, and promoting Cronin to play in the everyday lineup at third base. He did not get off to a very good start at the plate, and was hitting just .233 after the month of May. In June he got hot and lifted his batting average to .260, but just as things were looking good, he went into a slump again and his average fell back into the .240s.

It couldn't get any lower than this for Cronin, once a promising prospect, now considered a bust with his career hitting rock bottom. He became depressed with trying to play third base, and playing in a city he didn't care for, where the humidity drove him crazy. He wanted out of this situation, and he began to attend Mass every day, praying for a change of scenery.

As the season moved into late July, Cronin's play continued to suffer. In one game he made an error at a crucial time. The next day he went 0 for 5 at the plate, and late in the game, with Kansas City trying to come from behind, he failed to lay down a bunt with two men on base.

Cronin's batting average was now at .242, and he was failing to make the plays when needed. Muehlebach and Zwilling could not go on with him costing them ball games, and now were sure of what they had thought to be a major league prospect had turned out to be a major bust. They questioned if he was even good enough to play in the American Association, and there was talk about sending the struggling infielder to Wichita, a lower level minor league team.

For the thirtieth consecutive day Cronin attended Mass, and this time his prayer was answered when Joe Engel came back to town.

4

The Strange Season of 1928

"Griff groaned a few times and mumbled something to the effect that
Engel must be going 'goofy.'"
— Frank Young, sportswriter for the *Washington Post*, recalling
Griffith's reaction when Joe Engel had purchased Joe Cronin.

When Washington's starting shortstop, Bobby Reeves, reported to Fenway
Park on June 29, he told Bucky Harris he was "worn to a frazzle" and asked the
Senators' manager for a day off. During the 1928 season Reeves was required
to play every day, and play a second position as Goose Goslin's assistant in left
field. The extra work combined with a humid summer wore out the twenty-
four-year-old shortstop.

Reeves was forced to play every day due to injuries, and because Griffith
had decided to limit the Nats' roster to only a few reserves, with a shortstop
not among them. The team got off to a slow start in 1928 and fell out of contention early, leading to a lack of fan interest. With attendance below expectations Griffith lost money, and to help soften his financial losses he reduced his
team's payroll by having fewer reserves.

It was necessary for Reeves to work as Goslin's assistant, or "caddy" as
Frank Young put it, after Washington's left fielder injured his shoulder during
spring training. While the Senators were on the field one day Goslin looked
beyond the outfield and noticed a high school track and field team throwing
the discus. A few minutes later the high school athletes had a guest, and after
trying to throw the disc as far as he could while not using the proper form,
Goslin injured his right shoulder. It affected his throwing arm and he was barely
able to throw a baseball hard enough to crack a windowpane. The last thing
Griffith needed was an outfielder who couldn't throw.

The injury had no effect on Goslin's hitting, however, and because his
big bat was needed in the lineup, Harris had no choice but to play him. To
compensate for his lame arm Bobby Reeves was needed, and each time Goslin
fielded the ball, Reeves sprinted into left field to take Goslin's lob and make

a relay throw to the infield, thus creating a new position — the assistant left fielder.

Both Reeves and Goslin batted well throughout the spring, Reeves lifting his batting average to .362 after going four for four on June 13. But as spring turned to summer and the weather became hotter, Reeves began to lose weight and wear out. On June 19, Reeves stepped on the scale before a double-header and weighed 167 pounds. A few hours later, after starting in both games and collecting five hits while playing in eighty-three degree weather, he weighed himself again and found he had lost 13½ pounds.

In July, with Washington's mercury reaching the upper nineties, the heat combined with the extra work began to take its toll on the blond-haired blue-eyed shortstop. On July 4, with the temperature reaching ninety-seven, Reeves went 0 for 9 in a double-header, and a week later he committed three errors in one game.

Griffith was reluctant to bring in another player, but realized he had to rest Reeves. He gave Joe Engel a blank check and instructed him to buy a minor league infielder, but warned him not to spend too much. Engel knew exactly where to go, and he traveled to Kansas City to talk with George Muehlebach about the purchase of an infielder he had seen in April.

When Engel told the Kansas City owner he wanted to purchase Joe Cronin, Muehlebach thought he was joking. What major league scout in his right mind would want a minor league infielder who was hitting .242, and about to be demoted to a lower-level minor league? When Muehlebach realized Engel was serious, and understood Washington's need for another infielder, he became serious and played hardball. He set the purchase price at $7,500, a lot of money for a struggling infielder, and told Engel to take it or leave it. Engel took it. He filled out the check, and Cronin was a Washington Senator.

Cronin couldn't have been happier to leave Kansas City. As he his quickly packed and got ready to travel to Washington, Engel called to Griffith to tell him the news.

"How much did you pay for him?" asked Griffith.

"Seventy-five hundred," Engel replied.

"You paid how much for him?" asked a surprised Griffith.

"Seventy-five hundred," repeated Engel.

"You paid seventy-five hundred for him!" Griffith blasted into the phone.

"Yes sir," said Engel, who began to talk about bringing Cronin to Washington.

"You bought him for yourself! Not for me! You keep him!" screamed Griffith, who then slammed down the receiver with nearly enough force to put it through his desk. After flinching at the loud click at the other end of the line, Engel wanted to call Griffith back to explain, then made a wiser decision to allow his boss to cool off. When he did speak to a much calmer Griffith he made plans to bring his recruit by Griffith's residence. Or maybe the reason was to introduce him to Mildred, who worked in the Senators' front office as a secretary, and before leaving Kansas City he sent a telegram to her.

Thursday

Dear Mildred

Am bringing home a real sweetie.
Is Joe Cronin so be dolled up Wednesday or Thursday to meet him.
Tall and handsome. Hold all mail. Don't show this to anyone.

Yours

Joe

Engel arrived with Cronin at the Griffith residence after a long train ride. Cronin was tired, his clothes were wrinkled, his hair was messy, and he hardly looked like the Prince Charming Mildred had expected. She wasn't impressed.

Cronin reported to Bucky Harris at Griffith Stadium on the morning of July 16. He met his new teammates, was given a uniform, and sat in the dugout, where he watched his new teammates lose to the Browns in extra innings. Reeves, still desperately needing a day off, made two errors in the defeat. The following day Cronin observed again as Lefty Stewart shut out Washington 5–0, the sixth loss in a row for the Nats.

With no game scheduled for the following day, the Washington players looked forward to a day off and a break from the heat, but their plans changed when Harris called for a morning practice. The players complained and grumbled but followed orders and came out to Griffith Stadium. The practice gave Harris a chance to get a look at Cronin and he liked what he saw. He was pleased how he handled himself at shortstop and so were the writers who were on hand. "He goes to his left and right equally well, and he possesses a strong throwing arm," wrote a sportswriter from the *Washington Star*.

During the practice both Harris and coach Clyde Milan worked with Cronin on his hitting and noticed he stood flatfooted at the plate with a faulty stance, causing him to take a weak cut at the ball. They corrected the stance, and it made a difference in his swing.

Bobby Reeves's wish was granted. Cronin took his place in the starting lineup, and as Goslin's caddy. The extra work didn't seem to bother Cronin, who was thrilled to be back in the Big Show. He didn't seem to mind the temperature and played all eighteen innings of a double-header in ninety-five degree heat. The visiting Detroit Tigers won the first game to extend the Washington losing streak to seven, but the Nats took the nightcap 7–2, as Cronin collected two hits and handled all his fielding chances in both games. Frank Young was pleased with Cronin's performance and wrote, "Cronin fielded his position well today and showed a strong accurate arm."

Cronin started the next day and collected two more hits in Washington's win, and with Cronin in the lineup a day later the Nats won again. Suddenly they had a three-game winning streak.

There was a big difference with Cronin in the lineup. Along with winning three of the four games he started, the Senators made no errors, and Cronin handled all of his twenty-two fielding chances. The Griffith Stadium fans noticed the difference. So did Frank Young, who wrote that Cronin was making a big hit with the fans both for his fine fielding and for his timely hitting, which Young was pleasantly surprised with. "He was not reported as being particularly strong on the attack when he was signed."

On the attack Cronin pounded out seventeen hits in his first fifty at bats for a .340 batting average. The difference was his new stance, allowing him to take a better swing and hit the ball harder, thanks to the tutelage of Harris and Milan. Harris stuck with Cronin for the next two games and the result was two more errorless games, and two more wins to increase the winning streak to five.

While most were impressed with the new shortstop, Griffith was not. His boy was Bobby Reeves, whom he had envisioned of being his team's starting shortstop for years to come. Cronin was Engel's boy, not his, and he refused to acknowledge that Cronin played a role in the team's recent success. When asked about Cronin's being a better fielder than Reeves, Griffith came up with an explanation out of the book of 1,001 excuses. "His [Reeves's] uniform has been too small for him, and because of this tightness, he has been unable to bend over with comfort." Griffith intended to order a new uniform.

With their winning streak at five, the Senators headed west for a long road trip while Griffith remained in Washington and followed his team's results in the sports sections of the Washington newspapers. He wasn't happy when seeing Cronin's name in the box scores instead of Reeves's. He dispatched a telegram to Harris: "Keep Reeves in the line-up. He'll never be a Ball Player if you don't." Harris, who never second-guessed a player, sent a wire back to Griffith. "Neither will Cronin."

Cronin needed to learn to avoid base runners breaking up attempted double plays by jarring into the shortstop with a hard slide while the shortstop covered second base. After taking several hard knocks from opposing base runners, Cronin was forced to sit out a few days to let his bruises heal. Reeves went back into the lineup until Cronin felt fit enough to return.

At Yankee Stadium, with the powerful Yankees in a tight race for the pennant with the Athletics, the Senators played the part of spoiler and swept a double-header by scores of 6–1 and 11–0. Cronin started both games and banged out six hits on the day while over in the Yankees' dugout, manager Miller Huggins became frustrated as he watched in confusion. He had never seen Cronin before and was baffled by his hitting display. He thought he could slow him down by distracting him, and when Cronin came up to bat the Yankees' 5' 4" skipper squealed out, "Curve him! Curve the Busher!"

All season long, opponents took advantage of Goslin's injured throwing arm and were able to take an extra base each time he handled the ball. Harris decided to take him out of the lineup to give his injury time to heal, but after a few weeks of rest Goslin's shoulder was no better. While the team was in Detroit, a specialist named R.C. "Bonesetter" Sweet was called in from Battle Creek, Michigan, to examine Goslin's shoulder. For one hour he worked on Goslin, and his diagnosis was that the collarbone was out of place, causing soreness across his ribs and tying up his arm muscles. The injury was preventing the arm from rotating properly, and his solution was to nurse the arm for a few days, then start throwing easily and naturally. He guaranteed he would be throwing as well as ever after ten days. The next day Goslin was sore from the examination, but was excited, especially since the knots in his shoulder were gone and he assumed a full recovery would happen. But his shoulder didn't heal after ten days, and he became depressed.

In June, Goslin returned to the lineup, still unable to throw, but hitting the ball as well as any time in his career. By the end of June his average stood at .423, but as the season progressed his shoulder continued to ache, and feeling he needed time off to let his injury heal, he asked Griffith if he could take a few weeks off and go back to his farm in Salem, New Jersey. Griffith thought to himself for a moment before he came up with an idea, and he suggested time in Ocean City, thinking the salt water might do a lot of good. His leave of absence lasted just a day, however, after Sam Rice took a pitch on his already injured elbow and would be sidelined for a while.

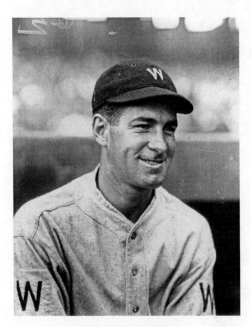

Bucky Harris (pictured) insisted on keeping Cronin in the lineup, regardless of how Clark Griffith felt.

Griffith placed a call to Ocean City to inform Goslin to report right away, and was shocked to learn he wasn't there. He then placed a call to the Goslin residence in Salem, and after hearing the ballplayer wasn't there either, he became worried. The mystery came to an end when Goslin called from, of all places, Atlantic City. It didn't make Griffith very happy to know his star had taken advantage of him, but he had no time to lecture the free-spirited outfielder. He needed him in the lineup and ordered him to report right away.

The Bucky Harris era appeared to be coming to an end in Washington. After his first two seasons he was on top of the world, leading the Senators to their first pennant and World Series championship in 1924, then winning another pennant the following season. Not bad for a manager with no experience, who was tabbed "Griffith's folly" when hired at age twenty-seven.

For Harris's two successful seasons, Griffith rewarded him with a $100,000 contract for the next three seasons. In 1926 and 1927 the Senators didn't win the pennant, but were good, winning eighty-one and eighty-five games respectively. In 1928 they were heading for a losing season, and since 1928 was the last year of Harris's contract, rumors began to swirl about a managerial change. Harris knew what he was up against and told Frank Young, "I consider my position at stake."

It didn't help Harris's chances to remain that he was hearing it from the fans who were not only unhappy about the Nationals' 1928 performance, but were bitter over two trades made during the 1927 season which backfired in 1928. One player traded was Buddy Myer, a favorite among the Griffith Stadium fans, who applauded him each time he came to bat in Washington wearing a Red Sox uniform. The other unpopular trade was that of pitcher General Crowder to the St. Louis Browns in a waiver deal. Both players starred in their new surroundings, with Myer batting .313 in 1928 and leading the league in stolen bases, while Crowder won twenty-one games during the season. At the time of the two trades Harris said the Nats were better off, claiming Myer wasn't ready for the major leagues, and that Crowder couldn't think, but now, one year later, he admitted he had made two big mistakes.

Before the 1928 season, Griffith had a feeling he would part with Harris after the season. He had an opportunity before the start of spring training when new Cleveland Indians owner Alva Bradley sent his general manager, Billy Evans Jr., to Washington to talk with Griffith about purchasing Harris. Evans wrote a check for $125,000 and put it on the table, but feeling Harris deserved to be in Washington for the last year of his contract, Griffith declined. With Harris not available Bradley settled for former Senators shortstop Roger Peckinpaugh to manage his ball club.

When asked if he would rehire Harris for 1929, Griffith remained silent, but did talk about the kind of team he wanted: "What I want is a bunch of fast, peppy, hard-hitting youngsters who, once they find themselves, will be stars for many years." One player who fit the bill was Buddy Myer, and Griffith wasted no time in going to work on bringing him back to Washington. He spoke with Red Sox president Bob Quinn, who made it clear to Griffith he wanted ballplayers, not cash.

After July, Goslin was still hitting above .400, and had a comfortable lead in the batting race. He cooled off in August, but by the end of the month was still leading the league and appeared on his way to his first batting title. In September, St. Louis Browns outfielder Heinie Manush got hot and was closing in on Goslin, setting the stage for an unusual conclusion to the season.

As luck would have it the Senators were scheduled to play the last four games of the season in St. Louis, with Goslin's average at .376, Manush's at

.372. In the first two games Manush went five for eight, but Goslin retained his lead by going two for three in the third game and had a two-point lead with one game left to be played. Players on both teams wanted to help their respective teammate win the title, and the umpiring crew was fully aware of the close battle, including the man who would get the assignment to work behind the plate for the final game of the season — Bill Guthrie.

Guthrie was a large man, known as the "Bull" for his bowlegged, barrel-chested physique. He was also known as "Dese-Dem-Dose" for his ability to butcher the English language, and his way of speaking often left players, coaches, and managers speechless. Most of all he was known for his famous line, "It's either dis or dat."

Goslin struck out and grounded out the first two times he came to the plate, then got hold of one and sent it over the center field fence. But in his next at bat he grounded out to fall three-tenths of a point behind. Manush, however, made an out in his last at bat of the day to give Goslin a one-point lead.

With the game headed into the top of the ninth, Goslin was due to bat. A note came to the dugout from the press box updating Goslin on the batting race, with the author including his advice to sit out the at bat, reminding him if he batted and made an out he would lose the title. Joe Judge warned him Manush might think he was yellow if a pinch hitter batted for him. The other players got involved in the conference, with everyone giving his opinion, and as the debate went on Goslin made a decision. He would bat.

In no time Goslin was in trouble with two strikes, no balls, and his batting title in jeopardy. He thought of an idea to save his title: if could make the umpire angry enough to throw him out of the game, he therefore wouldn't be charged with an out and would preserve the batting title. And what better umpire was there than Bull Guthrie, who had a short fuse, and was known to be quick to eject a player.

"Why, those pitches weren't even close," Goslin told Guthrie.

"Listen, wise guy, there's no such thing as close or not close. It's either dis or dat," responded Guthrie.

Goslin responded by acting mad; he yelled, stepped on Guthrie's big feet, and called him names. Guthrie waited for Goslin to finish before speaking.

"OK, are you ready to bat now? You are not going to get thrown out of this ball game not matter what you do, so you might as well get up to the plate. If I wanted to throw you out, I'd throw you to Oshkosh. But you are going to bat, and you better be up there swinging. No bases on balls, do you hear me?"

He heard him all right. The next pitch Goslin swung and hit a fly ball to right-center field. Browns right fielder Beauty McGowan, knowing if he made the catch Manush would win the batting title, ran hard, reached out with his glove hand, but couldn't get to the ball in time, and when the ball landed on the outfield grass Goslin won the batting title.

Washington's final record was 75–79, but with Cronin in the lineup they were 37–26.

"This kid is a natural fielder and a much better hitter than people give him credit for," Harris said of Cronin. "He has saved a number of games by brilliant fielding."

Griffith, however, was set on retaining Reeves and putting Cronin in the deal for Myer. Harris and Coach Al Schacht both pleaded with Griffith to keep Cronin, but the Washington owner had made his mind up. Reeves would stay.

Frank Young, who spoke highly of Cronin when he first arrived, sided with Griffith: "Reeves is a diamond in the rough who will develop into a star someday," stated Young, who also pointed out that Reeves came to the Nationals directly from college and never had the chance to develop in the minor leagues. Another point made was that Reeves would've been better had he not had the extra job as Goslin's caddy.

Young wrote a second article to promote Reeves, claiming he showed fielding excellence that had far exceeded Cronin, but the statistics didn't back this up. Reeves made thirty-six errors on the year, and had a fielding percentage of .908. Cronin posted a .953 fielding percentage, second best among American League shortstops. Young would have had a better argument had he compared the two in hitting. Reeves did have the higher batting average, finishing with a .303 average, while Cronin cooled off after his fast start and finished at .243.

One thing was certain for Cronin in 1929. He would be in the major leagues. The question was where.

5

THE 1929 SEASON

"I don't mind saying that Joe made a big hit with me and I believe he
will be a great player one of these days."
— Walter Johnson

Two days after the conclusion of the 1928 season, Bucky Harris emerged
from Clark Griffith's office and faced the sportswriters. "Well, boys, I'm
through," Harris told them. "President Griffith is the boss and that's his decision."

Griffith promised Harris he'd find him another managing job in the American League. Remembering his conversation with Billy Evans Jr. from the previous year, he contacted the Indians' general manager, but was told he was
content with Roger Peckinpaugh. The job was open in Detroit, however, and
the Tigers didn't hesitate to hire Harris.

Who would be the next manager of the Senators? There was excitement
in the nation's capital when Walter Johnson was mentioned, and on October
12 it became official. The Big Train was hired and received a three-year contract.

What kind of manager would Walter Johnson be? Most thought he was
too nice, too easygoing, to manage a major league team, but one thing was
sure — everyone was pulling for him, including the opposition. "I never knew
Walter well, but I've heard plenty about him and all good," said Lou Gehrig
during a visit to Washington for a New Year's Eve party. "I certainly hope he
will make a good manager."

Johnson pitched three more seasons after his dream came true when pitching the win in Game Seven of the 1924 World Series. In 1925 he won twenty
games, the twelfth time in his career he won twenty or more games in a season, and Washington won its second consecutive pennant. In the first game of
the World Series, Johnson was great, pitching a 4–1 win at Pittsburgh, allowing only five hits while striking out ten Pirates. In Game Four he shut out the
Pirates to give the Nats a three-games-to-one series lead, and Washington

Walter Johnson, who became Washington's manager in 1929, knew Cronin was a ballplayer right from the beginning.

appeared headed to another World Series championship. The Pirates won the next two games, however, to even the series and force a seventh game, and for the deciding game Harris had the Big Train rested and ready.

The weather and field conditions in Pittsburgh were ridiculous for Game Seven. It had rained the day before, forcing a postponement, and the rain continued into the next day. Puddles lined the outfield while the infield and pitcher's mound were a quagmire, but Commissioner Kenesaw Mountain Landis wanted to get the series over with and ordered the game to be played. As the game progressed the clouds opened and the later innings were played in a downpour. Johnson struggled with the elements, and the Pirates capitalized for fifteen hits and erased an early 4–0 deficit. Late in the game, with Washington leading by a run, Pittsburgh rallied for three runs in the bottom of the eighth inning, and held on for a 9–7 win.

In 1926 Johnson opened the season with an incredible performance by blanking the Athletics in fifteen innings while allowing only six hits and striking out twelve in a 1–0 win. He won six of his first seven decisions and appeared to be heading for another twenty-win season, but then he lost seven consecutive games. Age caught up to Johnson, who was now thirty-eight, and he finished the season a disappointing 15–16.

In 1927 Johnson came to spring training in great shape and ready to regain his superstar status, but sustained a fractured ankle when a batted ball hit him as he pitched batting practice. He was sidelined until late May. After he returned he said the injury took a lot out of him and he didn't feel the same. When he did pitch he resorted to curve balls rather than his legendary fastball, which wasn't what it used to be, and after the season the Big Train called it a career.

In 1928 Johnson accepted a managing job with the Newark Bears of the International League, but his debut was delayed when he became so ill with influenza he lost twenty pounds and was in bed for several weeks. After regaining his health and rejoining his team in mid–May, they didn't do very well, finishing in seventh place with an 81–84 record.

After taking care of his managerial situation, Griffith went to work on bringing Buddy Myer back to Washington, but found he had competition. Knowing Boston wanted to unload Myer, the Yankees and the Indians expressed interest, as did Bucky Harris, the man who had traded him, but now wanted him in Detroit. Griffith and Johnson traveled to Toronto for the minor league baseball meetings and met with Red Sox management, who set the cost for Myer at two pitchers and three shortstops—Cronin, Reeves, and Gillis. "The Red Sox seem to value Myer as highly as the Yankees do of [sic] Babe Ruth," said Johnson. "We can't afford to give them our entire team for one player."

At the major league winter meetings in Chicago, Griffith wined and dined the president and the manager of the Red Sox, Bob Quinn and Bill Carrigan, and the two men weren't bashful about eating, drinking, and running up a bill.

Griffith kept the food coming, and between each mouthful his guests spoke about the deal for Myer. When Griffith left Chicago a trade wasn't made, but the teams agreed on three of the five players the Red Sox requested. The holdup was that they wanted Cronin and Reeves, and Griffith was only willing to part with Cronin: "I'd be willing to part with both Reeves and Cronin if I were absolutely positive Myer would prove to be a first class third baseman."

After returning home, Griffith was able to get the Red Sox to agree on either Reeves or Cronin. The fifth player in the deal would be a minor league outfielder, Eliot Bigelow, the Southern Association's leading hitter in 1928 while under contract with the Senators. As far as Griffith was concerned the deal was done. He would keep Reeves and trade Cronin, but Al Schacht again insisted he'd regret the day he traded Cronin.

There was another question about who would start at shortstop. Both Griffith and Johnson planned on using Reeves (or Cronin) as a backup and switching Ossie Bluege from third base, but before this could be done, and the trade for Myer completed, there was a question about whether Bluege's ailing knee could hold up to the strain of playing shortstop. Bluege was called in to meet with Griffith and Johnson, and was asked how he felt about making the change, and if his knee would hold up. Bluege replied he was OK with the change, and assured them his knee would be fine.

There was another question for Bluege: who would he rather have, Cronin or Reeves? His answer was Cronin.

On December 15 the long-awaited trade was made, and the story appeared on the front page of the *Washington Post*: "The third baseman who was not deemed as big league caliber and traded to the Red Sox in 1927 was reclaimed by the Washington ball club yesterday." The cost was five players, with an estimated value of $75,000. They were Gillis, Lisenbee, Gaston, Bigelow, and Reeves.

Throughout the winter the question was: who got the best of the deal? Those who said Boston viewed Reeves as up and coming, and compared pitcher Hod Lisenbee to General Crowder. Those who favored Washington viewed Myer as an established star and said he would only get better. Bill Carrigan was sure Boston got the best of it and felt confident enough to tell the press, "We pulled one over on the Old Fox." By 1933 Milt Gaston was the only one of the five players still in the major leagues, and he was pitching for the White Sox.

It took a long time and a lot of work to get Myer, but there was another question to be answered. Would Myer sign his contract? Both Griffith and Johnson worried he wouldn't. Being traded for five players gave him power, and in the past Myer had proved to be shrewd in contract negotiations. The Indians had found that out after they had recruited him off the campus of Mississippi A&M. In 1925 they had him in spring training, where Indians manager Tris Speaker was impressed and saw a star in Myer. At the end of spring training Speaker offered a contract, and explained he wanted to send him to Dallas of the Texas League, where he would play every day and get professional experience. Myer was OK with that but insisted on a $1,000 signing bonus. Speaker refused to honor such a request for an unproven college kid, and the Indians management backed him up.

Myer left the Indians and went to New Orleans of the Southern Association for a tryout, bringing his older brother Jesse along for moral support. New Orleans manager Larry Gilbert and team owner A.J. Heinemann were impressed and offered a contract.

"How much bonus do I get?" asked Myer.

Bonus? Gilbert was shocked by the request. A college kid was thankful to get a tryout, but to ask for a bonus? Never had Heinemann given a signing bonus, but he made an exception, and his investment paid off when Washington paid $25,000 and sent two players to New Orleans for Myer during the 1925 season.

Griffith received Myer's 1929 contract in the mail, and assumed it was unsigned, but to his surprise it was signed, and he called Walter Johnson to tell him the good news.

After playing two seasons for last-place teams, Myer was so happy to be back with Washington, he drove through the night from his home in Ellisville, Mississippi, to Tampa. When he arrived, he entered the clubhouse with a smile from ear to ear. "I'm delighted to be back," Myer announced. "It seems mighty natural to be back with the Griffmen. I hated to leave the Capital two years ago. You can imagine my joy in returning." Myer, who hadn't slept in a day, was so happy to be back he put on a uniform and went to work. The *Washington Post* reported he was the happiest man in camp.

On the morning of May 2, 1927, Myer, who was Washington's starting shortstop, entered the clubhouse looking forward to the upcoming series with the New York Yankees. The other players said something to him about being in the wrong clubhouse. He didn't get it. A member of the front office asked him to step aside and informed him he had been traded to the Boston Red Sox. Myer couldn't believe what he was hearing, but it sunk in when he heard, "You are to report to the Red Sox in Philadelphia." Myer was shocked, heartbroken. How could the best prospect in baseball, who was supposed to be the Senators starting shortstop for many years, possibly be traded? He took a seat in front of his locker and began to cry. The other players felt for him and came over, sat by him, and tried to cheer him up, but couldn't. For five minutes he wept before finally gaining his composure, and when he did it was explained that this was the business of baseball, and could happen to anyone.

After his first workout back in the Senators, Myer found himself surrounded by sportswriters. "Naturally I am delighted to return as a regular," Myer told them. "I consider it a compliment indeed to be traded for such a large outlay of players. I hope I can make it a worth while deal for the Griffmen."

"Which club got the better deal?" a writer asked. Myer wouldn't answer the question, but replied, "Griffith obtained what he needed for what Carrigan wanted." Myer continued, "Understand I do not consider myself superior to the players traded. Rather it seems to me a case of Washington building for the present and Boston for the future. Carrigan is gaining some highly promising players. I consider Bob Reeves the best infield prospect in baseball."

Joe Cronin arrived in Tampa after a winter of playing tennis and hiking over hills in California to keep fit. His role was to be Bluege's backup, and his playing time was to be limited. After the first day of fielding practice reserve infielder Stuffy Stewart warned Cronin was no reserve. "This kid is going to give someone a terrible argument before a regular lineup is devised," Stewart said. "You can't find 'em any steadier, and he goes after everything."

For Walter Johnson it was his first look at Cronin, and he had no idea of what to expect. He had received mixed reports about his playing ability, but was aware that the Nats had played their best baseball of the 1928 season when Cronin was in the lineup. After two weeks Johnson was convinced. "He's a real ballplayer," he said. He was convinced that Cronin would be a regular for several other teams, and felt bad that he would have to play backup to Bluege, but he was determined to give Cronin considerable playing time. "He's a fine personality in addition and all I can say is I wish I had nine Cronins on my team."

Cronin had a great spring, batting .500, and there was talk he'd move into the lineup as the shortstop and Bluege would play second base. "He really has a good baseball future in my opinion," said Johnson.

The question of the spring was: did Goslin's injury heal? After winning the 1928 batting title, he was relieved the season ended, and was certain the time away from baseball would allow his shoulder to heal. He went back to the family farm in Salem, New Jersey, and after a few weeks of rest nothing changed. He went to see specialists, spent $500 of his own money, but still no change. He began to consider retirement.

One day he accompanied a friend to a wrestling match in Philadelphia, featuring the former world champion, Ed "Strangler" Lewis. Afterwards his friend took him to the locker room to meet Lewis, and during their conversation Goslin mentioned his shoulder injury. Strangler had suffered the same injury years earlier, and he said his shoulder healed when he eliminated meat from his diet. Goslin thanked Lewis for the advice, and after two weeks of no meat the shoulder healed.

Before reporting to Tampa, Goslin met Joe Judge in Hot Springs, Arkansas, and the two played several games of catch. When they reported to Tampa, Judge talked about Goslin's arm, the best among American League outfielders before his injury, and said it was as good as ever. Their games of catch were from a short distance, however, because Goslin was afraid to cut loose. In Tampa the Senators' trainer Mike Martin tried to convince Goslin to do so but he refused.

In the first exhibition game Davey Bancroft of the Dodgers singled to left field, and thinking Goslin couldn't throw, he attempted to stretch his hit into a double. Goslin cut loose with a powerful throw and Bancroft was out at second base by a wide margin. There were no more questions about Goslin's shoulder.

Going into the season there were high expectations for Washington, by the team and around the league. During spring training they won twenty-one of twenty-seven games. After a win, as Goslin and Nick Altrock walked off the field, Goslin said to the coach, "Gosh, what a team we're going to have this year."

Miller Huggins predicted the Senators to be the Yankees' biggest competitor, bigger than the Athletics, who had finished second the year before. Baseball writer Fred Lieb predicted Washington would win ninety-five games and the pennant. But when the season began, Washington came down to earth, losing eleven of their first fifteen games.

Buddy Myer, trying too hard to justify his trade, got off to a bad start, making only four hits in thirty-three at bats. In the field he was a liability with an inability to go to his right. To compensate for his lack of range he was instructed to play close to the third base bag, but this left a big gap between Myer and the shortstop for opposing batters. One day Johnson came up with a brainstorm and shifted Myer to second base, thinking his range might show up better at the position. In his first start he handled eleven chances without a problem, but Johnson was unsure he wanted to make the move permanent, and shifted Myer back to third base.

In May, Myer began to hit, and he hit safely in twenty-four consecutive games. Cronin, who got into the lineup when Bluege twisted an ankle, also began to hit, and in late May, after getting eleven hits in eighteen at bats to lift his average to .318, he won a job in the lineup. During his hot streak he hit his first career home run off Athletics pitcher George Earnshaw. In late August he hit four home runs on a nineteen-game road trip. "He may now almost be called a slugger, as attested by his four extra base hits," said Johnson.

In 1929 Cronin improved at the plate, batting .283, forty points over the previous year, and he hit nine home runs. Defensively he showed great range, more than most shortstops, and he never gave up on a ground ball. It isn't unusual for an infielder with great range to make more errors, but in 1929 Cronin made too many and led all American League shortstops with fifty-five. Mysteriously, most of his errors were balls hit directly at him. "I know Joe is a good fielder, and so I am not worried about his occasional slumps," his manager said. "He will have a few of them."

When Bluege returned to the lineup, it was Myer, not Cronin, who went to the bench, and Johnson said the move was permanent. Cronin remained at shortstop, Bluege went to third base, and Jackie Hayes played second base. Myer was hitting .316 and his manager's decision to bench him was baffling. Johnson explained his team was slumping and the move wouldn't hurt. The team, however, continued to slump and Johnson decided to put Myer back into the lineup, and at second base, but even with Myer's presence the Nationals lost nine of ten games. After they were swept by Boston, Griffith was fuming, and promised no more Mr. Nice Guy next season when dealing with salaries. If a player wasn't playing to his full potential he could expect a cut.

Ossie Bluege had played with a bad knee the past few seasons. When asked by both Griffith and Johnson if the knee could hold up, he said it would, but after he'd made a great stop of a batted ball his knee gave in, causing him to tumble and fall on his back. While on his back he threw to Myer at second base to force the runner. He then tried to get up, but couldn't. He was carried off the field, and six days later was on the operating table, his 1929 season over.

A more serious operation involved Clark Griffith. With a meeting scheduled with Judge Landis at the commissioner's office in Chicago, Griffith accompanied his team to the Windy City. At six o'clock in the morning of the meeting he was rushed to Mercy Hospital with a high fever and a low pulse, the result of appendicitis. Surgery was performed, his fever went down, and his pulse returned to normal.

With Bluege out for the season, Myer took over third base and Hayes went to second base, but on July 23 Johnson decided to have Myer and Hayes switch positions, and for the rest of his career Myer would be a second baseman. "Myer's hitting ability has never been questioned and I wanted to make room for him in the Washington infield," Johnson said. He played a hunch that Myer's range would show up better at second base, and he was right.

Adjusting to a new position didn't affect Myer's hitting. On August 5 he delighted the Griffith Stadium crowd by going four for four, including an inside-the-park home run, seven RBI, and four runs scored. At Yankee Stadium the following day Myer got four hits the first four times he batted and drove in three runs to give him ten RBI in his last two games, but it was the four consecutive hits people paid attention to. He now had a streak of eight consecutive hits, putting him three away from the record, held by Tris Speaker. In his fifth at bat of the day, Myer made an out to end the streak. With eight straight hits Myer's batting average increased to .320, but he then slumped and finished the season with a .300 average. Due to Johnson's conservative style, he stole eighteen bases, twelve fewer than the previous year, when he had led the league.

The big disappointment of the season was the decline of Goose Goslin's offensive production. His final batting average was .288, a ninety-one point drop from the previous season, and his total runs batted in was ninety-one, his lowest since his rookie season. The Washington baseball fans grew impatient with Goslin and began to boo each time he came to the plate, but they also wondered what had happened to their hero. Goslin blamed the background at Griffith Stadium, explaining the ads on the outfield wall were higher and brighter than other stadiums in the league. His statistics showed he was hitting twenty points higher on the road, but he was still having his worst season. The truth was he didn't get along with his manager, and it affected his performance.

The Goslin-Johnson feud had begun during the 1926 season when the Senators entered the season as two-time American League champions, and expected to be in contention for a third consecutive pennant. But it didn't turn out that way, mostly for a lack of pitching depth, and because age finally caught up to Walter Johnson. In mid-season Goslin was suspended by Bucky Harris for "indifferent play" after loafing on a fly ball and playing it into a double. When Goslin returned he went on a hitting rampage, but each time Goslin produced runs, the struggling pitching staff gave them back. Goslin became frustrated and complained to the press without thinking of the impact of his words: "Every time I 'bust' one for four bags, the other club always manages to come through with a rally that makes my hit as useful as a sieve for eating soup."

A few weeks later Johnson spoke before the entire team and vented his frustration at the team's lackadaisical attitude, singling a few players out and backing up his accusations with facts. Who he named is unknown, but Goslin, who had served a suspension for not hustling, was probably one of them.

When Johnson became Washington's manager it appeared he and Goslin would let bygones be bygones, but one day on the golf course their feud was rejuvenated when the two argued about whether one of them had not counted a stroke. During the course of the 1929 season their relationship continued to sour.

During a game Goslin came back to the dugout after grounding out and was informed he was fined for swinging when signaled the take sign. "Your failure to follow signaled orders will cost you one hundred dollars," Johnson told him.

"I didn't look for a sign because there were no runners on base," explained Goslin. His explanation wasn't accepted and the fine stood.

With the team struggling and in the second division, many wondered if Johnson would be back the following season. It was clear he was too easygoing, and his players took advantage. He never lectured, he tolerated anger and poor behavior, never argued with the umpires, didn't have team rules, didn't ban golf during the season, never called a team practice or meeting on an off day. With practices never being scheduled, and without a rule against playing golf, Muddy Ruel and Garland Braxton took advantage and played forty holes. When they reported to the clubhouse the next day both were too tired to play.

Rumors began to spread about Johnson's dismissal, and the rumors reached Griffith's hospital bed in Chicago, where he remained for nearly three weeks following surgery. He immediately made a statement about Johnson's future. "I want to make it as strong as possible that I am particularly satisfied with the manner in which Johnson is handling this team." Griffith spoke about the things he felt Johnson did well, particularly about his idea to move Myer to second base. "Buddy is showing up so well in his new berth that I do not believe Bucky Harris will be missed here."

Washington finished the season a disappointing 71–81, in fifth place, their first second division finish since 1922. Johnson wasn't happy with his team's showing or with his own job as manager. He realized he was too easy on his players because he wanted to be accepted by them and be one of the guys. He knew he had to get tougher in 1930, and he vowed he would. His players would find out next season their manager would no longer be Mr. Nice Guy.

6

THE SURPRISING SENATORS (1930)

"This kid Cronin at shortstop makes a big difference. He's there, that boy."

— Mickey Cochrane

When the new decade began Griffith had much to be concerned with, and it wasn't limited to the effects of the recent stock market crash. The Old Fox was unsure where the Senators would spring train, was threatening a lawsuit against the Atlanta Crackers and the Southern Association, and wasn't sure what to do about Goose Goslin, who was coming off his worst season, wasn't getting along with his manager, and wouldn't sign his 1930 contract. In November talks began with the St. Louis Browns about trading Goslin for outfielder Heinie Manush, who was also disputing his salary. The deal died for the time being, and both teams worked on getting their outfielders signed.

Griffith had warned he'd reduce the salary of anyone who wasn't playing up to par. With this in mind, and with a depression going on, Goslin's contract called for a $6,000 salary reduction. He refused to sign even after a $6,000 bonus scale was added. When spring training began Goslin remained unsigned and didn't report.

With spring quickly approaching Griffith needed to decide where his team would train. One thing was for sure: he wouldn't go back to Tampa, where he was fed up with poor field conditions, and with city officials who continuously ignored his requests to improve the field. He also wanted a mild climate, believing the humidity of the Sunshine State made it difficult for his players to adjust to the cooler East Coast weather when the season began. He attributed his team's poor starts in 1928 and 1929 to this lack of adjustment.

Led by the enthusiasm of "Mr. Biloxi," Tony Ragusin, who was a member of the Biloxi Chamber of Commerce, the city pitched Griffith on bringing his team to the Mississippi Gulf Coast. To help persuade him, they sent a package of shrimp along with their proposal.

Griffith decided on Biloxi, but had one condition: the baseball field had to be in tip-top shape. He got more than he asked for. At Biloxi Stadium the grass was bright green, and the field was so smooth, it looked more like a giant pool table cover than a baseball field. "The field is a whole lot better than most major league playing fields," said Mike Martin, who was thankful. A good field meant fewer blisters and shin splints, and would give him more time to work on other things.

Joe Engel was finding it harder to get players from the minor leagues. He had scouted a catcher named Bill Dickey a few years earlier and wanted to buy his contract, but was informed he was under contract with the Yankees. Engel was running into this problem too often.

Griffith and Engel looked at Branch Rickey's farm system, known as the "chain store" back then. Rickey signed his own prospects and assigned them to one of the Cardinals' minor league teams for development. When they were added to the St. Louis roster, Rickey and the Cardinals wouldn't have to pay a dime for their contracts.

Griffith went to work on imitating Rickey's chain store and looked for a minor league team for sale. He found one, the Atlanta Crackers of the Southern Association, and made a partial payment on the $650,000 sale price. But a week later the sale was nullified when three-fourths of the Southern Association's owners didn't approve. When Griffith heard this he exploded, especially since he hadn't been informed about this rule, and he demanded his money back. The Atlanta owners told him to stay cool and assured him they'd get the sale approved, but Griffith didn't want to be in a league where he wasn't welcomed and demanded the return of his deposit. After his request was denied he called his lawyer and prepared to file a lawsuit. Things would be settled, however, and Griffith worked out a deal with the Southern Association for the purchase of the Chattanooga Lookouts.

In Chattanooga, Griffith and Engel had a challenge. The Lookouts were the worst team in the Southern Association, with just four winning seasons in team history. They were in the smallest city in the Southern Association, and there was hardly any local interest in the team. Engel, who was assigned to run the team, went to work on putting a winning team on the field, and on his vision of creating a fun atmosphere that would attract fans to the ballpark. The first step was to oversee the construction of the new ballpark, which would be made of modern steel, have new seats, and have bird cages hanging from the rafters with each cage housing a canary.

It was discovered that Goslin's holdout wasn't about money, but was due to his poor relationship with his manager, who he claimed was too much on his case last season. As Griffith was learning more about Goslin's anger, a story broke quoting Goslin as saying he would never play for Walter Johnson. Griffith read the quote and demanded an apology, but Goslin denied saying such a thing and sent a letter to Griffith stating he would never apologize for something he never said.

Soon the trade rumors heated up again, with Bucky Harris interested in bringing Goslin to Detroit, but Griffith denied the rumors. Ray Cahill, a scout from the St. Louis Browns, made a visit to Biloxi, probably to talk to Griffith about a Goslin-Manush trade. After their closed-door meeting, nothing happened.

When the team left Biloxi and traveled to Chattanooga, word came that Goslin had accepted Griffith's terms and signed his contract. "I'm tickled to death," said Johnson. "We need his punch in the lineup and all I ask of him is to give me his best."

While the Senators were in Biloxi, bad news was received about an accident involving Johnson's son, Walter Jr., who was struck by an automobile while roller skating a block from the Johnsons' residence in Bethesda, Maryland. He was rushed to the hospital, where X-rays revealed two broken legs and a lacerated hand. He remained in the hospital with both legs in casts and his right hand bandaged. Johnson decided to stay with his team since Junior's condition was not life-threatening. His blood was circulating well and he had sustained no head injuries. Towards the end of the exhibition season Johnson left the team and went home to spend time with Walter Jr. and his family.

Joe Cronin reported to Biloxi after working hard during the winter in San Francisco by hiking, playing tennis, and swinging an ax at his job as a lumberjack, which added fifteen pounds of muscle to his frame. He spent time working on his game, concentrating on developing a new batting stance, and came up with one he said would make him a better hitter. He opened his stance by moving his left foot back, turned more towards the pitcher to allow him to see the ball better, and held the bat high and on an angle like Heinie Groh, the former batting star of the Giants.

Buddy Myer arrived, thrilled over the team's decision to spring train in Biloxi, which was located only 100 miles from his home in Ellisville, Mississippi. The people of Ellisville were delighted about Biloxi since the short distance allowed them to see their hometown player perform, and Myer could always count on having a big cheering section.

Both Cronin and Myer were determined to improve defensively and the two worked hard, Cronin on cutting down errors, Myer on picking up the finer points of second base. Both worked overtime on executing double plays, often remaining on the field after practice. Myer showed improvement at his position but couldn't break a habit of making the pivot off the wrong foot on double play relay throws.

As hard as Cronin and Myer worked, their starting jobs weren't secure, and their manager talked about a new double play tandem of Jackie Hayes at second base, and nineteen-year-old rookie Jim McLeod at shortstop. "Hayes is as good a second baseman as I have seen, bar none," Johnson said. Of McLeod, Johnson said, "If he could hit, then there is a possibility he could become our starting shortstop."

This kind of talk didn't sit well with Cronin and Myer, especially with Cronin, who worried about experiencing Pittsburgh again and became so nervous he couldn't focus. Johnson picked up on it, took him aside, and assured him he would be the starting shortstop. Both Cronin and Myer started on opening day, and both got off to a good start. Myer hit safely in the first fourteen games while handling all of his fielding chances. Cronin made a statement on what was to come during the second game of the year by hammering a home run and knocking in four runs in a Washington win at Boston. Also contributing to Washington's great start that propelled them into first place at the end of April was Sam Rice, who showed no signs of slowing down at age forty by hitting safely in his first twenty-eight games of the season.

Another reason for the great start was Walter Johnson did what he had vowed to do: get tougher. His first chance to show his team things would be different came during the third game of the season when pitcher Sam Jones threw his mitt in anger after Johnson ordered him to yield to an amateur to pitch batting practice. Johnson responded differently than expected. "I don't like your attitude," Johnson told the angry pitcher. "If you can't cheerfully follow orders then pack your bags and go home. Go inside the clubhouse and take off your uniform."

The next morning in the hotel lobby Jones approached Johnson and asked what was going on. Johnson answered by telling him he didn't appreciate his spirit, and ordered him to see Ed Eynon, the team's traveling secretary, who had a ticket for him to Washington.

Later Johnson spoke to the press about his interaction with Jones. He also accepted the blame for being too easy with his team last season and admitted it resulted in no discipline on his team. "Things this season will be entirely different, and I do not intend on taking anything off of my players."

When Jones arrived back in Washington he was greeted by sportswriters who asked him for his side of the story but the pitcher didn't have a statement. He appeared to be calm, and seemed to have no resentment towards Johnson. When the team arrived back from their road trip, Johnson and Jones talked, and the two shook hands.

In 1929 the Athletics won thirteen of the first fourteen games with Washington, and took seventeen of the twenty-two season meetings. The wins included a game which the Nats led 9–0, but the A's rallied for a 10–9 win, a trick the Mackmen would repeat in Game Four of the World Series with the Cubs, when the A's rallied for a 10–8 win after trailing 8–0. In the first meeting of 1930 the A's creamed Washington 9–0, and afterwards the Senators appeared calm and confident, which baffled the sportswriters. They found out why when the Senators won their next seven meetings with the A's and made a believer of Connie Mack, who was so impressed, he congratulated a member of the Washington front office on their "probable pennant." "The team that beats the Nationals will win the pennant," Mack said.

After winning seven in a row from the Athletics, the Nationals threatened to take a big lead in the pennant race. Mack needed to slow down the Nats, who were pulverizing his pitchers and batting .319 as a team. He turned to the golden arm of his ace, Lefty Grove, to cool off the Washington batters. Johnson countered with Lloyd Brown, who matched Grove for five innings by allowing no runs. In the top of the sixth the Athletics threatened with runners on first and third and only one out. With the dangerous Jimmie Foxx at the plate, Brown needed a double play and thought he had it when Foxx grounded to Cronin, who made a nifty stop and flipped the ball to Myer to force out the base runner, Al Simmons. Myer, still having problems in making the pivot, made it off the wrong foot, and just as Simmons jarred him after making a hard slide. The combination of the improper pivot and Simmons's aggressiveness caused Myer to throw the ball with little power, allowing Foxx to beat the throw, and the other base runner to tally. Grove went on to complete a 1–0 shutout, and in the process snapped Rice's twenty-eight-game hitting streak.

The loss didn't faze the Nats, who swept all five games from Boston in their next series while outscoring them, 37–6. Cronin made five hits in one game, and Sam Rice, who began a new hitting streak of seventeen in a row, went four for five in one game, and collected three hits in two other games. For the series he made thirteen hits in twenty at bats. Rice was a good hitter throughout his career but never was he this hot. Through the first forty-seven games of the season he hit safely in forty-five of them. The two he didn't get a hit in were the Lefty Grove shutout, and one game he sat out with an injury.

After the Senators won two straight at Yankee Stadium, Johnson found his room at the Waldorf Astoria Hotel packed with sportswriters who asked, "How come?" Johnson answered, "We are simply getting good hitting, good pitching, good fielding, and playing heads up ball. All in all I've got a team I'm proud of."

While the press was giving credit and respect to the Senators, the Philadelphia A's were not. Al Simmons, always with something to say, spoke about the pennant race and the Senators. "We ought to win [the pennant] and the Yankees are good for second. I don't think the Senators have the power to stay up there." Mickey Cochrane agreed but was concerned, especially because Goslin wasn't hitting. "If he hits like years past then it makes for a lot of trouble."

Bucky Harris was convinced this Washington team was better than the two he managed to a pennant and gave this team the nod in all eight starting positions, plus liked this pitching staff more than his. "Does this mean Washington will win the pennant?" asked a sportswriter.

"I don't mean to say Washington will win the pennant," Harris answered. "A pennant team needs breaks."

On Memorial Day the Nationals traveled to Philadelphia to play a morning-afternoon double-header with the Athletics, who trailed the Nats by three games. In the morning game, before twenty-five thousand fans, Washington had no problem with Lefty Grove, and led 6–3 in the bottom of the ninth. Spencer Harris of the A's hit a foul ball that catcher Muddy Ruel assumed was heading to the seats and made no effort to go after. The ball dropped to the ground in play. On the next pitch, Harris singled. Another hit was made, and with two outs, two men on base, Al Simmons came up to the plate, and the Athletics slugger hit the first pitch by Washington's submarine-style pitcher Ad Liska, and sent it over the left field roof for a three-run homer to tie the game. It took fourteen innings before the A's won.

Several Washingtonians made the trip for the afternoon game and were among the overflow crowd of thirty-five thousand. In the fifth inning Simmons hobbled up to the plate with the bases loaded. In the thirteenth inning of the morning game the star had injured his ankle while sliding into third base. With the score 7–5 in favor of Washington, Connie Mack called on Simmons to pinch-hit. Garland Braxton, Washington's pitcher, threw a screwball. Simmons swung and connected. The overflow crowd jumped to their feet as the ball headed to left center field and disappeared into the bleachers for a grand slam, giving Philadelphia a 9–7 lead. The A's went on to win and swept the twin bill to pull within a game of Washington.

The next day Connie Mack had a patched-up lineup with four of his regulars out, including Cochrane and Simmons, who had checked into the Garfield Hospital due to the pain and swelling of his ankle. The A's won, and also won the next day in Washington to take over the lead in the American League.

Feeling changes were needed to win the 1930 pennant, Griffith traveled with the team on their trip to the Midwest with trades in mind as the trading deadline approached. After the team arrived in Chicago he made a deal by sending a rarely used outfielder, Red Barnes, to Chicago for outfielder Dave Harris, who at the time had a .255 lifetime average with 113 career hits, of which ten were home runs. The trade turned out to be another lopsided one in Griffith's favor, as Harris would become one of the league's top pinch-hitters while Barnes would be out of the major leagues after the season.

After their series in Chicago the Senators traveled by train during the night, bound for St. Louis. Griffith remained in Chicago and put in a call to Phil Ball, the owner of the St. Louis Browns, to make another trade. This one involved Goose Goslin, who was having another disappointing season, and was currently slumping with four hits in his last seventeen at bats. His 1930 batting average of .271 was sixty points below his current .331 lifetime average, and both Griffith and Johnson agreed it was time to part with him.

The next morning in St. Louis, as Goslin was out and about, his teammates heard the news he had been traded and congregated in the hotel lobby to greet him upon his return. When he arrived someone said, "Go on to your own clubhouse." Goslin didn't get it. Someone mentioned he had been traded, but Goslin was sure he was joking and laughed. The bellboy handed to him a telegram and he read it. "They weren't kidding me, were they?" he said.

The trade was for Heinie Manush and pitcher General Crowder, who was a National once again. The baseball world was baffled and wondered what Phil Ball was thinking. Goslin for Manush was considered an even trade, but to get a pitcher of Crowder's caliber put another feather in the cap of the Old Fox.

Walter Johnson was thrilled and had a big smile when he spoke with the sportswriters. "I am very pleased with the deal. I believe Manush will prove just the man we need to hit us in to the pennant. We have a good club. Its record proves it. With a little more punch we'll have a great ball club, and I look to Manush to provide us with the extra punch."

"How about Crowder?" asked one of the writers. "He doesn't have such a fine record [in 1930]."

"Don't count Crowder as on the way out," responded Johnson. "He's a good pitcher. I expect him to prove mighty valuable to the Nationals." Johnson then turned the subject to the outfielder who he had traded. "I don't consider Goose as through. Not by a long shot. But he was through as far as the Washington club was concerned. He tried hard to swing into his batting stride this season, but he couldn't make it. As things were going it was up to us to help ourselves and we took advantage of the best offer made."

"Gee, I hate to leave Washington," Goslin said. "I simply haven't been able to get going this year, nor last. Perhaps a change of scenery will do me good." One thing Goslin wouldn't miss were the long outfield dimensions at Griffith Stadium, and the thirty-foot wall in right field. "This trade is likely to make a hero out of me," he said. "For sure I can hit the ball in the St. Louis Park."

"Great," responded Manush when asked about the trade. "I will perform well enough to prevent Washington from regretting the trade. I believe we have a fine chance to cop the flag this year. And everyone may be assured I'll do all I can to help cop it. "

"Back to the old Capital," said General Crowder. "Well, I didn't do so well when I was with Washington before but I think the fans in Washington know that all I lacked was experience. I have gained that since and I feel I will pitch winning ball for the Nationals this time." Like both Goslin and Manush, Crowder had held out for more money in the spring and the time off affected him. He was off to a slow start, winning just three of ten decisions, but people knew this was misleading based on his thirty-eight wins in the previous two seasons.

"Outrage" was how St. Louis reacted to the trade. One St. Louis newspaper called it "A crime" and "The most ridiculous trade ever made in baseball." In Washington the reaction was surprisingly similar. It didn't seem to matter what the Nationals received in return. Goslin was a hero to the fans and now their hero was gone.

A "Standing Room Only" sign appeared above the ticket window at Griffith Stadium on the morning of July 4, with the Yankees in town for a doubleheader. By 11:30 all parking yards around the stadium were filled, and traffic along Georgia Avenue was diverted. Every seat was occupied, and those who weren't fortunate enough to get a seat sat in the aisles, or stood in back of the last row, or literally hung from the rafters. A few fans got an idea to climb and find a spot in the structure beneath the upper deck. The police spotted these fans hanging over the box seat customers and ordered them to get down.

A crowd had remained outside hoping to somehow get into the game when admission was granted to them. They paid for the privilege of watching from a roped-off area on the field, located in front of the left field bleachers. The total attendance on the day was 33,900, the second biggest baseball crowd in the Washington, D.C. history. The largest had been for Game Four of the 1925 World Series, when additional bleachers were installed and 38,701 packed Griffith Stadium.

Sam Jones, now on great terms with his manager, pitched a five-hit shutout in the first game in Washington's 8–0 win. Jones began the season by winning his first six decisions, then lost two in a row before taking five weeks off to attend to his ailing mother. When he returned Johnson told him to be ready for the Yankees, and he was.

Washington won the nightcap 7–3, and completed the series sweep with wins the next two days, including one over Yankees left-hander Herb Pennock, who lost his personal seven-game winning streak. Before leaving town he told reporters he believed in Washington. "I believe Washington's infield is twice as tight as the Athletics,' that their pitching staff is equally as good and is made up of almost as good hitters."

After the sweep of the Yankees, Johnson received more good news. Walter Jr., who had recovered from his injuries, pitched his first game of the summer for the Bethesda Juniors of the Capital City League, a competitive sandlot league. He threw two innings, gave up only one hit, and struck out three before leaving the game for a pinch-hitter per Dad's instructions, who told him not to bat.

The red-hot Senators won eighteen of nineteen games and trailed the Athletics by one game. They became the talk of Washington, D.C., with everyone predicting a pennant and World Series Championship. With so much buzzing, the *Washington Post* put the Senators on the front page to follow their drive to the American League crown. The Washington players were confident they were going to win it and were speaking openly about it. "We're going to win the pennant as sure as I'm a foot high," said Manush.

There was a new opinion of Manush, who won the admiration of the Washington fans after playing on an injured ankle, sustained against New York when rookie third baseman Ben Chapman landed on him as he slid into third base. The Big Guy had made thirty-eights hits in ninety-five at bats for a .400 batting average since joining Washington, and he continued to win the fans when they heard he made three hits, including a home run, in Washington's win at Boston. Suddenly Manush was becoming as popular as Goslin, and the old cheer of "Come on, Goose" was now "Come on, Heinie."

Crowder was doing his part, winning his first five decisions since the trade, and the other starting pitchers were doing well. But there was a question about the team's pitching depth, especially since Johnson elected to send off his relief specialist, Garland Braxton, to Chicago. The writers counted two games lost that would have been won had Braxton been around, but Johnson disagreed, and explained the departure of the relief specialist had "a good psychological effect on his pitchers." "Braxton was always warmed up as a relief man. The pitchers used to figure if they did not halt the enemy in a few rounds they would get help from Braxton. Now they go in the box determined to stay the limit."

Washington finished their series in Boston by winning two of the next three games, and after the series Red Sox manager Heinie Wagner, told the press he believed he saw the best team in his league. "The addition of Manush assures them of the pennant." But what would happen without Manush? He re-injured his ankle in the Boston series, and this time it was enough to put him out of action. He went back to Washington to recover.

His teammates headed for the worst place to be in July of 1930 — the Midwest — where temperatures were soaring to record highs, the hottest spot being Sikeston, Missouri, where the mercury reached 112. In Omaha a few citizens took their own lives rather than have to endure another day of one hundred degrees. In St. Louis the thermometer in the Senators' clubhouse showed 104 as they got ready to play the Browns, and since there never has been a rule to reschedule because of hot weather, the contest went on. Ossie Bluege claimed the hottest spot in America was at third base, and to find out, someone ran to the clubhouse to fetch the thermometer and threw it towards the third base area. Sure enough, the reading was 114 degrees. The heat reached the east coast a few days later, and the temperature reached a record high of 106 in Washington. To escape the heat people headed to the parks, pools, and beaches.

Hazel Johnson drove through the intense heat with her children from Bethesda to Coffeyville, Kansas, for a family reunion. It was a difficult trip for Mrs. Johnson since she had recently recovered from pleurisy, plus she was occupied with taking care of Walter Jr., who needed for her to move him around the house while his broken legs healed. The previous year she had had her appendix removed, while not saying a word to her husband until after the surgery because she didn't want to distract him from his first spring training as the Nats manager. She had spent time taking care of her husband after he sustained a leg fracture in 1927, and again in 1928 after he became so ill he was ordered to bed rest. With so much to deal with, Hazel was exhausted and worn out.

The Big Train got to be part of his family reunion when family members drove up from Coffeyville to see the Nationals play the Browns in St. Louis. Hazel made the trip and intended to drive home after the series. Both Walter and Griffith suggested she put the car on the train and travel with the team rather than tolerate the heat on the drive back to the East Coast with her children. Wanting to get back home as soon as possible, she declined their offer, and when she reached Bethesda she was so fatigued she checked into the Georgetown Hospital. She was suffering from heat exhaustion, with lots of rest required to restore her health.

Washington hit a slump in the Midwest, and after a loss to the Browns, where the Nats out-hit St. Louis but played sloppily and gave away the game, Johnson called for a team meeting. The next morning he gave his boys a lecture they wouldn't soon forget. The manager singled out a few players to let them know they needed to perform better, and when these players emerged from the meeting they didn't look happy.

After Johnson grilled his team, the Nats lost again to the Browns after out-hitting them again, but the next day they managed to salvage a win before leaving town. The Nationals blew an 8–2 lead, then trailed 9–8 in the ninth until Cronin saved the day by hitting his second home run of the game. In the eleventh inning Cronin got his fourth hit on the day, and scored on Myer's double.

In their next game, at Chicago, Washington led 4–1 as the White Sox threatened. A ground ball looked like a double play that would kill the threat, but Myer once again made the pivot off the wrong foot and only a force out was made. The play should have been a double play and the failure to execute turned into a four-run rally and another loss. After the game Johnson benched Myer.

The phone rang in Sam West's room at Chicago's Del Prado Hotel. It was Griffith, who requested his presence. He wanted to talk with the twenty-five-year-old, left-handed hitting center fielder who had a developed a psychological problem batting against southpaws since 1926, after he was beaned by a lefty while playing for Birmingham. This forced Johnson to platoon West with George Loepp. But no longer was Griffith willing to platoon, and after he told West he had just sent Loepp to the minor leagues, he spelled things out. "You either learn to hit lefties and become the full time center fielder, or you yield the position to someone who can hit pitchers from both sides." West understood the message and later that day he started against Dutch Henry, a lefty, and banged out a pair of hits.

With Washington's slump in the Midwest, they now trailed Philadelphia by six games, but would have a chance to gain when the A's came to Griffith Stadium for a two-game series. President Herbert Hoover was present. "I'm here to lead your team out of its slump," he told Griffith, but it would take more than the president to do the job. The Nats played poorly in a 7–4 loss, and fell seven games behind the A's. In one inning their defense collapsed and gave up two runs without the A's getting a hit.

After the game Johnson went directly to the hospital to check on Hazel, who was growing weaker. The next day Johnson received a phone call in the dugout during the game and was told to come to the hospital immediately.

Hazel was now in grave condition, and she was fading fast. Walter sat in a chair next to her hospital bed, hoping for a miracle, and intent on staying until that happened. But her fate was sealed, and knowing the end was near, she thought of her children. She made a request to her husband to keep the family together. Walter vowed to fulfill it.

At 4:30 A.M. on August 1, with her hand clasped between her husband's hands, the end came. Hazel was thirty-six years old — was Walter's biggest fan — was his partner for life since they had been married sixteen years earlier.

Johnson ignored his closest friends, who pleaded with him to go home. He remained at his wife's bedside for hours and continued to hold her hand as he wept. He finally left and went home to his children, who were unaware of what had happened except for his oldest son, Walter Jr. Later that day the kids were at play in the living room as Walter and Walter Jr. watched, both wearing fake smiles. As the day progressed, Johnson was in the thoughts of many who stopped by to give their condolences. President Hoover and his wife had the Big Train in their thoughts and sent a large wreath.

Every member of the Nationals stopped by to give Johnson their sympathy. Joe Judge, who served as the acting manager in Johnson's absence, came by and Johnson took a minute to talk to him about the team. He left the team in his hands, giving him no instructions, but did suggest he put Myer back in the starting lineup.

After visiting their manager, the players went directly to Union Station, where they boarded a train for New York City. Deep in thought and feeling sad, no one said a word until someone spoke up about sweeping the Yankees as a tribute to Hazel. All the players were in agreement, and that was what the Nats did, with the help of Heinie Manush, who returned to the lineup. The star continued to swing a hot bat by pounding out six hits, three that left the yard. The next day Manush was four for four in Washington's 11–2 win over the Red Sox.

As his team was destroying the Yankees and the Red Sox, Johnson sat by his wife's coffin, rarely leaving, not even to eat or sleep. He was not a religious man, never attended church services, but spoke to God, continually asking how this could happen.

On August 8, Johnson went back to work and threw nearly the entire session of batting practice in one-hundred-degree heat. The next day he repeated the session with the temperature at 102, and the following day he reported looking so tired and worn-out that Mike Martin sent him home. When he returned he announced he was going to watch the game from the stands "and second guess 'em."

People noticed something happening with Cronin and Griffith's niece. Cronin was spending more time in the office, talking with Mildred, who worked as one of the secretaries. The players always thought of her as one of the boys on the team. She loved baseball, loved talking baseball, and knew a lot about the game, a seemingly perfect match for Cronin who ate, drank, and slept baseball.

The Washington shortstop bought a new car, showed it off to everyone, offered rides to his teammates and members of the visiting teams. He impressed his friends who were visiting him from California, and further impressed them when he told them he knew the president and would drive them to the White House to meet him. The truth was he didn't know the president, but he wanted to put one over. He drove into the White House driveway, something people could do back then, and parked at the front door.

"Oh, the Pres' isn't home," said Cronin.

"How do you know?" asked a friend.

"I could see his office light is off," Cronin replied.

"Oh yes, too bad," said a friend.

With twenty-five games left in the season, and trailing the Athletics by 8½ games, the Senators needed a sweep in their three-game series with Philadelphia. Cronin, hitting .338 on the year, delighted the twenty-five thousand on hand at Griffith Stadium by going three for three at the plate to help lead his team to a 7–3 win. In the eighth inning, with Simmons on first base, Foxx hit a ground ball to Myer, who flipped the ball to Cronin to force out Simmons. As Cronin attempted to complete the double play, Simmons grabbed his arm. Cronin told Simmons what he thought of his tactic and Simmons shouted back. The crowd yelled out for an interference call, but didn't get it. Umpire Bill McGowan was the only one in the stadium who missed the play, and up in the press box, Frank Young was in disbelief. "Umpire McGowan then showed why arbitrators are referred to as blind men. It's things like this that cause riots at games," Young wrote about the play. He went on to blast the other two umpires, Tommy Connolly and Ray Van Graflan, for not overruling the call.

The series moved to Philadelphia, where Lefty Grove, with a season record of 21–4 and a personal seven-game winning streak, faced Washington. Cronin tagged him for a home run and later drove in the winning run in the Nats' 3–2 win. Washington appeared to be heading for a sweep to keep their pennant hopes alive when they led 9–5 in the series' final game, but the A's came back behind home runs by Cochrane and Simmons, who had four hits on the day. The Athletics won 10–9 to all but sew up the pennant.

The heat was relentless in the summer of 1930, and on Labor Day the temperature in Washington hit 100 with the Red Sox in town for a double-header. In the top of the ninth of the first game the Senators were clinging to a 2–1 lead, a runner was on third base with two outs, and Bobby Reeves came to the plate. Griffith's boy, Bobby Reeves, had proved to be a bust as a shortstop and was switched to third base. At the plate he hit a disappointing .248 in 1929, and in 1930, due to illness and a knee injury, batted .217.

Reeves drilled a pitch towards left field, looking like a sure hit. Cronin leaped high, managed to tip the ball with his glove, and as he fell to the ground he reached out, gloved the ball, and landed on his back. He took the ball out of his mitt, held it up for the umpire to see that he had made the catch for the final out of the game. "Easily the greatest play seen here in years," wrote Frank Young. There simply wasn't anything Cronin couldn't do in 1930.

The Athletics were at Griffith Stadium for a one-game series on September 7 before a crowd of twenty-five thousand fans who were hoping that somehow the Nationals could rally to win the pennant. They watched the A's take a 5–0 lead, but saw Fred Marberry take the mound and hold the A's as the Nats got back in the game.

In the top of the seventh Al Simmons came to the plate to a chorus of boos. He had worn down the Washington pitchers all season long and had further angered the Washington fans when he had grabbed Cronin's arm.

Marberry's first pitch was high and inside, and Simmons didn't like how close it came to hitting him. He shouted at the Washington hurler. Marberry resented Simmons' comments and shouted back. When things calmed down Simmons finished his at bat by flying out, and on his way back to the dugout, with the crowd booing and shouting, a bottle was thrown and almost struck the star.

A few minutes later Marberry got the third out and knew exactly where he wanted to go. Muddy Ruel sprinted from his position behind home plate to head off the angry pitcher, and several Philadelphia players held Marberry to prevent him from getting to Simmons.

In the bottom of the ninth Washington rallied to win the game. Ruel and Bluege executed a perfect hit-and-run play, and Sam Rice followed with a hit to drive in the winning run. Marberry was credited with the win but wouldn't be satisfied until he evened the score with Simmons. He waited outside of the Athletics' clubhouse, and Griffith spotted him. Knowing his motive, he walked over to Marberry, spoke with him, and walked him into the Washington clubhouse.

The Senators were on the road when they received the news that the Athletics clinched the American League pennant. With the race now decided, Johnson left his team and went home to take care of his kids. When his train arrived back in Washington he was greeted by a group of sportswriters. "I am more than satisfied with our showing this season," Johnson told them. "I'll admit that we even did better than I thought we would." He believed his team was as good as Philadelphia with two factors making the difference: Lefty Grove and timely hitting.

Later that evening Johnson was at home when he heard his team won in Detroit 8–4, to clinch second place. The Nats won ninety-four games in 1930, second most in team history, and it was more than the 1924 team had won. They finished eight games behind the Athletics, but eight ahead of New York. At the box office the Senators enjoyed their best attendance since 1925, with 614,474 clicking the turnstiles.

Joe Cronin was brilliant all season and his stats told the story. He hit .346, banged out 203 hits, scored 127 runs, drove in 126 teammates, hit thirteen home

"This kid Cronin at shortstop makes a big difference." There simply wasn't anything Cronin couldn't do in 1930.

runs, and stole seventeen bases. And to think two years earlier he had struggled in the minor leagues.

Cronin's productive stats were aided by the use of the "rabbit ball" during the 1930 season. Thomas Shibe, the president of the Athletics, who was also vice president for A.J. Reach, the company that manufactured baseballs for both leagues, denied the acquisitions that livelier baseballs were being made. He also denied Ruth's charge that the National League baseballs had more pop: "The only difference is one is sewed with red and black thread, the other in black and blue thread." All this was probably true, but there was definitely a difference. According to the pitchers these baseballs were wound tighter, making them difficult to grip, and nearly impossible for throwing breaking balls.

Johnson called his shortstop's performance the biggest surprise of the season, and insisted he was no flash in the pan: "When a player unexpectedly has a good year, it is usually the result of several flashes between slumps. Cronin has been hitting and fielding consistently well all season."

Before leaving for San Francisco for the winter, Cronin stopped by the Nationals' office to say goodbye to Mildred and the others, when he heard Griffith call him into his office. The Washington owner told him he would get a pay raise in 1931, then reached into his desk drawer and pulled out a blank check, filled it out, handed it to Cronin and thanked him for his hard work.

After returning home to San Francisco the twenty-three-year-old star was informed that he had been chosen as the American League's Most Valuable Player.

7

THE 1931 SEASON

"I wanted Cronin for my Braves but the Judge [owner of the Braves, Judge Fuchs] didn't have the money to spend on more ballplayers at the time.

"I thought Cronin was one of the best young players I had ever seen and I wondered why he had not become a regular with a major league club."
— Rogers Hornsby, manager of the Boston Braves in 1928

In 1930 the Nationals proved they could take the Yankees, but could they take both the Yankees and the Athletics in 1931? Most didn't think they could beat the Athletics, but Walter Johnson and his team believed they were the best team in the league and 1931 would be the year they'd kick the door in on the Athletics dynasty.

Johnson felt he had the best pitching staff in the league and had good reason to. In 1930 his staff had the lowest ERA in baseball, and had outstanding depth with four fifteen game winners (General Crowder, Bump Hadley, Sam Jones, and Fred Marberry), a sixteen-game winner (Lloyd Brown), and a nine-game winner (Ad Liska).

The Athletics were coming off their second consecutive World Series championship, had the league's best pitcher in Lefty Grove, and also had George Earnshaw, who had won over twenty games in each of the last two seasons. The Yankees had Red Ruffing, whom they acquired from Boston during the 1930 season, but both teams lacked pitching depth and Johnson commented on it: "If the A's and Yankees don't uncover some good pitchers, we'll beat them out easier than a lot of people expect." Connie Mack responded to Johnson's comment by predicting a third consecutive pennant for his Athletics, but predicted a close race.

Unhappy with his team's third-place finish in 1930, Yankees owner Colonel Jacob Ruppert dismissed manager Bob Shawkey and signed Joe McCarthy, who had managed the Cubs to the 1929 National League pennant before being mysteriously terminated after a second-place finish in 1930. McCarthy was

73

offered a lucrative contract by Bob Quinn to manage the Red Sox but turned it down, saying he would rather manage a ready-made team that needed little or no managing than one that needed attention. "I am a stranger to the American League and can't predict where they will finish, but my Yankees will have a better showing in 1931 than in 1930," McCarthy said at his press conference.

After McCarthy signed a two-year contract for $30,000, Colonel Ruppert assured him that he was in charge. "Thank you, Colonel Huston," McCarthy said, unaware he called Ruppert by the name of his former ownership partner. "I hope the next one I sign will be for five years."

"I hope so too, Mr. McCarthy," Ruppert said. "And the name is Colonel Ruppert."

There was another change in management, this one coming at the top of the American League due to the untimely death of League President Ernest Barnard. The American League owners nominated Wil Harridge, who had served in the league office as Ban Johnson's secretary for seventeen years, and as Barnard's right-hand man for three years. "It is not necessary for me to say that I will do everything possible to keep up the traditions of the former two presidents, Mr. Johnson and Mr. Barnard," Harridge said after being elected. "I do not propose nor look for any additional clauses although I shall always be open to suggestions from anyone."

Another change in 1931 was to the ball, this change coming as a relief to pitchers who were thankful the rabbit ball wouldn't be used. The Washington pitchers claimed the 1931 baseball was easier to grip, and was better for throwing curves and other breaking stuff. The Big Train took a close look at the new baseball and threw several pitches. As usual, when Johnson pitched everyone paid attention. "I believe that bird could still win in our league if he decided to make a comeback," declared Sam Rice. Johnson assured his right fielder it would never happen.

The pitching staff Johnson was so proud of reported to Biloxi out of shape. General Crowder, expected to have a big season, reported overweight, and it affected his performance. His fastballs weren't fast, his curve balls didn't break, and he needed more time than spring training to regain his effectiveness. Marberry reported ten pounds overweight and loafed during practice. In one drill Johnson would hit balls into the outfield and his pitchers would sprint after them, but Marberry jogged, and Johnson lectured him after practice before the entire team. Marberry replied in anger, Johnson got mad, and words were exchanged that neither meant to say. Later Marberry said he regretted the incident and the following day he was on the field hustling, sprinting after fly balls, and all seemed to be forgotten, but Johnson and Marberry would have other disagreements during the season.

After the Nats finished spring training in Biloxi, they headed to Chattanooga to face a seventeen-year-old pitcher on the Lookouts staff who wasn't your average teenager. The pitcher was a female named Jackie Mitchell, a Chattanooga high school student signed by Joe Engel, who knew her presence would fill the seats in his Stadium.

Before the Nationals got their chance to face young Jackie Mitchell, she made her debut against the Yankees in front of nearly 4,000 fans at Engel Stadium. After Murderer's Row pounded the Lookouts pitchers to build a big lead, Mitchell entered the game to face the most feared heart of the order in baseball: Babe Ruth, Lou Gehrig, and Tony Lazzeri.

Mitchell nervously tugged her pants as Babe Ruth stepped to the plate. She threw her first pitch, Ruth swung hard and missed, and the crowd went wild. The Babe swung at the second pitch and missed, and swung so hard he stumbled and almost fell. Then Ruth watched the next pitch go by and the umpire called strike three. As the crowd cheered Ruth argued with the umpire, then stormed back to the dugout.

Lou Gehrig came up next and swung three times and missed, and the great first baseman quietly headed to the dugout as Mitchell's second strikeout victim. Lazzeri came next as the crowd cheered for another strikeout, but he broke the string by drawing a walk, and that was all for Mitchell, who headed for the dugout to an ovation.

The story of Jackie Mitchell's heroics was covered by every newspaper in the country and had people asking how good she really was. A Chattanooga sportswriter who was at the game gave his opinion: "Jackie is a better cook than she is a pitcher, and I've never tasted her cooking."

The Nationals arrived in Chattanooga expecting to face the teenage heroine, but wouldn't get the opportunity. Mitchell sustained a sore shoulder in her debut, and her pitching arm was placed in a sling. From there Mitchell would go on to pitch for barnstorming teams before she got tired of being a sideshow, and returned to Chattanooga to work in her father's optical shop.

Washington got the season off to a good start by taking three straight from Philadelphia following an opening-day loss to Lefty Grove, and the Nats were in first place for one week before the Athletics passed them. Johnson didn't panic and felt his pitching depth would make the difference. "Wait until the Athletics have to play double-headers," he said, believing twin bills would expose their lack of pitching depth.

In May the Athletics took control of the pennant race by winning seventeen consecutive games, and while the A's were winning the Nationals were not. In early May they fell below .500, and after a loss to their nemesis Earl Whitehill, Johnson decided it was time for another lecture: "We're not playing half as well as we can, and we better snap out of it right away." Johnson finished by telling his team that they were playing like "like cellar champs at worst."

The Big train got through to his players. They won their next six games, and in June they won sixteen of seventeen games, beating Whitehill in the process. Suddenly they were breathing down the necks of the Athletics.

Leading the way for the Nats was Cronin, who was looking every bit as good as in 1930. In June his batting average was up to .353, while Sammy West, who found out he could hit left-handers as well as right-handers, was batting .362. Leading the pitching staff was left-handed rookie Carl Fischer, who started the season as an unknown and worked out of the bullpen, but after being inserted into the starting rotation won eight of nine decisions.

Johnson had more than his share of problems with his starting rotation. Marberry missed over a month with a pulled groin, Sam Jones left the team to attend to his mom, who was in failing health, Crowder got off to a bad start, and Ad Liska, who had won nine games in 1930 and had the lowest ERA on the staff, developed a sore arm that didn't respond to treatment. He was sent home to recuperate but when he returned he re-injured his arm after being struck by a wild throw during pregame practice. When he returned he was unable to put anything on his pitches. His arm was dead, and he was placed on the voluntary retired list.

A blow to the Washington lineup was the loss of team captain and first baseman Joe Judge, who hit .326 in 1930. While the Nats were in Boston, Judge was rushed to a hospital to have his appendix removed. He remained at the hospital for two weeks, then after returning to Washington he suffered post-surgery complications, and the rest of his season was limited to just twenty pinch-hit at bats.

With Judge out of action the starting first baseman's job went to Joe Kuhel, a former teammate of Cronin's at Kansas City in 1928. Kuhel got off to a great start in 1928 and was about to be purchased by the Cubs until he became ill. When he recovered and returned to the lineup the Cubs withdrew interest, while other interested teams were turned off by his high price tag. Engel, who called him the best first baseman in the minor leagues, convinced Griffith to pay the $65,000 cost, the highest amount he ever paid for a minor leaguer. The total became $50,000 after Kansas City agreed to take two players from Washington's farm club in Chattanooga, and Joe Kuhel became a National in July of 1930. He made an immediate impression on Johnson after he knocked out two hits in his first starting assignment. "I am going on record right now to say that Kuhel is here to stay."

Kuhel hit .286 in 1930 while playing in eighteen games. The plan for him in 1931 was to play every day in Baltimore rather than sit on the bench as Joe Judge's backup, but after Judge became ill Kuhel was called up and became the starting first baseman. For the season he would drive in eighty-five runs, hit eight home runs, bat .269, play well in the field, and leave Washington fans debating who should start at first base in 1932.

On July 13 the Nationals entered Shibe Park to play the Athletics in a double-header, trailing the world champs by six games. With people turning to baseball to get their minds off the Depression, a huge crowd came out to see the twin bill. Shortly after the ticket window opened at 10 A.M. all tickets were sold, and the "Standing Room Only" sign was removed.

The majority of fans who couldn't get a ticket went home, but several thousand remained, determined to see the two games. They stood shoulder-to-shoulder as they congregated on a sidewalk across the street from the left field gate. With game time getting close they charged the ballpark and crashed the gate. The policemen stationed there couldn't hold back the sudden rush of fans, and once inside the ballpark the fans dropped from the left field wall and joined the other fans that paid for a spot on the outfield grass. The umpires delayed the start of the game. After fifteen minutes, with fans still falling onto the field, they decided to start the double-header.

Fred Marberry pitched the first game, and was still looking to get even with Al Simmons for his remarks from the previous season. The first time the two had faced one another in 1931 was back in April, when Johnson called Marberry from the bullpen to pitch to Simmons with the bases loaded, and with Washington clinging to a 2–1 lead. Marberry came through with a strikeout.

A week later in Philadelphia the two faced off under surprising circumstances. Late in the game, with a runner on second, with two outs, and with Simmons on deck, Johnson elected to have Marberry intentionally walk Cochrane, a piece of strategy that had the sportswriters scratching their heads. After the game Johnson told them his pitcher had requested to face Simmons. No pitcher would want to face Simmons with runners on base, but for Marberry it was a chance to show up the arrogant outfielder. The strategy backfired, however, when Simmons knocked out a two-run triple to win the game.

The next time Marberry faced Simmons the star hit an RBI single in his first at bat, and when he came up again Marberry plunked him, which amused the capacity crowd at Griffith Stadium.

Now in the third inning on July 13, Marberry took pleasure in showing up Simmons by fanning him. Two innings later his first pitch sent Simmons ducking for cover. He then proceeded to throw the next three pitches inside, and after ball four Simmons walked toward the mound. Marberry threw away his glove and put his dukes in the air as both dugouts emptied. Home plate umpire Bill McGowan stood between the two players and ordered Simmons to go to first base. "There's too big a crowd out here for us to start anything, but I'll be seeing yuh," said Simmons.

"That's OK with me," said Marberry.

As he stood on first base, Simmons took the opportunity to lash insults at Marberry as the hurler focused on the next batter. After Marberry struck out Foxx to end the inning the hometown crowd showered him with seat cushions and debris before he entered the safety of the Nats' dugout.

The rest of the game and the following game went by without further incident as the two teams split the double-header, but Marberry wasn't through with Simmons. The next time they met the Big Texan dusted him off again and continued to pitch him inside. For the season Marberry got the better of Simmons by limiting him to three hits in fifteen at bats.

The next confrontation Marberry had was with his manager in mid–September, when he was removed from a game after being hit on the hand by a line drive. Marberry didn't want to come out of the game, but Johnson insisted. After entering the dugout the pitcher made a comment as he passed by his manager. Johnson was stunned by the remark: his eyes got big, his face turned red, and he responded by telling the angry pitcher that he was suspended for the season. After the game, however, the two men had a calm conversation and apologized to one another. "I told Marberry to put on his uniform tomorrow," Johnson told the press. "I told him to report as usual tomorrow and we'll forget the whole argument." Johnson did fine the pitcher for his outburst, but wouldn't mention the amount.

Bobby Burke had been a rarely used left-handed pitcher since breaking in with the Nats in 1927. His lack of playing time had the Washington sportswriters questioning why he was kept on the roster for five years, and they felt he belonged in the minor leagues. Due to injuries on the pitching staff, Burke entered the rotation and won five of seven starts, his best outing a 2–1 win over Detroit. In July, Marberry and Jones returned to the rotation and Burke went back to the bullpen until August 8, when Johnson went with a gut feeling and started him against the Red Sox before only three thousand fans at Griffith Stadium. "Cut loose," Johnson told Burke before the game, and cut loose he did, and he became the first pitcher to throw a no-hitter for the Nationals since the Big Train did it back in 1920.

"I'm too nervous to talk," Burke told the sportswriters after the game as he shook under a shower in the Nats clubhouse. The writers were surprised the pitcher wasn't more excited. "Sure, I'm tickled to death," Burke said. "Gee, I'm glad that's over."

"Burke didn't throw more than a half dozen curves all afternoon," said home plate umpire George Moriarty, who described the performance as "flawless."

The Nats gave Burke five runs and played good defense behind him. He issued three walks while striking out eight. Earl Webb, who was on his way to setting the all-time record for most doubles in a season with sixty-seven, came to bat in the ninth inning with two outs. But he had no intention of getting a hit, and he stood in the batter's box and let three pitches go by to end the game.

Burke now had a spot in Johnson's starting rotation, and in his next start in Chicago he received an ovation from the crowd, who considered him a Chicagoan since he was from the nearby town of Joliet. In the first inning he extended his hitless streak to ten innings by sending the While Sox down in order, but in the second the White Sox pounded him for four runs to end his honeymoon. He would make four more starts, got pounded each time, and was demoted back to the bullpen.

Johnson hoped the no-hitter would give his team a boost, but August turned out to be another mediocre month for the Nats and dashed their pennant hopes. The 1931 season was labeled a disappointment by the Washington baseball fans and they spoke out about it. They cited poor managing, lack of team play, weak hitting, poor fielding, poor pitching, and mistakes on the base paths. In other words, everything was wrong with the Nationals in 1931.

The fans may have been too critical, but there wasn't much doubt the team fell short of expectations. The hitting fell off, especially after the month of June, as did that of all other teams due to the new baseball. But regardless of the new ball Washington's hitters hit lower than expected, especially Cronin and Manush. Cronin's batting average fell after June and he finished at .306. He did match his RBI total from 1930 by driving in 126 teammates, but the fans expected more from last year's MVP and began to boo him. Heinie Manush's batting average dropped from .362 to .307, and combined with Crowder's poor start to the season, made the Washington fans question the trade of Goslin, who had a good season in St. Louis.

Buddy Myer's batting average fell to .293, but he improved in the field and finished the year tied for the highest fielding percentage for American League second basemen. Best of all he broke the habit of making the double play pivot off the wrong foot, and despite looking awkward when pivoting he got the job done.

The Athletics were on their way to 107 wins and their third consecutive pennant. They did it with Simmons, Foxx, and Cochrane once again leading the hitting attack, and with the kind of pitching depth Walter Johnson thought they didn't have. Lefty Grove was practically unbeatable in 1931, winning thirty-one of thirty-five decisions, and equaling the American League record set by Walter Johnson and Smokey Joe Wood of sixteen consecutive wins. His streak ended in St. Louis when left fielder Jimmy Moore, who was subbing for Simmons, misplayed a fly ball into an RBI double, and his teammates got only three hits in a 1–0 loss. Afterwards Grove was furious, mostly with Simmons, who elected to stay in Philadelphia to nurse an injury.

With the pennant race decided, the Nationals battled the Yankees for second place. The Nats held an 8½ game lead over New York in June, but the Yankees were improving under their new manager and put things together in July with a record of 22–9.

The New Yorkers needed time to adjust to their new manager, with Tony Lazzeri having the most difficulty, and finding himself riding the bench. Soon there were trade talks with Washington, who offered pitcher Bump Hadley and reserve infielder Jackie Hayes for Lazzeri. The Yankees were OK with Hadley, but insisted on Myer instead of Hayes. Griffith didn't want to repeat the mistake he had made four years earlier in trading Myer, and declined the deal.

In August the Yankees won ten games in a row and moved past Washington in the standings, but Washington bounced back and led the race for sec-

Goose Goslin was traded to the Browns during the 1930 season. In 1931, the Washington baseball fans wanted him back.

ond place until the second-to-last day of the season, when they were swept in a doubleheader at Yankee Stadium that clinched the runner-up spot for New York. As the disappointed Nationals headed home not a word was spoken during the train ride. They did win ninety-two games, but viewed their 1931 season as a disappointment.

8

Damn Yankees (1932)

"The day before Roy Johnson knocked Dickey down, loosening a couple of teeth. Dickey said the next man who roughed him up had better watch out."

— Joe McCarthy

The Nationals arrived in Biloxi believing 1932 would be their year. The Cardinals proved the Athletics weren't invincible by beating them in the 1931 World Series, and the Nats considered themselves better than the Yankees based on their having finished eight games ahead of them in 1930, and felt they should've finished ahead of New York in 1931.

Walter Johnson's three-year contract expired at the end of 1931, but he was hired to manage another season. Along with Griffith, he worked on getting another outfielder to replace Sam Rice, who could still hit at age forty-two, but couldn't field his position.

Griffith wanted Goose Goslin back. He wouldn't solve the fielding problem, but he could hit, and Griffith hoped his popularity in the Capital would help at the box office. Goslin made it clear, however, he wouldn't play for Walter Johnson, and he would remain in St. Louis for another season.

The White Sox had an outfielder available, and a trade was made for twenty-nine-year old Carl Reynolds, a good all-around player, who hit for average and power, could field, and possessed a strong throwing arm. He was known to be a hard-nosed player who had a reputation for being aggressive on the base paths, and wouldn't hesitate to use his college football experience to knock over any catcher who blocked the plate to prevent him from scoring.

To get Reynolds the Nats traded pitchers Sam Jones and Bump Hadley, and infielder Jackie Hayes. Most were critical of the trade, claiming two pitchers was too much to give, but Johnson disagreed, believing Carl Fischer and Bobby Burke would fill in, and he was high on rookie Monte Weaver.

Weaver was a former mathematics professor at the University of Virginia who had burned out on teaching and decided to concentrate on his pitching career. He had a good fastball and an excellent curve; he won twenty-one games for Baltimore in 1931, and defeated the Nationals in an April exhibition game. Joe Engel scouted him after being told by Griffith to spend less time promoting in Chattanooga and more time scouting, and he was impressed enough to arrange for Weaver's purchase. The Orioles insisted that Weaver be allowed to complete his 1931 season in Baltimore, and the Nats agreed, but that changed when the Orioles pitched him in both ends of a double-header in ninety-degree weather. Griffith was furious when he heard the news, and he instructed the Orioles to send Weaver to Washington before they wore him out. On September 20 he made his major-league debut and defeated the White Sox.

"He'll win twenty for us," Griffith said of Weaver in Biloxi.

"He knows how to pitch," said Johnson, who claimed his curve ball was among the best in the league.

"Weaver is the finished product," said Joe Cronin.

While in Biloxi, the Nationals were joined by a catcher who was one of baseball's most interesting personalities. Shirley Povich described the new catcher to his readers: "The average mentality of the Washington ball club was hiked several degrees with the acquisition of the eminent Moe Berg." Berg was a Princeton graduate, who had a law degree from Columbia, and was believed to fluently speak one dozen languages. He was known to read bilingual newspapers each day, and to give signals on the field in Hindu and Yiddish.

The Nats were able to obtain Berg after the Indians gave him his unconditional release, but because a knee injury had limited him to just thirty games the previous two seasons, there was doubt about his being a major league–caliber player. Both Carl Reynolds and John Kerr (who was obtained in the trade with Reynolds), teammates of Berg's in Chicago, assured everyone the Nats were getting a good catcher.

Berg had begun his career in Brooklyn in 1923 as a shortstop. From there he became a utility infielder with the White Sox until an emergency situation in 1927. Injuries had left the White Sox with just one catcher, and catcher-manager Ray Schalk, who was among the injured, spoke about bringing in a backup from a class C or D minor league. Berg overheard Schalk talk about his plan and said, "Don't worry, you have a pretty good catcher sitting on the bench."

"The funny part of it is I wasn't thinking about myself," Berg told Povich shortly after he arrived. "I was referring to Earl Sheeley, our first baseman." Berg was aware that Sheeley did some catching in the Pacific Coast League and figured he could do the job. As luck would have it, Chicago's catcher, Harry McCurdy, was injured in a collision at home plate, and the White Sox were now out of catchers. "OK, Berg, get in there and catch," said Schalk.

There was no way to back out now, and Berg, whose only catching experience was during his sandlot days, entered the game and did the job. The real test came the next day when Berg was penciled in as Chicago's starting catcher against the 1927 New York Yankees. Berg proved he could handle a pitched ball, but how would he do on a play at the plate? The answer came in the seventh inning when Cedric Durst of the Yankees singled with teammate Joe Dugan on second base. Dugan rounded third and headed for home. Berg caught the throw from outfielder Bib Falk and tagged Dugan for an out. The other eight White Sox on the field came over to home plate to give Berg a pat on the back. Chicago won that day 6–3, and for better or for worse Berg was a catcher for the rest of his career.

Joe Judge reported to Biloxi in great shape, eager to get his starting job back after a season limited to seventy-four at bats due to illness. There were rumors he would go to Detroit to be Bucky Harris's everyday first baseman, and he was OK with that. Judge didn't care where he played if it gave him the chance to play every day. But a hand injury to Kuhel put the younger first baseman out of action and Judge had an excellent spring, hitting .375 to win the starting job.

The Nationals began the season without Cronin, who was sidelined with a sinus infection and tonsillitis. With Kerr filling in at shortstop, they won their first game over Boston, their first opening day win since 1927, and proceeded to sweep the four-game series. Cronin returned to the lineup and the Nats won seven of their next eleven games for an 11–4 start. In May the Nationals began the month with a three-game sweep over the other American League team off to a good start, the Yankees. One of those wins was a 10–3 drubbing of New York's pitching ace, Lefty Gomez.

Leading the way in Washington's fast start was Carl Reynolds, who was eating up opposing pitchers. In May he was hitting .420, but after American League pitchers got wise to the fact he was getting his hits on fastballs, Reynolds began to see curve balls, and went 0 for his next nineteen at bats.

Washington remained hot, even though Reynolds wasn't, and in mid–May their record was 19–5. Maybe 1932 was going to be their year.

Around this time a group of worn-out and financially ruined World War I veterans entered the nation's capital, determined to collect the bonuses that were promised for their service to their country. Their bonuses weren't due to be paid until 1945, but with the Depression in full swing, and with few jobs available, they wanted them now.

The veterans were welcomed, and were told to stay as long as they wanted as long as there were no Reds or Socialists among them. They set up their camps in vacated buildings, and acted in an orderly manner, cooperated with the district, and kept their camps clean. Several organizations supported them by chipping in to keep them fed and supplied with necessities. Clark Griffith gave his support by loaning his stadium for no charge, and the bonus seekers took advantage by staging boxing matches on the evening of June 7. Fifteen thousand Washingtonians came out to watch the bouts that began at 8:15 and lasted until 12:30. Admission was free but donations were requested. The crowd contributed $3,000, a total of twenty cents per attendee.

"Well, well, well. Keep up the good work until the Browns knock you off."

These were the words on Phil Ball's telegram to Clark Griffith after the Nationals swept the Yankees. The St. Louis owner's words turned out to be a promise instead of a threat after the Browns came to Griffith Stadium and swept the four game series, with Goslin doing damage by collecting ten hits in seventeen at bats. After the Browns left town the Nats lost their momentum and began to sink in the standings. By the end of June they were in fourth place, apparently headed for another disappointing season. Frank Young attributed the slide to the team's "lack of mental toughness."

The season was turning into another one of underachieving performances. As a team the Nats were fifth in the league in hitting with a .274 batting average. Pitching was a disappointment, especially Bobby Burke and Carl Fischer. To add strength to the pitching department Fischer was traded to the Browns for Dick Coffman, the pitcher who had hurled a three-hit shutout against the A's the previous August to snap Grove's sixteen-game winning streak. Coffman turned out to be a bust, however, winning only one game. Tommy Thomas was obtained from the White Sox and pitched well, but got little support from the slumping hitters, as indicated by his four-hit loss to the Yankees.

Walter Johnson became fed up with his players performing below expectations, especially Buddy Myer. In late May against the Yankees, Myer returned to the dugout after flying out to drop his batting average below .260. Johnson glowered at him as he sat on the bench, then made a sarcastic comment about his hitting. Myer replied and Johnson responded by taking him out of the game. After the game Johnson said all was forgotten and Myer would play in the next day's double-header in Philadelphia.

In mid–June, after a lopsided win over he Browns, Johnson predicted his team would go on a winning streak. The next day, however, his team dropped a pair to St. Louis, and Johnson was heartbroken. "That double loss makes me want to go back to the farm where I can communicate with nature and have no worries." The following day the Nats were pounded by St. Louis, 17–3.

The New York Yankees were dominating the American League. They came to Griffith Stadium for a Fourth of July double-header with a record of 50–21, and were 8½ games ahead of the second-place Athletics. Their hitting attack was as strong as ever with Babe Ruth, now thirty-seven years old and showing no signs of age, Bill Dickey blossoming into a star, Tony Lazzeri reclaiming his star status and now on good terms with his manager, and first baseman Lou Gehrig having a great season as usual, plus an unbelievable day on June 2 when he hit four home runs in one game at Philadelphia in a 20–13 Yankees win.

The New York pitching staff was the best in the American League. Lefty Gomez was leading the way with a 14–1 record, and leading the league with 114 strikeouts. Currently he had an eleven-game winning streak since losing his only game of the year in Washington back on May 2. Rookie Johnny Allen had a 6–1 record, and like Gomez, his only loss was to Washington. Red Ruffing had a

Moe Berg joined the Senators before the 1932 season.

7–2 record, and was second in the league to Gomez in strikeouts with eighty-five.

Bill Dickey was batting .332 with eleven home runs and fifty-five runs batted in, but his season wasn't all trouble-free. During the series the Yankees were swept by Washington in May, he argued with an umpire, and lost his cool to the point he drew a three-game suspension. In late June a tipped ball struck his leg and sidelined him for a few days with a deep thigh bruise. He returned to the lineup in Boston on July 3, and was lucky to avoid serious injury when bowled over on a play at the plate. The play occurred after a Red Sox hit, and Roy Johnson, who was the runner on second, rounded third and headed for home. Dickey took off his mask, blocked the plate, and caught a perfect throw from Babe Ruth that arrived ahead of the runner. Johnson, knowing he would be tagged out, plowed into Dickey and knocked the catcher flat on his back. Dickey lost consciousness and later discovered a few of his teeth were knocked loose. The Yankees screamed bloody murder, protesting that Johnson's play was too aggressive and unnecessary, but the umpires ruled it part of the game, and since Dickey was unable to hang onto the ball, Johnson was safe. The Yankees showed Roy Johnson he couldn't get away with roughing up one of their guys: the next time he came to the plate pitcher George Pipgras winged one past his ear.

One day later, in the bottom of the seventh of the first game at Griffith Stadium, the Nationals were trailing 3–2, but threatening. Carl Reynolds, who was now batting .302, singled and advanced to third on another single. Johnny Kerr was sent up as a pinch hitter, and was instructed to squeeze. Kerr squared to bunt but missed the ball, and Reynolds, who was halfway down the line, quickly scampered back towards third. Dickey whipped the ball to third baseman Joe Sewell, but the throw hit Reynolds in the back and the ball bounced sideways towards the Yankees dugout. Reynolds broke for home as Sewell ran to retrieve the ball, and Bill Dickey got ready for a play by taking off his mask and stepping forward to block the plate. Reynolds and Sewell's throw both arrived at the same time, and Reynolds slammed into the catcher, knocking him on his back for the second consecutive day. The ball rolled towards the backstop, and Dickey got up, but didn't retrieve the ball. Instead he clenched his fist and trailed Reynolds, who walked towards the Washington dugout. The Nats outfielder shook the batboy's hand, then thought he may have missed home plate during the collision, and decided to go back and touch home to be sure. As he did an about face he was greeted by a right cross from Dickey.

Both dugouts emptied, and the players congregated at home plate, but no punches were thrown. The crowd of fifteen thousand, stunned by what they had witnessed, was in an uproar. "Why don't you put your mask back on? You have all of your other equipment on!" a fan shouted to Dickey. A few fans ran onto the field, hoping to get into the action, but policemen headed them off. One fan, a middle-aged man, was able to make it to the group of angry ballplayers, and he was arrested.

After being punched, Reynolds stumbled backwards before a teammate caught him. Everything had gone blank, and when he came to his senses he thought he had been hit by the bat or ball. The next thing he knew an umpire was warning him against retaliation while another umpire was informing Dickey that he was disqualified (and a player who is disqualified from the first game of a double-header is ineligible to play in the nightcap).

Reynolds was helped to the dugout, where Mike Martin examined him. The Washington trainer suspected he had a broken jaw and made arrangements to get him to a hospital right away for X-rays. Martin's hunch was right. Reynolds's jaw was broken in two places. His jaw was wired, and he would be on a liquid diet for a while. He managed to open his mouth wide enough to form words and talk about the incident: "The only regret I have is I didn't get to hit Dickey back."

Back at Griffith Stadium, Griffith received the news and immediately dispatched a telegram to Will Harridge, requesting suspension for Dickey equal to the time Reynolds would be out. He also requested either Dickey or the Yankees to pay the medical bills.

The Nationals defeated the Yankees, 5–3, and in the process snapped Lefty Gomez's eleven-game winning streak. Another game remained to be played and there wasn't much doubt there would be trouble. It didn't take long for things to heat up when in the bottom of the first Johnny Allen knocked down Buddy Myer with his first pitch of the game. Nationals coach Patsy Gharrity, who was beside himself in the Washington dugout, came on to the field and made his way towards Allen. Johnson came over from the first base coach's box to head off the angry coach and persuaded him to get back into the dugout and remain there.

After ducking Allen's knockdown pitch, Myer belted a double, and later in the inning tallied the first run of the game. In the third inning Allen delivered a pitch that struck Myer on the right elbow. Myer was in pain and the game was delayed for five minutes while Walter Johnson and Mike Martin attended to him. The tough second baseman remained in the game, took his base, and the game continued.

The next batter was Heinie Manush, and he hit one over the right field wall. As Myer rounded third base, he shouted for Allen's attention. "At least you're a fair hotel clerk!" he told him, a reference to the pitcher's former job, and a not so nice reference to what he thought about his pitching.

After three innings Washington led 4–0, and Myer wouldn't have to worry about Allen since he was removed from the game, and on his way to his second loss of the season. The Yankees, however, weren't finished with Myer, and in the fourth inning Gehrig knocked him down with a hard slide into second base. Myer retaliated an inning later by purposely chopping one to the pitcher, and as he approached first base slid with his spikes up and ripped Gehrig's trousers. Myer quickly got up in anticipation of a fight, but the Yankees first baseman gave a good-natured smile and said nothing.

An inning later Babe Ruth knocked down Myer with a hard slide. Manush, fed up with the Yankees' going after Myer, decided to retaliate, and after hitting a triple he slid hard into third base and sent third baseman Joe Sewell backpedaling ten feet.

When the second game ended, with a 12–6 Washington win to complete the double-header sweep, the question was how long Dickey would be suspended. The Yankees catcher received a telegram from Harridge the next day informing him he was suspended indefinitely for his "malicious and unwarranted" attack. Later that afternoon Buddy Myer puffed on a cigar as he spoke with Tom Doerer, sportswriter from the *Washington Evening Star*. Myer was at Washington's Hamilton Hotel, working with a committee in planning Sam Rice Day, a special day set aside for the long-time Washington outfielder at Griffith Stadium, scheduled to take place on July 19. Myer and Doerer discussed the actions of Bill Dickey the previous day. The Nats second baseman didn't condemn the Yankee catcher, but spoke about thinking twice before reacting, or suffering the consequences during these "hard times." "You've got to take a lot on the field today and like it," Myer said. "When you figure a poke on the chin is going to cost you a couple hundred bucks and a parking spot on the bench for a few days, a ball player is going to take a lot before smacking the sender."

For Dickey a cost of a few hundred dollars and a parking spot on the bench for a few days would have been a gift. When Harridge announced his verdict, it was for $1,000 and a thirty-day suspension. McCarthy and Colonel Ruppert were shocked by the severity of the penalty, and both complained it was too harsh. After they let Harridge know how they felt, the league president told them they had the right to appeal, and they would get their chance within the next few days when the league board, a group made up of three American League owners, would meet in Cleveland during the American League's summer meeting.

Griffith also complained about the penalty, saying it wasn't enough. "That was no fight. It was an assault and you could quote me," he told Frank Young.

Harridge made another announcement that day that would change baseball forever, and it may have been motivated by Johnny Allen's dusting off Myer. He instructed his umpires to eject any pitcher caught in the act of attempting to intimidate batters by "dusting them off" and throwing the "bean ball." At the summer meeting he informed the American League owners of the consequences for all offenders. A first offense would be a game ejection. A second offense would be a ten-game suspension without pay. And a third offense would be a thirty-game suspension without pay. For Myer the announcement came too late, but at least he knew Allen would think twice before throwing at him.

Another meeting in Cleveland took place before the American League Board of Alva Bradley, Bob Quinn, and Harry Grabiner, the long-time White Sox vice president and secretary, who represented Louis Comiskey. The Board upheld Harridge's decision on Bill Dickey.

"So far as I'm concerned, it is all over," announced Colonel Ruppert.

"We'll have to make the best it," said McCarthy.

When Dickey was asked how he felt he shrugged his shoulders and said nothing.

Two weeks after having his jaw wired and living on a liquid diet, Reynolds and his wife came out of a movie theater on a humid evening, and climbed into a taxi to get back to their summer home at the Wardman Park Hotel. During their ride Reynolds complained of nausea, then began to cough and vomit. With his mouth wired he couldn't breathe nor could he heave, and he was in danger of strangling to death. He may have if not for the quick thinking of Mrs. Reynolds, who reached into her purse for her manicure scissors and ordered the cab driver to pull over by a light post. Reynolds and his wife got out of the taxi where luckily there was enough light for Mrs. Reynolds to see the wires, which she cut with her scissors, and her husband was able to open his mouth. Quick thinking and her actions made Mrs. Reynolds an all-star.

Sam Rice and Dave Harris filled in for Reynolds in right field. At age forty-two, Rice was on his way to another season of batting over .300 (he finished at .323). For eighteen seasons Sam Rice wore the uniform of the Washington Nationals, and for his service to the team, and to Washington, D.C., he was honored on July 19, Sam Rice Day.

Up to this point of the 1932 season, Rice had a lifetime batting average of .324. He hit over .300 thirteen times. He played in over 2,200 games, scored over 1,500 runs, and made 2,864 hits, the most among all active players in 1932. He was an outstanding citizen, who often attended the theater with his wife, visited bowling alleys and pool halls, and kept up on politics and with the happenings in society. A large turnout was expected, with a percentage of the gate receipts to go to Rice, but for whatever reason, perhaps due to the presence of the Bonus Army, a small crowd turned out. Griffith was surprised and disappointed, but was determined to make sure Rice got a nice payday on his special day.

After Griffith instructed his secretary, Elizabeth King, to connect him with Frank Nevin, the president of the Detroit Tigers, he explained the situation to Nevin. The attendance on Sam Rice day was just 5,093, and this would give Rice a check for just $100. To increase the amount Griffith was willing to take his end out of a 3,500 crowd in Detroit, and give the difference to Rice. "Why stop at 3,500?" Nevin replied. "We'll call it a 3,000 crowd and give the difference. That's the way the Detroit Club feels about Sam Rice."

Rice received a check for $2,235 and was showered with gifts from the Washington, D.C. community, including a Studebaker, a massive suitably engraved silver cup, an electric clock, a wristwatch, a portrait, a set of golf clubs, and letters from President Hoover and Will Harridge. In his letter Harridge wrote he regretted his absence due to a prior commitment, but expressed his appreciation to Rice for his character and told him he was a credit to the game of baseball.

Rice approached the microphone and thanked the people of Washington, and said this was the greatest day of his career. And to put an explanation point on his day he singled in his first at bat. Umpire Brick Owens called time out, called for the baseball, tossed it to Walter Johnson and told him to give it to Rice as a souvenir.

It was not known if the small turnout for Sam Rice Day was due to the Bonus Army, but there was no doubt their presence was having an effect on Washington's everyday business. They had become a threat to the safety and security of Washingtonians, who were annoyed with their constant begging, with their roaming through the streets intoxicated, and by their thefts.

The citizens of Washington had been curious when the Bonus Army first arrived. Many of them traveled to their camps to see them, and when they staged a march through the capital on June 6, over 100,000 came out to watch. There was hope for the Bonus Army in June when the Bonus Bill passed the House of Representatives, but it died in the Senate. The disappointed bonus seekers vowed to remain in the capital until they were assured their payments. Congress made it clear they weren't welcome and gave them an incentive to leave by offering to pay their fare home. Some took up the offer, while most elected to stay.

The Bonus Army made their homes in three camps around the city. Two were on Capitol Hill, where they occupied vacated buildings, set up tents, and built wooden shanties, while the other camp, known as Camp Marks, was located across the Anacostia River. Throughout the summer the camps' population grew, and there was doubt as to how many of the bonus seekers were actual veterans.

The day after Sam Rice Day the bonus seekers were instructed to leave the city by August 1. Later the date was moved up to July 27, and as that date approached, the largest number of patrolmen since the race riots of 1919 appeared in Washington.

July 27 passed, and the Bonus Army remained. On the morning of July 28, treasury agents showed up with a police escort at the camp located at Third and Pennsylvania. They entered a building the veterans occupied and announced it had to be evacuated for a construction crew that was due to knock it down later that day. A group of Bonus Men on the ground floor, their bags packed, peacefully obliged. On the second level were those who refused to leave and the treasury agents literally carried them down the steps, one by one, and out of the building.

As policemen watched the treasury agents do their work, they were informed two troops of veterans from Camp Marks were heading their way. When those veterans arrived they were ready to fight and began by throwing bricks. The policemen fought back, using their nightsticks. Two veterans were shot; one of them died. An officer was hit over the head and fell unconscious, his skull fractured. Pelham Glassford, the Washington police superintendent, realized his police force was going against a hostile group and worried for their safety. He quickly spoke up and announced, "Come on, boys, let's call an armistice for lunch anyhow." The fighting stopped and men from both sides cheered.

During the afternoon the citizens of Washington couldn't believe their eyes as they lined the sidewalks and watched the cavalry and tanks move down Pennsylvania Avenue. Among the spectators were three members of the Bonus Army who taunted the troops. "To hell with Hoover!" they shouted. A captain on horseback heard their insults and directed his horse towards the sidewalk. The three men saw him coming and ran away as fast as they could. "Get the hell out of here!" the Captain shouted.

It was an eerie sight to see the U.S Army line up against the veterans who had preceded them and fought in the Great War fourteen years before, but this was the scene at Pennsylvania and Third. Eighteen members of the current Army stepped forward, fixed bayonets, and put on gas masks as the veterans jeered them. An officer yelled a command, and three men stepped forward and hurled something at the veterans that hit the ground with a plop. "It's gas," one observer said to another.

The soldiers moved forward and the veterans began to scatter in disarray. A few veterans threw bricks, while another picked up a gas bomb and threw it back at the soldiers. As the veterans ran, the soldiers began to set fire to their shanties. Black smoke hovered over the capital, and was visible from the White House. Tear gas wafted across Pennsylvania Avenue and traveled for seven blocks, affecting several citizens. General Douglas MacArthur, in charge of the troops, elected not to wear a mask, and led the troops to the other camp on Capitol Hill, where tear gas was used, the veterans evacuated, and fire set to their shanties.

With his eyes red, his cheeks covered with tears, MacArthur issued controversial orders to have Camp Marks evacuated. Camp Marks was located across the Anacostia, and wasn't a threat like the other two camps on Capitol Hill. Many of its occupants were there with their families, with no income, and without homes. MacArthur didn't sympathize with them, and since there was uncertainty about how many were really veterans, he considered them a threat and went through with his plan. As the last of the veterans ran from the camp, one yelled, "We'll be back next winter." "Yes, and not so peaceful next time," shouted another veteran.

The next day Washingtonians went about their business, coughing and rubbing their irritated eyes from the effects of the tear gas. The cavalry followed orders to stop and check buses for veterans who might still be around. Newspapers around the country, all having stories and pictures of the events from Washington, questioned if such action taken by the government and cavalry was necessary. Readers were outraged and sent letters of protest to Congress and the White House.

On August 4, Bill Dickey was greeted with a chorus of boos and catcalls by the crowd at Comiskey Park in his first game back from his suspension. His second time at bat the crowd was louder, but Dickey quieted them by socking a grand slam. The Yankees catcher went four for six with five runs batted in on the day, and on his last trip to the plate the crowd cheered him.

The following day the Nats were trailing in Detroit, 13–0, and couldn't get a hit off Tigers pitcher Tommy Bridges, who had a perfect game through 8²/₃ innings. The twenty-five-year-old right-hander was one out away from immortality, and with the pitcher due up next, it appeared he had it. Then Walter Johnson made a surprise move when he sent up the league's best pinch hitter, Dave Harris. With eight thousand fans at Briggs Stadium holding their breath, Harris swung and hit the first pitch into left field for a single. A moment later Sam Rice grounded out to end the game, and Bridges would have to settle for a one-hit shutout. Johnson was criticized for his decision to send up Harris in a hopeless situation. Griffith wasn't happy about his manager's decision, especially since the Tigers had been so supportive on Sam Rice Day.

One week later the Yankees were back in Washington for the first time since the Fourth of July fiasco, and with Bill Dickey in their lineup. In the crowd of eight thousand was Will Harridge, who wanted to be sure there was order between the two teams, and with the league president on hand both teams were on their best behavior.

With two outs in the top of the tenth, Red Ruffing broke a scoreless tie by hitting a home run off Tommy Thomas into the left field bleachers. In the bottom of the tenth Johnson sent up a pinch hitter, someone who was unrecognizable when he first emerged from the dugout. Then it was realized that the player was Carl Reynolds, who was hard to identify because he was below his playing weight due to his liquid diet, and wasn't expected to return for another week. The crowd stood up and cheered as Reynolds swung the two bats and walked towards home plate. He walked directly at Dickey and stood very close to the catcher while swinging. Frank Young described the distance as "dangerously close."

Reynolds put down the extra bat and stepped into the batter's box. As he got ready Dickey took one step forward, leaned in, and mumbled something. An apology? "Ask Reynolds," Dickey said when asked after the game. "Ask Dickey," said Reynolds when he was asked.

Red Ruffing threw a fastball. Reynolds took a healthy cut and connected. The ball traveled towards the deepest part of the ballpark in right center field. The crowd roared, thinking how perfect for Reynolds to do this to the Yankees on his first at bat back from injury. Center fielder Earle Combs sprinted back towards the outfield wall, his back turned to the infield as he looked over his right shoulder to keep the ball in view. Without missing a stride the speedy outfielder made a leap, reached up, and plucked the ball out of the air for a long out. The crowd let out a groan of disappointment. A moment later Ruffing got the third out for a 1–0 Yankees win.

The next day the Yankees won again, with Reynolds appearing as a pinch hitter in the sixth inning with the bases loaded. Lefty Gomez struck him out on three curve balls. "Gomez made Reynolds look as foolish with three hooks as Dickey did with one," joked a New York sportswriter.

The two losses to the Yankees dropped the Senators' season record to 61–51. They were still in fourth place and their season, which had started off so well, was now written off as a disappointment. Washington baseball fans began to talk about 1933 and wondered if Johnson would be back as manager. Griffith refused to comment, but the assumption was Johnson could have the job as long as he pleased for his great service to the Nationals organization.

What was Griffith really thinking about 1933? One day Al Schacht was in his office when he let the cat out of the bag. "Al, I'm going to have to do something soon which I've been hoping to avoid. It breaks my heart." He paused for a moment. "I feel I must get rid of Johnson."

Schacht wasn't surprised to hear this, but thought it best to keep quiet and listen. Griffith continued, "He was my best pitcher, at times my only pitcher, my bread and butter. We've been together for so many years I have actually idolized the man. But I can't kid myself any longer. I don't think he's proven to be a good manager. It's time for a change."

Schacht asked Griffith if he had a replacement in mind. Griffith mentioned Ossie Vitt, who was having a successful season managing the Oakland Oaks of the Pacific Coast League, but wasn't sure he wanted him. Griffith stared out his office window and said nothing as he rolled a pencil between his fingers. Schacht got up and left Griffith to his thoughts.

Schacht had his own idea as to whom he wanted to manage. Later that day in the clubhouse he called out to Joe Cronin, who was in the showers: "Joe, have you ever thought about managing some day?"

"Yeah, probably, when my playing days are over," Cronin said. "I'd like to stay in baseball ... why?"

"Just asking," said Schacht.

"I am likely to ruin a great shortstop," Griffith said to Schacht.

"My eye!" replied Schacht. "When you made Harris your manager, he became a greater player.... Give it to Cronin, Griff."

"I'll think it over," said Griffith.

Walter Johnson was back on the pitcher's mound. Bucky Harris took his familiar position at second base. Peckinpaugh, Ruel, McNeeley, Zachary, Goslin, and the rest of the 1924 Nationals were all back to play a game at Griffith Stadium against the current Washington team before 11,561 fans, who came to cheer on the old-timers.

Johnson, Harris, and Peckinpaugh were all currently managing in the American League, and were the only three players from the 1924 team whose playing careers were finished. All of the other former Nats on hand were playing for major or minor league teams, and were granted permission by their teams to take the day off to be in Washington.

Earl McNeeley, who was currently player-manager for the Sacramento Senators of the Pacific Coast League, wanted to be in Washington so badly he flew in and arrived at the airport in time to get to Griffith Stadium to watch the current team play the Yankees.

As the old gang met in the clubhouse before the game, they all shook hands and said how nice it was to be back.

"Say, Bucky, are we going to have any signals today, or is it every man for himself?" asked Goslin.

Packinpaugh requested a pair of sliding pads. "I don't want to hurt myself bending over for a grounder."

The current team defeated the former World Champions, 6–2. Johnson pitched three innings, gave up five runs on eight hits, and had no strikeouts. In the ninth inning Earl McNeeley came to the plate, and Nick Altrock called time out, then carried a rock onto the field and placed it in front of third base. Hoping to recreate the dramatic game-winning hit from the 1924 World Series, McNeeley aimed for it, barely missed, and the result was a grounder to the third baseman and a double play.

The Nationals appeared to be inspired by the 1924 team, and they began to play their best baseball of the season. They finished the month of August by winning thirteen of sixteen games, then traveled to New York to play the Yankees.

In the first game General Crowder, who was having his best season, pitched his twentieth win of the year. He would finish the season by winning his last fifteen decisions and led the league with twenty-six victories. In the bottom of the ninth, Crowder was working on a shutout and trying to become the first pitcher to blank the Yankees since Wilcy Moore of the Red Sox did it on August 2, 1931. Two days earlier the Yankees had surpassed the American League record, set by the 1927 Yankees, who went 110 games before being shut out, and now were closing in on the all-time record set back in 1884 by Boston and Philadelphia, who each went that entire season of 136 games without being shut out.

With two outs to go, Crowder suddenly couldn't throw strikes. After he had put two men on by throwing eight consecutive balls, Red Ruffing came up as a pinch hitter and singled in a run to keep the Yankees' steak alive.

The next day Fred Marberry was on the verge of shutting out the Yankees, with Sam West helping out by making a leaping one-handed catch at the fence to rob Gehrig of a home run. With one out in the ninth inning Babe Ruth drew a walk, then Gehrig tripled to score Ruth.

Earle Combs kept the Yankees' streak intact in the final game of the series when he hit Monte Weaver's fourth pitch of the day over the right field wall. Although the chance to shut out the Yankees was gone, the game still had meaning for the Nats. If they could win to complete the series sweep, they would be the only team to win the 1932 season series with New York. In the ninth inning they led 5–4, and lefty pitcher Lloyd Brown was in the game to face Ruth and Gehrig. He struck out Ruth for the second out of the inning, but walked Gehrig. Then Lazzeri knocked one into the right field seats for a 6–5 Yankees win to prevent Washington from winning the season series.

The grudge match between the two teams continued during the series. Ben Chapman of the Yankees decided to get involved in the feud by spiking Buddy Myer on a play at second base, leaving a scar for life on Myer's leg. Myer didn't retaliate and he said nothing; he just gave Chapman an angry look to communicate he knew his actions were intentional.

After leaving New York the Nats remained hot, winning their next nine in a row, and during their winning streak Monte Weaver became a twenty-game winner, just as Griffith had predicted in the spring. The former mathematics professor won twenty-two games in his rookie season, and along with Crowder, Washington had two twenty-game winners.

Leading the hitting attack were Heinie Manush and Joe Cronin. Manush had a great second half, finishing with a .342 batting average, and led the league with 214 total hits. Cronin hit .318, drove in 116 runs, and led the league with eighteen triples.

Another bright spot was the performance of Joe Kuhel, who moved into the starting lineup in mid-season. Many fans, however, wanted the popular Joe Judge to start, and at times were too tough on Kuhel. A fan was giving it to the young first baseman after he made a misplay. "Aw, give him time," another fan said.

"Yeah, I'll give him time. Time in Leavenworth [federal penitentiary]," the fan shot back.

After playing the 1924 team, the Nationals finished the season by winning thirty-two of their last forty-two games. They finished with ninety-three wins, the third consecutive season they had won over ninety games, but without coming close to winning the pennant. In 1932, they finished third, fourteen games behind the Yankees and a game behind the Athletics.

A frustrated Clark Griffith wondered what it would take to win the pennant. He wasn't sure, but knew where to start.

9

New Deal for the Senators

"Boy, what a victory," Babe Ruth bellowed in the jubilant Yankees clubhouse following New York's 13–6 win at Wrigley Field, to win the 1932 World Series.

"My hat is off to you, Mac," Ruth told the Yankees manager as he shook his hand.

"I'm the happiest man in the world," McCarthy announced, as his players congratulated him with handshakes and a few pats on the back.

For McCarthy, sweeping the Cubs was sweet revenge. The late William Wrigley had fired him two years before, explaining he had to have a winner, after McCarthy had inherited a last-place team in 1926 and led them to five consecutive winning seasons, including the National League pennant in 1929.

"Boys, how about a little song?" hollered Yankees coach Art Fletcher. With arms over shoulders, the Yankees broke into the popular turn-of-the-century song, "The Sidewalks of New York."

> East Side, West Side, all around the town. The tots sang "Ring around the rosie," "London Bridge is falling down."
> Boys and girls together, me and Mammie O'Roarke.
> We tripped the light fantastic on the sidewalks of New York.

Two days after the singing Yankees celebrated, Clark Griffith made an announcement to the Washington sportswriters: "Walter Johnson will not manage in 1933. We have yet to pick a successor." The sportswriters wanted to know who was being considered, but Griffith would not budge. "I haven't even given the matter a thought," he told them.

The press speculated Joe Judge, Sam Rice, or Bucky Harris as the front-runners. Harris, whose closest friends claimed he had a verbal agreement with Griffith, was contacted at his Washington residence, but he refused to comment. A day later he signed for two more seasons with his current employer, the Detroit Tigers.

Most were predicting Joe Judge, based on his experience, his leadership, and years of service to the Senators. Frank Young had a hunch that Griffith was thinking about Joe Cronin, and reminiscing about nine years earlier, when he hired Bucky Harris to manage at the age of twenty-seven. Shirley Povich wasn't making any prognostications, but was intrigued over the idea of Griffith's coming out of retirement. It was a long shot, but Griffith said he would manage in case of an emergency.

As Washingtonians made their guesses, and answered the polls conducted by the Washington newspapers, Joe Cronin lay in a hospital bed, following surgery to remove his tonsils. Having no idea he was a candidate, he was more interested in being discharged and heading back home to San Francisco than who the next Washington manager would be. After leaving the hospital, he went to his rented room at the Wardman Park Hotel and began to pack his belongings. He planned to take an evening train to San Francisco, but his plans changed when his phone rang. It was Griffith, who requested his immediate presence at his office.

Cronin was eager to accept the job, but Griffith warned him not to jump at it. Not until he told him the ins and outs of managing. For two hours behind closed doors the Old Fox did everything to discourage him from wanting the position. He told him about his own experiences, and about Bucky Harris's being atop the World after winning two pennants and a World Series, then being booed out of town.

Cronin listened. Asked questions. He thought to himself, and he was more eager than ever to accept the position.

His boss was impressed. To Griffith this proved his new manager not only had confidence, but also had a fighting heart. "Cronin is a scrapper," Griffith said at the press conference the following morning. "He thinks nothing but baseball. I like these young fellows who fight for everything."

Cronin, who was four days shy of his twenty-sixth birthday, was so excited he could hardly speak. "I had ambitions to be a manager, but never had any idea I would have a chance so soon," he said, his voice still hoarse from surgery. "Naturally I'm tickled to death."

That afternoon Cronin returned to Griffith Stadium, this time as a spectator for a college football game, and watched Alabama defeat George Washington, 28–6. Throughout the game he shook hands and acknowledged the many who congratulated him and wished him well. Later that evening he received several phone calls, including one from Walter Johnson, who gave him his best wishes. Of all the praise he had received, the Big Train's meant the most to him.

"You have a lot of constructing to do before you win that first pennant, young fella," Griffith told his manager, as the two met on the following Monday. They examined their roster, and the rosters of the seven other American League teams, especially the powerful lineup of the New York Yankees. The 1932 Yankees had scored over one thousand runs for the third consecutive season. They had set a record by going an entire 154-game schedule without being shut out. In the World Series they had batted .313, scored thirty-seven runs, and belted eight home runs in just four games.

During the season Babe Ruth and Lou Gehrig batted over .340 and combined for seventy-five home runs and 288 RBIs. In the World Series the Cubs couldn't get Gehrig out. Baseball's Iron Man hit .529 with three home runs and eight RBIs. Ruth, showing no signs of aging at thirty-seven, batted .333 and smacked two home runs, including his "called shot."

The rest of the lineup included catcher Bill Dickey, who overcame his difficulties on the field, and capped a great season by hitting .438 in the World Series. Second baseman Tony Lazzeri had a great comeback season and hit a pair of home runs in Game Four of the World Series. Shortstop Frankie Crosetti showed promise, but clearly needed more time. The twenty-one-year-old rookie batted just .241, and committed twenty-five errors while posting a .937 fielding percentage, second worst among American League shortstops. At third base was Joe Sewell, the older brother of Washington's catcher, Luke Sewell. At age thirty-four, Joe was slowing down, but could still hit as he had proved by batting .333 in the World Series.

Joining Ruth in the outfield were Earle Combs and Ben Chapman. In addition the Yankees had a promising rookie named Dixie Walker. Earle Combs, the thirty-four-year-old Yankees leadoff man, could hit, run, and field, as he had proven to Carl Reynolds and the Senators during the 1932 season, when he had robbed Reynolds by making a beautiful running catch to ice a 1–0 Yankees victory. Ben Chapman, twenty-four years old, was a good all-around player who was considered an up and coming star. His first job in baseball had been as the batboy for the 1923 Birmingham Barons, a team that had pitchers Lefty Stewart and Earl Whitehill. He began his major league career as an infielder for the Yankees in 1930. When Joe McCarthy took over in 1931, he took advantage of Chapman's blazing speed by switching him to the outfield, and instructing him to steal as often as possible. Chapman swiped sixty-one bases in '31, the most since Sam Rice stole sixty-three in 1920.

"To win the pennant, we have to beat the Yankees," Cronin said. "We need some pitchers who can beat them." To stop New York's left-handed power hitters—Ruth, Gehrig, and Dickey—Griffith and Cronin agreed they needed stronger left-handed pitching. The best two lefties in the league were Lefty Grove and Lefty Gomez, and they knew they hadn't a prayer in obtaining them.

Left-handed hurlers were scarce in the American League. There were only eleven, two on the Senators roster. Griffith and Cronin believed there were better lefties in the league than their duo of Lloyd Brown and Bobby Burke. In their study of the American League rosters, they found two they wanted. One was Walter "Lefty" Stewart of the St. Louis Browns. The other was Earl Whitehill of the Detroit Tigers. Both pitchers were experienced. Both consistently defeated the Senators. If Washington could acquire Stewart and Whitehill, they could have their cake and eat it too. The Senators would have their two biggest nemeses on their side, and would pitch them against the Yankees.

Someone else Griffith wanted was Goose Goslin, and now since Walter Johnson was gone, Goslin wanted to return to the nation's capital. He was so confident of a trade he took a train to Washington so he could meet with Griffith to discuss salary.

The four o'clock hour was approaching, and the meeting ended so Cronin could catch his train for San Francisco. He said goodbye, and thanked Griffith for giving him the opportunity to manage. The two men would meet again in two months, and would travel to New York City for baseball's winter meetings, their best opportunity to negotiate trades.

The lobby of New York's Roosevelt Hotel was buzzing, with managers from all sixteen major league teams talking trades before the dinner hour. The most interesting sight was Giants manager Bill Terry talking with the Dodgers manager Max Carey. For years the two teams' legendary managers, John McGraw and Wilbert Robinson, had refused to speak. But now with the old guard gone, the Giants and Dodgers appeared to have a deal in the making.

Joe McCarthy was among the managers in the trade talks, and this baffled the sportswriters. Why would the manager of the World Champions want to make a trade? "If you don't trade, you'll fall behind," McCarthy explained, who was in the process of negotiating a trade with White Sox manager Lou Fonseca — shortstop Luke Appling for a Yankees pitcher. The trade never materialized, and McCarthy would not make any deals before the start of the 1933 season.

Joe Cronin, the youngest manager in the crowd, was trying to fit in. He looked dapper, shook hands, and spoke with the managers and sportswriters. He listened as others did the talking. It was this kind of baseball talk he loved, and he wanted to join in, but since he knew little about negotiating he chose to remain quiet ... for now.

Griffith met with his good friend, St. Louis Browns owner Phil Ball. The two made an immediate trade by undoing their deal made during the 1932 season, when they had swapped pitchers Carl Fischer and Dick Coffman. Coffman had won only one game for Washington, St. Louis wasn't happy with Fischer, and both owners were willing to re-exchange the pitchers and pretend the trade had never happened.

The next day Cleveland Indians General Manager Billy Evans Jr. approached Griffith and asked about the availability of Harley Boss, a first baseman whom the Nats assigned to Chattanooga for the 1932 season, where he batted .338, scored 114 runs, and drove in 99 runs. While Griffith negotiated, Cronin found Bucky Harris and asked about Earl Whitehill. Harris set the cost at Fred Marberry and another player. After a few hours of negotiating, both managers agreed upon Carl Fischer, and Joe Cronin made his first trade.

Cronin was excited about getting Whitehill, while Harris thought he pulled one over on the rookie manager. Not only was he getting Marberry and Fischer, he was getting rid of Whitehill, whom he believed was washed up and detrimental to his team. Whitehill had a violent temper, didn't listen to feedback, and would be thirty-four in 1933. During the 1930 season Harris had offered the temperamental pitcher to Walter Johnson, but the Nats' skipper wasn't interested. If Harris had intended to give his pitcher a wakeup call, he succeeded. The left-hander began to listen to his manager, and to his teammates, and he put together a string of eleven consecutive wins.

At seven o'clock Griffith and Cronin sat down with Phil Ball and Browns manager Bill Killefer, and began to talk about Goose Goslin and Lefty Stewart. In return the Browns wanted Carl Reynolds and Lloyd Brown. Since Brown was a left-handed pitcher, Griffith was reluctant to trade him, but Ball insisted on getting a left-hander if he was going to trade Stewart. Feeling Stewart was better than Brown, Griffith agreed.

Washington's president and manager took a look at their lineup and realized the addition of Goslin gave them an unbalanced starting lineup of five left-handed and three right-handed batters. To balance their lineup they added to the trade by swapping center fielders. Sam West was a hard-working, good all-around player, but batted from the left side. Fred Schulte wasn't quite as good, but was more valuable to the Nats since he batted right-handed.

Still wanting more in the deal, the stubborn Phil Ball insisted on cash. The amount would be determined later, but $20,000 was mentioned. Meanwhile, it was past midnight, and six hours since the meeting had begun. The four men agreed it was enough baseball talk for one day, and walked through the deserted lobby to the elevators. As the four men rode up in the same elevator, Cronin learned why they called his boss the "Old Fox."

"I'll tell you what, Phil," said Griffith. "I'll buy back Lloyd Brown for twenty-thousand dollars." Ball never even looked at Griffith as he slowly shook his head from side to side.

Walter Johnson was at the Roosevelt Hotel, seeking a managerial position. When he realized his chances were not good for the upcoming season, he taxied over to the hotel where the owners of the Pacific Coast League were meeting. He made contacts, made the owners aware he was interested in managing, and sat in the lobby as he awaited an offer. An offer never came.

Johnson traveled back home to Bethesda, Maryland, to live a secluded life with his five children.

Also at the Roosevelt Hotel was thirty-eight-year-old Joe Judge, who attempted to negotiate a sale that would allow him to play elsewhere. The Nationals had decided Joe Kuhel was ready to take over as the starting first baseman, and since the major league rosters were reduced to twenty-three players due to the state of the economy, the Nats didn't have a spot for Joe Judge. Griffith believed that Judge had a few more good years left, and Dodgers man-

Earl Whitehill, seen here with his daughter, Earlinda, welcomed the trade to Washington.

ager Max Carey agreed. After the winter meetings the Dodgers worked out a deal, and Judge was on his way to Brooklyn.

Before heading back to Washington, Griffith finished with Billy Evans Jr. by trading Harley Boss. The Senators president wanted two players in exchange, one a first baseman who could replace Boss in Chattanooga, and any player off the current Indians roster. That player was sinkerball specialist Jack Russell, considered one of the worst pitchers in the American League, with a lifetime record of 46–98. After having his best season in 1928 by going 11–14 with two shutouts for the last-place Red Sox, he lost seventy games in his next four seasons. The Indians believed he would be better on a winning team, but after trading for him during the 1932 season, they concluded it wasn't a case of playing for the Red Sox. It was that Russell stunk, and they were happy to unload him, while Griffith was happy to get another player in the deal.

Griffith would keep in touch with Evans after the meetings, and three weeks later they made another trade by swapping catchers, Roy Spencer for Luke Sewell. Sewell was a twelve-year veteran, known to be good at handling pitchers, and Griffith and Cronin considered him superior to Spencer.

After heading back to Washington, Griffith and Cronin sat down and reviewed their new roster. Their big question was who would lead off in 1933. Myer, the usual leadoff hitter, batted a disappointing .279 in 1932, and they thought maybe it would be better to try either Bluege or Kuhel.

A few hours later Cronin boarded a train and headed back to San Francisco. His next trip to Washington would be for the start of the 1933 baseball season.

10

OPENING DAY, 1933

Shortly after midnight on Friday, April 7, the nation's capital celebrated. People sounded their horns as they drove in heavy traffic. Pedestrians shouted the words "Pros It!" Nightclubs, hotels, and restaurants were packed. The pouring rain bothered no one who wanted to quench a thirst for beer and rejoice in the end of Prohibition. Spirits were high, the highest since the prosperous years of the Roaring Twenties.

During the celebration a truck moved through downtown Washington, escorted by two policemen on motorcycles. In the back of the truck was a shipment of beer, bound for the White House, and a band, which played the song from President Franklin D. Roosevelt's 1932 presidential campaign, "Happy Days Are Here Again." On one side of the truck was a banner which read, "Here's to you — President Roosevelt — The Nation's first real beer is yours."

Earlier that evening the president greeted two guests at the White House: Clark Griffith and National League president John Heydler. Griffith presented the president with two season passes, one built into a purse for the First Lady, and he invited him to throw out the ball for the home opener on April 12, against the Athletics. Roosevelt accepted the invitation.

"Will beer be sold at your ballparks?" asked the president. The two men cringed. They had hoped he wouldn't ask that question. Griffith said beer had never been sold at his stadium, and it wouldn't happen now. Heydler said his league would permit the operation of bars in the few stadiums that had sold beer prior to Prohibition. Roosevelt turned the subject back to baseball and told the two men that baseball had done as much as anything to keep up the spirits of the people during these difficult times.

Five weeks earlier Franklin D. Roosevelt had arrived in Washington for his inauguration during the peak of the Depression. One out of four Americans were unemployed, the national suicide rate had tripled, whole families stood in bread lines, and people had lost their homes, their life savings, and their dignity.

Roosevelt seemed to be what the country needed — a miracle worker who was a powerful symbol of success against the odds. Over a decade earlier he

Luke Sewell was a smart catcher who brought experience and leadership to the Washington starting lineup in 1933.

had been stricken with polio and refused to let it stop him. The nation elected him by an overwhelming margin over Herbert Hoover in November of 1932, and his confidence and enthusiasm won the love and respect of the American people, who believed in him, and in his "New Deal" to help bring recovery to the economy and the people.

Joe Cronin woke up early on the morning of April 12 and went to Mass. As he walked through the rain under his umbrella, he wondered if his managerial debut would be postponed. The skies were dark, and showers were forecast for the afternoon.

In Harrisburg, Pennsylvania, Connie Mack was certain that the game would be rained out, and that was good news. An extra day would give Jimmie Foxx time to heal from a shin injury, and would give him more time in the state capital to talk with the politicians about legalizing Sunday baseball in Pennsylvania. Something he overlooked was the possibility of a Roosevelt miracle. While making his point to the lawmakers, he was informed that the skies over Washington were clearing and the game would be played. Mack excused himself and hustled to the Harrisburg airport, but arrived too late to catch his flight for Washington, and the Athletics would have to play their season opener without their leader.

After attending Mass, Cronin returned to his room at the Wardman Park Hotel and called his proud parents back in San Francisco before leaving for Griffith Stadium. When he arrived and entered the clubhouse he was surprised to see his starting pitcher, General Crowder, asleep on the floor. He hoped it wasn't due to the repeal of Prohibition. That wouldn't be the ideal way to start his managing career.

Crowder was worn out from excessive thinking — about winning, extending his fifteen-game winning streak, and performing before the president. He decided he needed a quick snooze, and when he awoke Cronin asked him if he was nervous. Crowder didn't reply.

The Nationals broke out their new home uniforms, the plainest in baseball due to Griffith's request to keep the cost to under $20 per uniform. The new home uniforms were white, featured pinstripes, and had midnight blue hats and socks to match. The hats and shirt chests were plain. There was a blue "W" on each sleeve, blue numbers on the shirt backs, and a white stripe on each sock. Their new road uniforms were identical, except were gray and without pinstripes.

Shortly before game time, the president's cavalcade entered through the open doors in the right field fence. As the automobile crept along the first base side and headed to the president's box, the band played "Hail to the Chief," and a crowd of 23,359 came to their feet and applauded. When Roosevelt was escorted to his seat, the band broke into the National Anthem.

Griffith and Cronin accompanied the president in his box as he threw out the game's first ball. After Roosevelt was handed the baseball, he cocked his right arm, and a cameraman cried out, "Hold it, hold it, hold it," so he could adjust his lens. "If any of you photographers get killed, don't say I didn't warn you," said Roosevelt, who didn't have as much confidence in his throwing accuracy as he had in his New Deal. The president threw the ball and Johnny Kerr moved in front of Nick Altrock to make the catch. Cronin shook the president's hand as they engaged in a conversation, with Roosevelt finishing by wishing the rookie manager good luck.

Someone handed Roosevelt a scorecard, which he pretended not to see. He then accepted it and handed it to Eleanor, who knew nothing about keeping score. The First Lady passed it on.

Washington started the season on a good note, with a 4–1 win. Cronin, who was greeted with a deafening ovation when he made his first plate appearance, helped make his managerial debut a success by hammering three hits. Ossie Bluege drove in three runs, and General Crowder won his sixteenth consecutive game to tie Walter Johnson, Smokey Joe Wood, and Lefty Grove for the most consecutive wins by an American League pitcher.

After the final out, Cronin dashed for the tunnel leading to the Nats' clubhouse, which was located in the Washington dugout. On his way he heard the president call his name, and saw him motion him over to his box. "Great stuff, Joe. Keep it up," Roosevelt told him as he shook his hand. "He called me over," Cronin said afterwards. "'Where's Joe Cronin?' he said. Gosh, that's wonderful. Think of it."

Out of respect for the president the crowd remained in their seats as the cavalcade pulled up to his box. After Roosevelt got into the automobile the crowd cheered, and the president gave a prizefighter's salute by clasping his hands together and waving them above his head. The cheering continued until the cavalcade disappeared through the right field exit.

Cronin's day was not finished. After leaving the stadium, he went directly to the Georgetown Hospital to visit Tom Flaherty, Washington's leading baseball fan, who had missed the game due to an operation. After he listened to Cronin give him the recap of the Senators' victory, Flaherty said, "Gosh, if I could have only been there," and a look of sadness covered his face. "Well, Tom, how's tricks?" Cronin asked in an attempt to cheer him up. Flaherty responded with a big smile.

Earl Whitehill made his debut for the Nats the following day and looked good. The curve-ball specialist allowed only two hits through the first six innings, and earned his first win with Washington in an 11–4 triumph over Philadelphia. Goose Goslin responded to the crowd's loud ovations, and to the cheer of "Come on, Goose!" by belting the first Washington home run of 1933 over the right field wall.

The next day Lefty Grove allowed just six hits while sending the Nats to their first loss of the season, and Jimmie Foxx knocked out two hits and drove in two runs, after going 0 for three in his season debut the day before.

"You'll find Pa down in the potato patch," Walter Johnson Jr. told *Washington Herald* writer George Garner, who paid a visit to Johnson's residence. Garner walked through Johnson's 8½ acre baby farm: past the Rhode Island reds, the apple and pear orchards, four grazing cows, and found the Big Train peeling potatoes with four of his children. After some small talk, Garner asked the game's greatest pitcher about the Senators and the American League pennant race. "While I have not followed the game closely since what is sometimes called my 'retirement' I believe the Yankees will repeat," Johnson said.

The conversation was interrupted when Babs, Johnson's youngest child, wanted to know what to do with the pile of spuds. After attending to her, Johnson returned to the conversation: "This year's Nats team is the better of the two teams [comparing it to the 1932 team]. However, I think Sam West will be missed. Schulte is not in Sam's class. Goslin will give the team the punch it needs. I suspect he's delighted to get away from St. Louis.

"The pitching staff shores up to be one of the best Washington has ever had. Crowder, Whitehill, and Stewart are the big three in my opinion. Weaver is still on trial. He was mighty lucky a few times last season."

"The infield stacks up all right, although I've been unable to draw an accurate line on Kuhel. Perhaps Joe will make better lead way now that he has no competition.

"Cronin? A capable player and managerial material; however, it may turn out that Cronin might have done better to postpone his managing for a few years. I think both he and Griffith are taking a gamble. Managing and playing at the same time may affect his work at shortstop," Johnson concluded.

Carolyn, Walter's other daughter, appeared with a handful of worms, and asked if she should feed the chickens. Walter told her she should.

Garner asked the Big Train if he ever threw the baseball around. He said he did, once in a while with Junior, but he was not planning on making any comebacks. He did mention he was not retiring, and wanted to get back into baseball as a manager or minor league club owner.

The weather in Washington was so cold the pipes froze at Griffith Stadium. So did the bats of the Nationals. Against the lowly Red Sox they dropped the last two of a three-game series. Both Crowder and Whitehill were defeated, and for Crowder it was the end of his sixteen-game winning streak. The Nats' batting slump continued into the next series in Philadelphia, where they scored one run in each of the two losses, and saw their losing streak reach four to make their record 3–5. The critics were quick to point to Cronin, who had had just three hits in twenty-five at bats since his three hits on opening day. They also claimed he didn't look sharp in the field, and one writer wrote that he was throwing the ball as if it were a beanbag. "Bosh!" was Cronin's response to the critics. "All bosh. Last year if I made the same kind of stops and throws nothing would have been said about it. Now I'm on the spot."

Cronin and the Senators broke the slump the next day with a 10–7 win in

Philadelphia, with the shortstop collecting three hits and driving in three runs. But the hitting star was Goslin, who made four hits, including his second home run of the season. The Goose was in excellent spirits on the train afterwards, as the Nationals headed home to play three games against the Yankees.

The Yankees started the season where they had left off in 1932: by winning their first seven games, and appearing to be as invincible as the sportswriters had predicted.

"Hey Goose, what are we going to do with the Yankees?" asked Dave Harris.

"We're going to knock the beer out of them, and we're going to show them New York Mugs that we are 'World Serious,'" Goslin replied.

A Sunday crowd of 25,000 came out to Griffith Stadium to cheer the Nats and boo the Yankees, especially Bill Dickey. Lefty Gomez was New York's starting pitcher, and Washington countered with Whitehill, who was tabbed in Biloxi as the man who would oppose Gomez each time he pitched against the Nats. "I could beat Gomez anytime we meet," Whitehill said during spring training, and now was his first chance to prove it. He showed he meant business in the first inning by sending the Yankees down in order and delighted the home crowd by fanning Babe Ruth. In the fourth inning Lazzeri belted a two-run triple to give the Yanks a 2–0 lead. Myer evened the score by hitting a two-run triple over Chapman, and Schulte singled to score Myer to give the Nats a 3–2 lead.

In the top of the sixth, Lou Gehrig came to the plate. He was playing in his 1,205th consecutive game, and if he remained healthy for 103 more consecutive games, he would eclipse Everett Scott's record of 1,307 in mid–August. On this day, however, his streak appeared to come to an abrupt end. Whitehill threw a high, inside fastball. Gehrig turned his head, and the ball crashed against the back of his crown. The ball took off as if it had been batted, and bounced through the infield. Gehrig slowly fell "like he had been poleaxed," and lost consciousness. Joe McCarthy and the New York trainer ran to the scene. The tough first baseman regained consciousness, asked for water, then was helped to his feet, and to the amazement of everyone, he remained in the game.

Visibly shaken by the incident, Whitehill lost his concentration and gave up a double to Dickey, which scored Gehrig and another base runner to give New York a one-run lead.

In the bottom of the ninth, with Washington still down by a run, Cy Moore, New York's relief specialist, was on the mound. Moore had replaced Gomez in the seventh, and breezed through the Nats lineup in the seventh and eighth innings.

Cronin showed his players the way by opening the ninth with a single. While standing on first base, the manager signaled for a pinch-hitter, and his decision didn't make Dave Harris happy. Feeling insulted by being lifted for a pinch-hitter, Harris stomped back to the dugout, and Henie Manush, who had been sidelined due to a wrist injury, came to the plate. The move paid off as Manush lined one past Gehrig and into right field. Ruth looked all of his thirty-eight yeas as he chased the ball "at a snail's pace." Cronin scored the tying run, and Manush made it all the way to third base. A few batters later, Cronin called on forty-three-year-old Sam Rice to pinch-hit, and he came through with a single to score Manush for a Washington win.

Afterwards the Nationals were loud and enthusiastic in their clubhouse, except for Dave Harris, who sat by himself with his head down. "Howzit, Dave?" asked Cronin.

"Oh, so-so," Harris replied.

"Well, we won the game, didn't we?" said Cronin, and Harris smiled.

The next day the Nats and Yankees continued their feud. In the third inning Ruth was caught in a rundown between third and home, and as he lumbered towards third base he barreled in with a headfirst slide at Cronin, who saw Ruth coming and applied a hard tag. Ruth didn't approve of the aggressive tag, and as he lay on his stomach he looked up at Cronin and "told him what he thought of his glorious ancestors."

In the top of the sixth, Ben Chapman continued his assault on Buddy Myer by sliding into second base with his spikes aimed at Myer. He sliced a four-inch cut into the second baseman's calf, leaving a scar for life to go along with the one Chapman had carved into Myer the previous September. Heinie Manush had retaliated the previous season, and he decided to do it again. While running out a groundball, he hit the dirt and made a sprawling slide. Luckily Gehrig was able to sidestep him in time.

In the bottom of the sixth, shortly after Chapman had spiked Myer, the second baseman got his revenge by smashing a two-run triple to tie the game. In the bottom of the eighth, with the game tied 9–9, Goslin doubled off the top of the right field wall, and scored when Cronin doubled down the left field line. Schulte doubled to score Cronin and give the Nats a two-run lead. In the ninth the Yankees threatened, but fell short by a run, and Washington won another one-run game over New York.

After the game Myer was happy about the win, but angry about being spiked by Chapman, and he vowed vengeance against the Yankee outfielder if he ever spiked him again. His biggest concern, however, was the health of his wife, who was recovering at Washington's Emergency Hospital following surgery to remove her appendix a few days earlier. He quickly showered, got dressed, and went to the hospital to check on Mrs. Myer, leaving his thoughts about baseball and Ben Chapman in the clubhouse.

11

WAR AT GRIFFITH STADIUM

"I'll step on Chapman's face the next time he slides into second base! I regret that I did not think of that yesterday."
— Buddy Myer

It didn't matter to Buddy Myer that Ben Chapman was 1½ inches taller and thirteen pounds heavier. If he dared to spike him today, "he would wreak vengeance immediately," according to John Keller of the *Washington Evening Star,* who overheard Myer before the Nats took the field. Washington's second baseman knew something might happen after Chapman poked a single in the top of the fourth. And with Tony Lazzeri due up, a right-handed batter, there was a good chance the ball would be hit to the left side of the infield, giving Myer the responsibility of covering second base as the pivot man in a double play attempt. This would make him a target for Chapman and his gleaming spikes. To be safe, Myer moved closer to second base so he could receive the ball and make his relay throw in plenty of time before Chapman arrived.

Sure enough, Lazzeri grounded one to Cronin, and after Myer caught the shortstop's throw, he stepped towards the infield to give Chapman a clear path to the base. The Yankees left fielder was no less than three yards from second when Myer had the ball, but he kept running, then lunged forward with a hard slide, and aimed his cleats at the second baseman's right foot.

Myer stumbled and was unable to make a throw. He felt the pain, looked down, and noticed he had been spiked so hard the heel was separated from the sole of his shoe.

That was it! Payback time. This meant war.

As Chapman sat on the ground after sliding, Myer wheeled around, swung his foot, and kicked him in the back of his thigh as hard as he could. He swung his foot and booted his enemy a second time. He kicked him again and again. Chapman quickly rose to his feet. Myer threw his glove away. The two seized each other and began to throw punches. Both dugouts emptied, and Cronin and Umpire George Moriarty, who were closest to the fight, tried to separate the two. Players from both teams swore and exchanged insults when they arrived on the scene. They pried to two ballplayers apart, and a few of Myer's teammates pulled him away from Chapman.

Myer didn't wait for the umpires to inform him that fighting was an automatic ejection. He trotted towards the tunnel in the Nats' dugout, which led to both teams' clubhouses, as eight thousand hometown fans applauded.

Chapman remained on the field and surveyed the Nationals as if he were looking for another player to fight. An umpire told him he was disqualified and ordered him off the field. To a salvo of boos, Chapman walked to the New York dugout to retrieve his mitt, then headed for the Washington dugout, since it was the only route to the New York clubhouse, and this meant trouble.

After sending both teams back to their dugouts, the two umpires, Moriarty and Harry Geisel, were so engaged in listening to Cronin and McCarthy scream over which players should be ejected, they failed to notice that Chapman was unescorted as he headed towards the Washington dugout. His roommate Dixie Walker did notice, and he joined Chapman to make sure he made it to the safety of the Yankees' clubhouse. As they approached the dugout, Chapman heard it from the Senators. "You're yellow! That's right, you are yellow!" they told him, but he hardly noticed their taunts. Instead he focused on Buddy

 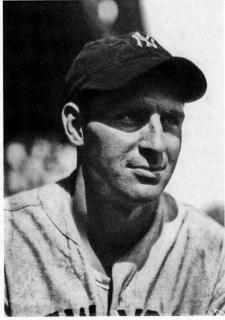

Myer (above, left) and Chapman (above, right) were the center of attention in the Senators-Yankees feud that erupted into a riot on April 25, 1933.

Myer, who waited for him inside the tunnel. When he saw Chapman, he charged. Then, for whatever reason, he halted and remained in the tunnel.

After Chapman entered the Nats' dugout, he encountered Earl Whitehill, who didn't care that this was the guy who had retrieved his bats in Birmingham ten years earlier. He had something to say and blurted it out. Chapman resented whatever was said and threw a right hook that connected with Whitehill's mouth. Whitehill grabbed Chapman and the two began to duke it out. Chapman connected with another punch, sending Whitehill to the floor. He toppled onto the pitcher, and aware whose dugout he was in, he covered up. The Washington players pulled him off their teammate and began to punch him. Walker came to his roommate's rescue, while the rest of the Yankees cleared their dugout and stormed across the field.

Gomez grabbed a bat, and Dickey, whose life was not safe in Washington, grabbed one of Ruth's fifty-four ounce clubs. A few of the Yankees grabbed him, pulled him back into the dugout, and advised him to stay there for his own safety.

The Yankees' rampage incited the customers behind the Nats dugout, and around three hundred of them spilled onto the field. Fearing a riot was about to erupt, someone made an anonymous phone call to Washington's second precinct station. A radio call went out, and when the police arrived, the police already on duty, who believed they could handle the situation, were unhappy to see them.

One Yankee reserve belted a fan in the face, knocking him to the turf. Lazzeri punched his way through a crowd. "Don't let Tony Lazzeri get in there, he'll kill somebody!" yelled a young female fan. Lazzeri heard the compliment and laughed. "I didn't realize I was supposed to be such a tough guy," he later said with a smile. "I didn't kill anybody, but I threw a few good punches, and for a minute I had a lot of fun."

Chapman, buried under a sea of bodies, punched away for his life. He heard a voice say, "I'm going to throw you in jail!" Realizing he was socking a policeman instead of a Senators player, he replied, "All right, but take me to the clubhouse so I can change my clothes."

Gomez was placed under arrest after striking a detective (wisely with his fist instead of his bat). He was handcuffed, and as two officers walked him towards the right field gate, Ed Eynon, an executive in the Nationals' front office, came out of the stands and convinced the officers to release him.

A fan on top of the dugout roof wanted to join in. Like someone afraid to dive into the pool, he sat down on the ledge, then dropped into the melee. He was placed under arrest along with another fan that got too involved.

After the Yankees returned to their dugout, and Chapman made it to the clubhouse (and did not encounter Myer on the way), another fight broke out, this one in the stands down the right field line between two men named George. The George who won the fight lost the decision by becoming the third fan to be apprehended by police.

During the fireworks, Babe Ruth and Lou Gehrig remained in the dugout, and were amused by the action. When asked why he did not partake, Ruth replied, "My cold was too bad to mix in anything like that these days. It might make my nose run more."

"What is a fellow supposed to do? Take it every day?" Myer asked the sportswriters in the Washington clubhouse. "Chapman deliberately spiked me. The day before he spiked me. I've stood it and haven't done anything. But I figured I wasn't going to take it any longer."

"Yeah, I'll talk to them," said Chapman to a reporter who poked his head into the shower in the New York clubhouse. Chapman appeared before the sportswriters with a towel around his waist. He had cuts and bruises on his body. His upper body bore several visible bruises. His cheek had a ripe red cut, and he had a lump on the back of his head. When asked if he was in pain he answered, "I'm not hurt."

"I had a right to the bag and I went in," Chapman said. "What kind of softies are there here anyhow? When a man goes into the bag he has every right to tie up the player to prevent a double play. That's all I was doing. After I got to the bag I did what I always do. That's baseball. I wasn't going to stop and wouldn't if we hadn't been separated."

Asked about his tussle with Whitehill, Chapman replied, "Well, Earl Whitehill got up and said something I didn't like. Why should he ride me? So I took a poke at him right in the nose."

"He socked me and I socked him back," said Whitehill. "I told him he was yellow, and he is. We rolled on the concrete and finally some others took a sock at him."

"I did," Mike Martin said with pride.

"I'm not making any report to you guys," umpire Moriarty told the press. "Any report will be to the president of the league. I haven't consulted with Geisel yet. Our report will go by wire tonight after we confer."

Everyone who had an opinion about the brawl pointed the finger at the opposition. The Nats claimed the Yankees had been after Myer for the past few seasons. The Yankees claimed Myer was "the roughest base runner in the American League," and picked on Gehrig by running across his feet at first base and by raising his spikes while sliding. Griffith backed up Myer, saying he had every right to retaliate. Colonel Ruppert said Chapman was within his rights, and Myer was the instigator, who should be kicked out of baseball.

Both managers spoke out. "There is such a thing as legally interfering with an attempted double play — but then there is such a thing as overstepping the bounds of propriety, and that is what Chapman did today," said Cronin.

"If it hadn't been for Whitehill, there wouldn't have been anything to it but the row at second base," according to McCarthy. "After all, it was none of Whitehill's business, and he should have kept his mouth shut."

After leaving the stadium, Myer went directly to the Emergency Hospital to check on his wife, who was surprised to see him at an early hour. "Hello, Buddy, how is it you got away so early from the game today?" Mrs. Myer asked.

"I got into an argument with one of those punk umpires and he put me out of the game. There's nothing to worry about," Buddy replied.

When play resumed, with New York ahead 2–0, Bill Dickey singled, and Crosetti cleared the bases with a triple. Cronin changed pitchers and replaced Weaver with Tommy Thomas, who was greeted by an RBI single by the pitcher Russ Van Atta. The Yankees continued to pummel the Washington pitchers for the rest of the afternoon. Gehrig hit one high over the right field wall, Lazzeri hit one into the left field seats, Ruth made two hits for four RBIs, Combs went five for five, Crosetti got three hits, rookie pitcher Russ Van Atta went four for four while hurling a five-hit shutout. The Yankees looked awesome by getting twenty-one hits in a 16–0 romp.

Later that evening Myer joined his teammates at Union Station, where they took a late night train to Boston for a two-game series. As they strolled along the platform, Myer walked with Griffith as he told him his side of the story. As Griffith listened he had an arm around Myer's shoulder, like a father who was supporting his own son. The two boarded the train, sat away from the rest of the team, and had a long talk.

During the train ride the Senators spoke about the day's events, and about Chapman, instead of playing their usual poker games.

"It was a clear case of provocation," said Moe Berg.

"I'd like to punch that guy on the schnoz," said Harris.

"One of these days Chapman is going to be trapped in a rundown, and very accidentally he is going to catch one of my pegs on the bean," said one of the pitchers.

Will Harridge intended to make a full investigation of the free-for-all. He suspended Chapman, Myer, and Whitehill indefinitely before leaving his home in the Chicago suburb of Wilmette and heading to the East Coast to conduct several interviews. Before the league president arrived in Philadelphia to interview Ben Chapman, umpires Moriarty and Geisel, and a few other Yankees, Chapman spoke with sportswriter James Isaminger of the *Philadelphia Inquirer* about the hurts and pains inflicted upon him by the Washington police. "They gave me this lump here on the back of my head," he said as he removed his cap to show the sportswriter. "And they ripped me here on the cheek," he said as he pointed to a cut. Isaminger reported that the left side of Chapman's face was lacerated and bruised. Chapman also spoke about his roommate Dixie Walker, who he said knocked down four or five detectives. "What a roomie. He belted those guys around like nobody's business."

When Harridge arrived and spoke with Chapman, the outfielder asked him, "What would you do if I, a trained athlete, called you the name Whitehill called me?"

"I'd punch you right in the nose," replied Harridge.

"That is what I did to Whitehill," said Chapman.

In Boston, Red Sox manager Marty McManus was concerned about the possibility that the Senators, being riled up, might take it out on his team. "I'm gonna tell my fellows that if they find that the Senators are inclined to carry yesterday's battle against the Yankees right into our camp, to be not only on guard to protect themselves but to come right back with all they have," the Red Sox manager told Melville Webb Jr. of the *Boston Globe*. McManus and his "fellows" found out the Senators held no misplaced grudges, and came to play ball.

Cronin sent Ed Linke to the mound for his first major league start. "The cocky kid from Chicago," who had slimmed down since reporting to Biloxi forty pounds overweight, pitched 8⅓ innings while limiting the Red Sox to just three hits, struck out four, and had a 3–1 lead before he gave up a double and two walks. Cronin called McAfee out of the bullpen to put out the fire, which he did, to secure a 3–2 Washington win. While earning his first major league victory, Linke yielded seven walks, and after he was wild in his next start, Cronin shipped him to Chattanooga to work on his control.

After beating Boston, the Senators traveled to New York for a two-game series with their record at 7–6, three games behind the Yankees. Harridge arrived the following morning to interview the Nats at their hotel. Myer went into detail with Harridge about the problems he had had last year with the Yankees: with Johnny Allen knocking him down ten times and hitting him with two pitches. He mentioned the Yankees had been after him, knocking him down on the base paths, and Chapman had spiked him the day before the fight and one time last season.

When Harridge finished his interviews, the questions were: who would be fined? Who would be suspended? Who would be fined and suspended? The *New York Times* reported how Myer might receive special consideration due to his wife's recent surgery. In the meantime Chapman had his own problems off the field. Back in his hometown of Birmingham his wife filed for separation. In her petition she alleged that Chapman showed evidence that he was determined to divorce her two months after their marriage in 1931, and there had been friction between them throughout the previous winter. She also claimed he left her with no means to support herself, except for small change adding up to less than three dollars. No one was aware of it at the time, but soon the story became public.

Later that afternoon, Myer and Whitehill participated in the pre-game warmup at Yankee Stadium as they waited for 2:30, the time when Harridge was due to announce his decision. At that exact time the American League president spoke, and his decision came as a shock to the Senators. "It didn't look to me as if the spiking was intentional," Harridge said. "Chapman went into second hard to break up a double play, which he had a perfect right to do. I fined Myer for kicking Chapman, and I fined Whitehill and Chapman because they were equally guilty in their parts they played in precipitating a riot. With the facts evening themselves out, I decided that a warning, five games and one hundred dollars would be sufficient punishment."

Myer and Whitehill had expected heavier fines, and were relieved it would cost them only $100. They headed for the train station and traveled back to Washington to serve their suspensions. When asked how he felt, Myer replied, "The president of the league has made his decision, and it is not for me to make any comment."

Clark Griffith, fuming over the decision, had plenty to comment about. "Chapman should've been suspended for a total amount of days equal to the amount given to Whitehill and Myer. He was the one who provoked the affair at second base, and he started the business in the dugout."

Griffith also had something to say about the umpires. "If the umpires said in their report to Mr. Harridge that Chapman didn't go out of his way to spike Myer, then they either didn't see the play or they are trying to make themselves look good. Whenever they make a report to the league president they are thinking about their jobs, and you could quote me!"

12

THE INCREDIBLE DOUBLE PLAY

GRIFFITH: "The greatest play I've ever seen."
SPORTSWRITER: "Greater than McNeeley's hit [in the twelfth inning of the last World Series game in 1924]?"
GRIFFITH: "Yes, a greater play."
SPORTSWRITER: "But it did not mean as much money?"
GRIFFITH: "It might. You never can tell."

Four days after the free-for-all at Griffith Stadium, the Senators and Yankees resumed their bitter rivalry before a Friday afternoon crowd of twenty-five thousand at Yankee Stadium. There would be no fights in this series, but there would be plenty of jockeying, beginning with the Yankees' dugout calling for pitcher George Pipgras to throw one at Cronin's head. The Nats manager showed the Yanks he would not be intimidated by belting a two-run double in the first inning. One inning later, Goslin's RBI single gave the Nats a 3–0 lead. The Yankees came back to tie the score on Ruth's fourth homer of the year, and Dickey's home run. In the tenth inning Cronin did it again, by drilling a single to propel the winning run across the plate.

The following day the Senators were on the verge of sweeping the two-game series. Going into the bottom of the ninth they led 6–2, but no lead was safe against the Yankees; not to mention that it was close to the five o'clock hour, the time when "five o'clock lightning" often struck for a Yankees rally and a come-from-behind win. Lightning was about to strike, but not the way the Yankees had hoped.

Three consecutive singles by Ruth, Gehrig, and Walker cut the Washington lead to 6–3. With Gehrig on second, Walker on first, nobody out, and the crowd cheering for a rally, Tony Lazzeri got hold of a pitch by Monte Weaver and sent 35,455 fans into hysteria when his long fly ball sailed over the extended reach of Goose Goslin. Walker sprinted towards second base, then stopped. Lou Gehrig was still by the second base bag, making sure the ball fell for a hit, and when Gehrig began to run, Walker was right on his heels.

Goslin quickly got to the ball, picked it up off the grass, and heaved it on a direct line to the cutoff man. Cronin, who assigned himself as Washington's designated cutoff man since he had the strongest arm among the Washington infielders, caught Goslin's throw, and when he turned towards the infield, Gehrig had rounded third base and Walker was about to round third. Cronin reared back and fired a strike to Luke Sewell. Gehrig was surprised to see the ball arrive before he did, and he made a quick slide to the outside of home plate. Sewell tagged him, skipped over his slide, and tagged Walker, who slid to the inside, to complete the sort of incredible double play "that is seen only once in a lifetime."

Gehrig and Walker remained in a reclining position, both in disbelief over what had just happened. The stunned crowd groaned as they dropped back into their seats.

"It was a swell job by Goslin and Cronin," Sewell said after the game. "I didn't even have to move for the ball. It was easy. Cronin can sure pitch the ball."

After the double play, the veteran catcher thought it would be wise to check on his pitcher, believing he was bewildered by what had transpired. As he approached Weaver, he held up two fingers. "It's two outs, Monte," he said.

"Oh, do we have two outs?" said the confused pitcher.

Sewell had to laugh. He turned away and covered his face with his big catcher's mitt. Here was Monte Weaver, a former mathematics professor, who was so dazed he couldn't add one and one.

Sewell talked about pitching to the next batter, Bill Dickey, to get the pitcher refocused. A moment later Dickey grounded out to end the game.

The Senators celebrated their victory, and after they converged in the infield to congratulate one another, an angry voice was heard from the Yankees' dugout. "We'll get you next time, you __." The Nats were not bashful about answering back, and they unloaded on the defeated Yankees.

Afterwards in the Washington clubhouse, Cronin was handed a mailed letter, forwarded to Yankee Stadium after missing him at their hotel in Boston. After he opened the envelope and read the letter, he began to laugh.

> Myer and Whitehill marked for a ride. Watch your step in New York Friday. Your team in danger of bricks and bottles.
> Signed "Eastside Gangster"

One week later the Senators made their first venture through the Midwest, with both Myer and Whitehill back in the lineup on May 6 in Detroit. Whitehill, making his first trip back to Detroit since being traded, was soundly booed until late in the game when the jeers were directed at the Tigers' big rookie first baseman, Hank Greenberg. The Detroit fans liked Detroit's regular first baseman Harry Davis, and they wanted to see him in the lineup, until Greenberg changed their jeers to cheers by launching his first career home run over the center field fence. It wasn't enough, however, as Washington won, 6–2.

In the top of the eighth came a scary moment with Myer at the plate. Tigers pitcher Whit Wyatt threw an inside fastball. Myer turned, and the ball struck him in the back of the head, then ricocheted into the box seats along the first base side. After a sickening thud echoed throughout Briggs Stadium, Myer fell to the ground, and to Shirley Povich it looked like "a lifeless body lying on the dirt of Briggs Field."

The Senators quickly ran to aid Myer, and after he regained consciousness Dave Harris and Cliff Bolton carried him to the clubhouse and placed him on Mike Martin's training table. The Washington trainer examined him and noticed a long tear on his scalp, but doubted there was a skull fracture. He immediately arranged for an ambulance to take Myer to the Providence Hospital, and to be safe, he requested X-rays.

The next morning Myer was in good spirits while resting at the hospital. He was propped up in bed, reading the newspaper, when his teammates came by while on their way to their game. One of them asked if his skull was the thickest to ever be X-rayed. Myer did not answer the question, but he did laugh.

Just as Martin had expected, the X-rays showed no skull fracture. As a precaution Myer spent the next few days in the hospital. Each evening he had a visitor in Clark Griffith, who intended to stay in Detroit until his second baseman was discharged. Myer rejoined his teammates a few days later, but could not help them avoid their usual sub-par showing against the American League's weaker Midwest teams. The Nats finished their first trip out west with six wins and five losses.

When the Midwest teams came through Washington, the Senators faced the Tigers' Tommy Bridges, who had thrown a near-perfect game against them back in August. Dave Harris had spoiled it with a pinch-hit single after Walter Johnson sent him to the plate with two outs in the ninth and with the Nats down, 13–0.

This time Bridges held the Senators hitless through 7⅔ innings. With four more outs needed for immortality, Kuhel hit one over the right field wall. After that, Bridges did not allow another hit, completing another one-hit win over Washington.

The day before, Fred Marberry poked his head into the Nats' clubhouse and made an announcement to his former teammates. "I'm bearing down on you guys, and I don't mean maybe. You're entitled to all you get. Now come on out and see who's who in this ball game."

Marberry fired a three-hitter in Detroit's 7–1 win, but it did not happen without controversy. The Senators complained about Marberry using his sweat to create spitballs, and also charged that Hank Greenberg was cutting the cover of the baseball with his belt buckle. Heinie Manush retaliated by kicking Greenberg's mitt as it lay on the ground between innings. Greenberg yelled at Manush, and Washington's left fielder fired back. After the inning Cronin gave Greenberg a piece of his mind, and then Marberry took matters into his own hands

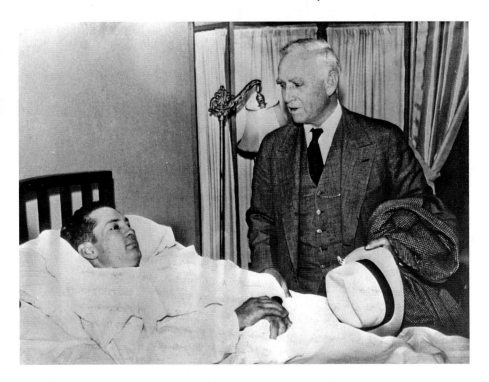

Griffith pays Myer a visit at the Providence Hospital in Detroit after the second baseman was hit on the noggin by a pitch from Whit Wyatt.

by throwing one close to Manush. Washington's big left fielder walked towards the pitcher, and Marberry walked towards the plate. Before the two came to blows home plate umpire Red Ormsby stepped between the two big guys and instructed them to return to their positions.

They had promised they would return, and they did: on the evening of May 8 the Bonus Army entered the nation's capital, hoping that this time, with a new president in office, they could get their bonuses. When they arrived, fifteen army trucks and policemen on motorcycles greeted them and escorted them fourteen miles into Virginia to Fort Hunt, where they pitched their tents and set up camp. One day they received a visit from the First Lady, who spoke to them about her experience as a volunteer during the Great War while having coffee with the men. When she said goodbye, a veteran commented, "Hoover sent the army, Roosevelt sent his wife."

The veterans were once again denied their checks, but were informed about job opportunities created by the president's New Deal, and several took advantage by heading down to the Florida Keys to work on a road construction project.

Ossie Bluege injured his foot while running out a ground ball in Chicago, and would be sidelined for nine days. The next day the Nats announced they were bringing up Cecil Travis from Chattanooga, who was tearing up the Southern Association with a .400 batting average. After hitting a grand slam on opening day, the nineteen-year-old went on a hitting spree, and had a .452 batting average until he was slowed down by a hand injury.

After reporting to Griffith Stadium a few hours before game time on May 16, Travis was informed he would be taking Bluege's place in the lineup. With no time to think about being nervous, he knocked out five hits to help the Senators defeat the Indians 11–10 in twelve innings. The next day he got two more hits while batting in his first major league run.

The scouting report on Travis was he could not field bunts, and could not hit low balls. His auspicious start at the plate clarified that the report was wrong about his hitting, but there was still the question of his fielding. The White Sox came to town wanting to know the answer. What Chicago did not know was Cronin had worked with the teenager in Biloxi on his fielding, and had showed him the proper way to whip the ball across the diamond. After Travis turned five bunts into five outs, the White Sox abandoned their game plan.

Travis made eight hits in his first fifteen at bats before cooling off by going one for his next fourteen. When Bluege returned to the lineup, Travis went to the bench, and would remain with Washington until Cronin was convinced that Bluege's injured foot had completely healed. On June 3, Travis was on his way back to Chattanooga.

A sellout crowd was projected for a Memorial Day double-header at Griffith Stadium with the Yankees in town, their first trip back since the brawl on April 25. Myer, Whitehill, and Chapman were all in uniform, with Whitehill scheduled to pitch the first game. In uniform, but out of the starting lineup because of a recurring stomach illness, was Buddy Myer, who was missing action for already the third time this season.

Myer's stomach problems had begun during spring training in 1931, when it was reported he was suffering from ptomaine poisoning after "eating too much good food." When he reported to Griffith Stadium on the morning of May 28, he told Cronin about his stomach pains, but also said he would play. He played in pain throughout the game until it became so intense he passed out on the field. In the bottom of the eighth, with the score tied at 4–4 against the A's, Myer sprinted from first to third on Sewell's single. After sliding into the base he lost consciousness.

Washington came into the three-game series at Griffith Stadium with a record of 23–16, two games behind the league-leading Yankees. The day was rainy and cold, and the start of the game was delayed for an hour. When the game finally began, a steady downpour continued.

The Griffith Stadium fans greeted Chapman with a Bronx cheer they had been saving for him for over a month. He replied by hitting an RBI single off Whitehill to give the Yankees the early lead. Cronin evened the score when he tripled in a run.

Both Whitehill and Yankees rookie lefthander Russ Van Atta held the hitters in check. Whitehill, as usual, wanted to win this one, and he baited home plate umpire Brick Owens for every call.

In the eighth inning, with the score still tied at 1–1, Whitehill threw Gehrig a fastball. Gehrig swung and drove the ball deep to right field. It cleared the wall, but to the foul side of the foul pole, before disappearing in the trees across the avenue. Gerhig rounded first base, saw the ball curve, then turned around and took a few steps toward home plate. Then, to everyone's surprise, Brick Owens ruled a fair ball. A surprised Gehrig did an about-face and trotted around the bases.

The Senators were in disbelief. All four infielders charged towards home plate, and so did Whitehill, who unloaded on Owens with his finest language. Cronin got in front of the irate pitcher to make his point. Bill McAfee and Tommy Thomas, both in the Nats' bullpen down the right field line, had had a perfect view of the ball, and they ran towards the home plate conference to give their point of view. But they were headed off by first base umpire Roy Van Grafflin, who ordered them back to the bullpen.

Cronin sprinted down the first base line to talk with Van Grafflin, but the umpire would not talk unless called upon by Owens. He sprinted back to Owens, who was hearing it from Whitehill, and now Bluege, who normally was calm and quiet. Cronin asked the umpire to talk with Van Grafflin. Owens, who never removed his mask during the argument, flat out refused to. In the meantime Whitehill could not calm down, and Cronin ordered him to the bench. As Whitehill walked towards the dugout he saw an object in the wet grass. It was Owens's whisk broom, dropped by the umpire during the course of the game. The angry pitcher picked it up, and the crowd gasped when he hurled it over the grandstand roof. Luckily for him, the umpires did not notice.

In the press box the writers agreed the wrong call was made, including Marshall Hunt of the *New York Daily News,* who wrote what he saw: "From the enclosure housing the Gentlemen of the press the ball seemed to travel foul."

Owens would not listen to Cronin's plea to confer with Van Grafflin. As the Nats continued to rave, Owens did an old umpire's trick to communicate that the dispute was finished, by bending over to sweep home plate. He frantically frisked his waist for his broom with no idea why he couldn't find it.

Cronin placed the game under protest, on the grounds of Owens's refusal to confer with Van Grafflin. He headed to the dugout to check on Whitehill to be sure the pitcher was calm enough to continue the game. Convinced he was, Cronin walked him to the pitcher's mound.

When play resumed the rain fell harder, and there was a question about how much longer before the game would be called. After Chapman drilled a single, Whitehill decided to take advantage of the conditions by stalling for a rainout. He continuously threw to first base, acting as if he was trying to keep the runner close to the base. Chapman caught on and remained on the base.

Owens also knew what the pitcher was trying to do, and he informed White-hill he wasn't going to call this game, so he may as well pitch.

Meanwhile the umpire was hearing it from the Washington dugout, from Mike Martin in particular. As Owens walked over to eject the Nats trainer, three pop bottles flew from the crowd and landed by his feet. For Martin it was the second time in his career he had been ejected, both times by Brick Owens.

Joe Cronin came through again with an RBI single to tie the score in the eighth inning. In the ninth, New York pushed across another run against White-hill for a 3–2 win. Due to the driving rainstorm and the darkening skies, Game Two of the holiday twin bill was postponed, and would be played the following day as part of a double-header.

The next day during batting practice, Babe Ruth hit one into the same trees as Gehrig's home run from the day before. The Washington fans sarcastically cried out, "Fair ball! Fair ball!" In regular business Washington took the first game, 11–7, with Cronin doing it in the clutch again by hitting a double to score two runs to break a 7–7 tie. In the nightcap Cronin sent Weaver to the mound, hoping to get another good performance from him like the one in New York when Washington won the miracle double play game. This time New York was ready, and they scored eight runs in the first two innings to send Weaver to an early shower. The Nats fought back but lost, 9–7.

Joe Sewell was the hitting star for New York in the nightcap with three hits and five runs batted in. "The little bugger can hit anything," Luke said of his brother after the game, when asked about his hitting. Off the field the Sewells enjoyed a close relationship. On the field ... one played for Washington, the other for New York. That tells the story.

The Yankees left town by adding a game to their first-place lead, and closed out May at 24–13. Winners of seven of their last nine games, they were on a roll, and were believed to be heading towards another pennant.

13

THE OLD WASHINGTON
WRECKING CREW

"I am here to tell you that Joe Cronin is piloting the best-looking club
I have seen in the majors in several years."
— Ed Bang of the *Cleveland News*

Once upon a time the Boston Red Sox were four-time World Champions
and the toast of Boston, before team owner Harry Frazee stripped the team of
its stars, including Babe Ruth, whom he sold to the Yankees in 1920. In 1923
Frazee was out after selling the Red Sox to Bob Quinn and his syndicate.

Quinn did not sell Babe Ruth, but did Boston no favors by waiving pitcher
Jack Quinn and trading Howard Ehmke, Buddy Myer, and Red Ruffing. After the
Athletics claimed Jack Quinn, he accumulated ten or more victories in each of
his next four seasons. Ehmke won fifty games for the A's, including one in the
1929 World Series, while the three players dealt to Boston in the deal were all out
of the majors within three years. For Myer, Quinn received five players that never
panned out. In exchange for Ruffing, the Red Sox received outfielder Cedric
Durst, who played 102 games for Boston before disappearing into obscurity.

Eight times the Red Sox finished last during the ten-year era of Bob Quinn,
and in 1932 they hit rock bottom, winning only forty-three games against 111
losses. To add insult to injury, the demise of the Red Sox allowed their National
League counterpart to become Boston's favorite team, and aided the Boston
Braves in becoming major league baseball's only team to enjoy a spike in attendance during the early 1930s.

Quinn knew the time had come to sell. A buyer was found in a young,
wealthy New York businessman named Tom Yawkey, a Yale graduate who vowed
to make the Red Sox better, but warned it would take time. "It will not change
in a day or month or even a season. It is going to be a long, hard job, but we
are going through until the end, and eventually we will put the Red Sox back
on their rightful heights."

The sale amount, during the peak of the Depression, was less than a million dollars. Ten years earlier the Quinn group had paid $1.2 million. In a generous act of kindness, Yawkey offered Quinn the option to retain his share. "I refused because I have not the money to stay in Boston baseball, and I won't be a hanger-on," Quinn said, after he apologized to the Boston public for his "failure to achieve ambitions." "I am not being driven out," Quinn explained. "If I did not think it was for the best interest of the Red Sox, I would have refused to sell."

Yawkey immediately hired the man he believed would help support his goal of building a winner. "A month ago, I had no idea I would be leaving the Athletics and Connie Mack to take over an interest in the Red Sox," said Eddie Collins, who was hired as the Red Sox vice president and treasurer.

"No owners wish to stand in the way of a good baseball man, and I wish Eddie every success," said Connie Mack. "We considered him a vital factor on our team."

Eddie Collins was one of the best second basemen to play the game. He was a great all-around player, known as a smart ballplayer who knew how to win. He starred on Connie Mack's World Series championship teams of 1910, 1911, and 1913, and starred for another World Champion for the Chicago White Sox in 1917. He served as a coach for Philadelphia during their recent string of three consecutive pennants. In his baseball career, as a player and coach, Collins was associated with nine pennant winners.

When the Nationals came to Fenway Park, Yawkey and Collins sat together for the final game of the series (after Washington had won the first two of three games), and watched their Red Sox imitate the Keystone Cops during an inning by stumbling and booting the ball around the infield to allow three runs on only one hit. In the next inning Kuhel's routine fly ball was dropped by outfielder Roy Johnson. An inning later Goslin broke for second base in an attempt to steal, and when the shortstop and second baseman assumed each other would cover second base, the catcher's throw sailed into center field. Goslin continued to third base, and after the center fielder threw the ball over the third baseman and into the crowd, Collins plunged his face into his hands and shook his head. Maybe Yawkey forgot to tell him that rebuilding the Red Sox would not be easy.

After winning their last three games in Boston, Washington swept the Athletics, scoring twenty-three runs in the two-game series. Schulte, hitting .346 on the year, belted a home run deep into the left-center field bleachers, called one of the furthest ever hit at Griffith Stadium. Goslin, who was back in the lineup after being benched for a batting slump and his poor glove work, hit his fifth home run of the year. The Goose was hot again, with ten hits in his last fourteen at bats to raise his average to .295. Manush was the hottest hitter on the team, and in the American League. After going five for five in the second game against Philadelphia, his consecutive-game hitting streak increased to nineteen.

As the Senators were about to make their second tour through the Midwest, the manager made a bold statement about catching the Yankees, whom they trailed by a game and a half. "We'll catch them before we leave St. Louis," Cronin predicted.

The players believed their recent hitting barrage and current five-game winning streak were partly due to their fifteen-year-old batboy, Jimmy Mahorney, handling their bats. Believing his "Midas touch" was needed to keep their strong hitting attack and winning streak alive, the players funded his trip through the Midwest.

Another member of the Washington baseball family would be making the trip. Twenty-one-year-old Calvin Griffith was assigned to pitch batting practice. Three years earlier he had served as the team's batting practice catcher. Before that he was the batboy. It was all part of his training from the ground up, to become a club executive and to take over for Uncle Clark some day.

Young Griffith and Mahorney learned the thrill of traveling with a major league baseball team had its downside. With temperatures near one hundred, the train ride to St. Louis was miserable. The players had previously asked Griffith about booking them on trains with fans blowing ice-filled lockers to create "air conditioning," but the Washington owner, never one to spend more money than necessary, said something about cooler trains being hazardous to their pitching arms. During this train ride the players approached Griffith with the same question, and volunteered to pay the difference. "You know, this idea might work after all," replied Griffith.

The legendary heat in St. Louis was relentless. After a few innings Moe Berg entered the dugout dripping wet, his uniform completely soaked, and announced, "Gentlemen, I believe Satan's joined the team and I'm confident he's inside my uniform." Berg lay across the dugout bench, his teammates covering him with wet towels and ice.

The only things hotter than the St. Louis weather were the bats of the Washington Senators. The Senators rallied for six runs in the top of the ninth in a 10–3 win, with the heart of the batting order, Goslin-Manush-Cronin, combining for seven hits. As Povich viewed the Washington trio's performance from the press box, he decided they needed a nickname, and he came up with "the Old Washington Wrecking Crew."

The following day the Old Washington Wrecking Crew, and the rest of the lineup, totaled fourteen hits in a 14–1 win over the Browns. While winning their seventh in a row, the Nats scored in double digits for the fourth consecutive game. They cooled off in the nightcap, however, dropping a 3–2 decision. Manush got a hit in the loss to extend his streak to twenty-two.

The Washington bats cooled off for just one game. They came back to pound the St. Louis pitchers for twenty-two hits, with four leaving the yard, in a 10–4 win. Cronin, who was red-hot, pounded out five hits, and Manush, who had seventeen multi-hit games in his last twenty-six contests, batting .444 during that stretch, also had five hits.

The Nats took three of four in their series with St. Louis, but still trailed the Yankees by half a game. In Chicago they continued to hit, with the Wrecking Crew combining for nine hits, in their 9–0 win over the White Sox. Manush enjoyed another perfect day by going four for four, for a total of twenty-three hits in his last forty-one at bats.

Overshadowed by Washington's Wrecking Crew and Manush's hitting streak was the work of the pitching staff. Whitehill pitched the 9–0 win over the White Sox for his eighth win of the season, and General Crowder won his tenth game the following day, with his teammates supporting him by scoring eleven runs. During that game Manush was hitless in his first five at bats, but in his sixth trip to the plate he smacked a base hit to extend the hitting streak to twenty-five.

Joe Cronin continued his batting rampage by going four for four in Washington's 7–3 win the next day. The win finally moved the Nats ahead of the Yankees, who were defeated in St. Louis for the twelfth time in their last eighteen games.

Cronin got more great news when he received word that the fans had voted for him as the American League's starting shortstop in the "Game of the Century"—one of the names used for baseball's first All-Star Game, scheduled to be played at Comiskey Park on July 6.

In the 7–3 win, Manush extended his streak to twenty-six, while lifting his season average to .345. The next day his streak ended, but Cronin picked up the slack by going three for four to extend his personal streak to six straight multi-hit games. The Senators' 7–5 win completed a series sweep at Chicago.

The shortstop they said would not be able to play and manage was hitting .359, with 55 runs batted in, and his first-place Nationals had won twelve of their last thirteen games. Suddenly, all those doubting Thomases, who had been so insistent at the beginning of the year, were speechless.

When Washington traveled to Cleveland for their next series, they would be playing against a familiar face. Two weeks before, Walter Johnson had been hired to manage the Indians.

"That's swell," said Cronin upon hearing the news. "It is a great spot for Walter out there with these pitchers the Indians have."

"I am certainly glad he landed," Griffith said. "Baseball needs fellows like him."

Johnson said he had no idea he was being considered for the job. He got a call from Billy Evans, who asked him if he would be interested. Johnson told the general manager he was, but not at the expense of his good friend, and current Cleveland manager, Roger Peckinpaugh. When informed Peckinpaugh was out, Johnson grabbed the job. "I love the game," Johnson said. "I like Cleveland and I feel the Indians have a chance to go somewhere."

From left to right: Joe Cronin, Heinie Manush, and Joe Kuhel. Cronin and Manush were so hot at the plate in June that Shirley Povich was inspired to nickname the heart of the Washington lineup "The Old Washington Wrecking Crew." Overshadowed by the Wrecking Crew was Joe Kuhel, who had a productive season in 1933.

Shortly after the Nats arrived in Cleveland, they went directly to their hotel for breakfast. They were in excellent spirits as they ate and chatted in the dining room, until someone pointed towards the back of the room. Everyone turned to look, and saw Walter Johnson, sitting by himself as he quietly ate his oatmeal. He appeared to be uncomfortable after he got up and passed by his former players, and as he walked to the door, a few whispered, "Poor Walter."

The Washington bats continued to sizzle. They scored nineteen runs on twenty-nine hits in a double win over the Tribe. Cronin knocked out two hits in each game, three for extra bases, and Manush, hitless in the first game, had three hits in the nightcap. In the first game Johnson started his ace, Wes Ferrell, who was working on a five-game winning streak. The Nats sent him to an early shower by scoring five runs in the fifth inning, which was more than enough runs for Whitehill, who pitched his second shutout in a row.

Afterwards, a more relaxed Walter Johnson greeted each player with a smile and a handshake as they arrived in the hotel lobby. "How bout lending me a few hitters, Joe?" he said when Cronin came through the door. "Sorry, can't spare 'em, Walt," Cronin replied with a laugh. After the two managers shook hands and chatted for a few minutes, Cronin's smile disappeared when he made a reference to 1932. "Tough that we could not hit for you like that last year," he told his former manager.

While Washington was in the process of winning two in Cleveland, the Yankees split a double-header in Detroit to fall a game and a half behind. In the first game pitcher Johnny Allen, who missed the first five weeks of the season with an injury, objected to two calls by umpire George Hildebrand. He vented his frustration by grabbing and violently shaking the arbiter before Lou Gehrig intervened. The pitcher drew a fine and suspension for his outburst.

Babe Ruth acted like he was not fazed by Washington's current hot streak. When asked who would win the American League pennant, his answer was the Yankees, and he said the A's would finish second. Not once did he mention the Senators in the conversation.

Age was catching up to the Babe. The intense heat was difficult for him to handle at age thirty-eight, and it took its toll. Ruth had just two hits in his last seventeen at bats. He requested to be benched for the second game of the double-header in Detroit, and he sat out the following day. The rest appeared to do him good. When he returned to the lineup, he came to bat in the top of the eighth, with two men on base, and with the New Yorkers trailing Detroit 7–2. Ruth picked the right time to come out of his slump, launching one 455 feet into the center field seats. Inspired by the Great One, the Yankees rallied for five more runs and won 10–7. The next day Ruth collected three hits in New York's 9–3 win, and suddenly New York had a four-game winning streak.

Heading into the eighth inning in Cleveland, the Nats trailed 3–2. With the game on the line, Cronin rose to the occasion again by following Goslin's triple with a single to tie the score. When Schulte followed with a routine fly out to right field, Cronin stood idle at first base until the Cleveland outfielder made a lackadaisical return throw to the infield. As quick as a flash, Cronin took off for second, and made it without a play. Bluege followed with a single to score his manager, giving the Nats a 4–3 lead that held up for another win, Washington's fifteenth in the last sixteen games.

Tris Speaker watched the Senators in Cleveland and was impressed, especially with Cronin. Maybe he saw something of himself in Washington's player-manager. Back in 1920 player-manager Speaker had batted .388 to help lead his Indians to the World Championship.

"Say, Joe, have lunch with me today," Speaker offered the next morning.

Cronin declined. "Sorry, I can't do it. I've been eating with Johnny Kerr and we haven't lost a game since then."

Percy De Haven, alias "Baltimore," a black baseball fan who attended games in Cleveland, was well known around the American League for his ability to get under people's skin and make the nicest persons angry. He directed his insults at visiting ballplayers and visiting owners, and once made Al Simmons so angry the outfielder began to climb the wall before his teammates pulled him down and persuaded him not to pulverize Baltimore. Another time he hassled Athletics owner Ben Shibe and Mrs. Shibe.

Baltimore found his victim during the Washington series in Bill McAfee, and he began his harassment routine when the pitcher began to warm up in the bullpen. Before entering the game, the pitcher told his teammates how badly he wanted to punch the loudmouth. McAfee came on in the bottom of the eighth with the Nats leading 6–3, but Cleveland was threatening with two runners on base. To add to the tension, Baltimore had relocated to a seat closer to the infield, and continued to hurl insults.

The first batter McAfee faced was Joe Vosmik, who hit a routine fly ball that Sam Rice lost in the sun, and after the ball landed on the turf, a run scored. The next batter, Glenn Myatt, hit a clean single to drive in another run, cutting the lead to 6–5.

McAfee managed to stop the rally, but began another threat in the ninth by walking the leadoff man, and throwing two consecutive balls to the next batter. Cronin called on Jack Russell to finish up, and McAfee, who was still hearing it from Baltimore as he headed for the dugout, was seething. He walked through the dugout to the doorway leading to the Nats' clubhouse, continued through the back exit, and found Baltimore standing in a runway. He grabbed the heckler, punched him in the jaw, punched him again before two policemen pulled him off, and as they escorted Baltimore out of the stadium, McAfee returned to the dugout to watch the conclusion of the game.

The Indians had tied the score and had the bases loaded, and with two outs, there were three balls on the batter. Russell threw his next pitch, which looked like a strike, but home plate umpire Moriarty saw it differently. "Ball four, take your base," called the umpire, and the Tribe won 7–6. Enraged over the call,

Cronin charged in, got in Moriarty's face, and gave the umpire an evaluation of his eyesight. McAfee bolted out of the dugout, and verbally assaulted the umpire, using all the emotions he felt about Baltimore, and about losing the game.

After the game, Indians owner Alva Bradley heard about McAfee's assault on Baltimore, and it did not help the pitcher when Moriarty told Bradley about his tantrum following the game. Bradley dispatched a telegram to Will Harridge. The American League president sent a telegram to McAfee, informing him he was fined $250 for his actions.

"Hell's bells. The Cleveland team ought to be fined, not McAfee," said Clark Griffith. "This Baltimore is a notorious heckler. The Cleveland club never has done anything about him. In Washington, we protect the players. If a patron resorts to abusive language we go to him and tell him to shut up or to go to the gate and get your money back."

Griffith admitted McAfee made a mistake by not reporting the incident to the Senators' management. If he had, Griffith said he would have filed a protest to the Cleveland club. He also said he did not intend to glorify the pitcher for his actions, and mentioned that he ought to know better. "But Baltimore is no credit to the genus of baseball fans," Griffith added.

After hearing from the league president, McAfee felt depressed. His teammates cheered him up by telling him he warmed the hearts of ballplayers everywhere who have always wanted to take a poke at Baltimore. The Washington baseball fans talked about raising cash to pay the pitcher's fine. McAfee was touched by this gesture, but said he would have to decline.

Motivated by the events from the day before, the Nats took their emotions out on the Cleveland pitchers, and crushed the Tribe, 15–2. The Washington Wrecking Crew delivered eight of the thirteen hits, and Manush went four for four. Unnoticed and underrated in the Washington attack were Joe Kuhel and Luke Sewell. Kuhel had a fifteen-game hitting streak, while the Nats receiver was hitting .385 on the road trip. Kuhel extended his hitting streak in Detroit with a home run in his first at bat to help Washington to a 3–0 lead after four innings.

Whitehill looked prime for another shutout by allowing only one hit through the first four innings. In the fifth frame Hank Greenberg, who now was becoming a favorite among the Detroit fans, launched a double, and when the next two batters singled, Whitehill was suddenly in a jam. The next batter, Gee Walker, hit one down the left field line that clearly landed in foul territory. In the press box a play-by-play announcer declared a foul ball, while Manush made no effort to go after the ball.

In an era when the responsibility for the foul lines fell to the home plate umpire, the call went to Roy Van Graflan, and he declared a fair ball. Both runners scored to tie the game, and Walker ended up on second base. Sewell could not believe the call, and he heaved his mask high into the air. Whitehill was beside himself, and he was so upset that Cronin was forced to remove him from the game. Cronin argued but got nowhere with Van Graflan. He ran to third base umpire Bill Summers, and requested him to overrule, but Summers backed Van Graflan. Later in the game the umpires did not help their position with the Nats when the first base umpire, Red Ormsby, called Sewell out after the catcher had apparently beaten the throw.

In the bottom of the ninth, with the Nats clinging to a one-run lead, the Tigers had two men on base with only one out. Cronin turned the game over to Bill McAfee, who overran the ball after the first batter he faced bunted. With the bases loaded, Gee Walker followed with a single over Cronin to score two runs and win the game for Detroit.

After the loss, not a word was spoken in the Washington clubhouse, until an intense discussion was heard coming from the umpires' room. A few minutes later Bill Summers appeared in the clubhouse, and requested to speak with Cronin and Whitehill. The umpire told them the ball was foul, and said it was Van Graflan who had made the call. A few minutes later Van Graflan appeared, and asked to speak with Sewell. He told the catcher he did not see the ball land, therefore he could not make the call.

Later the two umpires made their peace, and covered themselves in their report to the league office by agreeing the ball had landed in fair territory. The Senators were baffled, especially since the umpires had admitted the ball was foul. To make matters worse, New York had won, and were now tied with Washington for first place.

Washington bounced back to win the remaining two games in Detroit, including a 2–1 victory against their nemesis Tommy Bridges, with Crowder pitching a beauty in earning his twelfth win. The next day the Wrecking Crew was back at it, getting eight of the team's fifteen hits, and combining to drive in ten of the eleven runs.

The player-manager they said would buckle under pressure was now batting .365, second in the league to Simmons (.372). His 66 RBIs were second to Gehrig (70). His twenty-seven doubles were highest in the league. His team was leading the league in defense, was hitting a league-high .308, with 444 runs scored, just one less than the Yankees. Six regulars were hitting over .300: along with Cronin, Schulte was hitting .350, Goslin was now up to .331, Manush was at .340, Kuhel .311, and Bluege .323. They had won seventeen of their last twenty games, including twelve of fifteen on their Midwest trip. And most important, the Senators had regained the American League lead by a half game.

The story of the Yankees' season was their lack of pitching. They lost another half game to the Nats when their pitchers were unable to hold a 9–2 lead. The next day the Yankees kept pace with Washington by rallying for two runs in the ninth inning, with Johnny Allen, back from his suspension, pitching the win. New York moved back to within a half game with a 7–3 win to close out their road trip.

The Senators and Yankees were about clash in a Fourth of July double-header at Yankee Stadium, with first place on the line. Cronin was ready. He had planned ahead by saving his lefthanders Whitehill and Stewart for the twin bill, believing the duo would contain New York's left-handed power hitters.

The Washington baseball fans were also ready. All season they had followed their team's success in the newspapers, and by watching the electric scoreboard outside the *Washington Post* building, which showed every play of every game, including the ball traveling from the catcher back to the pitcher. Also included was the voice of Shirley Povich, describing the play-by-play. It was not television or a Web site, but it was the most advanced coverage at the time.

The several Senators fans who intended to make the trip to New York had an option of choosing from two trains, both with reduced costs. The Ohio and Pennsylvania offered a round-trip ticket for five dollars. Another special train would leave early on the morning of July 4, and would return after the game, for a cost of $3.50.

After arriving in New York City on the morning of July 3, the Senators went directly to the Waldorf Astoria Hotel to rest. Cronin would not get time to rest. After he checked in, his room quickly filled up with reporters. "Well, I was telling our batboy, Jimmy Mahorney, this morning, to keep those bats hot. Howdaya like the way we've been hitting?" Cronin asked the writers as he smiled.

The manager changed the subject to the amazing pitching performances that everyone around baseball was talking about: twenty-seven innings of shutout pitching by the Giants. The day before, New York Giants pitchers Carl Hubbell and Roy Parmelee had each hurled a 1–0 shutout against the Cardinals. Hubbell pitched all eighteen innings in the first game, allowed only six hits and no walks, and struck out twelve. In the nightcap Parmelee pitched the 1–0 shutout, defeating Dizzy Dean.

On the Cardinals' train after the game, Dean wandered off to the observation car to take a nap. When he awoke there was no sign of his teammates, who had changed trains in Harrisburg. Dean's bill for his snooze was a $100 fine, courtesy of Cardinals manager Gabby Street.

The surprising National League–leading New York Giants were 43–25 and were winning with Carl Hubbell, solid pitching, good fielding, team play, and the leadership of player-manager Bill Terry. The Cardinals were in second, and after losing the two 1–0 games, they trailed the Giants by 5½ games. The Pirates closely followed, 7½ games behind. The Cubs, who were favored to repeat as National League champions, were in fourth place, with a 37–37 record.

The American League was shaping up to be a two-team race. Philadelphia was a distant third, just two games over .500, and nine full games behind the Nationals.

July 4 was a muggy day in the Big Apple, with clouds hovering over the Bronx. A slight chance of rain did not bother the 77,365 who packed Yankee

Stadium to become the second biggest crowd in baseball history up to that time (85,264 had filled Yankee Stadium on September 9, 1928). Five thousand Washingtonians took their seats along the third base side, with their scattered cheering section extending from behind the Washington dugout to the left field foul pole. Among the visiting fans was Griffith, in his familiar front row seat beside the Nats' dugout.

The Washington Wrecking Crew wasted no time against Lefty Gomez. Cronin rifled a single to score the game's first run. The Yankees tallied in the bottom of the first, when Dixie Walker hit Whitehill's first pitch into the right field seats. An inning later Lazzeri sent one over the wall with a man on, and Cronin, knowing today was not Whitehill's day, called General Crowder, who had been selected to join Cronin in Chicago. The All-Star pitcher kept his team in the game until the seventh, when the Yankees rallied for two runs to extend their lead to 5–1.

Meanwhile Gomez was breezing along. When he came out to pitch the eighth inning, he had ten strikeouts, and had not allowed a hit since the third inning. In the eighth he quickly disposed of the first two batters, and appeared to be heading for another easy inning when Bob Boken, who batted for Crowder, hit a routine popup to the left side of the infield. But Tony Lazzeri had a mental lapse, running over from his second base position, calling off Frank Crosetti and Joe Sewell, who both had an easy play, and dropping the ball.

Attempting to capitalize and spark a rally, Cronin played a hunch by sending Harris to bat for Myer, and Harris delivered a double to score Boken to cut the home team's lead to 5–2.

Throughout the game the Washington fans had little to cheer about, but in the top of the ninth they came alive after both Schulte and Bluege singled, and Gomez, known to lose his composure once in awhile, hit a batter and uncorked two wild pitches to allow two runs to score. Boken followed by sending the game into extra innings with a sacrifice fly.

Russell had entered the game in the eighth, and he took care of business with his sinkerball in the bottom of the ninth. In the tenth Manush doubled, and Cronin once again produced in the clutch, with an RBI single, to make the exuberant Washington crowd "a case for St. Elizabeth's [a federal mental institution]." In the bottom half of the tenth, Russell pitched his third successive scoreless inning to ice a 6–5 Nats' win.

In the nightcap Lefty Stewart was magnificent, throwing strikes and keeping the New York batters off balance. Through the first five innings the southpaw did not allow a hit, but the Nats were faring no better against Yankees pitcher Russ Van Atta. In the sixth Washington broke through with two runs, one on a wild pitch, the third wild pitch of the day to result in a tally for the Nats. In the bottom of the ninth, with one out, and with Washington leading 3–1, Ruth connected for a solo home run, his only hit on the day. Stewart got Gehrig, who went 0 for 8 in the twin bill, to fly out, and when Chapman followed with a fly out, the Nats had swept the Yankees to increase their league lead to 2½ games. Cronin celebrated by riding Stewart piggyback style to the dugout. The shortstop had good reason to rejoice. Not only had his team swept the Yankees, but he had had four hits on the day to take the lead in the American League with a .368 batting average.

Before Cronin and Crowder boarded their train for the All-Star Game in Chicago, the manager reminded Mahorney to keep those bats hot. The rest of the first-place Washington Senators traveled back to the capital, where 150,000 people were enjoying an impressive display of fireworks. At the beginning of the show a scaffold blazed in bright colors, and spelled out a greeting: "Welcome 1933. The New Deal year. Good luck."

Six thousand loyal fans bypassed the fireworks for the opportunity to greet their team at Union Station. When the train arrived, the crowd cheered, and as each player stepped off and appeared in view, his name rang out. Heinie Manush, who surprisingly was not among the eighteen players picked to represent the American League in Chicago, was the first to appear, and as the crowd went wild he kissed his wife, then was led to a microphone to say a few words to the radio audience. He spoke about the pennant, and said hello to his three blonde-haired daughters.

With over half the season remaining, it was too early to discuss a pennant, but this did not seem to matter to the confident Washington baseball fans. On July 5 World Series ticket requests began to arrive in the Griffith Stadium mailbox.

14

BASEBALL'S DREAM GAME

"This is the long-awaited dream day of all baseball fans."
— Harvey Woodruff, *Chicago Tribune*, July 6, 1933

American League Starting Lineup	*National League Starting Lineup*
Ben Chapman CF	Pepper Martin 3B
Charlie Gehringer 2B	Frank Frisch 2B
Babe Ruth RF	Chuck Klein RF
Lou Gehrig 1B	Chick Hafey LF
Al Simmons LF	Bill Terry 1B
Jimmy Dykes 3B	Wally Berger CF
Joe Cronin SS	Dick Bartell SS
Rick Ferrell C	Jimmie Wilson C
Lefty Gomez P	Wild Bill Hallahan P

For years baseball fans had talked about a dream game, between two dream teams composed of baseball's best from each league. On Thursday afternoon, July 6, 1933, forty-nine thousand fans crammed into Comiskey Park to witness a dream come true, which would go down in history as baseball's first All-Star Game.

Baseball's dream game became a reality after *Chicago Tribune* sports editor Arch Ward promoted the game as baseball's contribution to Chicago's A Century of Progress Exposition. As in today's game, the fans voted for the starters, and with the game's sponsor, the *Tribune*, printing the ballots in their daily newspapers, Chicago's baseball fans cast the majority of votes, which explains why Al Simmons of the White Sox received the most, with 346,291.

Joining Cronin and Crowder on the American League All-Star roster was former teammate Sam West, the lone representative for the St. Louis Browns. He had had a great start to the season by collecting nine hits in his first seventeen at bats, and continued to swing a hot bat through the first half of the season to remain among the top ten hitters, with a .333 average at the All-Star break.

Starting as Cronin's counterpart for the National League was Dick Bartell, the rookie once highly touted by Pittsburgh's manager Donie Bush, who won the last utility infielder's spot on the Pirates' 1928 roster to force Cronin's departure to Kansas City. Bartell played in Pittsburgh for three years before being traded to the Phillies. Since 1928 he had hit over .300 four times, scored over one hundred runs two times, and developed into a solid defensive shortstop.

For their great years of service to the game, Connie Mack and John McGraw, considered the two greatest generals in the game's history, were assigned the honor to manage. For McGraw it meant coming out of retirement to lead the National League.

Cronin took care of the senior circuit in their first at bat, by fielding three consecutive groundballs, and winging three perfect throws to Gehrig. In the bottom of the second, with one out, and with Jimmy Dykes on first base, Cronin drew a walk. After Red Sox catcher Rick Ferrell flew out, it was up to the pitcher to produce with a man in scoring position.

Going into the season Lefty Gomez had a .155 lifetime batting average. During his rookie year, Babe Ruth bet him that he would not accumulate ten hits for the entire season. In the season's 145th game, Gomez became $250 richer by hitting a scratch single. Nobody would have wagered on Gomez to drive in the first run in the history of the All-Star Game, but the pitcher singled to left center field to score Dykes and give the American League a 1–0 lead.

More predictable was Babe Ruth's hitting the first home run, when in the third inning he sent a line drive over the right field wall. Eddie Collins, serving as the first base coach, did a dance, and slapped the Babe on the back as he rounded first base. His clout off Cardinals lefty Wild Bill Hallahan came with a man on, to open a 3–0 lead for the junior circuit.

In the fourth inning Crowder replaced Gomez, and his finesse style following Gomez's fastballs baffled the batters in the fourth and fifth innings. In the sixth inning the National Leaguers adjusted to Crowder and began to rally. With one out, Cubs pitcher Lon Warneke tripled, and tallied on Pepper Martin's groundout. Frank Frisch followed by belting a Crowder curve ball into the right field seats to cut the lead to 3–2. Things got nerve-wracking for the pitcher, and the American League, when Chuck Klein followed with a single, but Washington's pitching ace got out of the inning by getting a groundout from Chick Hafey.

Up to this point the American League's leading hitter was hitless. Then, in the bottom of the sixth, Cronin singled off Warneke, and after advancing to second on a bunt, he scored when pinch batter Earl Averill singled to increase the American League's lead to 4–2.

Hubbell silenced the American League bats after entering the game in the seventh inning to keep his league in the game. The National League threatened in the seventh against Lefty Grove, but Grove got out of the jam by striking out Gabby Hartnett, and by getting a fly out from Woody English. In the eighth inning, with a man on first, Hafey hit one far into right field. McGraw cheered in the dugout, thinking the ball was gone, but Babe Ruth saved the day when he backed up to the wall, leaped, and caught the ball for an out. "That old boy certainly came through when they needed him," McGraw said after the game.

Grove retired the side in the top of the ninth to seal a 4–2 win for the American League.

"Did you have a good trip?" a sportswriter asked Cronin when he stepped off the train at Union Station.

"Ga-reat!" replied Cronin. "It was one of the greatest experiences I had in baseball. It was great playing under Connie Mack. And say, this Warneke, this Hubbell — great."

Cronin was spotted by a group of kids, who ran over to the All-Star shortstop with their pens and autograph books in hand. The All-Star took a break from the interview to attend to his young admirers.

"Did you bring your bat back?" Griffith nervously asked, hoping that his shortstop had his red-hot bat for the rest of the season. Cronin was on the same wavelength as Griffith. Not wanting to risk something happening to his bat, he had taken one of Bluege's to Chicago, "but I used one of Foxx's bats. It had a lot of hits in it."

The Senators resumed their schedule at home on Saturday, July 8, with a double-header against the Indians. The day was special in the hearts of the 28,000 fans that came to honor Walter Johnson in his return to the capital. The Big Train received several gifts during a pre-game ceremony. Joe Cronin closed the event by stepping up to the microphone to say a few words about his former manager, a man he respected and admired.

It appeared Jimmy Mahorney had heard Cronin's message to keep the bats hot. The Washington batters picked up where they had left off at the All-Star break by pounding out a sweep in the double-header. Heinie Manush led the attack in the nightcap by going three for five, and Fred Schulte, the batting star of the day, went five for nine in the twin bill, with four runs batted in, and had the Washington fans forgetting about Sam West.

Washington's sweep over the Indians kept their 1933 undefeated Saturday record intact, and aided by New York's two losses following the All-Star break, the Nats now led by 4½ games.

A day later Washington scored three unearned runs in the first inning, and held on for a 3–2 win. Tommy Thomas pitched a good game for the win, and McAfee pitched the last two innings for the save. "Cronin has the boys playing heads-up baseball," Walter Johnson said after watching his team fall for the third time in two days. He had complimented the Senators' hitting attack a month before, and now he praised them for their fielding. Above all, he believed the Nats were getting the breaks. "The breaks helped Washington in 1924, and it looks like this season is a repetition of that one."

The three wins over Cleveland increased Washington's winning streak to seven, and their season record to a major league best 50–25. They were leading their league in hitting and fielding, and appeared to be heading for the American League Championship ... until they were struck by an episode that can change the complexion of a team's entire season, known as "Old Joe Slump."

The Washington bats cooled as fast as they had gotten hot in June, and they dropped four of their next five. Suddenly their fans, so supportive during the course of the season, were riding them. When they lost three of four games to the White Sox the crowd got restless to the point where *Chicago Tribune* sportswriter Irving Vaughn wrote, "Washington patrons are never kind with their remarks."

Shirley Povich had initially told the fans not to worry, but after the White Sox series he was worrying. "This is getting serious," he wrote. This did not make Griffith very happy. He reminded Povich that he had stuck with them during the good times of the first half of the season. But now, with the team in a slump, Grififth told him, "you begin to view us with alarm. That is no way to treat our ball club. I did not think you were one of our fair-weather friends."

Here come the Yankees!

After dropping their first two games following the All-Star Game they began to win, and in one week they made up the 4½-game deficit to pull even with Washington. Their winning streak began with three straight come-from-behind wins, with Ruth leading the way by blasting four home runs, and getting five hits in one of those games. "It's too bad Ruth had to go out there [to Chicago] and bust a home run," Griffith said. "It was an inspiration to the Yankees. Never disturb a sleeping lion."

The Yankees' winning streak continued when Tony Lazzeri belted a three-run homer. The Yankees kept on winning to extend their streak to nine. After finishing their home stand, they were in first place, and were now the favorites to win the pennant.

Al Simmons, never a favorite among the Washington fans, was usually marked for catcalls at Griffith Stadium. During Chicago's recent trip to the capital, Simmons had told a Washington sportswriter he did not want his playing style to be compared with Ty Cobb's. The Washington fans used his remark as more ammunition to fire at him, and each time Simmons came to bat he heard the fans shout out, "Ty! ... Ty! ... Ty!"

Simmons was about to shoot one back at Washington. After the White Sox were bombed by the Yankees in the first two games in the series at Yankee Stadium, to increase New York's winning streak to nine, Simmons spoke out about who he believed would win the American League flag. "The Yankees have the best team in the league. If they don't repeat they will have only themselves to blame. They dislike the Nationals so heartily that they've been pressing themselves out of a lot of games with them. If they can beat Washington in half of the twelve games they play the rest of the way, then they are right for another World Series."

The Nationals finished a disappointing home stand with a 9–8 record, and were blanked in three of their eight losses. Jake Miller of the White Sox, former Washington hurler Bump Hadley (who now pitched with the Browns), and Tommy Bridges (as usual) had shut them out. Bridges and Hadley both pitched four-hit shutouts, while Miller pitched his second shutout against the Nats in 1933, this time a three-hitter. Three days earlier Miller had defeated the Nats, and back in May he had shut them out on two hits. Three of Miller's four 1933 victories were against Washington, and all three were against Crowder, who was 8–0 versus Chicago in 1932.

The previous winter Miller had sent Griffith a letter, asking for a tryout. "I did not think that old fellow would ever be worth another trial," said Griffith. Back in December, at the winter meetings, Billy Evans joked about bring Miller back to the Indians, just so he had someone to pitch against Washington. "We laughed about the way he used to beat us when he was with the Indians."

It appeared that Mahorney's luck had worn off. The players desperately sought another good luck omen, when Calvin Griffith came to mind. Thinking back to their awesome hitting attack through the Midwest in June, it was remembered that it was Calvin Griffith who had pitched batting practice. He answered the players' request to return towards the end of their recent home stand, but this time he did not prove to be the lucky charm the Nats' slumping offense was counting on.

Slumping at the plate was Cronin, a result of taking a pitch on the left arm during the Chicago series. The injury had forced him to leave the game, miss the next game, and go to bed each night with his injured arm packed in ice.

Every day at 2:00, during a Washington home stand, Cronin took time to sit down on his stool in front of his locker and read his fan mail. "While we are winning our correspondence falls out. But just let us hit a slump and how the letters begin to pile in." And often mailed along with the letters were good luck charms like four-leaf clovers and rabbits' feet. Cronin once received a buckeye that he claimed had ended a batting slump.

According to Cronin, it's spring training when they get the real "beauties." Back in March a visitor, claiming to be good luck for the Senators, had wandered onto the Biloxi Stadium field and asked for a tryout. He wore a four-day beard and a shirt that was covered in layers of countryside grime. He rode the trains from town to town in hopes of getting a job. He did have some pitching experience, so why not get a job from a major league team?

When the visitor stepped onto the mound, the Washington pitchers covered their mouths or turned away to laugh. The prospect threw a few before Cronin told him thank you, but no thanks.

Connie Mack's Athletics were in third place, just where they were expected to be, with a 47–43 record, and ten games behind the first-place Yankees. Hitting and scoring runs remained a strong point for the Mackmen, with the departure of Dykes, Haas, and Simmons not having had much effect, as Mack had predicted. Their replacements were doing a good job, with third baseman Pinky Higgins hitting .320, Doc Cramer doing a better job than Haas in center field, and "Indian" Bob Johnson in left; although no Simmons, Johnson was batting over .320, and hitting with power. Best of all, Mack's lineup included Jimmie Foxx, who was on his way to his second consecutive MVP award. Also featured in Mack's lineup was the great all-around and inspirational play of catcher Mickey Cochrane.

Hitting was not the Athletics' problem, but lack of pitching depth was. Hurting the Athletics' pitching staff was a disappointing year from Tony Freitas, a twelve-game winner in 1932, whom Mack was counting on for 1933. His biggest disappointment was the poor season and bad attitude displayed by veteran pitcher George Earnshaw, who got into hot water before reporting to spring training by predicting the Yankees to win the pennant, and insisting the A's would greatly miss Simmons. He reported to spring training out of shape, and failed to get into shape after Mack allowed him time off to tune up. When Earnshaw did not follow orders to go to the bullpen to warm up during a game, Mack had had it, and he gave the pitcher his release.

Mack did have the brightest pitching star in Lefty Grove, who was having another great season, and owned a six-game wining streak when he pitched the first game of the series against Washington. Opposing Grove was seldom-used Bobby Burke, who had hurled a shutout against the Browns during Washington's last home stand. Burke had another great outing, by limiting the Athletics to two hits in five innings. In the sixth, Cronin gave the ball to Jack Russell, who was now the league's top relief specialist. Russell finished the game by striking out Foxx, Ed Coleman, and Johnson in succession. "He's got the best sinker in the Big Leagues today," Cronin said after the game. "Nine of ten batters hit the ball on the ground when Russell's pitching. They are either easy to get out, or turned into double plays." In the win, Washington's defense executed three double plays.

In the second game the Washington bats finally came alive in a 10–6 win. The batting star of the game, of all people, was Bill McAfee, who hit a triple and a home run.

The two wins moved the Nationals back into first place, and they increased their lead to a full game the next day when Whitehill hurled his twelfth win of the year. With a one-game lead over New York, the Nats headed back home to close out the month of July with a huge four-game series versus the Yankees.

15

HEAT OF THE PENNANT RACE

"If the Yankees still have any serious intention on winning that pennant, they had better brace immediately and take three out of four from the Senators at New York this week."

— Connie Mack

Lefty Stewart was cruising along with a 2–0 lead during the opener of the four-game series with the Yankees, before a crowd of fifteen thousand on a hot and humid day in the nation's capital. Through the first six innings Stewart allowed just one hit, and had New York's scoring streak of 303 consecutive games in jeopardy, until the Yankees broke through for a run in the top of the eighth.

In the top of the ninth, with Washington still clinging to a one-run lead, Cronin called on Russell, and Ben Chapman greeted Washington's closer with a double. Then Chapman went from hero to goat by getting trapped in a run-down between second and third. Ossie Bluege chased him back towards second base, then threw to Cronin, who made the tag. Umpire Harry Geisel began to signal the runner out, then changed his call, ruling that Cronin had missed the tag. After a lengthy argument, play resumed, and Luke Sewell rifled the ball to Cronin to catch Chapman leading off second base. Cronin made the tag, but Chapman's hard slide knocked the ball out of the shortstop's mitt. Dickey followed with a sacrifice, and Dixie Walker hit one deep enough to allow his roommate to tag up and score to tie the game.

With one out in the top of the tenth Combs doubled, and with Ruth, Gehrig and Chapman to follow, Washington appeared to be in trouble. Cronin instructed Russell to intentionally pass Ruth, and take his chances with Gehrig and Chapman. The strategy paid off when Gehrig flew out, and Chapman grounded out to end the inning.

In the bottom of the tenth the Senators loaded the bases. After Cronin was forced at the plate for the second out, he quickly got up from his slide, and motioned to the dugout for a pinch hitter. Off the bench came Cliff Bolton, not

Washington's twenty-game winners. From left to right: General Crowder, Monte Weaver, and Earl Whitehill. In 1933 Crowder won twenty-four games and Whitehill won twenty-two. Weaver won twenty-two games as a rookie in 1932, but dropped to ten in 1933 due to an injury that most believed was in his mind.

a popular choice among the Griffith Stadium grandstand managers. Cronin had already used his two best pinch hitters, Dave Harris and Sam Rice, but he still had Moe Berg, Bob Boken, and Johnny Kerr available, each seemingly a better choice than the third-string catcher who had batted only twelve times all season and produced just two hits. However, the twenty-six-year-old reserve came through, driving Red Ruffing's first offering past third baseman Joe Sewell to score the winning run.

After rain forced the second game of the series to be postponed, the hottest and most humid weather of the summer blanketed the country. In Washington, known to get quite humid, it was almost unbearable, but this did not seem to hamper the Washington batters, who shelled Johnny Allen for an 8–0 lead after seven innings.

With the game in hand, and with Washington about to chalk up another victory to increase their 1933 Saturday record to 18–0, the question remaining was if Crowder, on his way to his fifteenth win of the season, could finish the shutout. Babe Ruth answered that by socking a three-run homer with two outs in the top of the eighth. The Nats won 11–5, to increase their first-place lead to three games, and their season record to nine wins in twelve games against the Yankees.

On July 30 the temperature climbed into the upper nineties, but Griffith Stadium was the place to be, and Clark Griffith smiled when informed the attendance topped thirty thousand. The standing-room-only crowd liked what they saw in the early going, when Kuhel hit one over the thirty-foot wall in right field for his eighth home run of the season, and Washington's league-leading defense turned two double plays. Whitehill was pitching well, but the heat was too much for the veteran, and he requested to be replaced, a rarity for this pitcher, who resented being removed from any game he started. He would fight with managers, or throw a tantrum, or do both, but on a day like today, he was not making any arguments.

The Nats' defense uncharacteristically fell apart, committing three errors, two on bunted balls, and one by Goslin, after he threw the ball away in an attempt to cut down Ruth advancing from first to third on a single. The Yankees went on to win, 7–2.

For the final game of the series, with the temperature reaching ninety-nine, Cronin pitched Stewart on three days' rest. A ladies' day crowd of fifteen thousand watched the Yankees pound out eighteen hits in their win to reduce Washington's lead back to one game. Ruth led the attack with four hits, including a double off the top of the right field wall, and a bases-loaded triple. Frank Crosetti added four hits, and the New York offense exploded for seven runs in the fourth inning to send Stewart to the showers.

The fourth-place Cleveland Indians entered August with a season record of 49–52, and were 14½ games behind the Senators. Since Walter Johnson had taken control they had won 22 games and lost 27. Leading their pitching staff with twelve victories was right-hander Oral Hildebrand, winner of his first six decisions in 1933 to earn a spot on the All-Star team. After his brilliant start, the All-Star divided his next twelve decisions, and believed he had lost his momentum because his new manager had misused him. On August 1 Hildebrand had a confrontation with his boss, after Johnson came to the mound to remove him with the bases loaded, and with the Indians trailing. The outraged pitcher created a dust storm by kicking at the pitcher's mound several times, then heaved the resin bag and his glove. "That will cost you $100," Johnson informed him. As Hildebrand walked off the mound he lashed out at Johnson.

In the clubhouse after the game the angry pitcher continued with his verbal attack. Johnson tried to explain, but the pitcher refused to listen, and when Johnson finally did get a word in, he told the pitcher he was suspended, and he would not pitch until he was ready to pitch and restore his temper. "It would take quite a spell before I comply to this!" shouted Hildebrand. "And I don't care if I pitch another game for you!"

Hildebrand traveled back to Cleveland to tell his side of the story to Billy

Evans. When the two met, the general manager listened, and then he calmly explained that it was up to the pitcher to make his peace with his manager. Hildebrand understood and contacted Johnson to apologize. The Big Train appreciated the apology, told the pitcher to rejoin the team, and announced he intended to put him back in the starting rotation.

When the Senators met the Red Sox in their next series, Boston had a familiar face in their lineup. Joe Judge was back in the American League after the Dodgers had released him, and that was fine with him. "The National League reminded me of the minors," he said. "Why, the day I got an offer from the Red Sox, I got one from Bill Terry," and Judge declined his offer. Did he really choose the Red Sox because the managing position might open in the near future? "I am playing for McManus. They did not hire me as manager, and I would be deeply obliged if my well-wishers would not rush into print."

The Nats began August with a three-game sweep over the Red Sox. Crowder looked great in the first game, winning 2–1 for his sixteenth win of the season. The Nationals' bats came alive in their 8–4 win the next day to give Whitehill his thirteenth win. Whitehill aided his own cause by clouting an RBI triple to help his team to a 5–0 lead, but later in the game he got into a jam, and as usual, he refused to listen to his manager's advice. When Cronin walked towards the pitcher's mound, Whitehill walked off the hill, and kept on walking until Cronin retreated to his position. The pitcher continued to struggle, and when the Nats manager finally called for a relief pitcher, Whitehill picked up the resin bag and punted it into center field.

Cronin called for his closer, who finished the game for another save, but Russell did not stick around to enjoy it. With other matters on his mind, he rushed over to the hospital to see his wife, who became the second Washington player's wife to have her appendix removed during this season.

Monte Weaver, a twenty-two-game winner the previous season, had only four wins through the end of July. He had been out of action for over a month due to a sore arm, but was his arm really sore? The word was it was all in his mind and he should have been pitching. He returned to the starting rotation to complete the sweep over the Red Sox, and was impressive by striking out four and allowing no walks, much to the delight of ten thousand fans that watched the Senators win, 3–2.

While the Senators were sweeping the Red Sox, Philadelphia was taking it to New York. The Yankees looked awful while getting swept, and fell four games behind Washington. Their struggling pitching staff gave up thirty-one runs, and defensively the Yanks were slipping, especially Babe Ruth, who could no longer cover ground, and Earle Combs, now thirty-four, had slowed down, and could not back up Ruth as in previous years. To add to McCarthy's headaches, the most feared lineup in baseball was in a slump, scoring only six runs during the three-game series. One of the losses was a shutout thrown by Lefty Grove that snapped the Yankees' scoring streak at 308 games. For Grove the win was his sixteenth, to tie him with Crowder for the league lead.

In New York City fifty people died due to the heat wave. Macy's Department Store claimed to be a place for relief, and their ads in the *New York Times* encouraged people to take advantage of their basement floor, where the temperature was a "comfortable" eighty-five. Babe Ruth found his refuge by requesting to be removed during the contests. Father Time had caught up to Ruth. No longer could he tolerate the hottest days of summer for nine full innings.

Bill McAfee was traded to Rochester, with cash, for another pitcher. His season was a disappointment, especially after he had won six of his seven decisions in 1932. A good 1933 was expected, but he never did get on track, even before his confrontation with Baltimore. He did win his first three decisions, and saved three games early in the season, but in his only start he was bombed, and he won his second game after blowing a save. Following the All-Star break, he saved two games while pitching his best baseball of the year, but the Nats felt they could find a better pitcher. (Or was it due to something else? In his book, *Beyond the Shadow of the Senators*, Brad Snyder mentions that the first time McAfee warmed up during the home stand that followed his fight with Baltimore he was jeered by Washington's die-hard black fans, who occupied the right field pavilion next to the Senators' bullpen. Not wanting to lose support from his die-hards, or perhaps fear for the pitcher's safety, may have persuaded Griffith to make the deal).

From the Rochester Red Wings of the International League the Nats got Ed Chapman, a hard-throwing right-hander who was a former teammate of Buddy Myer's at Mississippi A&M College. Wanting to rest his starters for the upcoming series at Yankee Stadium, Cronin gave Chapman the starting assignment against Philadelphia, and he received a welcome to the Big Show that he would not forget. Foxx greeted the rookie by smacking his thirty-first home run into the next county, and Chapman gave up four runs before being removed during the third inning.

The Athletics extended their lead to 8–1 before Washington rallied, and when Manush extending his hitting streak to thirteen games by clearing the bases with a three-run triple, the game was tied, 8–8. Pinky Higgins untied it with a home run to complete his cycle for the day in Philadelphia's 12–8 win.

With Washington coming to New York for a four-game series, the Yankees had to make their move now. A win over Boston, while Higgins powered the Mackmen past Washington, put the Yanks within three games. When the series began, the two teams put the pennant race aside and worked on intensifying their rivalry. Cronin smacked a hard tag on Gehrig when the first baseman made an aggressive slide at the shortstop as he covered second base. Baseball's Iron Man did not appreciate the tag, and after he had his say he jogged back to the dugout to the applause of the home crowd, while Cronin kept on shouting as he limped back to his position. In the top of the inning Buddy Myer got caught in a rundown. Lazzeri chased him, and as he applied the tag from behind, he gave a hard shove, causing the base runner to fall to his knees. Myer quickly scrambled to his feet, and began to walk towards Lazzeri as he called him every name in the book. Did Myer's own words from the year before echo in his mind? "You have to take a lot on the field and learn to like it." He had said it himself, and he knew if he "smacked the sender," it would mean another suspension, and right now, in the heat of a pennant race, Washington could not afford to lose him.

Washington went to work in the second inning, and took a 5–0 lead against Van Atta, who was hurt by the Yankees' fielding woes. Lazerri made an error, and Cronin made him pay by knocking in two runs with a single.

The Washington manager was the most fired-up person on the field. As forty-five thousand fans booed him throughout the afternoon, Cronin was all over the umpires, and did not spare his players and coaches. After a Senators base runner was called out on a close play at third base, Schacht did not argue the call. When the inning ended, Cronin chewed out his third base coach. "I did not want to get thrown out of the game," Schacht explained. "Get thrown out!" blasted Cronin. "It'll do you good. And it will do the club some good."

General Crowder did not have it on this day, and after the Yankees rallied to cut the lead to 5–4, Cronin decided to bring Russell into the game in the fifth inning. In the ninth inning, with Washington still leading by a run, the Nats were one out away from a big win. The Yankees were threatening, with runners on second and third, and with Ben Chapman at bat. Russell threw a sinker. Chapman swung and hit the ball on the ground, directly at the sure-handed Cronin. Then came a shocking turn of events when Cronin flat out missed the ball. It scooted between his legs and into left field. Both runners scored, and just like that, an assumed victory became a heartbreaking defeat. (The hometown scorekeeper credited Chapman with a hit, although Povich insisted it was an error all the way.)

In the nightcap Lou Gehrig, playing in his 1,300th consecutive game, belted a home run, and later Ruth hit one, his twenty-sixth of the season. With New York leading 5–3, and two outs to go for a sweep of the double-header, Buddy Myer came to the plate with two of his teammates on base. The crowd booed the fiery second baseman, not only for his part in the rivalry, but also because he had been a "Yankee killer" at the plate. Joe McCarthy, aware a dangerous left-handed batter was stepping in, removed right-handed pitcher Red Ruffing. He called on left-handed veteran Herb Pennock, but Myer upset the strategy by making his fifth hit of the day to score both runners and tie the game. With Washington's Wrecking crew due up next, the Senators were in great position to rally. But Pennock struck out Goslin, and Manush hit a routine fly ball to end the inning.

General Crowder, ineffective in the first game, pitched in the bottom of the ninth. Dickey led off with a hit, and moved into scoring position on a sacrifice. After Crowder struck out Walker for the second out in the inning, Joe Sewell came the plate, and up in the press box the Washington sportswriters wanted Cronin to call for an intentional walk. Sewell was hitting .288, while the on-deck batter, Sammy Byrd, was batting .237. First base was open, and to the writers it made sense to pass Sewell and pitch to Byrd. But on the field Cronin overlooked the idea and elected to pitch to Sewell, who clubbed a hit to score Dickey with the winning run, sending the Yankee Stadium crowd into bedlam.

After a pair of 6–5 losses on ninth-inning rallies, the Washington lead was back to one game, and it looked as though a collapse was underway. The Nats' team batting average, a league-leading .308 at one time, was now down to .295, their run production had dropped, and they had now lost four in a row to the Yankees. With two games remaining in the series, and another game against the Yanks in a week, this was a time of urgency. Cronin had to think of something to get his team back into a winning habit, and it had to be done now!

16

THE WINNING STREAK

"Ever since we were kids we dreamed about playing in the World
Series.... The pennant is just laying there, waiting for us to take it."
— Joe Cronin's pep talk on August 8

From spring training through the morning of August 8, Joe Cronin never
mentioned the pennant to his team or to the press. Back in March he would
comment about why he believed his team was better than the Yankees, but
when asked about winning the pennant his reply was, "Pennant? What's that?"
He had patiently waited for the right moment, and before the third game of the
series at Yankee Stadium he called a team meeting to let the cat out of the bag.

It was Earl Whitehill's turn in the pitching rotation, and the added pressure of the Nats' needing a win, along with Cronin's pep talk, was the perfect
tonic for a competitor like Whitehill. Also serving as an inspiration was the
presence of his biggest fan, Violet Linda Whitehill, his beauteous wife of seven
years, a former model who claimed to be the young lady we know today on the
box of Sun-Maid Raisins. Being unable to handle the suspense, Mrs. Whitehill would stay away from the ballpark on days her husband pitched. But today
she summoned her courage, and sat in a front row seat beside the Senators'
dugout.

Yankees pitcher Johnny Allen showed he was going to play hardball today,
when in the second inning he knocked down Cronin with a high and inside
fastball. Two batters later he pitched one close to Kuhel. The first baseman
dropped his bat, put his hands on his hips, and glowered at the pitcher. After
the inning ended the usually calm Al Schacht headed from the third base coach's
box to the pitcher's mound and issued a challenge to Allen. The pitcher
accepted, and as he began to walk towards the Washington coach, home plate
umpire Bill McGowan stepped between the two, and ordered them to their
dugouts.

When Allen was not throwing at the Washington batters, he was perfect,
and after he retired Myer to begin the fourth inning, he had retired the first

The Senators got great pitching, timely hitting, and several players to step up to contribute to a great team effort. But Povich insisted in his column that the hero of the series was Buddy Myer. "He was the most talked about of the ballplayers of the entire four-game series, and with reason."

In the field, Myer had handled all thirty-four of his fielding chances, and came up with big stops and key plays "that did more to discourage the Yanks than all the Washington pitchers." At the plate, Myer made seven hits, including his home run, a late-inning RBI hit to deliver the tying run in the second game of the series, and in the final game of the series he delivered a key hit against Lefty Gomez.

The most talked-about ballplayer in Boston was Joe Cronin, the toast of the citizens with Irish heritage in South Boston, who looked upon him as one of their own. In Boston the Nats had three come-from-behind wins as they swept the three-game series. Joe Kuhel's bat, and his hustle on the base paths, decided the outcome in the first game. His two runs batted in cut Boston's lead to 3–2, and in the top of the eighth he made his fourth hit of the day. Manush followed with a sacrifice attempt, and Kuhel beat the throw to second base. He then arrived ahead of the throw to third base on Cronin's bunt. A walk to Harris tied the score, and Goslin followed with a two-run single that proved to be the game winner. The Goose came through the next day by smacking a two-run double to tie the game in the top of the ninth. After two walks, Schulte broke out of his second half slump with a double down the left field line to score two more runs. Kuhel, swinging a red-hot bat, then stroked a two-run single to complete a six-run rally in an 8–4 Washington win.

Earl Whitehill followed with another great game, limiting the Red Sox to five hits, to pick up his fifteenth win. Ossie Bluege tied the score with a home run, and in the eighth inning Myer tripled and scored on Cronin's long fly out.

The Yankees arrived in Washington needing a win after splitting a pair in Philadelphia the day before, and now trailing Washington by 4½ games. New York's pitching staff had let them down against the Athletics. After knocking out Lefty Grove in the first game with five runs, the hurlers failed to hold the lead. Jimmie Foxx led the rally with two home runs in an 11–9 A's win. In the nightcap New York jumped to a 4–0 lead, but the pitchers gave away that lead. The Yanks fought back to win, 8–6.

Before the game in Washington, as Ben Chapman walked along the first base line, he spotted Buddy Myer in the Washington dugout. "Say, Buddy," he called out, "we sure could've bought a lot of gasoline for that one hundred dollars we were fined."

"Yeah, there goes that bird dog I was saving up for," Myer replied, and the hatchet in the Myer-Chapman feud was officially buried.

A Sunday crowd of twenty-seven thousand came to Griffith Stadium to see if the Senators could take another one from the Yankees and increase their winning streak to six. In the fifth inning, with the game tied at 2–2, Dave Harris crushed a long drive against the wind that hit high off the left-center field wall, and Harris settled for a double. Kuhel followed with a routine fly ball to center. Combs was set to make the catch, then sprinted ahead when a gust of wind carried the ball towards the infield. Crosetti and Lazzeri each had an easy play, but stood idle, and the ball dropped in for a hit to score Harris.

In the top of the ninth Lefty Stewart, who had pitched a great game, got into trouble. With two men on base, and only one out in a one-run game, Cronin called on Russell to put out the fire, which he did.

In their twelfth win in nineteen meetings against New York, Joe Kuhel went three for four, and Buddy Myer, who was batting .420 against the Yankees in 1933, went four of five. Stewart held Ruth, Gehrig, Sewell, and Combs hitless, and Russell capped the day by striking out Dixie Walker to end the game.

The two teams had a three-game series remaining, scheduled for Yankee Stadium during the last week of the season. The Yanks, now 5½ games behind, had work to do if they intended to be within range of the pennant at that time.

Shirely Povich was confident that Washington would win the pennant, and he felt sure enough to ask Cronin a question on the train to Chicago. "Hey Joe, how many games are the Nats going to win the pennant by?"

"We gotta win tomorrow's game before we win the pennant," answered Cronin. "We're not talking pennant yet."

In Chicago, Crowder and Whitehill each hurled a 5–1 victory. For Crowder, who helped his own cause by going three for three at the plate, it was his nineteenth win, the most in the major leagues. For Whitehill the win was his sixteenth, just one shy of his career high. Manush hit safely in both games to extend his streak to twenty-three, and the Nats extended their winning streak to eight.

As the Nats were winning in Chicago, the Yankees lost one of their two games in St. Louis to fall 6½ games behind. The third game of the series was the one that put Gehrig ahead of Everett Scott as baseball's all-time leader for most consecutive games played. Before playing his 1,308th, the first baseman was honored during a modest pre-game ceremony. The Yankees dropped the game in ten innings as once again their pitchers failed to hold on to an early lead. The Senators picked up another game, extending their streak to nine by beating Jake Miller. Before the game Cronin instructed Nick Altrock to pitch batting practice, and his slow curves made Miller's look fast. The Nats knocked him out of the box before the first inning ended, and went on to pound out sixteen hits in a 14–1 win. Weaver continued to look like the pitcher from 1932 by limiting Chicago to just 4 hits.

Chicago manager Lou Fonseca pitched Miller the next day, and this time he made it through the first inning, and the second, but not the third, when the Nats rallied for four runs. After that the Washington bats died, and they did not make another hit through the next six innings. The White Sox evened

Buddy and Mina Myer. Buddy Myer wore out the Yankees during the month of August.

the score, and threatened to win in the ninth inning, but the Senators' infield turned a double play to end the inning. In the top of the tenth Cronin drew a walk to become the Senators' first base runner since the fourth inning. Goslin and Schulte followed with singles, and Bluege came through with a two-out hit that scored two runs to give the Nats a 6–4 lead. Russell was on to earn another save in the bottom of the tenth, and the White Sox were going to make him work for it. Evar Swanson led off with a single, but Myer stepped up once again by fielding a ground ball, tagging Swanson who was en route to second base, and throwing to Kuhel in time to complete the double play. A moment later Cronin fielded a ground ball and fired to Kuhel to finish the win, the tenth in a row.

The coming World Series was being discussed, and the vision was the Senators versus the Giants. Bill Terry, the outspoken player-manager of the Giants, fired the first shot by saying the Nats had only a few fellows who could hit, while the Yankees were tough right down the line. "I'd rather play the Senators any day."

At his desk Griffith read the newspaper, and saw Terry's statement. He tossed the paper onto a chair, took a bite out of his unlighted cheroot, and replied, "Why, the nerve of that guy!" He told the sportswriters, "He can't insult my ball team." Griffith vowed that if the Giants were in the World Series, his Senators would "show 'em some hitters."

The sportswriters agreed with Griffith. Wayne Otto, who covered the Cubs, for the *Chicago Herald American*, said a World Series of the Senators vs. the light-hitting Giants would be "a joke."

Terry's remarks made no difference to Cronin, who had other things to worry about, like finding another experienced pitcher to add depth to his staff. He had Sam Gray in mind, a ten-year veteran with the Browns. At the age of thirty-five, he was believed to be washed up, but Cronin saw value in Gray's experience and believed he could help his team. The manager picked up the phone and called the pitcher.

Cronin: "We've just bought you. We're going places this season and I think you can help out."

Gray: "Don't buy me, Joe. They're trying to unload a sore-armed pitcher on you. I can't do you any good. Make 'em call of the deal."

Cronin: "Gee, that's tough. Well, hold everything. I've gotta see Griff."

Knowing he was near the end of his career, and pitching for Washington would offer a chance to pitch in a World Series, Gray decided to call Cronin and explain that his ailing arm would recover within a few days. The deal, however, was called off, and Gray would remain with the last-place Browns.

The Senators extended their winning streak to eleven, with a 5–3 win in St. Louis, and Crowder won his twentieth game, allowing only six hits and fanning five. He was cheered throughout the game by the St. Louis fans, who remembered when he hurled for the Browns and won twenty-one games in

1928. Another former St. Louis Brown, Heinie Manush, was also applauded for extending his hitting streak to twenty-six, after swatting a home run.

In Chicago the New York pitchers blew a 7–0 lead, and the White Sox won 8–7 to drop the Yankees to 8½ in back of the streaking Senators. The following day, before 43,000 at Comiskey Park, New York put on a batting clinic, scoring twenty-five runs on twenty-eight hits in a double-header sweep. But they were unable to gain on the Senators, who extended their winning streak to thirteen after sweeping a pair in St. Louis. In the first game Earl Whitehill, closing in on twenty wins, pitched another dandy, facing only twenty-two batters through seven innings. In the ninth inning Bluege executed a perfect squeeze to score the winning run for a 2–1 win. In the nightcap Stewart pitched five innings, and Russell pitched the last four in a 4–3 win. In the bottom of the ninth the Browns had a runner on base with one out when Rollie Hemsley hit a scorching grounder. Myer gloved it and started a twin killing to finish another beautiful day.

Heinie Manush's hitting streak, now at twenty-eight, was just thirteen away from the American League record, set by George Sisler at forty-one. The major league record of forty-four had been set back in 1897 by Wee Willie Keeler. The minor league record was sixty-nine, set back in 1919, and was almost eclipsed during this season in the Pacific Coast League by an eighteen-year-old named Joe DiMaggio. His hitting streak had reached sixty-one before being snapped in late July by Ed Walsh Jr. His amazing accomplishment, however, would not be his immediate ticket to the Big Show, as the man who would become the Yankees' next great outfielder still had two more full seasons left in the minors.

The Senators were in excellent spirits as they waited in the St. Louis train station. Cronin stepped up to an imaginary plate and held his umbrella like a bat. "Throw something," he called to his teammates. Goslin grabbed the hat off Kerr's crown and pitched it. Cronin swung, hit the hat, and it landed in someone's cereal bowl. Suddenly hats were coming at Cronin from all directions, with Griffith also pitching his. Harris tossed Crowder's hat, Cronin swung, and on his follow-through he knocked a lamp off a table that smashed against the floor with a loud crash.

A few minutes later the team walked through a tunnel and onto the platform to board their train for Detroit when Myer decided to restart the game. He swiped Sewell's hat, and the catcher reacted by pulling Myer's bowtie right off his collar. Sewell held up the tie to show Myer he had it, and if he wanted it back he better give him his hat. Myer looked at his finger, and noticed he had cut it during the game. Mike Martin was annoyed when he was requested to unpack his big black medical bag to find a bandage.

During the train ride, Goslin, Myer, Sewell, and Whitehill each chomped on a cigar as they played an intense game of bridge. Bolton, Rice, Russell, and Thomas played rummy. Manush, Harris, Kerr, and Kuhel, the worst card players on the team, played hearts. Dave Harris read his detective magazine, Ossie Bluege sat by himself as he stared into space, Moe Berg was immersed in a book he had picked up in England about ancient law, and the sportswriters smoked as they tapped their typewriters.

Berg looked up from his book and noticed Schacht talking with Cronin. "Look at Schacht sitting on the manager's lap again," he called out. The catcher turned his attention to politics, and began a diligent conversation with Fred Schulte about Germany. During their conversation Berg made an uncomplimentary remark about the chancellor of Germany. Schulte, whose nationality was German, pretended to be offended, and he leaped onto Berg. As the two wrestled and laughed, their teammates paid no attention, and remained focused on whatever they were doing.

The Senators arrived in Detroit on the morning of an off day in their schedule. After they checked into the Cadillac Hotel, they headed to Briggs Stadium to see the Tigers play the Athletics. As they watched the game, Bob Considine of the *Washington Herald* watched the Nats, and he worried when he noticed the number of greasy hotdogs they were gobbling up, then washing down with sugar-filled drinks of every color of the rainbow. "It leads me to fear their thirteen-game winning streak may be laid to rest," wrote Considine.

During the game Hank Greenberg of the Tigers came to the plate. "This guy couldn't hit the ground," insisted Dave Harris. On the next pitch Greenberg got hold of one, and as the ball sailed high over the left field screen, Harris's teammates turned to look at him. Harris took a swig from his bottle of Coke, sat back, and said, "I still say he can't hit."

Before leaving for the stadium the next morning, Povich asked Cronin again about the pennant.

Cronin: "Didn't I tell you not to bring that up?"

Povich: "OK, Joe, but who you going to start in the first game of the World Series?"

Cronin: "Scram, Povich!"

The Detroit fans cheered when Hank Greenberg stepped into the batter's box in the sixth inning of a 2–2 ballgame. The rookie pleased his fans by crushing a Weaver pitch, sending the ball for a long ride to deep left field. The ball cleared the street and landed by a woodshed, some fifty yards beyond the left field fence. In the press box Povich was amazed by the rookie's power, and described it to his readers. "When Greenberg hits a ball on the nose it stays hit."

The Senators came back with three runs, led by Goslin, who had three hits on the day, and Manush, who also added three hits to extend his streak to twenty-nine. Kuhel delivered a big blow with a two-run single. The Tigers reclaimed the lead, then Buddy Myer hit a two-run double in the top of the ninth to give the Nats an 8–7 lead.

In the bottom of the ninth Cronin called on Crowder to finish off the Tigers. The league leader in wins was unable to find his mitt and asked Russell to loan him his. After he disposed of the first batter, he gave up back-to-back doubles to Pete Fox and Charlie Gehringer that tied the game. Cronin decided to change pitchers, and Crowder, believing Russell's mitt had brought him bad luck, hurled it towards the dugout as he walked off the mound. "That's twenty-five dollars!" Cronin shouted to Crowder.

Tommy Thomas came on to pitch, and he struck out Gee Walker for the second out of the inning. Hank Greenberg was the next hitter, and after backing the big first baseman away with two inside pitches, Thomas threw a fastball. Greenberg swung and connected, and the sound of his bat hitting the ball was like an explosion that was heard throughout the stadium. According to Povich, the ball was "bound for Lake Michigan. It was still climbing as it passed over the high screen in left field."

Greenberg had practically single-handedly defeated Washington to snap the thirteen-game winning streak. For the day he had three hits, four runs, four RBIs, and two home runs. Not a bad day for someone that Dave Harris said could not hit.

Afterwards in the clubhouse Cronin had a word with Crowder to make sure he understood his actions would not be tolerated, and he would have to pay the $25 fine. "Twenty-five dollars is a bush league fine. Why not make it a hundred and twenty-five?" the pitcher said. Cronin laughed. "Sorry Gen, got to do it."

The *Washington Post* scoreboard posted Greenberg's second home run to put a damper on the day for the Washington baseball fans, but little did they realize that the worst was yet to come. At 6:00 the following evening heavy rain began to fall, the wind picked up, and the barometer fell to 28.94, one of the lowest readings in Washington history. The capital was in the eye of a hurricane. The intensity of the storm, the worst in thirty-seven years, paralyzed the city. The devastating storm caused the Potomac to overflow, and soon streets were underwater, basements were flooded, and homes became islands. The fifty-one mile per hour wind ripped off rooftops and knocked down over four hundred trees. Power outages were widespread, forcing hospitals and police stations to work by candlelight. Some 250 operators were called to duty to help the police departments, and they were kept busy, as were the policemen in aiding motorists who drove into high standing water. When the casualties were tallied after the storm the total was four in Washington.

Tommy Bridges had been sidelined with an injury for three weeks, but hardly looked rusty in his return to action. And what better team was there for Bridges to come back to play against than the Senators? For Bridges it was just another start against Washington, and he hurled a 2–1 win. In the ninth inning he tripled off Crowder, and scored on a fly ball to win the game. The good news was Manush extended his hitting streak to thirty games.

Fred Marberry pitched the next day, hoping to end his personal slump. The former Washington ace started the season by winning thirteen of his first sixteen decisions, but then lost seven of his next eight. On this day he would not make it through the first inning as his former teammates scored four times en route to a 9–5 win. Manush made three hits in five at bats, and Goslin also made three hits. A day later the twosome destroyed the Tigers' pitching again, with Manush getting three more hits, and Goslin sending two over the fence in Washington's thirteen-run, seventeen-hit attack. Joe Kuhel, once again unnoticed in the offense, knocked out three hits, and the next day he went four for five with a home run in Washington's 5–4 win.

Six weeks earlier, lightning had struck against the White Sox, when Cronin did not see Manush's relay throw. The ball hit him between the shoulder blades, then rolled all the way to Berg behind the plate, who picked up the ball in time to tag the runner for an out. When it's your year, it is your year.

During that 5–4 win lightning had struck again, this time in the bottom of the third, after Pete Fox drew a walk, and Charlie Gehringer followed with a single. Gee Walker hit one over Goslin, resulting in a repeat of the double play that had occurred in New York three months before. As Fox waited to see if Goslin would make the catch, Gehringer started to run, and he became an automatic out after passing Fox on the base path. When the ball fell for a hit, Fox began to run. He rounded third base, and was out thrown out at the plate via Goslin to Cronin to Sewell.

On the train ride to Cleveland no one was happier than the manager, who roamed the two cars occupied by the Nationals, and had a broad smile as he slapped his players on he backs. "Can we come back?" he said to anyone who would listen. "What did we do after losing those two games in Detroit? We had a great opportunity to fold up, didn't we?"

In Cleveland, Walter Johnson was informed by Alva Bradley that the Indians ownership group agreed to give him a contract for the 1934 baseball season. "The Directors want me to tell you that we are most pleased and happy over your work as manager," Bradley told the Big Train. "We have high hopes for you next season." The Indians had a good August, with a seven-game-winning-streak that put them three games over .500, and past the Athletics for third place.

President Roosevelt was having a great year, and his New Deal was apparently working. He showed the evidence when submitting a report to the press from the Department of Labor. The report showed employment was up 21.3 percent over 1932. Manufacturing industries increased by 7.2 percent over June, and 21.9 percent over July of 1932. Wages paid in industries were up 7.9 percent over June, and 28.5 percent from July of 1932. July was the fifth consecutive month employment improved. Workers were being brought back to the mines, to the oil fields, and to various commercial branches, stores, and offices. The auto industry had already surpassed the entire 1932 output, just through the month of July. The president warned he would not rest, and would not let his staff rest on these laurels. There was still a lot of work ahead.

Also contributing to the improved economy was the repeal of Prohibition. In Washington an estimated five thousand jobs were created. Brewery companies needed plant help, clerical workers, salespeople, drivers, driver helpers, watchmen, executives, and wholesale dealers, not to mention employment opportunities created for restaurants and hotels.

In Chicago, A Century of Progress Exposition supported the need for employees, and with visitors coming from all four corners of the country, money was pumped into the economy. On August 19th, a total of 244,472 attended the fair, with over twenty-six thousand on the grounds before the gates opened. On June 3, attendance was 235,325 on Jewish Day. Children's Day and Agricultural Day also produced big turnouts.

In Cleveland, the Indians won, snapping Washington's streak of twenty straight Saturday wins. Manush's hitting streak had also ended, at thirty-three games. One of his at bats resulted in a questionable call at first base, with his teammates insisting that Manush had beaten the throw.

In the second game of the series, Whitehill pitched his eighteenth win to surpass his career high. For Whitehill it was his eighth consecutive win, and his teammates gave him support by scoring fourteen runs. He could have also thanked the Indians for committing nine errors, three away from the record set by Detroit in 1901. The Indians' fielding performance did not make Walter Johnson, and sixty thousand fans, very happy. Johnson was more pleased in the nightcap when his Indians committed no errors in a 6–3 win.

Another crowd of 60,000 came to Municipal Stadium the next day, and they watched the Nats win the first of two games, with Stewart winning his fourth consecutive game, thanks to Manush's RBI single in the top of the tenth. In the nightcap the Nats faced Monte Pearson, a rookie, and he hurled eight hitless innings. In the top of the ninth Bluege broke up the no-hit bid with a leadoff single, and after an out, Manush hit a triple, and scored on Cronin's fly out. The Nats still lost, 7–2.

Washington finished their final trip through the Midwest with a 12–5 record, now had an overall record of 82–43, and a lead of eight games over the Yankees. Their magic number to win the American League pennant was nineteen.

The Yankees returned home after a 9–7 road trip, and McCarthy conceded the pennant. "It's time to face facts," the Yankees skipper said. "We'll keep trying ... but, this doesn't blind me to the fact we have to rebuild and do it quickly." Close followers said the Yankees would clean house, and the only untouchables were Gehrig, Dickey, Chapman, Walker, Gomez, Ruffing, and Van Atta.

As for Babe Ruth, his future in New York was unknown, and there were rumors he would become player-manager for the Red Sox or the White Sox. There was also a story by the Associated Press of Ruth's plans to retire at the end of the season. Ruth read the story and called up the AP sports editor: "Say, where do those fellows get that stuff about me being washed up? When I'm ready to quit for good everyone will know it." Ruth made a statement to the sports editor about where he stood for 1934 and beyond. "I hope to play next year. I believe I will be able to, so for the present at least, I am not retiring from baseball."

17

WINNING THE PENNANT

"I just cried when I heard the news. He's been such a good son to us. I have been praying his team would win. It was such a responsibility for Joe, being so young, and his first year as manager."
— Mary Cronin, after hearing the news that the Nats had clinched the pennant.

According to the sportswriters, the noise for the Senators in the nation's capital was nothing like it had been nine years earlier when Washington experienced its first pennant. But Ruth Crowder and Betty Manush had a hard time believing this, after they glanced out a window from inside the *Washington Post* building, and were amazed to see the number of Nats fans congregated before the *Post*'s scoreboard to watch the results of their team at Philadelphia.

At Shibe Park, Earl Whitehill, winner of his last eight decisions, got into trouble in the first inning after throwing three consecutive balls to Jimmie Foxx. With a 3–0 count, two runners on base, and only one out, Whitehill threw a slow curve into Foxx's wheelhouse. The A's slugger made him pay by crushing his thirty-seventh homer of the season into the left field seats.

Back in Washington, Mrs. Crowder and Mrs. Manush, who were guests of the *Washington Post*'s sports department, became nervous upon hearing the news, and both began to chew gum. The entire sports department chewed gum after the Athletics scored four more in the fifth inning for a 7–0 lead. The Nats went on to lose 12–3, with Whitehill losing for the first time since July 16.

On September 2, Foxx hit number thirty-eight, and Lefty Grove defeated the Senators in the first game of a double-header for Washington's fifth loss in their last seven games. Nobody was panicking, however, since the Nats still owned a comfortable seven game lead.

General Crowder, wanting to end his team's slump, as well as his own personal dry spell, limbered up to pitch in the nightcap. Since winning his twentieth game he had lost four in a row. His manager suggested it was due to overworking, and he advised his pitching ace to ease up. Crowder was one who never rested. On days he was not scheduled to pitch he would grab a catcher's mitt and warm up the pitchers, or grab a bat and hit grounders and fly balls to warm up the fielders.

Joe Kuhel, batting .366 in his last fifty-six games, helped Crowder get back in the win column by breaking a 3–3 tie in the top of the seventh with a two-run blast over the right field wall for his tenth homer of the year.

Washington won their next three games over Boston to conclude their season series against the Red Sox with a 17–4 record. In the first game Cronin sent Cliff Bolton to the plate in the bottom of the ninth, with two outs in a tie game, and with the winning run aboard. Once again he came through with the game-winning hit. "He's a sweet little hitter," Cronin said about Bolton. "He led every minor league he ever played in hitting and you can't take that away from him." Well, not exactly, but Bolton was a fine hitter during his four seasons in the minor leagues, batting .403, .356, .380, and .338.

It had been a while since Cronin's bat was heard from. Since taking a fastball on the arm in mid–July, the Washington shortstop's batting average had dropped from .368 to .309. In the first game of a double-header on September 5, Cronin finally had a productive game by going four for six in a 5–4 win. In the nightcap Whitehill went to the mound, and for his second straight start was not sharp. After Earl gave up twelve hits in 6⅓ innings, Cronin called for a reliever, and the temperamental pitcher responded as expected, by stomping his way to the dugout. After he sat on he bench he began to stare at the water bucket as if it had made an insulting remark. He then came to his feet, and after punching out the poor water bucket, he booted it several times before sending it sliding across the dugout floor. Dave Harris decided to join in by kicking the bucket back to Whitehill, which the pitcher did not find amusing. In the end Harris came through with a pinch-hit RBI to help the Nats win, with Whitehill getting credit for his nineteenth victory.

In the ninth inning, when the Red Sox threatened, Cronin called on Crowder to put out the fire. "If you get the side out without a run I'll remit that twenty-five dollar fine," Cronin told Crowder.

"That's an easy twenty-five bucks," replied Crowder, who then backed up his words.

To fill a few opened roster spots, Cecil Travis was recalled from Chattanooga, left-handed pitcher Ray Prim, a purchase from Albany, was added, and one other pitcher joined the Nats, this one a thirty-nine-year-old, who had played all twenty-one years of his career in the minors. Four years earlier he had given up on his dream of pitching in the Big show, until Chattanooga Lookouts manager Bert Niehoff told him his forgotten dream was about to become a reality. "Well, Alex, how would you like to go the big leagues?" Niehoff asked.

Alex McColl assumed this was a joke. "I'm too old to be kiddin' at this late date, so cut it out, Bert."

"Why, dern your bald head, I'm a-kiddin' on the square," Niehoff replied.

He explained that the Senators were aware of his age, and knew he had never been to a major league spring training camp, but still wanted him.

On September 6 McColl made his first start, opposing Jake Miller and the White Sox. The thirty-nine-year-old rookie was erratic yet effective, giving up five walks, but only four hits, and went the distance to earn his first major league win by a score of 3–1. The difference was the unexpected timely hitting of McColl (a .184 hitter during five seasons in the Southern Association), who sliced a two-run double in the second inning.

After being shut out a day later by former Washington hurler Sad Sam Jones, the Senators manufactured eleven runs to help Crowder win his twenty-second. Cronin knocked out four hits, three of which were doubles.

September 9 was Ossie Bluege Day at Griffith Stadium, and like everyone else on his special day, the twelve-year veteran was showered with gifts and compliments during a pre-game ceremony. As for the game, Earl Whitehill started off slowly by giving up a first-inning run before settling down. In the fifth, sixth, and seventh innings he did not allow a hit, but in the eighth inning the White Sox added one to tie the score, 2–2. The game went into extra innings, and Whitehill took care of the White Sox in the tenth and eleventh. In the bottom of the eleventh, with the skies darkening, Chicago's shortstop Luke Appling booted Goslin's easy grounder. Manush followed with a single, then Schulte smacked a 3–2 pitch for a hit to score Goslin and make Whitehill a twenty-game winner.

Walter Johnson and his Indians came to town after losing four straight in Philadelphia to fall out of third place. Lefty Stewart and the Nats extended Cleveland's losing streak by beating them 7–3, for Washington's ninetieth win of the year, and it was now a matter of time before Washington would clinch the American League pennant. The Yankees were 8½ games back, and to make things tougher, three of their rained-out contests would not be made up. "The sooner this gets over with, the less I'll worry about it," said Griffith. "When things reach a stage like this, a fellow is more inclined to have more worries."

Cronin was talking beyond clinching the pennant. "We're going to keep on trying to win games through the last game of the season. I want to keep the boys in the winning habit."

After dividing the next two games with Cleveland, Washington swept a four-game series from Detroit. Afterwards Bucky Harris admitted, "The Nats have a great team." Before one of the games Marberry stopped by the Washington clubhouse and challenged Cronin to pitch his best against him, meaning Crowder. He got Stewart, instead which hardly mattered; the Nats kayoed Marberry with five runs on eight hits in the first two innings.

In another win, the Nationals came to bat in the bottom of the ninth, after Greenberg had made his third hit of the game in the top of the inning to increase the Tigers' lead to 3–1. With two outs, and with Rice on first base, the fans began to head for the exits when Myer hit a grounder to Greenberg. The scrappy second baseman raced down the baseline and beat Greenberg to the bag with a headfirst slide. Suddenly the fans began to scramble back to their seats. Goslin followed with a hit to score Rice, Manush walked to load the bases, and Cronin hit a wicked ground ball, too hot for third baseman Marv Owen to handle, to score Myer and Goslin to win the game.

Cliff Bolton was responsible for a win over Detroit, getting another pinch-hit RBI in the bottom of the tenth to lift Crowder to his twenty-third win. For Bolton it was his third game-winning hit during Washington's last at bat.

Sam Gray admitted he had a sore shoulder, but advised that it would quickly heal. The Senators were unsure and elected to take a pass on buying his contract. To Washington's surprise Gray was right, and he proved it by hurling a 4–2 win at Washington. For Gray it was the last game he would pitch in his ten-year major league career.

With a magic number of two to clinch the pennant, the Washington bats cooled off. They lost again to the last-place Browns when former Washington hurler Dick Coffman shut them out on six hits, and with the Yankees winning two over Chicago that day, the magic number remained at two. The Senators cut it in half the next day when they broke out their bats in a 13–5 win, Crowder's twenty-fourth victory. During the game Rogers Hornsby, who had become the Browns pilot when Bill Killefer resigned in late July, sent Garland Braxton to pitch in relief — an answer to a prayer, since this gave the Nats an opportunity to bat against a left-handed screwball pitcher. "It didn't seem to bother us much," Cronin said after the game. "From what I hear of Hubbell's screwball, Braxton's is the nearest thing to it."

That same day the New York Giants arrived at Grand Central Station, where they were greeted by ten thousand fans, following their clinching of the National League pennant the previous day in St. Louis. During the game Bill Terry was on deck when he looked up at the press box, where a writer had signaled down to him. Terry knew the gesture meant the second place Pirates had lost to the Phillies to officially make the Giants the National League Champions.

Thursday afternoon, September 21, was a beautiful day in the nation's capital as a ladies' day crowd of ten thousand filed into Griffith Stadium. The sun was bright, the temperature was a comfortable sixty-eight degrees, and the Senators got ready to face the Browns, with one more victory, or one more Yankees defeat, to wrap up the pennant. The good news was the Yankees were idle, meaning the Nats had the opportunity to clinch in a winning effort.

Washington got a run off Bump Hadley in the second inning. The Browns evened the score in the seventh against Lefty Stewart, and threatened to rally for more, but as they had done all season, the double play combination of Cronin-Myer-Kuhel turned another one to end the inning.

In the bottom of the seventh Kuhel got his second hit of the game, and Boken, today's starting third baseman, drew a walk. Sewell followed with a hit to deep center field, and the two base runners got tangled up in the base paths, much like Gehrig and Walker five months before. Kuehl recovered, rounded third, and made it home with a slide to give the Nats a 2–1 lead.

Stewart handled the Browns in the eighth inning, but in the ninth Carl Reynolds led off with a single. Bruce Campbell followed with a hard grounder, which Myer gloved, and once again he started a twin killing.

With one out to go for the pennant, the crowd began to buzz, as Browns second baseman Oscar Melillo was ready at the plate. In left field, Manush needed time to adjust his sunglasses, and he frantically waved his arms to get the umpire's attention. Cronin noticed and called out to Stewart, but the pitcher had already started his windup. Melillo swung and lifted a fly to left field. Manush ran to his left, his sunglasses dangling from his left hand, got under the ball, and snared it with his glove hand to clinch the 1933 American League pennant!

The Senators headed directly for the tunnel leading to their clubhouse as hundreds of fans stormed the field. Within a few minutes the entire team was in the safety of their clubhouse, and the celebration began. As players began to hug and congratulate one another, Bobo Baxter rolled in a cart filled with ice and bottled beer. He began to hand out the bottles, and he handed one to McColl, who was shy about asking for one. When asked what he thought of all the excitement, McColl responded with one word:

"Gaa-osh."

Griffith grabbed his youthful manager, grasped his hand, and pumped his arm for about five minutes as light bulbs popped, movie cameras went into motion, and a radio announcer reported the happenings. The announcer moved over to Cronin and asked about winning the pennant. The manager gave all the credit to his ballplayers, "who made it easy for any manager."

Rogers Hornsby entered the clubhouse to congratulate Cronin, and after the Nats manager convinced Griffith to release his hand, he shook hands with the St. Louis manager. "I hope you beat the Giants and believe that you will," Hornsby told Cronin. A writer overheard the Browns' skipper, and reminded him that he was quoted a few days before saying the Giants would win the World Series. Hornsby claimed he had been misquoted. "I'm for the Nats and wish 'em all the luck in the world."

Buddy Myer, who had participated in the clubhouse celebration when Washington clinched the 1925 pennant, decided he'd had enough, and was the first to dress and head for the exit. When he opened the door he saw the number of females lined up, with their autograph books in hand. He warned the others, then led a few of his teammates through a different exit, but the idea did not work. The ladies were everywhere, and they mobbed the ballplayers.

It was known that Joe Cronin, baseball's most eligible bachelor (since Lou Gehrig was about to marry Miss Eleanor Twitchell), was who the ladies were waiting for, and the handsome player-manager figured he could avoid them by exiting through the dugout, then walking across the field and sneaking out the right field gate. After he walked up the dugout steps and set foot on the field, there was a screech, and suddenly there was a group of teenage girls heading towards him. Cronin made a dash for the gate, with his admirers screaming while in pursuit. He won the race to the gate, but it was locked, and he was trapped. He quickly ran, weaved his way through the crowd, and sprinted for the center field gate with the fair ones on his trail. Luckily this gate was unlocked, and after exiting, he outran his admirers to his car. He drove directly to the Wardman Park Hotel, entered his apartment, and placed a long-distance call to his folks to tell them the good news.

After hearing the word from Washington, Biloxi erupted. Mayor Kennedy declared a half-holiday, and the city celebrated, starting with a parade through the streets. Throughout the evening horns sounded, speeches were made, bands played, and sideshows were everywhere, as Biloxi toasted the 1933 American League Champions.

On Friday, September 23, while the Senators enjoyed a day off, many of the players stopped by Griffith Stadium for no particular reason. They watched the workmen begin to add extra seats to increase the stadium's capacity to 35,743 for the World Series. Additional bleachers were erected in left and center field, and seats were constructed on top of the grandstand roof, along with a temporary press box. The stadium's permanent press box would be used for additional customer seating.

Inside the stadium office, the Washington Senators' four full-time secretaries—Aubrey Becker, Thelma Griffith, Elizabeth King, and Mildred Robertson—were busy going through World Series ticket applications and fulfilling orders. Most requests were for the more expensive $6.50 box seats, and the $5.50 upper deck seats. The bleacher seats, priced at $3.30, were not in demand, and this baffled Griffith, who projected these seats to sell as fast as the others.

Cronin came by to read the several telegrams sent by well-wishers, including family and friends, former President Herbert Hoover, the Biloxi Chamber of Commerce, Connie Mack, Walter Johnson, Joe McCarthy, Will Harridge, Colonel Ruppert, Tom Yawkey, and Eddie Collins.

With the American League pennant now sewed up, the Senators, who had won a franchise-high ninety-seven games, had one thing left to play for with six games remaining: a one-hundred-win season. They hosted Philadelphia for two games and lost both, including one by a score of 11–4, with Crowder getting bombed, and with Lefty Grove winning his twenty-fourth game to tie him with Crowder for the league lead.

Next up for Washington were three consecutive off days, placed on their schedule for the purpose of make-up games, no longer necessary since the pennant had been clinched. Cronin called for a 1:30 practice at Griffith Stadium each day.

The Washington manager had placed an order for National League baseballs, since these balls would be used for the World Series games at the Polo Grounds (while the American League ball would be used at Washington). Before the first day of practice Cronin emptied a bag of three dozen onto the pitcher's mound, and instructed his pitchers to use them. He was curious to find out if the other league's baseball, known to be less lively, had any rabbit to it. He got his answer when he hit the first pitch deep into the left field bleachers. "Gee, I must be in the wrong league," Cronin said.

Whack! He hit the second pitch over the left field wall. He gave the next pitch a ride, and it bounced off a hotel sign on the upper right field wall. "That ball's not going to make a difference," he declared.

Both Schulte and Harris knocked one into the left field bleachers, and Goslin and Myer both hit one high over the right field wall. The Senators were now convinced the National League ball had plenty of pop to it. As for its thicker cover and raised stitches, "If that helped the Giants' pitchers, it's going to help our pitchers, too," said Cronin.

Bill Terry disagreed. The overconfident manager said his Giants would beat Crowder and Whitehill in the first two games. "It would surprise me if they do," Cronin answered, who would not respond further. He also refused to comment about who his starting pitcher would be in Game One of the World Series. "I told my four starters to be ready."

After practice the Senators held a meeting to decide about splitting the World Series spoils, the issue the Cubs had been highly criticized for during the previous autumn by voting lesser shares, or no shares, to a few team members. Washington had problems of their own back in 1924 and 1925, when their decision to divide resulted in hurt feelings. This time the players voted everyone a share. Twenty-four full shares would be given, which included coaches Altrock and Schacht, and Mike Martin, who had each received a half share in 1924 and 1925. This year's half shares would go to Ed Eynon of the front office, Bobo Baxter, and Bill McAfee. The groundskeeper, Emil Haismith, would get $750, Travis and McColl would get $500 apiece, and the secretaries would be included. The players also agreed to make a pot for Jimmy Mahorney.

While the Nats practiced, both Sewell and Stewart were in New York to scout the Giants. Cronin had previously said there was no point in scouting the opposition, but he had every intention to, and he gave the battery mates instructions not be seen. Sure enough a photographer recognized them. Sewell got up from his chair and split, while Stewart remained, and even smiled for the cameraman. Word was received in the Giants' dugout; several players turned to look, and spotted Stewart seated several rows behind. They jokingly beckoned to the pitcher to let him know he was welcome to view the game from the Giants' bench. Stewart declined the invitation.

Garland Braxton accepted Cronin's invitation, and on his way back home to North Carolina for the winter, he attended a practice to pitch screwballs to the Washington lineup. For Braxton, who received a check for his time, it was quite a workout, hurling nothing but screwballs for over an hour. "That was harder than pitching a regular game," he claimed. The Nats did a good job against the screwball, hitting it far and to all directions of the outfield, and afterwards the consensus was, "Bring on Hubbell." "That screwball didn't look so tough to us, and Braxton knows how to throw it," Cronin said. "The only thing he lacks is Hubbell's speed."

The Senators were back in action at Yankee Stadium, with members of the Giants in attendance for the first two games of the series, which the teams split. If the Giants had attended the third game they would have witnessed history. The Washington infield turned a record of six double plays in their 7–2 win, with Myer and Cronin teaming up for four of those twin killings. "Buddy Myer is getting the ball away faster than any second baseman I have ever seen," said Cronin.

In 1933 Buddy Myer broke out and matured into the ballplayer that others knew he could be. At the beginning of the year, with his suspension, taking one on the bean, and his stomach ailment, he started off slowly. In mid–June he was batting just .276, and was demoted to the eighth spot in the batting order. Cronin and Griffith began to wonder if they were better off without him, and while in Boston, Cronin met with Collins and Yawkey behind closed doors where Myer's name was mentioned in a possible trade. Soon Myer was playing the best baseball of his nine-year career. He began to hit, especially against the Yankees, and soon he was back to being Washington's leadoff man. In mid–August he raised his batting average above .300, where it would remain for the rest of the season. In the field, Myer developed into a smooth-fielding and dependable second baseman, especially when starting, pivoting, and finishing double plays.

One year before Griffith and Cronin agreed that the pennant would be won or lost against the Yankees, and the Nats won fourteen of twenty-two games versus New York. The two men also agreed that trades were necessary for players they believed would help win the pennant, and their trades paid off. In the three-for-three trade with St. Louis, Goslin and Schulte for West and Reynolds turned out to be about even, but Washington got the better end of Stewart for Brown, with Stewart winning fifteen games, while Brown started off 1–6, and was sent to Boston in mid-season.

The two trades with Cleveland worked out better than expected. Sewell hit .264, and did a good job handling the Washington pitchers; Spencer batted just .203. In the Harley Boss for Jack Russell deal, Russell won twelve games and led the majors with thirteen saves, while Boss proved not to be a major league caliber first baseman.

The trade with Detroit was good for both teams, with Marberry winning sixteen games, while Fischer had a respectable season by winning eleven. White-hill won twenty-two, and proved valuable against the Yankees. His best asset was his unwillingness to accept losing, the kind of spirit Washington had lacked during the few years prior. In mid–May the Nats found that out after White-hill lost a 5–0 game in St. Louis. "Tough luck, Earl," his teammates told him afterwards, thinking this was what he wanted to hear.

"Tough luck, hell," Whitehill snapped back. "Those Yankees are coming down here and they'll knock a club like the Browns stiff. That's the only tough luck about it."

Cronin received the unfortunate news that his parents would not be able to attend the World Series. "I'd give anything if I could make the trip," said Mary Cronin, "but a sudden attack of neuritis has made it impossible for me to travel." Jeremiah Cronin would stay with her, but one of Joe's brothers was on his way.

Jesse Myer was also on his way to support his kid brother. The older Myer could not be prouder, and showed his admiration by hanging pictures of his brother throughout his "everything store" in Ellisville.

The A's came to Griffith Stadium for the last game of the season, with Washington a win shy of one hundred. Ray Prim got the starting assignment and pitched brilliantly, allowing only four hits through eleven innings, but he received no run support. In the twelfth inning Prim gave up three runs on five hits. In the bottom of the twelfth Cronin sent up fifty-seven-year-old coach Nick Altrock to pinch-hit. The Washington coach would pinch-hit once in a while, just for laughs. In 1929 he made a pinch hit, and his teammates joked about his one for one season making him the American League batting champion.

As Altrock stood at the plate, pitcher Rube Walberg called in his outfield-ers, and catcher Ed Madjeski took off his mitt to receive Walberg's lobs. Altrock hit one back to the pitcher, who ran to the base path and waited for the com-ical coach. The coach made the next move by running to the Nats' dugout, and when Walberg turned his back, he took off for first base, but the umpires declared him out for running out of the base path.

After the game, Povich spoke with Cronin, hoping to get the answer as to whom he planned to pitch in the first game of the World Series.

Cronin: "Drop around and see me Tuesday about 1:29. I'll have some news for you."

Povich: "Who's going to pitch the opening game?"

Cronin: "Scram, Povich!"

During the Giants' tumultuous 1932 season, John McGraw, New York's manager since 1902, resigned on June 3. Since McGraw also served as the Giants vice president, he was responsible for choosing his successor, and his selection was Bill Terry, who was surprised to receive the offer. He and McGraw had been at odds, especially when it came time to talk salary. Terry was interested, but said he wouldn't touch the job to be a puppet or front man for McGraw. He insisted on having a free hand, and McGraw assured him it wouldn't be any other way. "From now on I'm out and you're in running the Giants."

Terry was a relief to the ballplayers, who were burnt out on McGraw's dictator style of calling every pitch, his tongue-lashings, and his demands. Terry knew this was a problem and he eased up, only asking his players to follow his example of hustling and playing hard. "There is no tomorrow," Terry, known to be a bad loser, would tell his team. "Win that game today." He also wanted a winning spirit on his team and noted that many of his players in 1932 did not have it. "They are great players but I can't use them." Fred Lindstrom may have been among those whom Terry was referring to, and in a three-team trade, Lindstrom went to Pittsburgh, and the Giants received Phillies outfielder Kiddo Davis. In a five-player deal with St. Louis, the two teams swapped catchers, with the Giants getting Gus Mancuso. In mid-season the Giants bolstered their depth when a trade with the Dodgers brought them Lefty O'Doul.

The most productive trade was the one that did not seem to matter, when the Giants sent shortstop Doc Marshall to Buffalo of the International League for infielder Blondy Ryan. John "Blondy" Ryan's only major league experience was with the White Sox in 1930, when he played third base and batted .207 in twenty-eight games. Ryan was a weak hitter, a slow runner, did not draw walks, and was unspectacular in the minor leagues. But with Ryan, Terry had a good defensive player, and the type of character he wanted for his team. He was a confident leader, who wanted the ball hit to him when the game was on the line, and wanted to win as badly as the New York manager did.

New York's new shortstop took charge immediately. He was the leader in their well-known huddle system, which involved an infield conference at the pitcher's mound to discuss strategy. The huddle system proved to be valuable, and was great for team spirit.

In mid-season Ryan was injured, sustaining a spike wound on his shin, and the Giants began to slump. Without their leader, they headed to Chicago, where they were swept by the Cubs in a four-game series. After a loss in St. Louis to Dizzy Dean, New York was on a seven-game losing streak, with their first-place lead over the Cardinals down to 2½ games.

Back in New York, Ryan acted by dispatching a telegram, telling his teammates to hang in there, and letting them know he would be back soon. "They can't stop us," was his last sentence, and those words served as an inspiration to the team's drive to the pennant.

Hal Schumacher shut out the Cards the next day, followed by a victory by Hubbell, and then the New York batters bombed Dizzy Dean, 11–2. Soon Ryan was back, wearing a shin guard to protect his injury, and the Giants were on their way.

Joining Ryan to compose one of baseball's best infields was second baseman Hughie Critz (pronounced Crites). At first base was Bill Terry, an excellent fielder, and at third base was Johnny Vergez. The Giants' outfield had four solid players, the most notable being twenty-four-year-old Mel Ott. The others were Kiddo Davis, Jo-Jo Moore, and Lefty O'Doul. The catcher was Gus

Mancuso, an improvement over the last few seasons, who did an excellent job in handling the pitching staff.

The brightest unit of the Giants was their pitching staff, led by screwball specialist Carl Hubbell, Hal Schumacher, who threw an excellent sinker, and Fred Fitzsimmons, who threw a knuckleball.

The Senators were favored, based on a stronger attack. The Giants were credited with better pitching, but with Crowder, Whitehill, Stewart, Weaver, and Russell, Washington had a dependable staff that finished second in the American League (to Cleveland).

The Giants finished first in the National League in pitching, third in fielding, but were just fourth in hitting. Their attack was not weak by any means, with Bill Terry, who hit .401 in 1930, and .322 in 1933. The other dangerous hitter was Mel Ott, who swatted twenty-three home runs in 1933, scored ninety-eight runs, and drove home 103 teammates.

The National League champs suffered a setback when Johnny Vergez, the team's best right-handed threat, was rushed to a Boston hospital for an emergency appendix operation. In a nice gesture, Cronin paid a visit to New York's third baseman when the Nats were in Boston.

Taking over for Vergez was Travis Jackson, who had been slated as the team's starting shortstop before the season. But his ailing knees could not handle the required movement for the position on a daily basis, so he became a utility infielder.

Carl Hubbell was the name the Senators had heard throughout September. While in Boston, as the Washington batters struggled during a game, a few Boston fans laughed and taunted the Nats: "Wait until you meet Hubbell!"

How good was Hubbell? He won twenty-three games in 1933, ten by shutout, and posted an ERA of 1.66. In 309 innings pitched, he allowed just forty-seven walks. During the season he pitched forty-six straight innings without giving up an earned run, and he began the season by allowing only one earned run in his first thirty-two innings.

According to the Giants, Hubbell and their other pitchers would take it to the Senators.

"Our pitching is too strong for Washington," said Johnny Vergez.

"The Giants are ready," said Bill Terry. "I know what my ball team can do. We are the best when the going gets toughest. The Giants are confident of victory."

The Senators were not shy in speaking out themselves.

Cronin: "Our club is going to the World Series with the idea that it can not help but beat any team that wears a New York uniform."

Goslin: "Hubbell's not so hot — he's never been up against hitters like we got. We may spank the cover off the ball against him."

Berg: "I don't see how the Giants can beat us."

Sewell: "I seen many a pitcher in my career I've liked better than Hubbell; for instance, Lefty Grove. While I'll even go so far as to say our two southpaws, Whitehill and Stewart, are as good, if not better, because they've had to pitch to far superior hitters in the American League than Hubbell has in the National League."

Bluege: "Figures may not amount to everything in a short series like this one, but you certainly can't ignore them — and the figures all point to a Washington victory."

Dave Harris: "When those Giants get down to Griffith Stadium, provided they don't call it quits in the meantime, they'll believe they are playing on one of those million-acre cotton fields a fellow sees down near Greensboro, North Carolina, where I'm from."

The Nats departed for New York on the Sunday evening, following their last game of the season. The players' wives were on the train, and everyone was in great spirits. All the way to the Big City the confident ballplayers and their wives sang songs.

On Monday the Senators took the field at the Polo Grounds, following the Giants' workout. Batting practice was the first order of business, and as the Giants watched the Washington practice from the stands, they were awed when they saw twenty-six baseballs clear the outfield wall or travel over the roof. The Giants had batted only two balls out during their practice.

After practice the Senators showered, had dinner, and got to bed early, as each player secretly wondered how good Mr. Hubbell would be. The answer was about to come.

1933 American League standings

Team	Wins	Losses	Pct.	Games Back vs. Washington
Washington	99	53	0.651	
New York	91	59	0.607	7 (8–14)
Philadelphia	79	72	0.523	19½ (11–11)
Cleveland	75	76	0.497	23½ (8–13)
Detroit	75	79	0.487	25 (8–14)
Chicago	67	83	0.447	31 (7–15)
Boston	63	86	0.423	34½ (4–17)
St. Louis	55	96	0.364	43½ (7–15)

18

THE 1933 WORLD SERIES

"The Hubbell Hubbub and hullabaloo of the last three weeks unfolded
itself this afternoon as an awful truth to Washington."
— Shirley Povich

Game One

Buddy Myer was anything but calm when he arrived in the Washington
clubhouse on the morning of Game One. It was not due to the tension of the
World Series, but because of a fatality he had witnessed while taxiing to the
Polo Grounds. A pedestrian had stepped into the path of his cab, then dodged
the vehicle, but stumbled into the path of a truck that dashed him into a steel
structure of an elevated railroad, killing him instantly. The tragedy was clear
in Myer's mind, and instead of focusing on the game, his thoughts were on the
tragedy.

In Washington the fans were arriving as early as sunrise to claim the best
spot to view the play-by-play results on the *Washington Post* scoreboard. By
game time the crowd had expanded to over six thousand.

At the Polo Grounds the line at the outfield ticket window extended for
six blocks, with fans hoping to buy a $1.10 bleacher ticket. Better seats were
also available, but during these difficult times most could only afford to sit in
the bleachers. At 9:56 A.M., the outfield ticket window opened. As customers
purchased bleacher tickets and entered the stadium, people in the back of the
line began to push. The scene turned ugly when customers began to fall, while
others fought back. Clothes were torn, hats were smashed, and sack lunches
were crushed, causing the sidewalks to become slippery. Two people were
so overcome by fear they fainted, one of whom was a thirteen-year-old boy.
Others sustained injuries after slipping on the slick sidewalks and tumbling to
the pavement. The police arrived, many of them on horseback, and attempted
to restore order. As they worked to separate people, and help others back to
their feet, a riot was about to erupt at the ticket window when it was announced

Mrs. Stewart, Bobby Stewart (age 7), and Lefty, before Game One of the 1933 World Series.

that the bleachers were sold out. Frustrated customers that missed out began to boo the Giants' box office. Others said some things about the Giants' management.

In the press box Shirley Povich and 509 other sportswriters received the answer to the mystery of who would be the starting pitcher for Washington. Both Crowder and Whitehill were in the outfield shagging balls during batting practice, as Lefty Stewart sat alone in the dugout.

Cronin was playing a hunch with Stewart, who had enjoyed a successful season against the Yankees and currently owned a seven-game winning streak. If the southpaw had another win left in his streak, the Senators would be a game up with Crowder and Whitehill to follow. Something else appealing to the Nats manager was matching a left-hander against New York's three best hitters—Terry, Ott, and Moore—who each hit from the left side.

The Giants took the field, wearing new hats and socks for the World Series. Their hats were black with an orange interlocked "NY." Their socks were black with orange stripes. A crowd of 46,672 fans cheered and rang their cowbells, then stood for a rare playing of the Nationals Anthem, not done before each game in those days, but performed before the first game of the World Series.

Carl Hubbell stood on the mound, removed his hat, and placed it over his heart. As the band played, and the spectators sang, the Giants' pitching ace got a lump in his throat. Never before he had witnessed such a scene, and it was enough to inspire him to pitch a great game.

Buddy Myer's name was heard over the stadium's public address system. As Washington's leadoff man stepped in, his teammates shouted encouragement from their dugout along the first base side. Home plate umpire Charlie Moran cried out, "Play ball!" The crowd cheered as Hubbell went into his windup, and threw his first pitch. Myer turned his hips, took a cut, and the 1933 World Series was underway.

The ball skipped off Myer's bat, then crashed into the screen behind home plate. After fouling two more pitches, Myer looked at two balls before Hubbell threw a low screwball. Myer checked his swing, but Moran rang him up. Before heading back to the dugout as Hubbell's first strikeout victim, the Nats' leadoff man had some words for the home plate umpire.

Goose Goslin was up next, wearing his lucky sweater, which he refused to wash for fear it would change his luck. His garment was stained with perspiration, and as stiff as a board, but that did not bother Goslin, as long as he believed it brought him good luck. The Wild Goose looked at ball one, then swung and missed at two screwballs. After the next pitch, Goslin, who said he and his teammates might spank the cover off the ball against New York's pitching star, became Hubbell's second strikeout victim.

Next up was Heinie Manush, the American League's hit leader for the second consecutive season, who was projected to have a huge series at the plate. He could not touch Hubbell's screwball, and quickly became strikeout victim number three. The first World Series inning Hubbell had ever pitched, he struck out the side.

Lefty Stewart toed the rubber, knowing he was going to have to be exceptional this afternoon to match up with his counterpart. The first Giants batter he faced was Jo-Jo Moore, and Stewart induced the leadoff man to hit a ground ball directly to Myer, who failed to get his glove down. The ball scooted between his legs and rolled four feet into the outfield. Back in Washington the fans groaned when the error was posted.

Stewart was unfazed. He took care of the next two batters, Hughie Critz and Bill Terry. Mel Ott followed for his first World Series at bat. After looking at a strike, the Giants' cleanup hitter loaded in his unorthodox style of lifting his right foot into the air before striding into the next pitch with a powerful sweeping swing — and he connected. Goslin faded back to the right field wall, looked up, and watched the ball sail into the seats for a 2–0 New York lead.

People wondered which Joe Cronin would show up to the World Series, the one who hit .368 during the first half of the season, or the one who struggled with a .252 average in the second half. In the top of the second he became the first Washington batter to hit a Hubbell pitch into fair territory. Travis Jackson made a dive for the ball, but missed, and it rolled into leftfield for Washington's first hit. Schulte followed by hitting into a fielder's choice. Kuhel, who Terry warned Hubbell to be very careful with, swung and missed on a full count. Schulte attempted to steal on the play, but was gunned out by Giants catcher Gus Mancuso to end the inning.

In the top of the third, Hubbell sent the Nats down in order, while striking out Bluege and Stewart to give him a total of six. In the bottom of the third the Giants threatened to blow the game open. The first three batters, Critz, Terry, and Ott, all singled to score New York's third run of the game, and Cronin conceded that his gamble on starting Stewart had not worked. He called on Russell to get out of the jam, and his ace reliever came through, but the Giants were able to add another tally for a 4–0 lead.

Myer led off the top of the fourth, and this time he produced, with a base hit into centerfield. After an out and an error moved him up two bases, he scored Washington's first run on a fielder's choice. In the next three innings Hubbell retired the Senators in order.

"The boys are not so hot today," said someone at the *Post*'s scoreboard.

"This Hubbell certainly must be something," someone else added.

While Hubbell was at his best, Buddy Myer was not. Myer had been brilliant in Washington's drive to the pennant, but today was his day of infamy. In the bottom of the second he appeared to redeem himself for his earlier miscue by making a sensational diving stop. He quickly came to his feet and threw to first base, but Kuhel was unable to glove his low throw, and the Nats' second baseman was charged with another error.

In the seventh, Mel Ott singled off Russell's arm, to complete a four for four day at the plate. As Russell clutched his arm in pain, Ott broke for second base. Sewell picked up the ball and threw to Myer, who dropped it for another error to tie a record by becoming the fifth player to make three errors in a World Series game.

To begin the top of the eighth, Hubbell struck out Bluege for his ninth strikeout, and for his eleventh consecutive out. Sewell followed with a walk on a full count to end the streak. Then Harris came to the plate as a pinch hitter, and took three consecutive balls. The Giants huddled at the pitcher's mound, and when play resumed, Harris took ball four to give the Nats hope, with two men on, nobody out, and the top of the order coming up.

Back in Washington the crowd came alive. At the Polo Grounds, Myer hit a grounder directly to Ryan, a sure double play ball. However, Ryan booted it, but recovered in time to get a force out at second base. Goslin followed by sending a long drive to right field. The entire Washington dugout stood up, thinking a three-run homer would tie the game. The ball curved foul before landing in the upper deck, and the Senators shook their heads as they sat down on the bench. Goslin walloped the next pitch, and sent a scorching line drive headed for the right field corner. Terry leaped high and made the catch for the third out. It was clearly New York's day.

The Senators did not give up. In the top of the ninth Manush reached base on an error, and Cronin hit his second single of the game. Next up was Schulte. "Come on you, Schulte!" someone shouted in Washington. Schulte hit a hot grounder, too hot for Travis Jackson to handle, and the Washington centerfielder reached with a single to load the bases with nobody out, and with Kuhel due up. "A homer will do it!" yelled an excited Nats fan.

Kuhel hit into a fielder's choice, but a run scored to make the score 4–2, and there was only one out for Bluege. But the Nats' third baseman could not touch a Hubbell pitch, and he missed a screwball by a mile and a half for strike three.

Luke Sewell followed by hitting a grounder to Jackson, who threw across the diamond to Terry to end the game. Terry tossed the ball to Hubbell, a souvenir for a well-pitched game, and the Giants headed for the centerfield clubhouse.

"Yes, Hubbell is a great pitcher," Cronin said after the game. "He's a lot faster than we had expected." When asked who the starting pitcher would be for Game Two, Cronin made no secret about it. "Crowder will start. And he will win."

In the Giants' clubhouse, as Hubbell and Ott received several handshakes and pats on their backs from their teammates, Terry came bursting through the door. "Well, we showed 'em a pitcher, boy, and you can tell the World they'll see a lot more of him," the Giants' manager announced, and the clubhouse exploded with a loud cheer. A few minutes later the entire team sat down at two long banquet tables, broke out the beer, and chatted about their victory.

"The finest game he ever pitched," said Mancuso. "I never saw Carl mix 'em up better than today."

"They're great, all right," Hubbell said about the Washington lineup. "Don't make any mistake about that. But after we got the lead they tried to slug, couldn't play for one run, and that gave me an advantage."

In the Washington clubhouse the press approached Myer, baffled by his fielding difficulties. The second baseman was more interested in discussing the casualty he had witnessed. The last thing Myer wanted to talk about was Game One.

Game Two

When the Senators arrived at the Polo Grounds for Game Two, they were greeted by a group of college boys who hummed a funeral march. The boys hummed it again as the Nats walked down the stairs leading from their centerfield clubhouse to the field. The ballplayers looked at the chorus and smiled. A few hours later, Goose Goslin had a broad smile as he crossed home plate after tagging one off Giants pitcher Hal Schumacher that traveled on a direct line to the upper deck in right field.

General Crowder was moving along, shutting out the Giants through the first five innings while allowing just two hits. The All-Star pitcher did get into a jam in the second inning, when the Giants put runners on second and third with one out, but he got the next two batters to ground out. In the fifth inning the Cronin-Myer-Kuhel tandem turned a double play to end the inning and preserve the 1-0 lead.

Jo-Jo Moore started the Giants' sixth with a single to left field, but was erased after Critz's sacrifice attempt was turned into a force out from Kuhel to Cronin. Terry followed by hitting a fly ball down the left field line, which dropped into fair territory. Critz raced to third, and Terry made it to second for a double.

Cronin and Sewell made a trip to the mound to check on Crowder and talk strategy. They decided to take a chance on loading the bases by intentionally walking the next batter, Mel Ott, and as the crowd responded by booing the Washington manager's decision, Terry decided to play a hunch. He signaled to his dugout for a pinch hitter, and boos turned into cheers when the popular Lefty O'Doul emerged, a ten-year veteran with a .351 lifetime batting average.

With a 2–2 count, O'Doul tipped Crowder's next offering. The ball grazed the top of Sewell's big catcher's mitt, caromed off his chest, and fell to the ground. It would have been a tough play to make, but had Sewell hung on, it would have been a strikeout, just what Crowder and the Nats needed.

O'Doul sent Crowder's next pitch through the middle of the Washington infield. The crowd erupted as both Critz and Terry scored to give New York a 2–1 lead.

Jackson followed with another hit up the middle, again with two strikes. Ott rounded third and easily scored, while O'Doul scampered all the way to third base.

Terry played another hunch by opting to have Mancuso bunt. The Giants' catcher caught the Senators flatfooted, and he was safe without a play. O'Doul crossed home on the play with the fourth run of the inning, and he had a big smile as he trotted to the New York dugout.

Crowder struck out Ryan for the second out, but Schumacher followed with a hit to leftfield. Travis Jackson, wincing from the pain of his post-surgical knees, rounded third base and sprinted towards the plate. Manush fielded the hit and fired the ball to Sewell. Jackson slid under the catcher's tag for the fifth run of the inning, and the crowd let out a roar that was deafening. As the Polo Grounds celebrated, the Senators' wives pouted, and a few began to cry.

Jo-Jo Moore followed with his second hit of the inning to score another run, and Cronin decided to lift Crowder. He wanted to bring in Russell, but his relief specialist was hurting from taking Ott's drive off his arm the day before. Tommy Thomas came into the game, and he got the third out to stop the bleeding, but the damage was done. The Giants had rallied for six runs on seven hits.

A five-run lead was more than enough for Schumacher, who breezed through the last three innings to beat the Nats on five hits, and to give the New Yorkers a 2–0 World Series lead.

Afterwards the defeated Senators walked to their waiting cabs, when those college kids reappeared, humming their tune. The Nats were in no mood for music. Several issued a warning for the lads to desist or else. The boys understood the message and quietly walked away.

Three days earlier, the Senators had been singing, confident of victory during their train ride to New York. There was no singing on the ride back to Washington. The Nats were in the unexpected position of being down two games in the series, and the pressure was on. When the train arrived at Union Station, two thousand fans were there to greet them. As the players stepped off the train, one by one, they was cheered, with Manush and Crowder receiving loud ovations, but the loudest was for Goslin.

Myer heard the cheers when he appeared, and a worried expression formed across his face. He was having a tough series, and perhaps feeling those cheers were undeserved, he quickly disappeared.

Joe Cronin looked angry when he emerged. As he walked to the exit, hundreds trailed him while shouting encouragement. The Washington manager did not respond. He quickly hopped into a cab and vanished from the scene.

Game Three

Thursday morning, October 5, rain fell as dark clouds hung over the nation's capital, making it seem that Game Three would be postponed. For Washington baseball fans, a more important matter was if the Senators could bounce back from a 2–0 deficit. Al Schacht believed it would happen. "It'll be different in Washington," he told the press following Game Two.

"Yeah, it'll be different. When we beat Whitehill for a change," responded Giants second baseman Hughie Critz.

Capitol Hill was busy, with debt negotiations being discussed by U.S representatives and delegates from Great Britain. The ambassador from Argentina was in conference with U.S. officials discussing the Reciprocal Trade Treaties. The Senate committees were discussing the weighty condition of the stock market. It was still raining when the lunch hour arrived, but the game was still on, and scheduled to start on time at 1:30. With several congressmen, delegates, and other officials intending to join President Roosevelt at Griffith Stadium for game three, conferences ended abruptly, and lunch was served.

A few miles away, Cronin arrived at the Senators' clubhouse, where he found his team in disarray. His players were feeling the pressure, and a few were pacing the floors while talking to themselves. Cronin immediately called for a team meeting to get his team refocused.

"I hope all of you are as ashamed as I am of what happened in the first two series games," Cronin told his players. "We're a better ball club than the Giants, and now is the time to show it to a city that has supported us all season."

As Cronin gave his players a pep talk, Earl Whitehill, Washington's starting pitcher for Game Three, appeared calm as he did his pre-game ritual of mopping his face with ice.

After Cronin finished his speech, his team was in much better spirits. They took the field for their pre-game warmup, but the rain picked up. As the players headed back to the clubhouse, the ground crew quickly dragged the tarp over the infield. By one o'clock it was still raining, and the skies grew darker, but Game Three was still intended to begin at 1:30.

At the White House the president finished his busy morning in the Oval Office, then took a few minutes to have a quick lunch at his desk. As the president ate, a motor cavalcade surrounded by policemen on motorcycles waited in the driveway, ready to take the president to the game.

At Griffith Stadium, as the crowd awaited the president's arrival and the start of the game, several fans relocated to seats beneath the upper deck for protection from the rain. Others remained in their box seats and shielded themselves by holding up newspapers. In the right field bullpen Earl Whitehill began to warm up, throwing curve balls in preparation for the Giants' batters. The damp weather affected the hurler's pitching arm, and something popped in his left elbow. Whitehill ignored the injury. Throughout his ten-year major league career, he had dreamed of this moment — of starting a World Series game — and he was not going to miss this opportunity, not even for an injury.

Back at the White House, President Roosevelt finished his lunch, then grabbed his hat and a few other things before heading out the front door. He walked through the rain to his cavalcade and got into the automobile, where he joined a few high-ranking officials. The First Lady would not be with him today due to a previous social engagement.

Word arrived at Griffith Stadium at 1:25 that the president was on his way. The start of Game Three would be delayed until the president was comfortably seated in his box, followed by his throwing the ceremonial pitch.

At 1:36 the right field gate opened. Earl Whitehill, who was close to the gate, halted his warmup, and the president's cavalcade drove through the entrance. The automobile rode along the first base wall then stopped at the president's box, located next to the Washington dugout. As a band played, and the crowd applauded, the president was helped out of the vehicle, and escorted to his box.

Meanwhile Whitehill continued his warmup, when Cronin came by to check on him. One look at the pitcher's elbow and Cronin informed him to pack it in. He decided he would pitch Weaver instead. As expected, the pitcher did not take the news well. His blood began to boil, and he lashed out at his manager. Cronin resented whatever Whitehill had said, and was ready to fight, but realized that it would not look good for the manager to brawl against his own pitcher before the president, other delegates, and 25,727 fans. Whitehill was able to regain his composure and calmly asked, "Can I please pitch today?" Cronin looked into the pitcher's determined eyes, and decided to honor his request.

When Roosevelt entered his box, a miracle occurred. The rain stopped, and the sun made its first appearance of the day. "That is plain lucky," said a spectator. "Everything he touches, the sun shines on it."

Roosevelt knew he had a role for the game, and he was prepared. "Where's the ball?" he asked. Griffith, McGraw, and Judge Landis, who were all standing close by, looked at one another. Griffith began to frisk his pockets but found nothing. A policeman alertly ran to the Giants' dugout on the third base side, and then ran back with a baseball in hand. He tossed the ball to Roosevelt, who made a nifty catch. He then drew his arm back as he laughed. "All right, here it goes," he warned, then threw the ball. Manush leaped and made the catch. The Washington leftfielder wanted the president to sign it, but he was bashful about approaching his box, so he asked a policeman to do it for him.

Earl Whitehill threw his first curve ball for a strike, and the crowd applauded. The pitcher was ready. His injured elbow was swelling by the minute, but he was so focused, he hardly noticed. Jo-Jo Moore hit the next pitch, sending a high fly to right field. Goose Goslin ran to the base of the wall in foul territory, reached into the stands, and made the catch. Whitehill retired the next two batters to take care of New York in the first inning.

Through the first two games Buddy Myer did not do well, getting only one hit in seven at bats, and making three errors in Game One. The Washington fans, appreciative of Myer's performance during the season, gave him a cheer when he was announced for his first plate appearance of the afternoon. And he came through by knocking a Fred Fitzsimmons knuckleball into leftfield for a hit.

Goose Goslin received a loud ovation when he stepped in, and he brought the crowd to its feet with a long drive to right field, which looked as if it might clear the thirty-foot wall. The ball hit a barbershop sign, just a few feet shy of a home run. Myer went all the way to third base, and Goslin took second with a double.

The crowd cheered for Heinie Manush, who was overdue for a big hit. Through the first two games the star outfielder had had just one hit. This time he hit a knuckle ball for a weak pop fly into shallow leftfield that Ryan caught for the first out of the inning.

Cronin followed with a soft grounder to the left side of the infield. Myer, eager to get a run on the board, broke for the plate. Fitzsimmons came off the mound and quickly got to the ball. He had a play on Myer, but when he attempted to plant his feet, he skidded in the wet grass, and by the time he regained his balance, Myer was across home plate with the game's first run. Fitzsimmons made the throw to first base in time to get Cronin.

Schulte hit a 3–2 pitch into right field for a hit, and Goslin ran home for a 2–0 lead. Mel Ott fielded the ball and looked towards the infield, but failed to notice that Schulte had rounded first and was digging for second base. Ott made a soft throw to Ryan, and Schulte slid beneath his tag.

Kuhel followed with a slow roller to Jackson. The third baseman had no play, but Schulte danced a bit too far off second base. Jackson fired the ball to Critz, and Schulte found himself in a rundown before being tagged out to end the inning.

Mel Ott led off the top of the second inning, and saw only curve balls. The Giants' little slugger got hold of one, and sent it for a ride into leftfield, but in the spacious outfield of Griffith Stadium, Manush had more than enough room to make the catch.

The Giants got something going when Davis followed with a single, and Jackson drew a walk. Whitehill threw a sweeping curve to Mancuso, who hit the ball on the ground, and Cronin-Myer-Kuhel turned two to end the inning.

Ossie Bluege was 0 for New York with four strikeouts. In the ninth inning the previous day he had been removed for a pinch hitter. But to start the second inning he hit one down the line, out of Jackson's reach. He made it to second base for a double, and he moved up a base when Sewell followed with a ground out. Whitehill hit a grounder back to Fitzsimmons, who looked to third base to make sure Bluege was not going to try to score. He noticed Bluege was far off the bag, and he threw to Jackson, but Bluege made it back safely, and Whitehill made it safely to first base.

Myer came through in the clutch as he had all season, with a hit down the right field line. Terry made a desperate stab for the ball, but was not even close. Bluege easily scored the Nats' third run. Whitehill went to third base, and Myer to second with a double.

Washington now had a chance to break the game wide open with Goslin at the plate, and he hoisted a fly ball to centerfield. Moore made the catch. Whitehill tagged up, but the throw beat him to the plate for an easy out to end the inning.

Down 3–0, the Giants needed to do something. It looked like a good start to the top of the fourth, when Ryan hit a fast falling pop fly to right center-field. Myer, his back turned to the infield, ran into the outfield, made a leap, and made what one writer called "a hair raising catch." The stunned crowd remained silent for a moment then broke into a cheer. As Ryan headed back to the dugout, he shrugged his shoulders as if to ask how that ball did not fall for a hit.

Myer's catch proved to be important. The Giants made a pair of singles. With two men on base and two outs, Bill Terry came to the plate, a dangerous hitter. The New York manager hit a slow roller to Kuhel, who made the pickup and stepped on the bag to end the inning. After that, Whitehill was in complete command. In the fifth inning he sent the Giants down in order on just four pitches. In the sixth inning he retired the side on five pitches. In the seventh inning he retired the side on six pitches. Fifteen pitches and nine outs!

In the bottom of the seventh Myer made his third hit of the day, resulting in his second run batted in to make the score 4–0. During the inning the congressmen seated around the president began to talk about the "Roosevelt luck," and how it could even be injected into baseball. Roosevelt laughed, then said, "Well, it's a grand old game."

Whitehill retired the first batter in the eighth inning to extend his string to eleven retired in a row. The Giants mounted a threat when the next batter singled, and an error by Cronin put another man on base with only one out. Critz grounded out, but moved up the runners. Terry followed by hitting a curve straight up in the air, and in disgust, he lifted his bat over his head before slamming it to the ground. Sewell camped under the pop-up, and hauled it in to end the inning.

Whitehill had no problems in the ninth inning. When Manush squeezed Mancuso's fly ball for the final out of the game, the Senators were back in the series.

"Whitehill pitched a marvelous game, and we got hits when we needed them. That explains the result," Cronin said afterwards in the victorious Washington clubhouse. "I'll start Weaver tomorrow and see if we can't get even with them."

"I had a couple of chances myself to stick in a hit that would've counted, but it was Whitehill's day," said Terry, who'd had a hitless day at the plate. "He had plenty of stuff and used it with exceptional judgment."

Whitehill did not seem to be bothered by his injured elbow, which was now the size of a baseball. The pitching hero of the day received a couple of gifts, one from Manush, who gave him his signed baseball to perhaps start a tradition of giving out the game ball. Another gift was handed to Whitehill, this one being a telegram sent by his proud father back in Cedar Rapids, Iowa, who wired, "I'm the happiest man in Iowa — Dad."

Game Four

At the White House about one hundred members of the press gathered around two of the most beloved figures in America on Friday morning, October 6. Each had a grin as they listened to President Roosevelt tell a story about the man he had his arm around.

"In 1920, during the presidential campaign, I walked into the lobby and found the crowd, that I thought was waiting for me, with their backs turned. I was surprised. I could not figure out why they were ignoring me. I found the center of attention to be the Babe." Unsure what to say, Ruth grinned and shrugged his shoulders. When asked if he recalled the incident, he said he did not.

The weather was pleasant for Game Four, close to seventy degrees, as Monte Weaver took the mound to pitch the most important game in his two-year career. Among the crowd, and seated in a first row box, was Babe Ruth. Next to him was the empty president's box. Roosevelt had decided to spend the day working in the Oval Office.

Weaver began by missing with his first three pitches, and Cronin made a trip to the mound to talk to his pitcher. After their brief meeting, Weaver missed again to complete the walk.

Critz followed, and hit a bullet right to Myer, who made the catch, then fired the ball to Kuhel to double up the base runner. Terry followed with an infield hit, but Mel Ott hit a soft pop-up to Bluege to end the Giants' first inning. After that, Weaver was warm, and sent the Giants down in order in the second and third innings.

Carl Hubbell did not like the American League baseball. "I find I can get more speed on the ball, but nothing much in the way of 'stuff.'" The Senators found that hard to believe, especially since Hubbell retired the first nine he faced.

With no score in the fourth inning, Terry hit a line drive to centerfield. The ball barely cleared the four-foot-high fence, and landed in the temporary bleachers for a home run. This appeared to rattle Weaver, who immediately got into trouble by giving up an infield hit and two walks to load the bases with two outs. After the Senators' pitcher threw ball one to Ryan, Cronin signaled to the Washington bullpen, and both Russell and Stewart began to warm up.

After committing three errors and collecting only one hit in the first two games, Myer redeemed himself with a wonderful performance in Game Three.

Weaver buckled down, and threw the next three pitches past Ryan to end the inning.

In the bottom of the fourth, Myer bunted a beauty to the right side of the pitcher's mound. Hubbell hustled to the ball, slipped as he picked it up, and threw to first while in a seated position, apparently too late to get the fleet-footed Myer. But Moran, the first base umpire, ruled the play an out, and the grandstands went into an uproar. As Myer jogged back to the dugout, he had a few things to tell Moran.

Hubbell's streak of retiring ten in a row came to an end when Goslin hit a sharp grounder down the first base line that Terry was unable to handle. Manush followed with a walk, and suddenly the Nats were threatening. But Hubbell got out of the inning when Cronin flew out, and Schulte grounded out.

In the sixth inning Myer beat out a ground ball for an infield hit. Goslin moved him into scoring position with a sacrifice. Manush, who had just one hit in twelve at bats for the series, hit a sharp grounder, ticketed for a hit to right field. Terry ranged to his right and extended his right arm, but the ball was out of reach. Second baseman Hughie Critz, who was having a great series

The two World Series playing managers: Bill Terry and Joe Cronin.

in the field, got the ball by making a great glove-hand stop, then threw to Hubbell, who had hustled off the mound to cover first base. Hubbell caught the ball after Manush had crossed the base, or that was what Manush and 26,762 fans believed.

Manush turned around and walked back to the base, believing he was safe, then learned that Moran had called him out. Angry and frustrated, Manush stomped towards the umpire, slapped him across the chest with his left hand, and brushed the umpire's bow tie, knocking it loose. Realizing his mistake, Manush acted as if his actions were accidental, and immediately apologized. Umpire Moran raised his right arm, pointed his thumb, and yelled, "You're outta here!"

Reserve infielder Johnny Kerr, who was coaching first base, began to argue, and Cronin ran over from the on deck circle to partake in the debate, as did Sewell and Myer. As the crowd booed, a pop bottle was thrown from of the stands, and it landed close to the umpire. When Moran walked away from the debaters, two more bottles landed at his feet. Cronin peacefully followed the umpire, hoping to at least get him to reinstate his slugger. Myer also followed, but not as peacefully. Moriarty, the second base umpire, came over to warn Myer to cool it.

Order was restored. Myer was on third base, with two outs, and Cronin, apparently distracted by the events, struck out to end the inning.

Manush grabbed his glove and headed to the outfield for the start of the seventh. He said something as he passed by Moran. "And you're out of the game," the umpire reminded him. After Manush took his position in left field, Moran shouted to home plate umpire Red Ormsby, to inform him that he had ejected Manush. Ormsby looked into left field, and motioned to the outfielder to get off the field. Manush responded with a sarcastic wave that the crowd found humorous, and some began to cheer. Third base umpire Charles Pfirman jogged into left field to speak to Manush, and was able to persuade him to leave the field, but the angry outfielder warned that he was going to punch Moran on his way back to the clubhouse. As he approached the infield, Cronin and Myer, both aware they could not afford to lose Manush to a suspension, surrounded Manush and escorted him from the field. Moriarty followed, and whispered something into the outfielder's ear that appeared to have a calming effect.

In the bottom of the seventh the Senators finally broke through against Hubbell to tie the score at 1–1. Kuhel led off by laying down a bunt that Hubbell fumbled for an error. Bluege put down a perfect bunt to move Kuhel up a base, and Sewell came through with the hit to score Kuhel for the third run off Hubbell in the series, all of which were unearned.

The Giants threatened in both the eighth and ninth innings, but Weaver managed to escape both frames without allowing a run. In the bottom of the eighth the Senators put two runners on, but did not score, and in the ninth Hubbell sent the Nats down in order to send the game into extra innings.

In the tenth inning Weaver retired the heart of the New York lineup. The

Washington crowd anticipated a win after Myer got a one-out single in the bottom of the tenth, his second hit of the day. Goslin followed by moving Myer into scoring position with a sacrifice bunt. After a walk to Harris on four pitches, Cronin came to the plate with a chance to win the game, but grounded to Ryan, and Game Four moved into the eleventh inning.

Despite being two for fourteen in the series, Travis Jackson was confident before batting in the top of the eleventh. "I'm leading off this inning and I'm going to get on somehow, by taking one in the hip, or whatever. So have a pinch-runner ready for me," Jackson announced in the New York dugout.

"Strike him out, Monte!" yelled a fan when Jackson stepped in. He came through as promised, with a base hit, and as he stood on first base he stared in the direction of the New York dugout, expecting a pinch runner to replace him. But no one left the bench, and Jackson knew he was in the game for another batter.

Mancuso laid down a bunt, and while the Nats retired him, Jackson slid into second base, then looked toward the New York dugout, and once again nobody budged.

What Jackson did not know was that Terry had every intention of sending in a pinch runner, but when he told a player to get in there, the player shook like a leaf, and Terry decided it was best to leave Jackson in.

With Jackson on second, and one out, due up were Blondy Ryan and Carl Hubbell, the eighth- and ninth-place hitters. To everyone's surprise Ryan came through, with a sharp single to left, and Jackson, ailing knees and all, rounded third base and scored the go-ahead run. Hubbell followed with a hit, and realizing his pitcher was out of gas, Cronin made a call to the bullpen for Russell, who got the last two outs to end the inning.

Schulte came through in the do-or-die bottom of the eleventh with a hit. Then the "pebble" reappeared from the 1924 World Series. Kuhel bunted one down the first base line, and, believing the ball was heading foul, Terry let it roll, but the ball managed to stay fair after it apparently nicked a pebble, giving the Senators runners on first and second with no outs. Ossie Bluege followed by doing his job for the second straight at bat, laying down a bunt to move along the runners.

The Giants went into a huddle, and decided to intentionally pass Sewell to load the bases to set up a double play opportunity, and a force out at any base. Russell was due up, with Myer, who was five for his last eight, to follow. As expected, Cronin looked to his bench for a pinch hitter. The obvious choice of Harris could not be made since he had entered the game after Manush was ejected. This left Kerr, Berg, or Boken, all right-handed hitters, and left-handers Sam Rice, who had plenty of postseason experience, or Cliff Bolton, who was red-hot in the month of September, with nine hits in eighteen at bats, four of which were pinch-hits in the ninth inning, and two of his hits scored the game's winning run. Cronin's choice was Bolton.

The Giants were baffled. Who was this guy? How do you pitch to him? Terry looked around his infield, hoping someone had an answer. Bolton had batted once in the series, in Game Two, but one at bat was not enough to go by. Needing to come up with an idea, the New York infield huddled.

Two stories are told as to what happened next. One is that both Ryan and Critz requested to play back for a double play try. "If he hits the ball to me, we'll get a double play," Blondy Ryan assured his manger. Terry agreed to let his two middle infielders play back, "but not too far," he warned. The Giants' manger instructed Hubbell to pitch low and outside, in order to get a ground-ball. "Make him hit it to me, Hub," Ryan reminded the pitcher. "I'll get him."

The other story involves Chuck Dressen, a Giants reserve who was added to the roster in September to replace the ailing Johnny Vergez. Before joining the Giants, Dressen had served as a player-manager for the Nashville Vols of the Southern Association, the same league the Chattanooga Lookouts played in, and had given him the opportunity to see Bolton play during the 1932 season. Dressen came out of the dugout to join the huddle and give his advice to the New York manager. "Bill, I played with this bird down south. He's awful slow. Play the infield deep and you may get a double play."

"All right," Hubbell said after hearing Dressen. "Gus, let's give him plenty of dipsydoos [screwballs]," he told his catcher.

Cronin called Bolton back to the dugout. He shook his hand, gave him a big smile for confidence, and gave him a pat on the back as he turned to head towards the plate.

Bolton looked at ball one, then swung and missed by a lot.

"I can't look. I can't look," a spectator said as he closed his eyes and covered his face.

Hubbell threw a screwball. Bolton swung, and hit the ball on the ground — directly to Ryan — who threw to Critz for one out. Terry caught the relay throw to complete the double play and end the game.

The crowd quietly got up and headed for the exits. The Senators were now one game away from elimination.

Game Five

Washington's 1933 season appeared to be finished, after they fell behind 3–0, as game five headed into the bottom of the sixth. The Giants had taken care of Crowder in 5⅓ innings. Russell entered the game, and ended the Giants' sixth by striking out Ryan and Schumacher.

Schumacher had allowed only three hits through five innings, and appeared to be heading for an easy sixth inning after disposing of Myer and Goslin. Manush, who got the OK from Landis to play today following his game ejection the day before, kept the inning alive with a hit, only his second of the series. Cronin followed with a single, and up came Fred Schulte, one of the few Senators having a good series at the plate. He swung at the first pitch and hit the ball to deep left field. Moore went back to the temporary bleachers, and watched the ball land in the crowd for a home run to tie the game. After crossing home plate, Schulte shook hands with Jimmy Mahorney before heading to the jubilant Senators' dugout, where his teammates mobbed him.

Kuhel and Bluege followed with infield hits, and when Jackson threw wildly on Bluege's hit, Kuhel made it to third base. The Senators now had five consecutive hits in the inning, and Terry decided it was time for a pitching change. He called on forty-three year-old, hard-throwing Dolph Luque, a Cuban known for his red-hot temper, who had postseason experience by pitching for the Reds in the 1919 World Series. He got out of the jam by getting Sewell to ground out.

Both Russell and Luque breezed through the next two innings, and both pitched through the ninth to send the game into extra innings. In the top of the tenth, with two outs, Mel Ott, who was two for his last thirteen since going four for four in Game One, was at the plate. He took a powerful swing at a 2–2 pitch and connected. The ball traveled high and far to centerfield, and Schulte, who was playing in his customary position of shallow centerfield, sprinted toward the fence in front of the temporary bleachers. He reached up and leaped high, but his ankles hit the top of the four-foot-high barrier, causing him to topple into the seats. The ball tipped his mitt and rolled up the aisle steps. Cronin knew it was a home run, for the ball did leave the confines of the field, and that made it a home run regardless if the ball was touched or not, but he tried an old trick by making the call before the umpire made his. "Ground rule double!" Cronin shouted, and second base umpire Pfirman ordered Ott to stay at second base.

In centerfield, Schulte's body had disappeared into a sea of fans, except for his legs that draped over the fence. It was feared the outfielder was seriously injured, and his teammates, along with a few officers of the law, came running to aid him. Ott was also concerned, and walked into the outfield to observe.

Meanwhile Bill Terry was on the field, arguing with Pfirman, then appealing to Morarity and Moran. While the umpires huddled, Schulte reappeared, and limped back to his position. After a minute the umpires broke from their meeting, and waved Ott home. Cronin objected, and argued with the entire umpiring crew, but their decision stood.

The good news for the Senators was that in the bottom of the tenth the Old Washington Wrecking Crew was due up. Goslin led off, and grounded to Terry. The New York manager flipped the ball to Luque, who stepped on first base for one out. Manush, having a tough time in the series, hit one on the nose, but right at Critz for the second out. Cronin came through with a single, his seventh hit of the series, to keep his team's hopes alive. Schulte followed by taking four straight balls, and the Nats had two men on base for Joe Kuhel.

Luque settled down, and threw three straight past the Washington first baseman to end the 1933 World Series. The New York Giants were the World Champions of baseball.

One by one the Senators entered their clubhouse, headed to their lockers, and fell onto their stools. Dazed, heartbroken, and defeated, nobody said a word. Cronin was misty-eyed as he sat on his stool and stared into space in disbelief over losing to the Giants. A telegram appeared, and six players passed it down the line before it reached the Washington manager, who opened it, read it, then broke into a smile. Perhaps it was from his parents? Or was it from Mildred?

Most of the ballplayers quickly showered, got dressed, and left the clubhouse through the back exit. Cronin remained, seated before his locker, still wearing his uniform as if he were not ready for the season to end.

Terry entered the clubhouse with photographers trailing him. He congratulated each of the remaining players, then approached Cronin and extended his hand. The Nats' manager got up from his stool, smiled, shook Terry's hand, and congratulated him.

"Your boys are certainly great," Terry told him.

Cronin was the last player to leave. Before departing he said goodbye to Baxter and Mahorney and thanked them for their hard work. Then Joe Cronin walked out the back door. His 1933 season was now a memory.

19

ONE MORE CHEER
FOR THE SENATORS

MANUSH: "Goose, if you were hitting today against the live ball, what
do you think you'd hit for an average?"
GOSLIN: "Oh, about .350."
MANUSH: "Put me down for .375."

The old-timers greeted one another with a slap on the back, as if they had just arrived in Biloxi for spring training. Heinie Manush laughed as he chomped on a cigar. Earl Whitehill talked about his travels as a representative for Spaulding Sporting Goods. Fred Marberry was dressed like the distinguished businessman he had become in Texas. "Yeah, I hit that ball good," said Earl McNeely about his hit that won the 1924 World Series.

"Griff, you son of a gun, it's great to see you again," the former ballplayers said after entering his office. Seventy-eight-year-old Clark Griffith's eyes flickered as he smiled.

"Boy, this is great," said Jack Russell. "I'm managing Tampa now, and when I got the telegram, I said, 'I'm taking off Tuesday night.'"

"I wouldn't have missed this for anything in the world," said McNeely. "Just seeing these fellows, and being with Griff is something I'll never forget."

Members of the 1933 American League Champions, and others from the Senators' glory years of the 1920s and 1930s, returned to Griffith Stadium on the evening of August 17, 1948, for "Clark Griffith Night."

"My, what I'd give to have these boys in their prime," Griffith said. "How they could play baseball."

How the world had changed since Washington won the 1933 pennant! The Depression was over. The Bonus Army had won. President Roosevelt and Walter Johnson were gone. So was the Babe, who had died the day before of cancer at the age of fifty-three. "That's too bad," Griffith said upon hearing the news. "The poor fellow just couldn't make it. He was a great man and a great player."

"What a man he was," Joe Judge said. "There was nothing he couldn't or wouldn't do."

Since 1933, there had been another World War, racial integration among major league rosters, lights installed at Griffith Stadium, and just three winning seasons for Washington.

In 1934 injuries decimated the Senators. The entire everyday lineup, four of the reserves, and four pitchers, all missed action during the course of the season. Cronin broke his wrist and missed the last month of the season. The Nats finished in seventh place, with thirty-three fewer wins than the year before.

Cronin assigned his managerial duties to Al Schacht for the Nats' final road trip, while he remained in Washington to take care of his wrist and work on his wedding plans. On September 27, Joe and Mildred were married in Washington at St. Matthew's Church. They had planned for a quiet affair, but when the ceremony began at 10:00 A.M. every pew was occupied, while hundreds waited on the doorsteps and in the street in front of the church. When the newlyweds emerged, the police cleared a path to their car. From there they headed to New York City and boarded a ship bound for San Francisco.

After the 1933 season Tom Yawkey paid $150,000 for pitchers Lefty Grove and Wes Ferrell. Bucky Harris was hired to manage, and the Red Sox enjoyed their best season since the last time they had won the pennant, in 1918.

Surprisingly, Eddie Collins believed that Harris was not the man to manage his team. Who did he think the right man was? "Mickey Cochrane," he told Yawkey. The Red Sox owner laughed. They hadn't a prayer of buying the 1934 American League MVP, who had just managed the Tigers to the 1934 pennant.

"My second choice, Joe Cronin, is just as hard to get," Collins replied. "Griffith would never part with him."

"Perhaps he won't," Yawkey said, "but I'll make him an offer."

On October 22 the Cronins arrived in San Francisco, aboard the Panama Pacific Liner *Virginia*. Will Stevens, a sportswriter for the *San Francisco Chronicle*, was there to greet them. He asked the Washington manager about the 1935 season, and what new strengths would be added to the Senators. "We don't need any, if we get just an even break in injuries," Cronin replied. "We have the pitchers, the infielders, the outfielders—all we have to do is get them on the field at the same time."

A few days after the Cronins had checked into their suite at the Hotel St. Francis, Joe received a phone call from Griffith, and was floored over what he was hearing. "The price is enormous, Joe—the highest ever paid for a baseball player—much the highest," Griffith told him.

Yawkey had offered $225,000 and a shortstop. Griffith had declined, but changed his mind after careful consideration. Washington's 1934 attendance was the lowest since 1919, and the club fell into debt. Aware that Yawkey's offer would get his club out of the red, knowing that Yawkey could pay a higher salary, and certain that the Red Sox owner would take care of Joe and Mildred,

In 1946 Clark Griffith celebrated his seventy-seventh birthday with his grandchildren.

he decided to go ahead with the deal as long as it was OK with Joe — which it was.

"I'm naturally glad," said Cronin. "It is the greatest spot in baseball today. Naturally, it is going to hurt, too — leaving Washington." Cronin added, "I regret to leave Clark Griffith; he's been so nice to me and I have deep respect for him."

"But you have to expect anything in baseball — and this is one of those things."

"We were not dissatisfied with Harris," Collins explained. "He was successful as any man could be under the circumstances, but we need a manager of Cronin's magnetic fire."

Griffith brought Bucky Harris back to manage the Senators. In 1935, without Cronin, with an aging Heinie Manush, and a poor pitching staff, Washington finished with virtually the same record as in 1934.

In 1936 a funny thing happened. Griffith made a trade before the June 15 deadline for Ben Chapman. "Baseball makes strange teammates," wrote Povich. "Casting Earl Whitehill, who was punched by Chapman; Ben Chapman, who punched him; and Buddy Myer, who vowed eternal vengeance against Chapman."

"It's OK with me," said Chapman. "It's tough to leave a first-place club for a fifth-place team, but it's all in the game. Who are the Yankees getting?" When told he was traded straight up for second-year outfielder Jake Powell, he replied, "He's a fine ballplayer."

The word was that the trade was made because McCarthy had become fed up with the temperamental outfielder. Chapman insisted there was no trouble with the Yankees' manager, but said they were problems with the New York fans. "One day a fellow was riding me so unmercifully from the box and was calling me names a fellow just can't swallow. Finally I walked by him and told him what I thought of him. Well, the story got to one of those radical newspapers they have up there and everybody believed that I was anti-something or other. I took a beating, and I guess it did hurt my playing."

Chapman arrived at the Cadillac Hotel in Detroit in time to join his new teammates for breakfast. When he entered the dining room he looked for someone to join, and found someone sitting alone. After he sat down, the others stopped eating and went on guard in case a fight suddenly erupted.

The person Chapman elected to sit with was Buddy Myer.

The Washington second baseman displayed his Southern hospitality by being very cordial. Soon there was laughter between the two. The others sighed in relief and went back to eating breakfast.

Later that morning Chapman encountered Whitehill in the hotel lobby. The two shook hands and engaged in a friendly conversation. Chapman was probably relieved to know there were no grudges, and his new teammates accepted him.

In 1936 Chapman batted .332, represented Washington in the All-Star Game, and helped lead the Nats to a surprising winning season. His stay would not be for long, however. Midway through the next season, in an attempt to bolster the team's pitching and catching, he was traded to the Red Sox for the Ferrell brothers—pitcher Wes, and catcher Rick. In 1941 Chapman returned to the Senators for twenty-eight games before being dealt to the White Sox.

In 1947 Chapman was involved in another controversy, this time while serving as manager of the Philadelphia Phillies: he was highly criticized for his harsh treatment of Dodgers rookie Jackie Robinson. "I wasn't hard on Jackie Robinson," he said in later years. "I was tough on everybody. It had nothing to do with the color of his skin."

This may have been true, but Chapman would never be vindicated, partly due to his reputation during his playing days for harassing Jewish ballplayers and spectators. It was remembered that he had purposely spiked Buddy Myer, who some sportswriters believed was Jewish (he was not; his tie to Judaism was one Jewish great-great-great-grandfather).

During the 1948 season, with the Phillies struggling in sixth place, Chapman was terminated.

Before the 1937 season, Griffith added another player who had also been a target for jeers among the Washington fans. Al Simmons was on his way to Washington. "It certainly suits me," Simmons said when hearing the news. "And it looks like a great break for me, too. The Washington club looks to me like it is going places."

Simmons would spend two seasons in the capital before talking his way out of town. On the last day of the 1938 season he got into it with the fans after being taunted. During his final at bat of the season, he challenged three fans to meet him under the stands. He issued a second and third challenge, and even went as far as to dispatch the clubhouse boy with a note.

"No ballplayer of mine can conduct himself in such a manner," said Griffith, who announced that he was fining the outfielder $200, and was going to report Simmons to Will Harridge and Judge Landis. "The language displayed by Simmons was not only objectionable, but obscene."

"I knew it was coming," said Simmons, who accused Griffith of fining him to offset the bonus he had earned for batting over .300.

The three young men Simmons had threatened said it was a case of mistaken identity, and that the culprit was several rows behind. When asked if he knew who was riding him, Simmons admitted he was unsure. "And I don't agree with people who say a fan is entitled to call a player any name he thinks."

A few months later a deal was made, and Simmons was on his way to the Boston Braves.

During the late 1930s, Griffith concentrated on building for the future, and added several promising youngsters. With Buddy Lewis, Mickey Vernon, George Case, Walt Masterson, and Early Wynn, along with Cecil Travis, Washington appeared to have a bright future.

Buddy Lewis was only eighteen years old when he joined Chattanooga in 1935, and was considered the most promising prospect the Nats ever had. After hitting .303, and leading the Lookouts in home runs and runs batted in, he was promoted to the Senators at the end of the season. In 1936, as Washington's everyday third baseman, he hit .291 and scored 100 runs. Two years later he joined Travis on the American League All-Star team.

In 1941 Travis went unnoticed when finishing with a .359 batting average, and with a major league leading 218 hits. He hit two points higher than Joe DiMaggio, who had hit safely in fifty-six consecutive games that season, and he had thirty-three more hits than Ted Williams, who batted .406.

World War Two hurt the Senators more than any other team. Both Lewis and Travis served, missing 3½ years. When he returned during the 1945 season, Travis was not the same player. The layoff, along with frozen feet he had suffered while fighting in the Battle of the Bulge, resulted in a loss of his All-Star reflexes.

After the 1947 season Travis retired at the age of thirty-three, with a .314 lifetime batting average, and questions would always be asked about his full potential had he not served. He would also be remembered for his modesty and his sweet disposition. "If he was a woman, I would have married him," said Buddy Lewis.

Lewis batted .333 after returning in 1945, and had another good season in 1946. In 1947 he injured his hip in a collision in the outfield, and retired after the season at the age of thirty. On Clark Griffith Night he spoke about making a comeback. "I've been working out with the American Legion Junior baseball team, and I'm in fairly good shape. My hip hurts me a bit. I don't know yet whether I'll come back or not but it would be fun. I miss the road trips. When that telegram came I was off and running. Any excuse would have brought me up." Lewis would return in 1949 before retiring for good.

After the 1942 season, Griffith changed managers, replacing Harris with Ossie Bluege. Under Bluege's direction the Nats finished second in 1943, and came within one game of winning the pennant in 1945. After the 1947 season Bluege moved into the front office, and Joe Kuhel was hired to lead the Senators in 1948.

"Just one more winner, just one more and my life will be complete," said Griffith. It was not going to happen in 1948. The Nats entered Clark Griffith Night in sixth place, twenty-two games under .500, and trailed the first-place Indians by twenty-four games.

As a crowd of twenty-four thousand watched slides which depicted Griffith's career, the old-timers gathered by the Washington dugout. The current Washington team watched from their dugout, and perhaps they tried to imagine the days when Washington was atop the American League. Recently the entire team had seen *The Babe Ruth Story*, starring William Bendix, and they laughed during a scene when Colonel Ruppert said with sarcasm, "You even let the Washington Senators beat you ... of all teams."

At 8:45 Arch McDonald, the radio voice of the Senators, introduced each former player. One by one, they walked to home plate to shake hands with Griffith. As in the good old days, the loudest cheer was for Goslin, who hugged Griffith and gave him a big kiss.

"What a relief pitcher he was," a fan said after Marberry was introduced. "The best. The very best."

Joe Cronin, currently the general manager for the Red Sox, received a loud ovation. He walked over to his former boss, and gave him an enthusiastic handshake. The Red Sox were disappointing during Cronin's first three seasons, finishing no better than fourth, and no closer than sixteen games from the top. In 1938 Bobby Doerr joined Boston, and in 1939 another rookie, Ted Williams, came aboard. The Red Sox played more to their potential, but still could not capture the pennant.

By 1946 Cronin's playing days were finished, but he still managed the Red

Sox. During that season everything finally came together, and Boston won the American League pennant with 104 wins. In the World Series they met the Cardinals, and in what was one of the best series ever, the Red Sox lost a heartbreaker in seven games. After the 1947 season Cronin became the Red Sox general manager.

Two other members from the 1933 team had managed a team to the pennant. Luke Sewell did it with the St. Louis Browns. When he took over the Browns during the 1941 season, he inherited a team that had lost 111 games two years before, and had not had a winning season since 1929, but under his leadership things changed in a hurry. "Keep hustling," he kept reminding his team, and after Sewell took over, the Browns hustled to go 55–55 for the remainder of the season. In 1942 they posted a winning record, and in 1944 they won the pennant. A dream to see the underdog St. Louis Browns winning it all fell short by two games, after they lost to the Cardinals in six games in the World Series.

Tommy Thomas managed a pennant winner in 1944, when he guided the Baltimore Orioles to the International League flag, followed by a victory over the American Association champions, the Louisville Colonels, in the Junior World Series. In 1948 he was still managing the Orioles.

Bucky Harris managed the Yankees to the 1947 pennant, and won his second World Championship when the New Yorkers defeated Jackie Robinson and the Dodgers in the World Series. On Clark Griffith Night the once boy manager of the Senators stood with his former team while wearing the Yankee pinstripes.

Buddy and Mina Myer were the proud parents of two boys in Baton Rouge, and Buddy was on his way to becoming a successful banker. Lefty Stewart was in the furniture business, Dave Harris wore badge number 650 for the Atlanta police force, Fred Schulte owned a bowling alley, Monte Weaver was in the awning business, Bill McAfee was the father of two and a distributor for International Harvester Company in Albany, Georgia, and Cliff Bolton never reached his full potential. The Nats became annoyed with his continuous holdouts, and after he missed a team train in 1937, he was sent to Detroit. Four years later he was back in Washington during the tail end of the season, and went zero for eleven to finish up his disappointing career.

Goslin rented boats and fishing equipment, Rice was a chicken farmer, Crowder managed the minor league team in his hometown of Winston-Salem, later becoming a part owner, and Moe Berg had the most interesting life after baseball, with a career in espionage.

Where was Moe Berg? Did he receive a telegram? While he went undercover for the Office of Strategic Strategies (OSS) during World War Two, his stationery company was mismanaged and went under, and the IRS was looking for him.

After Cliff Bolton finally ended his holdout by signing his 1934 contract midway through the season, Griffith decided to send Berg to Chattanooga to make room for Bolton. Berg declined the demotion and was waived, then claimed by the Indians, which reunited him with Walter Johnson. He went on to play five more seasons with Cronin's Red Sox.

Following the 1934 season Berg was a member of the American League All-Star team that traveled to Japan to play a series of games against the Japanese All-Stars. During one of the games he snuck away from the dugout, entered the locker room, changed into a kimono, brushed his hair back and parted it down the middle, and held a bouquet of flowers to add to his cover.

He entered St. Luke's Hospital, and speaking fluent Japanese at the front desk, claimed he was there to visit the American ambassador's daughter and her newborn. But Berg had no such intention. Instead he went to the hospital roof, disposed of the flowers, and from under his robe he pulled out a movie camera to film the Tokyo skyline. In 1942, when Colonel James Doolittle plotted his air raid on Tokyo, for whatever reason, he opted not to refer to Berg's movie.

Berg went undercover again in 1944; this time his cover was as a Swiss graduate student. A German scientist named Werner Heisenberg came to Zurich to give a public lecture. Back in the United States physicists feared that Heisenberg was attempting to develop an atomic bomb. If during his lecture he evinced that he was, Berg was to reach for his concealed revolver, and in case he used it, he was to swallow a cyanide pill before being apprehended by Nazi agents who were guarding the lecture hall. Nothing happened that evening.

There were jobs in baseball, with law firms, and personal business opportunities, all of which would have helped Berg even up with the IRS. Instead he elected to work various jobs for the CIA, and he gradually paid off his reduced debt.

In later years he spoke to an editor from a publishing company about writing his autobiography.

"I enjoyed all your pictures," the editor told him.

"Pictures? Who do you think I am?" asked Berg.

"Aren't you Moe from the Three Stooges?" the editor asked.

Berg did not laugh. Instead, he got up and left the room.

Alex McColl pitched the last two innings of Game Two in the 1933 World Series, when the Nats were blown out at the Polo Grounds, 6–1. He was on the Washington pitching staff in 1934, went 3–4 with a 3.86 ERA, and saved a game before injuring his pitching arm (that required surgery). He bounced back to win twenty-two games for Chattanooga in 1935, and was invited to join the Nats in spring training in 1936. Povich got a kick out of seeing McColl on the roster, and noted that his age appeared at thirty-nine for the fourth straight season.

McColl returned to Chattanooga in 1936, won twelve games, and managed the Lookouts for part of the season. In 1938 he pitched and managed in the Sally League, and the following year he pitched for Springfield of the Eastern League. In 1941 he was named manager of the Warren, Ohio, team in the Pennsylvania State League, and it was reported that his pitching career was still intact ... at the age of thirty-nine.

At 102 E. 52nd Street in New York City, patrons ordered broiled Maine lobster tails for $5.95, or broiled beef flanken — the special for the evening — from the Al Schacht scorecard. "All meats I serve are Big League top prime only."

After Griffith sold Cronin, he sat down with Schacht to tell him that Cronin wanted him in Boston, and he would be part of the deal. "What did they do, throw in a bag of peanuts to get me?" joked Schacht.

"They can pay you better in Boston than I can," Griffith said, "but Al, if you don't like it there, you can always come back to this ball club. Remember that."

After the 1936 season Schacht decided that he had had enough coaching, and went into clowning full time. He entertained at ballparks from coast to coast, and once worked in 121 cities in 125 days. In 1947 he went into another venture — the restaurant business — and reduced his acting career to part time.

Seventy-one-year-old Nick Altrock, the other half of the former "Altrock and Schacht" comedy team, continued to entertain crowds, and still served as a coach for the Nats.

In Chattanooga they rode in Joe Engel cabs, smoked Joe Engel cigars, and still continued to pack Engel Stadium. Joe Engel never ran out of promotions, and one evening 24,000 packed his 16,000-seat stadium when he gave away a furnished home with a new car. "He was a very kind-hearted man," recalled one of his secretaries. "Every Christmas, he opened up his stadium and fed many hungry people."

Calvin Griffith joined the Washington front office in 1935. From 1936 to 1940 he helped run the operations in Chattanooga and Charlotte, and learned all phases of baseball operations, including field manager. In 1937 he managed the Lookouts for part of the season. In 1941 he returned to Washington to run the concessions at Griffith Stadium.

During the 1933 season and the World Series, over 500,000 fans passed through the turnstiles at Griffith Stadium, and the Senators made money. However, Griffith knew he had a price to pay for fielding a pennant winner, and knew there would be players who wanted to be compensated for their good seasons. With the Depression still going, something would have to give, and it was Goslin and his high salary.

Griffith explained the situation. Goslin understood, but had one request — not to be traded to a losing environment as when the Nats dealt him to the Browns in 1930. Griffith gave him his word.

In Detroit, Goslin fit in well in a powerful lineup that featured Cochrane, Gehringer, and Greenberg. In 1934 and 1935 the Tigers won the pennant, and won the 1935 World Series on Goslin's hit in the bottom of the ninth in game six.

In 1936 Goslin had one of his best seasons, but during the next season age caught up with him, and the following spring the Tigers released him. When Griffith heard the news he invited Goslin back to Washington to finish out his career: "You started with me eighteen years ago. Why don't you come back to Washington and finish up with me?"

"He was a wonderful man, always so helpful and kind," Goslin said about Griffith. "He was more than a father to me, that man."

Buddy Myer became a better hitter by becoming more patient at the plate, and by learning how to execute a drag bunt to perfection. "Myer was one of the finest drag bunters to ever play, and as a left-handed hitter he was particularly adept at dragging the ball for a base hit," recalled former player Billy Werber.

In 1935 sixty of Myer's 215 hits were bunt singles. That same year Myer won the batting title with a .349 average. What was most impressive was in the month of September, when he collected forty hits and went four for five on the final day of the season to edge out Joe Vosmik of the Indians by a single point.

After the season Myer was wanted by Yankees manager Joe McCarthy. The Yankees had had three consecutive second-place finishes since winning the World Series in 1932, and feeling Myer's competitive spirit was the missing ingredient, New York offered Griffith $200,000. But Griffith had no intention of selling Myer, and made the cost unattractive.

"Certainly I would to like get Buddy Myer," said McCarthy, "but when Griffith started mentioning $500,000, we thought he was talking about a franchise." When it was clarified it was the cost for Myer, the Yankees backed off.

In 1938 Myer was involved in another brawl, this time with Billy Werber following a play at third base. Both players were fined and suspended. "Buddy Myer and I had a good laugh about our fracas the next time we saw each other, and we remained good friends with no hard feelings," Werber recalled to author C. Paul Rogers III. "Myer was an intense competitor who just lost his cool that day. Not that I am throwing stones, because I lost my cool as well."

On July 22, 1935, Griffith Stadium celebrated another Walter Johnson Day, and Washington's greatest was presented with a silver cup and a scroll. For Johnson it was the support he needed during a difficult season as manager of the Indians. One week later he resigned.

In 1934 Johnson's Indians won a surprising eighty-five games and finished third, yet many did not appreciate the good job Johnson had done. The Cleveland sportswriters, who believed they were qualified to manage the team and should be heard, were unfair in their criticism of the Big Train. Others stood by Johnson, including Babe Ruth, who was so bothered by the criticism that he summoned Johnson's two daughters, who were staying at the same hotel as the Yankees, to his room. "I don't know whether you girls have seen any of the bad comments about your Dad, but if you have, don't pay a bit of attention to them, because he's a fine, fine person," he told the two girls, who were both unaware of the comments.

Most of the Cleveland players respected Johnson, including Indians pitching ace Mel Harder. "Johnson was a good manager, but he had a problem with a few of the players, and it snowballed on him."

Johnson also had the appreciation and support of Alva Bradley and the board of directors, who unanimously voted Johnson a contract for 1935. "I still think Walter Johnson is a pretty good fellow," Bradley said.

After his days in Cleveland, Johnson came home to where he was worshiped. When he appeared at Griffith Stadium, "It often took forever to get into the stadium, because he never brushed off an autograph request," recalled his daughter, Carolyn Thomas. "He would patiently sign all the way in, and my sister and I would roll our eyes."

In 1935 Walter Jr. had another accident after he fell asleep at the wheel and slammed his car into a telephone pole. He sustained several bruises and a few broken bones, but once again, he bounced back to continue his pitching career. After a friend of Connie Mack's saw him pitch, he was invited to the Athletics' spring training in 1939. After developing a sore arm he went to Des Moines, where he struggled and was eventually released. He would pitch for a few other minor league teams that summer but nothing would come of it, and by the end of the 1939 season, Junior's career was over.

In March of 1946 Johnson complained about numbness in his left arm. He checked into the Georgetown hospital where his condition was believed to be good, but then he suddenly took a turn for the worse. Later, an advance X-ray revealed he had a malignant, inoperable brain tumor.

As weeks passed by, the Johnson family became baffled over why they had not received a single bill. When they pulled a doctor aside and asked why, they were informed that Griffith was paying for everything.

With his family at his bedside on the evening of December 10, 1946, the Big Train passed on, at the age of fifty-nine.

Eight hundred seventeen members of the Bonus Army, employed under Roosevelt's New Deal, were sent to the Florida Keys in 1935 to build bridges, fix roads, and revitalize the bankrupt area into becoming a tourist attraction once again. On Labor Day a hurricane devastated the area. A week later it was reported that 144 bodies of veterans had been found, and 320 were reported missing. People everywhere asked why there was a failure to warn and evacuate the Bonus men. Charles C. Clark of the National Weather Bureau in Washington claimed "ample notice of the danger and approach of the hurricane was given."

Regardless if notice was given or not, most Americans felt enough was enough, and were in favor of the veterans' receiving their bonuses. In 1936 the Bonus bill passed, but was vetoed by Roosevelt, who feared this would destroy credit. The bill went back to Congress and the House overwhelmingly overrode the president's veto. The veterans patiently waited out the weekend that followed, and on Monday the Senate voted 77–19 in favor. The Bonus Army had finally won their battle. Victory became official in mid–June, when the veterans received neatly wrapped brown packages containing baby bonds.

After the old Senators were introduced, the speakers took center stage.

"As long as we have men of the spirit of Clark Griffith, this country will not fail," said Commissioner Happy Chandler.

Harridge praised Griffith for his contributions, and presented him with a gold watch, a gift from the American League.

"I am going to request that everyone in the audience sit down as I talk," said President Truman. "It is a privilege to be here tonight when we are honoring a hero who deserves everything he's got. He is a shining example of what this great country can produce. He worked on the diamond, became a manager, and now an executive. It takes stamina and ability to do that, and Mr. Griffith has that." "I salute him as a great citizen of Washington."

Truman then changed the subject to another hero. "I want to pay tribute to another baseball great, Babe Ruth."

On the final day of the 1934 season, 12,000 fans came to Griffith Stadium to see Babe Ruth play what many believed would be the final game of his career. The citizens of Washington presented him with a parchment of thousands of signatures in a pre-game ceremony. "It is with great satisfaction that I receive this from the fans in Washington," Ruth told the crowd. "This tribute is something I will cherish as long as I live."

Ruth would return in 1935, but as a member of the Boston Braves. In mid-season, with just six homers, and an embarrassing batting average of .181, Ruth finally retired.

"All of you saw those great stars of other years a few minutes before," Griffith said into the microphone. "They brought honor and glory to Washington. This is a great tribute — one I'll never forget."

The former American League champions sat together and watched the Yankees pound the Senators, 8–1. Afterwards, as $2,000 worth of fireworks capped the evening, the former players gathered in a small pressroom located behind the press box and were joined by the working press.

"Look, I don't know how many games you fellows see now, but you saw one tonight," a sportswriter said to Goslin and Marberry. "I see a game every night or every day and the only improvement over your days is the fielding. The infielding is better, but the pitching is worse, and the hitting is worse."

"Thanks, pal. But seriously, I might go along with you," replied Goslin.

When Whitehill heard "pitching," he decided to chime in. "You could go back to Abner Doubleday or Alexander Cartwright, but the first thing in pitching is to get a piece of that plate."

"And it's a roughhouse league," added Heinie Manush, who was currently employed as a scout for the Pirates. "There aren't many kids just now who get attention and those who do are asking for big bonuses. They're asking for $65,000, some of them, and it kind of sets me back on my heels. I used to play alongside a guy who didn't cost $400, so help me, and he was a fair country ball player. His name was Ty Cobb."

Shortly after the last firecracker exploded, and the stadium lights were turned off, the reunion came to an end. The ballplayers had their fun in reliving their glory days, but now it was time to return to their families and present careers. They said goodbye, mentioned how nice it was to see one another, and then they vanished — into history.

APPENDIX 1:
GAME BY GAME RESULTS
FOR THE 1933 SENATORS

Date	Opponent	Record	Place	Games Back or in Front	WINNING/ Losing Pitcher (Record)	Home Runs (Number on Season)
12-Apr	vs. Philadelphia, W,4–1	1–0	1	1	CROWDER (1–0)	
13-Apr	vs. Philadelphia, W,11–4	2–0	1	1	WHITEHILL (1–0)	Goslin (1)
14-Apr	vs. Philadelphia, L,1–5	2–1	4	-0.5	Stewart (0–1)	
15-Apr	vs. Boston, W,2–1	3–1	3	-0.5	WEAVER (1–0)	
17-Apr	vs. Boston,L,2–4	3–2	3	-1.5	Crowder (1–1)	
18-Apr	vs. Boston,L,4–6	3–3	4	-2.5	Whitehill(1–1)	
20-Apr	at Philadelphia,L,1–8	3–4	4	-3	Stewart (0–2)	Sewell (1)
21-Apr	at Philadelphia,L, 1–3	3–5	4	-4	Crowder (1–2)	Myer (1)
22-Apr	at Philadelphia,W,10–7	4–5	4	-4	THOMAS (1–0)	Goslin (2)
23-Apr	vs.New York,W,5–4	5–5	3	-3	WHITEHILL (2–1)	
24-Apr	vs.New York,W,11–10	6–5	4	-2	CROWDER (2–2)	Kuhel (1)
25-Apr	vs.New York,L,0–16	6–6	4	-3	Weaver (1–1)	
27-Apr	at Boston,W,3–2	7–6	3	-3	LINKE (1–0)	
28-Apr	at New York,W,4–3 (10 inns)	8–6	3	-2	STEWART (1–2)	
29-Apr	at New York,W,6–3	9–6	2	-1	WEAVER (2–1)	
30-Apr	vs.Philadelphia,W,5–4 (12 inns)	10–6	2	-1.5	MCAFEE (1–0)	
4-May	at Cleveland,L,6–5	10–7	4	-2	Thomas (1–1)	
6-May	at Detroit,W,6–5	11–7	3	-1	WHITEHILL (3–1)	Goslin (3)
7-May	at Detroit,L,9–10	11–8	3	-1	Thomas (1–2)	Bluege (1)
7-May	at Detroit,W,6–2	12–8	3	-1	STEWART (2–2)	Boken (1)
8-May	at St. Louis,W,10–8 (12)	13–8	2	-1	MCAFFE (2–0)	Boken (2) Sewell (2)
9-May	at St. Louis,W,7–5	14–8	2	-0.5	CROWDER (3–2)	
10-May	at St.Louis,L,0–5	14–9	3	-0.5	Whitehill (3–2)	
11-May	at St.Louis,L,3–4	14–10	3	-1.5	Stewart (2–3)	Bluege (2)
13-May	at Chicago,W,5–4 (10)	15–10	3	-0.5	CROWDER (4–2)	Boken (3)
14-May	at Chicago,L,8–10	15–11	3	-1.5	Whitehill (3–3)	Harris (1) Kuhel (2)
14-May	at Chicago,W,11–9	16–11	3	-1.5	MCAFFE (3–0)	Goslin (4)
16-May	vs.Cleveland,W,11–10 (12)	17–11	1	tied	CROWDER (5–2)	Kuhel (3)
17-May	vs.Cleveland,W,3–2	18–11	1	tied	CROWDER (6–2)	
18-May	vs.Cleveland,L,5–6	18–12	2	-1	Whitehill (3–4)	
19-May	vs.Chicago,L,1–10	18–13	2	-2	Thomas (1–3)	
20-May	vs.Chicago,W,7–0	19–13	2	-1	WEAVER (3–1)	
21-May	vs.Chicago,L,0–6	19–14	2	-1	Crowder (6–3)	
22-May	vs.Detroit,W,6–5	20–14	2	-1	WHITEHILL (4–4)	
23-May	vs.Detroit,L,1–7	20–15	2	-2	Stewart (2–4)	
24-May	vs.Detroit,L,1–3	20–16	2	-2.5	Weaver (3–2)	Kuhel (4)

Date	Opponent	Record	Place	Games Back or in Front	WINNING/ Losing Pitcher (Record)	Home Runs (Number on Season)
25-May	vs.St.Louis,W,7–2	21–16	2	-2	CROWDER (7–3)	
26-May	vs.St.Louis,W,5–2	22–16	2	-1.5	WHITEHILL (5–4)	
28-May	vs.Philadelphia,W,7–4	23–16	2	-2	THOMAS (2–3)	
30-May	vs.New York,L,2–3	23–17	2	-3	Whitehill (5–5)	
31-May	vs.New York,W,12–7	24–17	2	-2	THOMAS (3–3)	
31-May	vs.New York,L,7–9	24–18	2	-3	Weaver (3–3)	Cronin (1)
1-Jun	vs.Boston,L,5–7 (13)	24–19	2	-3.5	Thomas (3–4)	
2-Jun	vs.Boston,W,8–3	25–19	2	-3.5	WEAVER (4–2)	
3-Jun	vs.Boston,W,8–5	26–19	2	-3.5	RUSSELL (1–0)	
4-Jun	vs.Boston,W,4–3 (13)	27–19	2	-4	RUSSELL (2–0)	
5-Jun	at Philadelphia,L,4–7	27–20	2	-4.5	Crowder (7–4)	Schulte (1)
6-Jun	at Philadelphia,L,4–8	27–21	2	-6	Stewart (2–5)	
7-Jun	at Philadelphia,T,13–13		2	-6		Bluege (3) Berg (1)
8-Jun	at Boston,L,3–4	27–22	2	-5.5	Thomas (3–5)	
8-Jun	at Boston,W,12–2	28–22	2	-5.5	RUSSELL (3–0)	
9-Jun	at Boston,W,7–2	29–22	2	-5.5	WHITEHILL (6–5)	
10-Jun	at Boston,W,7–5	30–22	2	-4	STEWART (3–5)	Goslin (5)
11-Jun	vs.Philadelphia,W,13–6	31–22	2	-3.5	CROWDER (8–4)	Schulte (2)
13-Jun	vs.Philadelphia,W,10–6	32–22	2	-2.5	RUSSELL (4–0)	Goslin (6)
17-Jun	at St.Louis,W,10–3	33–22	2	-1.5	WHITEHILL (7–5)	
18-Jun	at St.Louis,W,14–1	34–22	2	-1.5	CROWDER (9–4)	Myer (2) Bluege (4)
18-Jun	at St.Louis,L,2–3	34–23	2	-1.5	Thomas (3–6)	Myer (3)
19-Jun	at St.Louis,W,10–4	35–23	2	-0.5	STEWART (4–5)	Harris (2) Cronin(2) Kuhel (5) Schulte (3)
21-Jun	at Chicago,W,9–0	36–23	1	-1	WHITEHILL (8–5)	
22-Jun	at Chicago,W,11–4	37–23	1	tied	CROWDER (10–4)	
23-Jun	at Chicago,W,7–3	38–23	1	0.5	THOMAS (4–6)	Manush (1)
24-Jun	at Chicago,W,7–5	39–23	1	0.5	STEWART (5–5)	Bluege (5)
25-Jun	at Cleveland,W,9–0	40–23	1	1.5	WHITEHILL (9–5)	
25-Jun	at Cleveland,W,10–1	41–23	1	1.5	BURKE (1–0)	
26-Jun	at Cleveland,W,4–3	42–23	1	2	CROWDER (11–4)	Kuhel (6)
27-Jun	at Cleveland,L,6–7	42–24	1	1	McAffe (3–1)	
28-Jun	at Cleveland,W,15–2	43–24	1	1	STEWART (5–2)	Manush (2)
29-Jun	at Detroit,L,4–5	43–25	1	tied	Burke (0–1)	Kuhel (7)
30-Jun	at Detroit,W,2–1	44–25	1	1	CROWDER (12–4)	
1-Jul	at Detroit,W,11–3	45–25	1	0.5	THOMAS (5–6)	Cronin (3)
4-Jul	at New York,W,6–5 (10)	46–25	1	1.5	RUSSELL (5–0)	
4-Jul	at New York,W,3–2	47–25	1	2.5	STEWART (7–5)	
	All-Star Break					
8-Jul	vs.Cleveland,W,6–2	48–25	1	4.5	CROWDER (13–4)	
8-Jul	vs.Cleveland,W,5–4	49–25	1	4.5	RUSSELL (6–0)	
9-Jul	vs.Cleveland,W,3–2	50–25	1	4	THOMAS (6–6)	
10-Jul	vs.Cleveland,L,2–3 (12)	50–26	1	3	McAffe (3–2)	
11-Jul	vs.Chicago,L,3–9	50–27	1	2	Crowder (13–5)	
12-Jul	vs.Chicago,W,4–1	51–27	1	2	WHITEHILL (10–5)	
13-Jul	vs.Chicago,L,6–9	51–28	1	1	Russell (6–1)	
14-Jul	vs.Chicago,L,0–4	51–29	1	tied	Crowder (13–6)	
15-Jul	vs.St.Louis,W,1–0	52–29	1	0.5	STEWART (8–5)	
15-Jul	vs.St.Louis,W,2–0	53–29	1	0.5	BURKE (2–1)	
16-Jul	vs.St.Louis,L,0–7	53–30	1	tied	Whitehill (10–6)	
18-Jul	vs.St.Louis,L,3–4	53–31	2	-1	Russell (6–2)	Goslin (7)
19-Jul	vs.St.Louis,W,8–7	54–31	1	tied	THOMAS (7–6)	
20-Jul	vs.Detroit,L,0–1	54–32	1	tied	Crowder (13–7)	
21-Jul	vs.Detroit,W,7–1	55–32	1	tied	WHITEHILL (11–6)	
22-Jul	vs.Detroit,W,4–3	56–32	1	1	RUSSELL (7–2)	
23-Jul	vs.Detroit,L,8–12	56–33	2	-0.5	Thomas (7–7)	
24-Jul	at Philadelphia,W,5–2	57–33	1	0.5	BURKE (3–1)	
24-Jul	at Philadelphia,W,10–6	58–33	1	0.5	CROWDER (14–7)	
25-Jul	at Philadelphia,W,5–1 (5 innings)	59–33	1	1	WHITEHILL (12–6)	
27-Jul	vs.New York, W,3–2 (10)	60–33	1	2	RUSSELL (8–2)	

Date	Opponent	Record	Place	Games Back or in Front	WINNING/ Losing Pitcher (Record)	Home Runs (Number on Season)
29-Jul	vs.New York,W,11–5	61–33	1	3	CROWDER (15–7)	
30-Jul	vs.New York,L,2–7	61–34	1	2	Russell (8–3)	Kuhel (8)
31-Jul	vs.New York,L,9–13	61–35	1	1	Stewart (8–6)	Harris 2 (3 & 4)
2-Aug	vs.Boston,W,2–1	62–35	1	2	CROWDER (16–7)	
3-Aug	vs.Boston,W,8–4	63–35	1	3	WHITEHILL (13–6)	
5-Aug	vs.Boston,W,3–2	64–35	1	4	WEAVER (5–3)	
6-Aug	vs.Philadelphia,L,8–12	64–36	1	3	Russell (8–4)	
7-Aug	at New York,L,5–6	64–37	1	2	Russell (8–5)	
7-Aug	at New York,L,5–6	64–38	1	1	Crowder (16–8)	
8-Aug	at New York,W,5–1	65–38	1	2	WHITEHILL (14–6)	Myer (4) Manush (3)
9-Aug	at New York,W,4–1	66–38	1	3	WEAVER (6–3)	
10-Aug	at Boston,W,5–3	67–38	1	3.5	CROWDER (17–8)	
11-Aug	at Boston,W,8–4	68–38	1	4	Crowder (18–8)	
12-Aug	at Boston,W,2–1	69–38	1	4.5	Whitehill (15–6)	Bluege (6)
13-Aug	vs.New York,W,4–3	70–38	1	5.5	Stewart (9–6)	
15-Aug	at Chicago,W,5–1	71–38	1	5.5	Crowder (19–8)	
16-Aug	at Chicago,W,5–1	72–38	1	6.5	Whitehill (16–6)	Cronin (4)
17-Aug	at Chicago,W,14–1	73–38	1	7.5	Weaver (7–3)	Berg (2)
18-Aug	at Chicago,W,6–4 (10)	74–38	1	7.5	Russell (9–5)	
19-Aug	at St.Louis,W,5–3	75–38	1	8.5	Crowder (20–8)	Manush (4)
20-Aug	at St.Louis,W,2–1	76–38	1	8.5	Whitehill (17–6)	
20-Aug	at St.Louis,W,4–3	77–38	1	8.5	STEWART (10–6)	
22-Aug	at Detroit,L,8–10	77–39	1	7.5	Crowder (20–9)	
23-Aug	at Detroit,L,1–2	77–40	1	8	Crowder (20–10)	
23-Aug	at Detroit,W,9–5	78–40	1	8	STEWART (11–6)	
24-Aug	at Detroit,W,13–6	79–40	1	8	RUSSELL (10–5)	Goslin 2 (8 & 9)
25-Aug	at Detroit,W,5–4	80–40	1	9	BURKE (4–1)	Kuhel (9)
26-Aug	at Cleveland,L,4–5 (11)	80–41	1	8	Crowder (20–11)	Schulte (4)
27-Aug	at Cleveland,W,14–1	81–41	1	8	WHITEHILL (18–6)	
27-Aug	at Cleveland,L,3–6	81–42	1	8	Crowder (20–12)	Rice (1)
29-Aug	at Cleveland,W,2–1 (10)	82–42	1	8	STEWART (12–6)	
29-Aug	at Cleveland,L,2–7	82–43	1	8	Burke (4–2)	
1-Sep	at Philadelphia,L,3–12	82–44	1	8.5	Whitehill (18–7)	Cronin (5)
2-Sep	at Philadelphia,L,3–7	82–45	1	8	Russell (10–6)	
2-Sep	at Philadelphia,W,8–4	83–45	1	8	CROWDER (21–12)	Kuhel (10)
3-Sep	vs.Boston,W,3–2	84–45	1	8.5	WEAVER (8–3)	
5-Sep	at Boston,W,5–4	85–45	1	9.5	RUSSELL (11–6)	
5-Sep	at Boston,W,9–6	86–45	1	9.5	WHITEHILL (19–7)	Schulte (5)
6-Sep	vs.Chicago,W,3–1	87–45	1	9.5	MCCOLL (1–0)	
7-Sep	vs.Chicago,L,0–1	87–46	1	8.5	Weaver (8–4)	
8-Sep	vs.Chicago,W,11–2	88–46	1	8.5	CROWDER (22–12)	
9-Sep	vs.Chicago,W,3–2 (11)	89–46	1	9	WHITEHILL (20–7)	
10-Sep	vs.Cleveland,W,7–3	90–46	1	8.5	STEWART (13–6)	
11-Sep	vs.Cleveland,W,5–1	91–46	1	9.5	WEAVER (9–4)	
12-Sep	vs.Cleveland,L,1–3	91–47	1	8.5	Crowder (22–13)	
14-Sep	vs.Detroit,W,4–3	92–47	1	9	WHITEHILL (21–7)	
16-Sep	vs.Detroit,W,11–2	93–47	1	10	STEWART (14–6)	Goslin (10) Kuhel (11)
16-Sep	vs.Detroit,W,4–3 (10)	94–47	1	10	CROWDER (23–13)	
17-Sep	vs.Detroit,W,4–3	95–47	1	9.5	RUSSELL (12–6)	
18-Sep	vs.St,Louis,L,2–4	95–48	1	9	Burke (4–3)	
19-Sep	vs.St.Louis,L,0–4	95–49	1	7.5	Whitehill (21–8)	
20-Sep	vs.St.Louis,W,13–5	96–49	1	7.5	CROWDER (24–13)	
21-Sep	vs.St.Louis,W,2–1	97–49	1	8	STEWART (15–6)	
23-Sep	vs.Philadelphia,L,1–3	97–50	1	7	Weaver (9–5)	
24-Sep	vs.Philadelphia,L,4–11	97–51	1	7	Crowder (24–14)	
28-Sep	at New York,L,9–11	97–52	1	6	Crowder (24–15)	
29-Sep	at New York,W,8–5	98–52	1	7	WHITEHILL (22–8)	Manush (5)
30-Sep	at New York,W,11–2	99–52	1	8	WEAVER (10–5)	
1-Oct	vs.Philadelphia,L,0–3 (12)	99–53	1	7	Prim (0–1)	

APPENDIX 2:
1933 SENATORS STATISTICS

Batters	Games	At Bats	Runs	Hits	Doubles	Triples	Home Runs	RBI	Batting Average
Joe Kuhel	153	602	89	194	34	10	11	107	.322
Buddy Myer	131	530	95	160	29	15	4	61	.302
Joe Cronin	152	602	89	186	45	11	5	118	.309
Ossie Bluege	140	501	63	131	14	0	6	71	.261
Goose Goslin	132	549	97	163	35	10	10	64	.297
Fred Schulte	144	550	98	162	30	7	5	87	.295
Heinie Manush	153	658	115	221	32	17	5	95	.336
Luke Sewell	141	474	64	125	30	4	2	61	.264
Dave Harris	82	177	33	46	9	2	5	38	.260
Sam Rice	73	85	19	25	4	3	1	12	.294
Cliff Bolton	33	39	4	16	1	1	0	6	.391
Cecil Travis	18	43	7	13	1	0	0	2	.302
Moe Berg	40	65	8	12	3	0	2	9	.185
Bob Boken	55	133	19	37	5	2	3	26	.278
John Kerr	28	40	5	8	0	0	0	0	.200
Nick Altrock	1	1	0	0	0	0	0	0	.000
Totals	153	5524	850	1586	281	86	60-2	793	.287

Pitchers	W-L	ERA	Saves	Innings Pitched	Hits	Walks	Strikeouts	Shutouts
General Crowder	24-15[1]	3.97	4	**299**	**311**	81	110	0
Earl Whitehill	22-8	3.33	1	270	271	100	96	2
Lefty Stewart	15-6	3.82	0	231	227	60	69	1
Monte Weaver	10-5	3.26	0	152	147	53	45	1
Jack Russell	12-6	2.69	**13**	124	119	32	28	0
Tommy Thomas	7-7	4.8	3	135	149	49	35	0
Bobby Burke	4-3	3.23	0	64	64	31	28	1
Bill McAffe	3-2	6.52	5	53	64	21	14	0
Ed Linke	1-0	5.06	0	16	15	11	6	0
Alex McColl	1-0	2.65	0	17	13	7	5	0
Ed Chapman	0-0	8	0	9	10	0	4	0
Ray Prim	0-1	3.21	0	14	13	2	6	0
Totals	99-53	3.82	26	1390	1415	452	447	5

Bold Indicates League Leader
1. tied for league lead

APPENDIX 3:
1933 WORLD SERIES STATISTICS

New York	*At Bats*	*Runs*	*Hits*	*Home Runs*	*RBI*	*Batting Average*
Bill Terry	22	3	6	1	1	.273
Hughie Critz	22	2	3	0	0	.136
Blondy Ryan	18	0	5	0	1	.278
Travis Jackson	18	3	4	0	2	.222
Mel Ott	18	3	7	2	4	.389
Kiddo Davis	19	1	7	0	0	.368
Jo-Jo Moore	22	1	5	0	1	.227
Gus Mancuso	17	2	2	0	2	.118
Lefty O'Doul	1	1	1	0	2	1.000
Homer Peel	2	0	1	0	0	.500
Carl Hubbell	7	0	2	0	0	.286
Hal Schumacher	7	0	2	0	3	.286
Fred Fitzsimmons	2	0	1	0	0	.500
Dolph Luque	1	0	1	0	0	1.000
Totals	176	16	47	3	16	.267

	W-L	*ERA*	*Innings Pitched*	*Hits*	*Walks*	*Strikeouts*
Carl Hubbell	2-0	0.00	20	13	6	15
Hal Schumacher	1-0	2.45	14.2	13	5	3
Fred Fitzsimmons	0-1	5.14	7	9	0	1
Dolph Luque	1-0	0.00	4.1	2	2	5
Hi Bell	0-0	0.00	1	0	0	0
Totals	4-1	1.52	47	37	13	24

Washington	*At Bats*	*Runs*	*Hits*	*Home Runs*	*RBI*	*Batting Average*
Joe Kuhel	20	1	3	0	1	.150
Buddy Myer	20	2	6	0	2	.300
Joe Cronin	22	1	7	0	2	.318
Ossie Bluege	16	1	2	0	0	.125
Goose Goslin	20	2	5	1	1	.250
Fred Schulte	21	1	7	1	4	.333
Heinie Manush	18	2	2	0	0	.111
Luke Sewell	17	1	3	0	1	.176
Dave Harris	2	0	0	0	0	.000
Cliff Bolton	2	0	0	0	0	.000
Sam Rice	1	0	1	0	0	1.000
Lefty Stewart	1	0	0	0	0	.000
General Crowder	4	0	1	0	0	.250
Earl Whitehill	3	0	0	0	0	.000
Monte Weaver	4	0	0	0	0	.000

Washington	At Bats	Runs	Hits	Home Runs	RBI	Batting Average
Jack Russell	2	0	0	0	0	.000
Totals	173	11	37	2	11	.214

	W-L	ERA	Innings Pitched	Hits	Walks	Strikeouts
Left Stewart	0-1	9.00	2	6	0	0
General Crowder	0-1	7.36	11	16	5	7
Earl Whitehill	1-0	.000	9	5	2	2
Monte Weaver	0-1	1.74	10.1	11	4	3
Jack Russell	0-1	0.87	10.1	8	0	7
Tommy Thomas	0-0	0.00	1.1	1	0	2
Alex Mccoll	0-0	0.00	2	0	0	0
Total	1-4	2.74	46	47	11	21

CHAPTER NOTES

Prologue

— Nats win flag by nosing out Browns, 2–1: *Washington Post,* September 22, 1933.

— "Heartiest congratulations to you and all members of your team on winning the American League": *Washington Times,* September 23, 1933.

— "Congratulations. You are a great boy, Joe": *Ibid.*

— "Congratulations on clinching the Pennant": *Washington Herald,* September 23, 1933.

— "When the news arrived, the city celebrated": *Washington Herald,* September 23, 1933.

— "Congratulations, Joe. I will be pulling hard for you in the World Series": *Washington Herald,* September 23, 1933.

— "Keep the World Series in San Francisco": *Washington Evening Star,* September 23, 1933.

— "Are you going to beat the Giants, Joe?" *Washington Post,* September 23, 1933.

— "Did I say that?" *Ibid.*

Chapter 1

— "When Clark Griffith hired Joe Cronin": *Washington Post,* October 27, 1934. "The Big Show": *Washington Post,* February 22, 1933.

— "But look here, Joe. I thought a manager had to be tough with the boys": *Ibid.*

— "Griffith's Folly": *Washington Post,* February 11, 1933.

— He would ask Al Simmons or Lou Gehrig what kind of pitch they hit: Clipping from the Joe Cronin player file at the A. Bartlett Giamatti Research Center.

— "Joe's going to make a few errors and is going to fail at bat at times": *Washington Post,* January 16, 1933.

— "I have no doubt Joe Cronin will prove successful as the new manager of the Washington club": *Washington Herald,* March 21, 1933.

— "Joe is an outstanding student": *Washington Post,* October 10, 1932.

— "We ought to get Goslin back": *Washington Post,* April 15, 1931.

— "What's the matter, pop?": *Washington Evening Star,* March 7, 1933.

— "Nothing now, Goose": *Ibid.*

— "It looks natural to see Goslin back in a Senators uniform": *New York Times,* March 9, 1933.

— "Sure I'm happy to be back": *Washington Evening Star,* March 30, 1933.

— "For nine years I have been with a losing club": *Washington Herald,* March 6, 1933.

— "To be with a winning club for a change will be a treat": *Ibid.*

— "I'm glad to get with Washington": *Washington Post,* February 23, 1933.

— "I expect to have a better year than I did with the Browns": *Washington Evening Star,* March 21, 1933.

— "I hope I could stay with the team long enough to make the trip to Philadelphia": *Washington Post,* March 31, 1933.

— Sewell's drawl being thick enough to make mud pies: *Washington Post,* February 25, 1933.

— "It should have everything": *Washington Post* March 1, 1933.

— "I always did like to play center field in Washington": *Washington Herald,* March 7, 1933.

— Schulte's value of $100,000: *Ibid.*

— "I felt a responsibility every time I stepped up to the plate, every time I went after a fly": *Washington Post,* February 18, 1933.

— "I never saw Schulte work so hard": *Washington Post,* March 24, 1933.

— "Did you bat fourth last year?": *Washington Post,* March 2, 1933.

— "No one is going to oust me this season": *Washington Herald,* March 8, 1933.

— "Better than Brooks Robinson": Walter Langford, *Legends of Baseball* (South Bend, IN: Diamond Communications, 1987), p. 141.

— "I've been throwing the wrong way for two years": *Washington Evening Star,* March 5, 1933.

—"I'll be up here someday, anyhow": *Washington Post*, March 1, 1933.

—"Frankenstein": *Washington Post*, March 17, 1933.

— Boken purchased for $12,000: *Ibid.*

— Best second baseman in the American League: *Washington Post*, March 8, 1933.

—"Incidentally, watch out for Joe Kuhel this year": *Washington Post*, March 4, 1933.

—"In Japan, 45,000 kids play the game": *Washington Evening Star*, March 1, 1933.

—"A pinch hitter bows to the catcher, umpire, and pitcher": *Ibid.*

—"Just think—chopsticks": *Washington Post*, February 28, 1933.

—"And then again the old sap of ambition starts to run up and down your muscles with greater speed when you have a pennant hanging over you": *Washington Post*, March 2, 1933.

—"You know, I'm a ballplayer first, manager second": *Washington Evening Star*, March 1, 1933.

—"Jo-Jo": *Washington Post*, April 5, 1933.

— Family squabble with Cronin and Schacht: Al Schacht, *My Own Particular Screwball* (Garden City, NJ: Doubleday, 1955), p. 192.

— The other businessman, Al Capone, would get a cut of the gate receipts: *Washington Post*, April 1, 1933.

— Al Capone, inmate #40886: *Chicago Tribune*, May 5, 1932.

—"The Yankees can't be any better than in 1932": *Washington Evening Star*, April 6, 1933.

—"If we could get a break with the Yankees": *Ibid.*

—"In the first three innings I was watching closely": *Washington Post*, May 10, 1931.

—"Boy, am I glad I don't have to bat against Whitehill this year": *Washington Herald*, March 8, 1933.

—"Those scores were close enough for me to have taken the Yanks": *Washington Evening Star*, March 6, 1933.

—"I could beat Gomez any time we meet": *Washington Herald*, March 6, 1933.

—"Our club won 107 games last season": *Washington Evening Star*, March 11, 1933.

—"Playing managers like Bucky Harris": *Washington Post*, April 3, 1933.

—"[T]hose Yankees should be twenty-five games in front": *Washington Post*, January 13, 1933.

—"If that isn't rank disloyalty then Benedict Arnold led the thirteen colonies": *Washington Post,* January 21, 1933.

Chapter 2

—"What an old fox you are": *Washington Herald*, May 19, 1933.

— Name changed from "Senators" to "Na-tionals": Marc Okkonen, *Baseball Uniforms of the 20th Century* (Lewisville, TX: Sterling Publications Company, Inc., 1991), p. 85.

— Griffith mortgaged his ranch for $27,000: *Washington Post*, October 28, 1955.

—"First in war": Hank W. Thomas, *Walter Johnson* (Washington, DC: Phenom Press, 1995), p. 33.

— Griffith once saddled a horse for Jesse James: *Washington Post*, October 28, 1955.

—"[F]irst honesty lesson in baseball": Clipping from Clark Griffith's file at the A. Bartlett Giamatti Research Center.

— Griffith would cut the baseball with his cleats: Mike Sowell, *July 2, 1903* (New York: Macmillan Publishing Company, 1992), p. 18.

—"Amos Rusie was faster": *Washington Post*, October 28, 1955.

—"What are you going to do? Pray or something?": *Washington Herald*, May 19, 1933.

—"Western League" to "American League": Sowell, p. 9.

— Griffith served on the board of Protective Association of Professional Players: *Ibid*, p. 17.

—"[H]e was the pitcher the American League said he was": *Washington Post*, January 30, 1933.

— He was personally responsible for the loss: Thomas, p. 101.

—"Well, I may have won the game 1–0, but don't let that fool you": Lawrence S. Ritter, *The Glory of their Times* (Woodstock, VT: Macmillan Publishing Company, 1966), p. 151.

—$16,000 a year, and he also received a signing bonus: Tom Murray, *Sport Magazine's All-Time Stars* (New York: Signet Books, 1977), p. 206.

— Fred Clarke's visit to Johnson in Kansas: *Ibid.*

— Already spent the $10,000 signing bonus: *Ibid.*

— Comiskey paid Mack $50,000 for Eddie Collins: *Ibid.*

— Legend of the nickname "The Big Train": Thomas, p. 140.

—"We want Johnson!": Murray, p. 212.

— The ball hit the ground in foul territory with a "plop": *Washington Post*, October 11, 1924.

—"Speech ... Speech": *New York Times*, October 11, 1924.

—"I'm too happy to speak right now": *Ibid.*

Chapter 3

—"Keep swinging, Joe": *Kansas City Star*, May 23, 1928.

— Wasn't bashful predicting it to his friends: Al Hirschberg, *From Sandlots to League President* (New York: Julian Messner, Inc., 1962), p. 22.

—"How would you like to help me, Joe?": Hirschberg, p. 20.

—"What are these for?": Hirschberg, p. 21.

—$7.50 per game; negotiated his payment to $12.50: Dick Dew, "Cronin Story." Joe Cronin player file at the A. Bartlett Giamatti Research Center.

—$200 bonus: *Ibid.*

—"Say, who is this kid with the do or die look on his face?": *Washington Post*, February 12, 1933.

—"This kid, Bartell, is a cinch to land a big league job": *Pittsburgh Press*, February 28, 1928.

—Bush reiterated to that press that he was not impressed with Cronin: *Pittsburgh Press*, March 17, 1928.

—Number 17: *Kansas City Star*, May 6, 1928.

—He would rather be in the minors and play every day: *Kansas City Star*, April 4, 1928.

—"Five hundred fans who should have their heads examined": *Chicago Tribune*, April 8, 1928.

—"Cronin will prove to be one of the fielding sensations": *Kansas City Star*, April 12, 1928.

—"But could he hit?": *Ibid.*

—"He looks like real class the way he gobbles up grounders": *Ibid.*

—Easier than that of the lower-level Western League: *Kansas City Star*, May 5, 1928.

—"Kuhel looks like a good find to me": *Kansas City Star*, May 22, 1928.

Chapter 4

—"Griff groaned a few times and mumbled something to the effect": *Washington Post*, August 23, 1931.

—"Worn to a frazzle": *Washington Post*, June 30, 1928.

—"Caddy": *Washington Post*, June 23, 1928.

—Reeves had lost 13½ pounds: *Washington Post*: June 20, 1928.

—"How much did you pay for him?": Clipping from the Joe Engel player file at the A. Bartlett Giamatti Research Center.

—Telegram sent by Joe Engel to Mildred Robertson: Murray, p. 66.

—"He goes to his left and right equally well": *Washington Evening Star*, July 20, 1928.

—"Cronin fielded his position well today": *Washington Post*, July, 20, 1928.

—"He was not reported as being particularly strong on the attack": *Washington Post*, July 23, 1928.

—"His uniform has been too small for him": *Washington Post*, July 21, 1928.

—"Keep Reeves in the line-up. He'll never be a Ball Player if you don't": Hirschberg, p. 55.

—"Curve him! Curve the Busher!": Clipping from the Joe Cronin Player File at the A. Bartlett Giamatti Research Center.

—$100,000 contract: *Washington Post*, August 5, 1928.

—"I consider my position at stake": *Washington Post*, July 19, 1928.

—Evans wrote a check for $125,000: *Washington Post*, November 18, 1928.

—"What I want is a bunch of fast, peppy, hard-hitting youngsters": *Washington Post*, July 12, 1928.

—Bill "Bull" Guthrie: *Sporting News*, March 15, 1950. Clipping from the Bill Guthrie umpire file at the A. Bartlett Giamatti Research Center.

—"Dese-Dem-Dose": *Ibid.*

—"It's either dis or dat": *Washington Post*, June 3, 1928.

—Joe Judge warned him Manush might think he was yellow: Ritter, p. 254.

—"Why, those pitches weren't even close": *Ibid.*, p. 255.

—"Listen, wise guy, there's no such thing as close or not close": *Ibid.*

—"OK, are you ready to bat now?": *Ibid.*

—"This kid is a natural fielder": *Washington Post*, September 20, 1928.

—"Reeves is a diamond in the rough": *Washington Post*, August 12, 1928.

Chapter 5

—"I don't mind saying that Joe made a big hit with me": *Washington Post*, August 26, 1929.

—"Well, boys, I'm through": *Washington Post*, October 3, 1928.

—"I never knew Walter well": *Washington Post*, January 1, 1929.

—He said the injury took a lot out of him: *Washington Post*, August 3, 1927.

—"The Red Sox seem to value Myer as highly as the Yankees do of [sic] Babe Ruth": *Washington Post*, December 9, 1928.

—"I'd be willing to part with both Reeves and Cronin": *Washington Post*, December 13, 1928.

—Bluege replied he was OK with the change, and assured them his knee would be fine: *Washington Post*, April 1, 1929.

—Who would he rather have, Cronin or Reeves?: Bob Addie, "The last time Washington won the World Series," *Washington Post*. Joe Cronin player files at the A. Bartlett Giamatti Research Center.

—"The third baseman who was not deemed as big league caliber and traded to the Red Sox in 1927": *Washington Post*, December 17, 1928.

—"We pulled one over on the Old Fox": *Washington Herald*, December 17, 1928.

—"How much bonus do I get?": Bud Montet, "Random shots." Buddy Myer player file at the A. Bartlett Giamatti Research Center.

—$25,000 and sent two players to New

Orleans for Myer: *Washington Evening Star*, August 26, 1925.
— "I'm delighted to be back": *Washington Herald*, March 5, 1929.
— "You are to report to the Red Sox in Philadelphia": *Washington Herald*, May 3, 1927.
— "Naturally I am delighted to return as a regular": *Washington Herald*, March 5, 1929.
— "Which club got the better deal?": *Ibid.*
— "Understand I do not consider myself superior to the players traded": *Ibid.*
— "This kid is going to give someone a terrible argument": *Washington Herald*, March 6, 1929.
— "He's a fine personality in addition": *Ibid.*
— "He really has a good baseball future in my opinion": *Washington Post*, April 3, 1929.
— Ed "Strangler" Lewis: *Washington Post*, April 6, 1929.
— Judge talked about Goslin's arm: *Washington Post*, March 11, 1929.
— "Gosh, what a team we're going to have this year": *Washington Post*, March 23, 1929.
— "He may now almost be called a slugger": *Washington Post*, December 15, 1929.
— "I know Joe is a good fielder": *Washington Post*, August 26, 1929.
— "Myer's hitting ability has never been questioned": *Washington Post*, July 24, 1929.
— Goslin blamed the background at Griffith Stadium: *Washington Evening Star*, July 2, 1929.
— "Indifferent play": *Washington Evening Star*, July 22, 1926.
— "Every time I 'bust' one for four bags": *Washington Evening Star*, March 9, 1926.
— "Your failure to follow signaled orders will cost you one hundred dollars": *Washington Post*, July 18, 1929.
— "I want it to make it as strong as possible": *Washington Post*, July 18, 1929.
— "Buddy is showing up so well in his new berth that I do not believe Bucky Harris will be missed": *Washington Post*, August 18, 1929.

Chapter 6

— "This kid Cronin at shortstop makes a big difference": *New York Times*, May 27, 1930.
— $6,000 salary reduction: *Washington Post*, March 9, 1930.
— "Mr. Biloxi": Interview with Murella Powers, Biloxi, Mississippi, historian, October 2, 2004.
— "The field is a whole lot better than most major league playing fields": *Washington Post*, February 28, 1930.
— "Chain store": *Chicago Tribune*, December 15, 1933.
— $650,000 sale price: *Washington Post*, June 5, 1929.

— "I'm tickled to death": *Washington Post*, April 3, 1930.
— "Hayes is as good a second baseman as I have seen, bar none": *Washington Post*, March 12, 1930.
— "If he could hit, then there is a possibility he could become our starting shortstop": *Ibid.*
— "I don't like your attitude": *Washington Post*, April 17, 1930.
— "Things this season will be entirely different, and I do not intend on taking anything off of my players": *Washington Post*, April 18, 1930.
— "Probable pennant": *Washington Post*, April 28, 1930.
— "The team that beats the Nationals will win the pennant": *Ibid.*
— "How come?": *Washington Post*, May 28, 1930.
— "We are simply getting good hitting, good pitching, good fielding": *Ibid.*
— "We ought to win [the pennant] and the Yankees are good for second": *New York Times*, May 27, 1930.
— "If he hits like years past then it makes for a lot of trouble": *Ibid.*
— "Does this mean Washington will win the pennant?": *Washington Post*, June 5, 1930
— "Go on to your own clubhouse": "Goslin last to hear he has been traded," *Washington Post*, June 15, 1930.
— "They weren't kidding me, were they?": *Ibid.*
— "I am very pleased with the deal": *Washington Evening Star*, June 15, 1930.
— "How about Crowder?": *Ibid.*
— "Don't count Crowder as on his way out": *Ibid.*
— "I don't consider Goose as through": *Washington Herald*, June 15, 1930.
— "Gee, I hate to leave Washington": *Washington Times*, July 15, 1930.
— "The trade is likely to make a hero out of me": "Manager sees pennant with new punch," *Washington Post*, July 15, 1930.
— "Great ... I will perform well enough to prevent Washington from regretting the trade": *Washington Herald*, July 15, 1930.
— "Back to the old Capital": *Washington Evening Star*, June 15, 1930.
— "Outrage ... A crime ... The most ridiculous trade ever made in baseball": *Washington Post*, June 16, 1930.
— "Standing Room Only": *Washington Post*, July 5, 1930.
— 33,900: *Washington Evening Star*, July 5, 1930.
— "I believe Washington's infield is twice as tight as the Athletics'": *Washington Post*, July 10, 1930.
— "We're going to win the pennant as sure as I'm a foot high": *Washington Post*, July 12, 1930.

—"Come on, Heinie": *Washington Herald*, July 22, 1930.

—"A good psychological effect on his pitchers": *Washington Post*, July 9, 1930.

—"Braxton was always warmed up as a relief man": William B. Mead, *Two Spectacular Seasons* (New York: Macmillan Publishing Company, 1990), p. 40.

—"The addition of Manush assures them of the pennant": *Washington Post*, July 10, 1930.

—112 degrees in Sikeston, Missouri: *Chicago Tribune*, July 21, 1930.

—104 and 114 degrees: *Washington Post*, July 21, 1930.

—106 degrees: *Washington Post*, July 21, 1930.

—Both Walter and Griffith suggested she put the car on the train and travel with the team: Thomas, p. 316.

—"You either learn to hit lefties and become the full time center fielder": *Washington Post*, July 28, 1930.

—"I'm here to lead your team out of its slump": *Washington Post*, July 31, 1930.

—Spoke up about sweeping the Yankees as a tribute to Hazel: *Washington Post*, August 2, 1930.

—Asking how this could happen: Murray, p. 216.

—"[A]nd second guess 'em": *Washington Post*, August 15, 1930.

—"Oh, the Pres' isn't home": Clipping from the Joe Cronin player files at the A. Bartlett Giamatti Library.

—"Umpire McGowan then showed why arbitrators are referred to as blind men": *Washington Post*, August 25, 1930.

—"Easily the greatest play seen here in years": *Washington Post*, September 2, 1930.

—He shouted at the Washington hurler. Marberry resented Simmons's comments and shouted back: *Washington Post*, September 8, 1930.

—"I am more than satisfied with our showing this season": *Washington Post*, September 20, 1930.

—"The only difference is one is sewed with red and black thread, the other in black and blue thread": Washington Post, June 12, 1930.

—"When a player unexpectedly has a good year": *Washington Post*, September 21, 1930.

Chapter 7

—"I wanted Cronin for my Braves but the Judge": *Washington Evening Star*, March 9, 1931.

—"If the A's and Yankees don't uncover some good pitchers": *Washington Post*, March 2, 1931.

—"I am a stranger to the American League and can't predict where they will finish": *Washington Post*, April, 12, 1931.

—"Thank you, Colonel Huston": *Washington Post*, October 15, 1930.

—"I hope so too, Mr. McCarthy. And the name is Colonel Ruppert": *Ibid*.

—"It is not necessary for me to say that I will do everything possible": *Chicago Tribune*, May 28, 1931.

—"I believe that bird could still win in our league if he decided to make a comeback": *Washington Post*, March 4, 1931.

—Marberry replied in anger, Johnson got mad: *Washington Post*, March 7, 1931.

—"Jackie is a better cook than she is a pitcher, and I've never tasted her cooking": *Washington Post*, April 5, 1931.

—"Wait until the Athletics have to play double-headers": *Washington Post*, May 28, 1931.

—"We're not playing half as well as we can, and we better snap out of it right away": *Washington Post*, May 9, 1931.

—"[L]ike cellar champs at worst": *Ibid*.

—$65,000: *Washington Post*, July 29, 1930.

—$50,000: *Ibid*.

—"I'm going on record right now to say that Kuhel is here to stay": *Washington Post*, August 21, 1930.

—"Standing Room Only": *Washington Post*, July 14, 1931.

—"There's too big a crowd out here for us to start anything, but I'll be seeing yuh": *Washington Post*, August 1, 1931.

—"That's OK with me": *Ibid*.

—"I told Marberry to put on his uniform tomorrow": *Washington Post*, September 16, 1931.

—"Cut loose": *Washington Post*, August 10, 1931.

—"I'm too nervous to talk": *Washington Post*, August, 9, 1931.

—"Burke didn't throw more than a half dozen curves all afternoon": *Ibid*.

—In other words, everything was wrong with the Nationals in 1931: *Washington Post*, August 30, 1931.

Chapter 8

—"The day before Roy Johnson knocked Dickey down": *Washington Post*, July 8, 1932.

—"He'll win twenty for us": *Washington Post*, March 30, 1932.

—"He knows how to pitch": *Washington Post*, March 21, 1932.

—"Weaver is the finished product": *Washington Post*, April 5, 1932.

—"The average mentality of the Washington ball club was hiked several degrees": Nicholas Dawidoff, *The Catcher Was a Spy* (New York: Pantheon Books, 1994), p. 72.

—"Don't worry, you have a pretty good catcher sitting on the bench": *Washington Post*, June 29, 1961.

—"The funny part of it is I wasn't thinking about myself": *Washington Post*, March 14, 1932.

—"OK, Berg, get in there": *Washington Post*, June 29, 1961.

—$3,000: *Washington Post*, June 9, 1932.

—"Well, well, well. Keep up the good work until the Browns knock you off": *Washington Post*, May 3, 1932.

—"[L]ack of mental toughness": *Washington Post*, June 9, 1932.

— Myer replied and Johnson responded: *Washington Post*, May 30, 1932.

—"That double loss makes me want to go back to the farm": *Washington Post*, June 14, 1932.

—"Why don't you put your mask back on?": *Washington Evening Star*, July 5, 1932.

—"The only regret I have is I didn't get to hit Dickey back": *Washington Herald*, July 5, 1932.

—"At least you're a fair hotel clerk!": *Ibid.*

—"[M]alicious and unwarranted": *Washington Herald*, July 6, 1932.

—"You've got to take a lot on the field today and like it": *Washington Evening Star*, July 6, 1932.

—"That was no fight. It was an assault and you could quote me": *Washington Post*, July 10, 1932.

—"[D]usting them off" and throwing the "bean ball": *Washington Post*, July 10, 1932

—"So far as I'm concerned, it is all over": *Washington Post*, July 11, 1932.

—"We'll have to make the best of it": *Ibid.*

—"Why stop at 3,500?": *Washington Post*, July 20, 1932.

—$2,235: *Ibid.*

— In his letter Harridge wrote: *Washington Post*, July 17, 1932.

—100,000: *Washington Post*, June 7, 1932.

—"Come on, boys, let's call an armistice for lunch anyhow": *Washington Evening Star*, July 29, 1932.

—"To hell with Hoover!": *Chicago Tribune*, July 29, 1932.

—"Get the hell out of here!": *Ibid.*

—"It's gas": *Ibid.*

— MacArthur issued controversial orders to have Camp Marks evacuated: *Washington Herald*, July 29, 1932.

—"We'll be back next winter": *Chicago Tribune*, July 29, 1932.

—"Yes, and not so peaceful next time": *Ibid.*

—"[D]angerously close": *Washington Post*, August 14, 1932.

—"Ask Reynolds": *Ibid.*

—"Ask Dickey": *Ibid.*

—"Gomez made Reynolds look as foolish with three hooks as Dickey did with one": *New York Herald-Tribune*, August 15, 1932.

—"Al, I'm going to have to do something

soon which I've been hoping to avoid": Schacht, pp. 195–196.

—"Joe, have you ever thought about managing some day?": Schacht, p. 196

—"I am likely to ruin a great shortstop": *Ibid.*

—11,561 fans— *Washington Post*, August 16, 1932.

—"Say, Bucky, are we going to have any signals today?": *Washington Post*, August 16, 1932.

—"I don't want to hurt myself bending over for a grounder": *Ibid.*

—"Aw, give him time": *Washington Post*, July 15, 1932.

Chapter 9

—"Boy, what a victory": *Chicago Tribune*, October 3, 1932.

—"My hat is off to you, Mac": *Ibid.*

—"I'm the happiest man in the world": *Ibid.*

—"The Sidewalks of New York": *Ibid.*

— Words to "The Sidewalks of New York": *New York Times*, October 28, 1928.

—"Walter Johnson will not manage in 1933. We have yet to pick a successor": *Chicago Tribune*, October 5, 1932.

—"I haven't even given the matter a thought": *Washington Post*, October 5, 1932.

—"I like these young fellows who fight for everything": Gene Schoor, *The History of the World Series* (Scranton, PA: William Morrow and Company, Inc., 1990), p. 147.

—"I had ambitions to be a manager, but never had any idea I would have a chance so soon": *Washington Post*, October 10, 1932.

—"You have a lot of constructing to do before you win that first pennant, young fella": Bob Addie, "The last time Washington won a World Series," *Washington Post*. Joe Cronin Player file at the A. Bartlett Giamatti Research Center.

—"To win the pennant, we have to beat the Yankees": Shirley Povich, *The Washington Senators: An Informal History* (New York: G.P. Putnam's Sons, 1954), p. 177.

—"If you don't trade, you'll fall behind": *Chicago Tribune*, December 15, 1932.

—$20,000: Bob Addie, "The last time Washington won the World Series," *Washington Post*. Joe Cronin player file at the A. Bartlett Giamatti Research Center.

—"I'll tell you what, Phil": *Ibid.*

Chapter 10

—"Pros It!": *Washington Post*, April 7, 1933.

—"Happy Days Are Here Again": *Washington Post*, April 3, 1933.

—"Here's to you — President Roosevelt — The Nation's first real beer is yours": *Washington Post*, April 7, 1933.

—"Will beer be sold at your ballparks?": *Philadelphia Inquirer,* April 7, 1933.

—$20 per uniform: *Washington Post,* February 14, 1933.

—"Hail to the Chief": *Washington Post,* April 13, 1933.

—23,359: *Ibid.*

—"Hold it, hold it, hold it": *Washington Herald,* April 13, 1933.

—"If any of you photographers get killed, don't say I didn't warn you": *Ibid.*

—"Great stuff, Joe. Keep it up": *Washington Evening Star,* April 13, 1933.

—"He called me over": *Washington Herald,* April 13, 1933.

—"Gosh, if I could have only been there": *Ibid.*

—"Well, Tom, how's tricks?": *Ibid.*

—"Come on, Goose!": *Washington Herald,* April 14, 1933.

—"You'll find Pa down in the potato patch": *Washington Herald,* April 10, 1933.

—"While I have not followed the game closely since what is sometimes called my 'retirement' I believe the Yankees will repeat": *Ibid.*

—"This year's Nats team is the better of the two teams": *Ibid.*

—"The pitching staff shores up to be one of the best Washington has ever had": *Ibid.*

—"The infield stacks up all right, although I've been unable to draw an accurate line on Kuhel": *Ibid.*

—"Cronin? A capable player and managerial material": *Ibid.*

—"Bosh! All bosh": *Washington Post,* April 20, 1933.

—"Hey Goose, what are we going to do with the Yankees?": *Washington Herald,* April 23, 1933.

—"I could beat Gomez anytime we meet": *Washington Herald,* March 6, 1933.

—"[L]ike he had been pole axed": *Washington Post,* April 24, 1933.

—"[A]t a snail's pace": *Washington Post,* April 25, 1933.

—"Howzit, Dave?": *Ibid.*

—"[T]old him what he thought of his glorious ancestors": *Ibid.*

Chapter 11

—"I'll step on Chapman's face the next time he slides into second base!": *Washington Herald,* April 27, 1933.

—"[H]e would wreak vengeance immediately": *Washington Evening Star,* April 27, 1933.

—"You're yellow! That's right, you are yellow!": *Washington Post,* April 28, 1933.

—"Don't let Tony Lazzeri get in there, he'll kill somebody!": *Philadelphia Inquirer,* April 27, 1933.

—"I didn't realize I was supposed to be such a tough guy": *Ibid.*

—"I'm going to throw you in jail!": *Washington Evening Star,* April, 27, 1933.

—"All right, but take me to the clubhouse so I can change my clothes": *Ibid.*

—"My cold was too bad to mix in anything like that these days": *Washington Evening Star,* April 27, 1933.

—"What's a fellow supposed to do? Take it every day?": *Philadelphia Inquirer,* April 27, 1933.

—"Yeah, I'll talk to them": *Washington Herald,* April 26, 1933.

—"I'm not hurt": *Washington Post,* April 26, 1933.

—"I had a right to the bag and I went in": *Washington Herald,* April 26, 1933.

—"Well, Earl Whitehill got up and said something I didn't like": *Washington Herald,* April 26, 1933.

—"He socked me and I socked him": *Ibid.*

—"I'm not making any report to you guys": *Ibid.*

—"[T]he roughest base runner in the American League": *Washington Evening Star,* April 28, 1933.

—"There is such a thing as legally interfering with an attempted double play": *Washington Herald,* April 26, 1933.

—"If it hadn't been for Whitehill, there wouldn't have been anything to it but the row at second base": *Washington Evening Star,* April 27, 1933.

—"Hello, Buddy, how is it you got away so early from the game today?": *Washington Herald,* April 26, 1933.

—"I got into an argument with one of those punk umpires": *Ibid.*

—"It was a clear case of provocation": *Washington Evening Star,* April 26, 1933.

—"I'd like to punch that guy on the schnoz": *Ibid.*

—"One of these days Chapman is going to be trapped in a rundown": *Washington Post,* April 26, 1933.

—"They gave me this lump here on the back of my head": *Philadelphia Inquirer,* April 27, 1933.

—"What a roomie. He belted those guys around like nobody's business": *Ibid.*

—"What would you do if I, a trained athlete, called you the name Whitehill called me?": *Washington Herald,* April 28, 1933.

—"I'm gonna tell my fellows": *Boston Globe,* April 27, 1933.

—"The cocky kid from Chicago": *Washington Post,* April 28, 1933.

—Myer went into detail with Harridge: *Washington Post,* April 29, 1933.

—Chapman's wife filed for separation: *Washington Post,* May 12, 1933.

—"It didn't look to me as if the spiking was intentional": *Washington Times*, April 29, 1933.

—"With the facts evening themselves out": *Washington Post*, April 29, 1933

—"The president of the league has made his decision": *Washington Evening Star*, April 30, 1933.

—"Chapman should've been suspended for a total amount of days equal to the amount given to Whitehill and Myer": *Washington Herald*, April 29, 1933.

—"If the umpires said in their report to Mr. Harridge that Chapman didn't go out of his way": *Ibid.*

Chapter 12

—"The greatest play I've ever seen": *Washington Post*, May 2, 1933.

—"[F]ive o'clock lightning": Gordon H. Fleming, *Murderers' Row* (New York: Wm. Morrow and Company, 1985), p. 12.

— 34,455 fans: *Washington Herald*, April 30, 1933.

—"[T]hat is seen only once in a lifetime": "Weaver goes route as double play in 9th halts uprising," *Washington Post*, April 30, 1933.

—"It was a swell job by Goslin and Cronin": "Greatest yes, says Griffith on double play by Sewell," *Washington Post*, April 30, 1933.

—"It's two outs, Monte": Fred R. Sammis, *This Great Game* (New York: Rutledge/Prentice Hall Inc., 1971), p. 157.

—"We'll get you next time, you __": "Weaver goes route as double play in 9th halts uprising," *Washington Post*, April 30, 1933.

—"Myer and Whitehill marked for a ride. Watch your step in New York Friday": *Washington Post*, April 30, 1933.

—"[A] lifeless body lying on the dirt of Briggs Field": *Washington Post*, May 7, 1933.

—"One of them asked if his skull was the thickest to ever be X-rayed": *Washington Post*, May 8, 1933.

—"I'm bearing down on you guys, and I don't mean maybe": *Washington Herald*, May 8, 1933.

—"Hoover sent the army, Roosevelt sent his wife": Paul Dickson and Thomas B Allen, *The Bonus Army: An American Epic* (New York: Walker & Company, 2006), p. 216.

—"[E]ating too much good food": *Biloxi Daily Herald*, March 29, 1931.

—"The little bugger can hit anything": *Washington Herald*, June 1, 1933.

Chapter 13

—"I am here to tell you that Joe Cronin is piloting the best-looking club I have seen in the majors in several years": *Washington Post*, June 27, 1933.

—"It will not change in a day or month or even a season": *New York Times*, February 27, 1933.

—"I refused because I have not the money to stay in Boston baseball": "McManus holds post as leader of Boston Hose," *Philadelphia Inquirer*, February 27, 1933.

—"A month ago, I had no idea I would be leaving the Athletics and Connie Mack": *Ibid.*

—"No owners wish to stand in the way of a good baseball man": "Ed Rommel may succeed Collins as Mack's aide," *Philadelphia Inquirer*, February 27, 1933.

—"We'll catch them before we leave St. Louis": *Washington Post*, June 15, 1933.

—"You know, this idea might work after all": Langford, p. 135.

—"Gentlemen, I believe Satan's joined the team and I'm confident he's inside my uniform": Louis Kaufman, Barbara Fitzgerald, and Tom Sewell, *Moe Berg: Athlete, Scholar, Spy* (Boston: Little, Brown and Company, 1974), p. 77.

—"The Old Washington Wrecking Crew": *Washington Post*, June 18, 1933.

—"Game of the Century": Robert Obojski, *All-Star Baseball Since 1933* (New York: Stein and Day Publishers), p. 1.

—"That's swell. It is a great spot for Walter out there with these pitchers the Indians have": *Washington Post*, June 10, 1933.

—"I am certainly glad he landed": *Ibid.*

—"I love the game": *Cleveland Plain Dealer*, June 10, 1933.

—"Poor Walter": *Washington Herald*, June 26, 1933.

—"How about lending me a few hitters, Joe?": *Washington Post*, June 26, 1933.

—His answer was the Yankees, and he said the A's would finish second: *Washington Herald*, June 25, 1933.

—"Say, Joe, have lunch with me today": *Washington Herald*, June 28, 1933.

—"Baltimore": *Washington Herald*, June 29, 1933.

—"Ball four, take your base": *Washington Herald*, June 28, 1933.

—Fined $250: *Washington Post*, June 29, 1933.

—"Hell's bells. The Cleveland team ought to be fined, not McAfee": *Washington Herald*, June 29, 1933.

—"But Baltimore is no credit to the genus of baseball fans": *Ibid.*

—"Well, I was telling our batboy, Jimmy Mahorney, this morning, to keep those bats hot": *Washington Post*, July 4, 1933.

—$100 fine: *Chicago Tribune*, July 5, 1933.

—77,365: *New York Times*, July 5, 1933.

—"[A] case for St. Elizabeth's": *Washington Post*, July 5, 1933.
—Reminded Mahorney to keep those bats hot: *Washington Post*, July 7, 1933.
—"Welcome 1933. The New Deal year. Good Luck": *Washington Post*, July 5, 1933.

Chapter 14

—"This is the long-awaited dream day": *Chicago Tribune*, July 6, 1933.
—Al Simmons of the White Sox received the most: *Chicago Tribune*, June 25, 1933.
—Gomez became $250 richer: *Washington Post*, September 18, 1931.
—"That old boy certainly came through when they needed him": *Chicago Tribune*, July 7, 1933.
—"Did you have a good trip?": *Washington Herald*, July 8, 1933.
—"It was one of the greatest experiences I had in baseball": *Ibid.*
—"Did you bring your bat back?": *Washington Post*, July 8, 1933.
—"I used one of Foxx's bats. It had a lot of hits in them": *Ibid.*
—28,000 fans: *Washington Post*, July 9, 1933.
—"Cronin has the boys playing heads-up baseball": *Washington Post*, July 10, 1933.
—"The breaks helped Washington in 1924": *Ibid.*
—"Washington patrons are never kind with their remarks": *Chicago Tribune*, July 15, 1933.
—"This is getting serious": *Washington Post*, July 14, 1933.
—"[Y]ou begin to view us with alarm. That is no way to treat our ball club": *Washington Post*, July, 15, 1933.
—"It's too bad Ruth had to go out there [to Chicago] and bust a home run": *Washington Post*, July 11, 1933.
—"Ty! ...Ty! ... Ty!": *Chicago Tribune*, July 13, 1933.
—"The Yankees have the best team in the league": *Chicago Tribune*, July 18, 1933.
—"If they can beat Washington in half of the twelve games": *Washington Post*, July 18, 1933.
—"I did not think that old fellow would ever be worth another trial": *Washington Post*, July 18, 1933.
—"We laughed about the way he used to beat us when he was with the Indians": *Ibid.*
—"While we are winning our correspondence falls out": *Washington Post*, July 23, 1933.
—"[I]t's spring training when they get the real 'beauties'": *Ibid.*
—"He's got the best sinker in the Big Leagues today": *Washington Herald*, July 7, 1933.

Chapter 15

—"If the Yankees have any serious intention on winning that pennant": *Washington Herald*, August 7, 1933.
—"That will cost you $100": *Washington Post*, August 2, 1933.
—"It would take quite a spell before I comply to this!": *Washington Post*, August 3, 1933.
—"The National League reminded me of the minors": *Washington Post*, August 3, 1933.
—"I am playing for McManus": *Washington Post*, August 5, 1933.
—The temperature was a "comfortable" eighty-five: *New York Times*, July 29, 1933.
—He was jeered by Washington's die-hard black fans, who occupied the right field pavilion next to the Senators' bullpen: Brad Snyder, *Beyond the Shadows of the Senators* (Blacklick, OH: McGraw-Hill Companies, 2003), p. 78.
—"You have to take a lot on the field and learn to take it": *Washington Evening Star*, July 5, 1932.
—"I did not want to get thrown out of the game": *Washington Post*, August 8, 1933.

Chapter 16

—"Ever since we were kids we dreamed about playing in the World Series": *Washington Post*, August 22, 1933.
—"Pennant? What's that?": *Washington Post*, March 12, 1933.
—"[O]ne of the hardest hits I had ever seen": *Washington Post*, August 9, 1933.
—"I sure wish they had moving pictures back then": *New York Times*, August 10, 1933.
—"We're going to win today": *Ibid.*
—Toppled onto the field: Donald Honig, *Baseball in the '30s* (New York: Crown, 1989), p. 73.
—"He was the most talked about of the ballplayers": *Washington Post*, August 11, 1933.
—"[T]hat did more to discourage the Yanks": *Ibid.*
—"Say, Buddy, we sure could've bought a lot of gasoline": *Biloxi Daily Herald*, February 28, 1934.
—"Hey Joe, how many games are the Nats going to win the pennant by?": *Washington Post*, August 16, 1933.
—"I'd rather play the Senators any day": *Washington Post*, August 17, 1933.
—"Why, the nerve of that guy!": *Washington Post*, August 17, 1933.
—"We've just bought you": *Washington Post*, August 18, 1933.
—"Don't buy me, Joe": Povich, p. 180.
—"Gee, that's tough": *Washington Post*, August 18, 1933.

— 43,000 at Comiskey Park: *New York Times*, August 21, 1933.

—"Throw something": *Washington Herald*, August 21, 1933.

—"Look at Schacht sitting on the manager's lap again": *Washington Herald*, August 21, 1933.

—"It leads me to fear their thirteen-game winning streak may be laid to rest": *Washington Herald*, August 22, 1933.

—"This guy couldn't hit the ground": *Ibid.*

—"I still say he can't hit": *Ibid.*

—"Didn't I tell you not to bring that up?": "This Morning with Shirley Povich," *Washington Post*, August 23, 1933.

—"When Greenberg hits the ball on the nose it stays hit": *Washington Post*, August 23, 1933.

—"That's twenty-five dollars!": *Washington Post,* August 25, 1933.

—"[B]ound for lake Michigan": *Washington Post*, August 23, 1933.

—"Twenty-five dollars is a bush league fine. Why not make it a hundred and twenty-five?": *Washington Post*, August 25, 1933.

— The barometer fell to 28.94, one of the lowest readings in Washington history: *Washington Post*, August 25, 1933.

— 250 operators were called to duty: *Ibid.*

—"Can we come back?": *Washington Post*, August 26, 1933.

—"The Directors want me to tell you that we are most pleased and happy over your work as manager": *Washington Post*, August 25, 1933.

— Report to the press from the Department of Labor: *Chicago Tribune*, August 17, 1933.

— Five thousand jobs: *Washington Post*, April 8, 1933.

— 244,472 attended the fair: *Chicago Tribune*, September 5, 1933.

— Attendance was 235,325 on Jewish Day: *Chicago Tribune*, August 20, 1933.

— 60,000 came to Municipal Stadium: *Washington Post*, August 20, 1933.

—"It's time to face facts": *Washington Post*, August 31, 1933.

—"Say, where do those fellows get that stuff about me being washed up?": *Chicago Tribune*, September 1, 1933.

Chapter 17

—"I just cried when I heard the news": *Washington Herald*, September 23, 1933.

—"He's a sweet little hitter": *Washington Post*, September 5, 1933.

—"If you get the side out without a run I'll remit that twenty-five dollar fine": *Washington Post*, September 21, 1933.

—"Well, Alex, how would you like to go to the big leagues?": *Chicago Tribune*, September 6, 1933.

—"The sooner this gets over with, the less I'll

worry about it": *Washington Post*, September 11, 1933.

—"We're going to keep on trying to win games through the last game of the season": *Washington Post*, September 13, 1933.

—"The Nats have a great team": *Washington Post*, September 18, 1933.

—"It didn't seem to bother us much": *Washington Post*, September 21, 1933.

—"Gaa-osh": *Washington Herald*, September 22, 1933.

—"[W]ho made it easy for any manager": "Boy Manager besieged in clubhouse," *Washington Post*, September 22, 1933.

—"I hope you beat the Giants and believe that you will": "Nats will take series, says Hornsby," *Washington Post*, September 22, 1933.

—"I'm for the Nats and wish 'em all the luck in the world": *Ibid.*

— Increase the stadium's capacity to 35,743: *Washington Post*, September 13, 1933.

— World Series ticket prices in Washington: *Washington Post*, September 10, 1933.

—"Gee, I must be in the wrong league": *New York Times*, September 26, 1933.

—"That ball's not going to make a difference": *Washington Post*, September 26, 1933.

—"If that helped the Giants' pitchers, it's going to help our pitchers, too": *Ibid.*

—"It would surprise me if they do": *Ibid.*

—"I told my four starters to be ready": *New York Times*, September 26, 1933.

— The Senators held a meeting to decide about splitting the World Series spoils: *Washington Post*, September 27, 1933.

—"That was harder than pitching a regular game": *New York Times*, September 28, 1933.

—"Bring on Hubbell": *Washington Post*, September 28, 1933.

—"That screwball didn't look so tough to us, and Braxton knows how to throw it": *Ibid.*

—"Buddy Myer is getting the ball away faster than any second baseman I have ever seen": *Washington Post*, October 2, 1933.

—"Tough luck, Earl": *Washington Post*, May 12, 1933.

—"I'd give anything if I could make the trip": "Cronin's mother kept from Series," *Washington Post*, September 26, 1933.

—"Everything store": Stevey Myer, phone interview on July 23, 2007.

—"Drop around and see me Tuesday about 1:29. I'll have some news for you": *Washington Post*, October 2, 1933.

—"From now on I'm out and you're in running the Giants": *Washington Post*, September 17, 1933.

—"Win that game today": *Ibid.*

—"They can't stop us": *Washington Post*, September 27, 1933.

—"Wait until you meet Hubbell": *Washington Post*, September 6, 1933.

—"Our pitching is too strong for Washington": "Vergez, of Giants, to root from coast," *Washington Post*, October 3, 1933.

—"The Giants are ready": *Washington Post*, October 3, 1933.

—"Our club is going to the World Series": *Washington Star*, October 3, 1933.

—"Hubbell's not so hot — he's never been up against hitters like we got": *Washington Post*, October 3, 1933.

—"I don't see how the Giants can beat us": *Washington Times*, September 30, 1933.

—"I seen many a pitcher in my career": *Washington Times*, October 28, 1933.

—"Figures may not amount to everything": *Chicago Herald American*, October 2, 1933.

—"When those Giants get down to Griffith": *Washington Herald*, October 3, 1933.

Chapter 18

Game One

—The Hubbell Hubbub and hullabaloo of the last three weeks unfolded itself this afternoon as an awful truth to Washington": "Odds shift as Nats bow to Giants in opener, 4–2," *Washington Post*, October 4, 1933.

—46,672: *New York Times*, October 4, 1933.

—Hubbell during the National Anthem: Langford, p. 50.

—"The boys are not so hot today": *New York Times*, October 4, 1933.

—"Come on you, Schulte": *Ibid.*

—"A homer will do it!": *Ibid.*

—"Yes, Hubbell is a great pitcher": *Chicago Tribune*, October 4, 1933.

—"Crowder will start. And he will win": "Crowder will hurl today for Nats," *Washington Post*, October 4, 1933.

—"Well, we showed 'em a pitcher, boy, and you can tell the world they'll see a lot more of him": *Chicago Tribune*, October 4, 1933.

—"The finest game he ever pitched": *San Francisco Chronicle*, October 4, 1933.

—"They're great all right": *Ibid.*

Game Two

—College boys who hummed a funeral march: *Washington Post*, October 5, 1933.

Game Three

—"It'll be different in Washington": *New York Times*, October 5, 1933.

—"Yeah, it'll be different. When we beat Whitehill for a change": *Ibid.*

—"I hope all of you are as ashamed as I am": Povich, p. 183.

—25,727 fans: *New York Times*, October 6, 1933.

—"Can I please pitch today?": Bob Addie, "The last time Washington won a World Series," *Washington Post*. Joe Cronin player file at the A. Bartlett Giamatti Research Center.

—"That is plain lucky": *Washington Herald*, October 6, 1933.

—"Where's the ball?": "Roosevelt enjoys contest in Capital," *New York Times*, October 6, 1933.

—"All right, here it goes": *Ibid.*

—"[A] hair-raising catch": "Story of the game told play by play," *New York Times*, October 6, 1933.

—"Roosevelt luck": "Roosevelt enjoys contest in Capital," *New York Times*, October 6, 1933.

—"Well, it's a grand old game": *Ibid.*

—"Whitehill pitched a marvelous game, and we got hits when we needed them": "Cronin confident, lauds new spirit," *New York Times*, October 6, 1933.

—"I'll start Weaver tomorrow and see if we can't get even with them": *Ibid.*

—"I had a couple chances myself to stick in a hit that would've counted, but it was Whitehill's day": *Washington Evening Star*, October 6, 1933.

—"I'm the happiest man in Iowa — Dad": *The Cedar Rapids Gazette*, October 6, 1933.

Game Four

—"In 1920, during the presidential campaign, I walked into the lobby and found the crowd": "Roosevelt tells a Babe Ruth story," *New York Times*, October 7, 1933.

—"I find I can get more speed on the ball, but nothing much in the way of 'stuff'": *Washington Herald*, October 7, 1933.

—26,762 fans: *New York Times*, October 7, 1933

—"You're outta here!": *Washington Post*, October 7, 1933.

—"And you're out of the game": *Chicago Tribune*, October 6, 1933.

—"I'm leading off this inning and I'm going to get on somehow": Langford, p. 94.

—"Strike him out, Monte!": *Washington Post*, October 7, 1933.

—But when he told a player to get in there, the player shook like a leaf: Langford, p. 95.

—"[P]ebble": *Chicago Tribune*, October 7, 1933.

—"If he hits the ball to me, we'll get a double play": "Ryan, Critz, draw Terry's acclaim," *New York Times*, October 7, 1933.

—"[B]ut not too far": *Ibid.*

—"Make him hit it to me, Hub, I'll get him": *New York Herald-Tribune*, October 7, 1933.

—"Bill, I played with this bird down south. He's awful slow": *Washington Times*, October 7, 1933.

—"Gus, let's give him plenty of dipsydoos": *Ibid.*

—"I can't look. I can't look": *Washington Post*, October 7, 1933.

Game Five

—"Ground rule double!": John Devaney and Burt Goldblatt, *The World Series* (Chicago: Rand McNally, 1981), p. 141.

—"You boys are certainly great": *Washington Post*, October 8, 1933.

Chapter 19

—"Goose, if you were hitting today": *Washington Post*, August 10, 1959.

—"Yeah, I hit that ball good": *Washington Evening Star*, August 18, 1948.

—"Griff, you son of a gun": "Old time greats bring joy to Griffith on his 'Night,'" *Washington Post*, August 18, 1948.

—"Boy, this is great": *Ibid.*

—"I wouldn't have missed this for anything in the world": *Washington Evening Star*, August 18, 1948.

—"Clark Griffith Night": *Washington Post*, August 17, 1948.

—"My, what I'd give to have these boys in their prime": *Washington Evening Star*, August 18, 1948.

—"That's too bad. The poor fellow just couldn't make it": *Washington Post*, August 17, 1948.

—"What a man he was": *Washington Herald*, August 18, 1948.

—Tom Yawkey paid $150,000 for pitchers Lefty Grove and Wes Ferrell: *Washington Post*, April 15, 1934.

—"My second choice, Joe Cronin, is just as hard to get": *Washington Post*, October 27, 1934.

—"We don't need any, if we get just an even break in injuries": *San Francisco Chronicle*, October 23, 1934.

—"The price is enormous, Joe": *San Francisco Chronicle*, October 27, 1933.

—Yawkey offered $225,000 and a shortstop: Dawidoff, p. 98.

—"I'm naturally glad. It is the greatest spot in baseball today": *San Francisco Chronicle*, October 27, 1934.

—"I regret to leave Clark Griffith; he's been so nice to me": *Washington Times*, October 27, 1933.

—"But you have to expect anything in baseball": *San Francisco Chronicle*, October 27, 1933.

—"We were not dissatisfied with Harris": *Washington Post*, October 27, 1934.

—"Baseball makes strange teammates": *Washington Post*, June 16, 1936.

—"It's OK with me": *Washington Herald*, June 17, 1936.

—"[E]verybody believed that I was anti-something or other": *Ibid.*

—The Washington second baseman displayed his Southern hospitality by being very cordial: *Washington Herald*, June 17, 1936.

—"I wasn't hard on Jackie Robinson": Bill Legg, Executive Director of the Alabama Sports Hall of Fame, phone interview on September 20, 2007.

—Jewish great-great-great-grandfather: Stevey Myer, phone interview on April 28, 2008.

—"It certainly suits me": *Washington Post*, April 6, 1937.

—"No ballplayer of mine can conduct himself in such a manner": *Washington Post*, October 3, 1938.

—"And I don't agree with people who say a fan is entitled to call a player any name he thinks": *Washington Herald*, October 3, 1938.

—"If he was a woman, I would have married him": Buddy Lewis, personal letter to author, dated September 21, 2007.

—"I've been working out with the American Legion Junior baseball team and I'm in fairly good shape": *Washington Herald-Times*, August 18, 1948.

—"Just one more winner, just one more and my life is complete": *Washington Evening Star*, August 18, 1948.

—Crowd of twenty-four thousand: *Washington Post*, August 18, 1948.

—"You even let the Washington Senators beat you": *Washington Herald-Times*, August 18, 1948.

—"What a relief pitcher he was": *Washington Post*, August 18, 1948.

—"Keep hustling": Clipping from the Luke Sewell Player file, at the A. Bartlett Giamatti Research Center.

—Dave Harris wore badge number 650 for the Atlanta police force: *Washington Post*, April 10, 1938.

—"Aren't you Moe from the Three Stooges?": Dan Gutman, *Baseball Babylon* (New York: Penguin Books, 1992), p. 314.

—"All meats I serve are Big League top prime only": Menu from Al Schacht's restaurant.

—"What did they do, throw in a bag of peanuts to get me?": Schacht, p. 211.

—24,000 packed his 16,000-seat stadium: Clipping from the Joe Engel Player file at the A. Bartlett Giamatti Research Center.

—"He was a very kind-hearted man": Cy Yoakman, "She struck out Babe Ruth," *Sports Heritage*. Jackie Mitchell player file at the A. Bartlett Giamatti Research Center.

—The Senators made money: *Washington Post*, October 14, 1933.

—"You started with me eighteen years ago": Ritter, p. 261.

—"He was more than a father to me, that man": *Ibid.*

—"Myer was one if the finest drag bunters to ever play": Bill Werber and C. Paul Rogers III, *Memories of a Ballplayer* (Cleveland, OH: Society for American Baseball Research, 2001), p. 39.

— New York offered Griffith $200,000: *Washington Post*, March 12, 1939.

—"Certainly I would like to get Buddy Myer": *Ibid.*

—"Buddy Myer and I had a good laugh about our fracas the next time we saw each other": Werber and Rogers III, pp. 40–41.

—"I don't know whether you girls have seen any of the bad comments about your Dad": Thomas, p. 324.

—"Johnson was a good manager": Langford, p. 70.

—"I still think Walter Johnson is a pretty good fellow": *Washington Post*, July 20, 1934.

—"[I]t often took forever to get into the stadium, because he never brushed off an autograph request": Carolyn Thomas, personal interview on October 22, 2007.

—"When they pulled a doctor aside and asked why, they were informed that Griffith was paying for everything": Henry W. Thomas, personal interview on September 27, 2004.

— 817 members of the Bonus Army, employed under Roosevelt's New Deal, were sent to the Florida Keys in 1935 to build bridges: *Washington Post*, September 8, 1935.

—144 bodies of veterans had been found, and 320 were reported missing: *Ibid.*

—"[A]mple notice of the danger and approach of the hurricane was given": *Ibid.*

— Senate voted 77–19 in favor: *Washington Post*, January 28, 1938.

—"As long as we have men of the spirit of Clark Griffith, this country will not fail": "President helps honor Nat Owner," *Washington Post*, August 18, 1948.

—"I am going to request that everyone in the audience to sit down as I talk": *Washington Herald-Times*, August 18, 1933.

—"It's a privilege to be here tonight when we are honoring a hero who deserves everything he's got": *Ibid.*

—"I want to pay tribute to another baseball great, Babe Ruth": *Ibid.*

—12,000 fans came to Griffith Stadium to see Babe Ruth: *Washington Post*, October 1, 1934.

—"It is with great satisfaction that I receive this from the fans in Washington": *Ibid.*

—"All of you saw those great stars of other years a few minutes before": *Washington Herald-Times*, August 18, 1948.

—"Look, I don't know how many games you fellows see now, but you saw one tonight": *Washington Evening Star*, August 19, 1948.

—"Thanks, pal": *Ibid.*

—"You could go back to Abner Doubleday or Alexander Cartwright, but the first thing in pitching is to get a piece of that plate": *Ibid.*

—"And it's a roughhouse league": *Ibid.*

—"They're asking for $65,000, some of them": *Ibid.*

BIBLIOGRAPHY

Dawidoff, Nicholas. *The Catcher Was a Spy*. New York: Pantheon Books, 1994.

Devaney, John, and Burt Goldblatt. *The World Series*. Chicago: Rand McNally, 1981.

Dickson, Paul, and Thomas B. Allen. *The Bonus Army: An American Epic*. New York: Walker, 2006.

Eig, Jonathan. *Opening Day*. New York: Simon & Shuster, 2007.

Fleming, Gordon H. *Murderers' Row*. New York: William Morrow, 1985.

Gutman, Dan. *Baseball Babylon*. New York: Penguin Books, 1992.

Hirschberg, Al. *From Sandlots to League President*. New York: Julian Messner, 1962.

Honig, Donald. *Baseball in the '30s* New York: Crown, 1989.

Kaufman, Louis, Barbara Fitzgerald, and Tom Sewell. *Moe Berg: Athlete, Scholar, Spy*. Boston: Little, Brown, 1974.

Kerr, Jon. *Calvin: Baseball's Last Dinosaur*. Madison, WI: Wm. C. Brown, 1990.

Langford, Walter. *Legends of Baseball*. South Bend, IN: Diamond Communications, 1987.

Mead, William B. *Two Spectacular Seasons*. New York: Macmillan, 1990.

Murray, Tom. *Sport Magazine's All-Time All-Stars*. New York: Signet Books, 1977.

Obojski, Robert. *All-Star Baseball Since 1933*. New York: Stein & Day, 1980.

Okkonen, Marc. *Baseball Uniforms of the 20th Century*. Lewisville, TX: Sterling Publications Company, 1991.

Povich, Shirley. *The Washington Senators*. New York: Putnam's, 1954.

Ritter, Lawrence S. *The Glory of Their Times*. Woodstock, VT: Macmillan, 1966.

Sammis, Fred R. *This Great Game*. New York: Rutledge/Prentice Hall, 1971.

Schacht, Al. *My Own Particular Screwball*. Garden City, NJ: Doubleday, 1955.

Schoor, Gene. *The History of the World Series*. Scranton, PA: William Morrow, 1990.

Snyder, Brad. *Beyond the Shadows of the Senators*. Blacklick, OH: McGraw-Hill, 2003.

Sowell, Mike. *July 2, 1903*. New York: Macmillan, 1992.

Thomas, Henry W. *Walter Johnson*. Washington, DC: Phenom Press, 1995.

Werber, Bill, and C. Paul Rogers III. *Memories of a Ballplayer*. Cleveland, OH: Society for American Baseball Research, 2001.

Wright, Marshall D. *The American Association*. Jefferson, NC: McFarland, 1997.

_____. *The International League*. Jefferson, NC: McFarland, 1998.

_____. *The Southern Association in Baseball*. Jefferson, NC: McFarland, 2002.

Internet

www.baseball-almanac.com
www.baseballlibrary.com
www.baseball-reference.com

Interviews

Cronin, Tom — July 14, 2007.
Legg, Bill — September 20, 2007.
Myer, Stevey — July 23, 2007 and April 28, 2008.
Powers, Murella — October 2, 2004.
Thomas, Carolyn — October 22, 2007.
Thomas, Henry W.— September 27, 2004.

Newspapers

Atlanta Journal
Biloxi Daily Herald
Boston Globe
Cedar Rapids Gazette
Chicago Herald American
Chicago Tribune
Kansas City Star
New York Herald-Tribune
New York Times
Philadelphia Inquirer
Pittsburgh Press
San Francisco Chronicle
Washington Evening Star
Washington Herald
Washington Herald-Times
Washington Post
Washington Times

INDEX

Numbers in **bold italics** indicate pages with photographs.

A MURDER OF INNOCENTS

A Christian Legal Thriller: Book Two

MICHAEL SWIGER

Cover design by: 100 Covers
Library of Congress Control Number: 2018675309
Printed in the United States of America

To Bill Wilder,
the world needs more men like you

Critical Acclaim For

A Trial of Innocents

"Michael Swiger tackles late-term abortion, murder charges against a brain-damaged suspect, official corruption involving drug dealing, and the ins and outs of a criminal trial in his first thriller A TRIAL OF INNOCENTS." - *Publishers Weekly*

"This book will leave you exhilarated and shaken, but above all it will make you think." - *Cleveland Connection Magazine*

"A fast-moving novel for readers who like action and suspense with a hint of John Grisham thrown in." - *The Writer's Edge*

"Michael Swiger's A TRIAL OF INNOCENTS is an effort so savvy and well-written, it's hard to believe it's a first novel." - *Upsouth Magazine*

"A TRIAL OF INNOCENTS has suspense, excitement, and even a smidgen of humor and romance." - *Herald-Star*

Nominated for the 2001 Pulitzer Prize for Fiction

Nominated for the Ohioana Book Award

Nominated for the 2001 New Century Writer Award

1

Monday, October 2, 2000
Wheeling, West Virginia
Oglebay Park
5:05 P.M.

A red-headed man, wearing a Cleveland Browns T-shirt, faded jeans and a gray backpack slipped into the employees restroom in an isolated brick building on the grounds of Oglebay Park near the famed Good Zoo. He walked over to the last stall and closed the door. The sterile scent of disinfectant assaulted his nostrils. He sat on the toilet, propped his feet up on the door, and checked his watch. *The security guard should be making his rounds any—*

The door swung open. Thick-soled boots thumped across the tile floor. The footsteps looped around the room and headed out the door. *I've got 20 minutes.*

He unzipped the backpack, pulled out a black jumpsuit and slid it over his clothes. He reached back inside the bag, grabbed a small flashlight and jammed it between his teeth. He thought he heard something and froze. *Nothing.*

He shouldered the pack, stepped on the toilet seat, then climbed onto the tank of the commode. He ripped open the Velcro pocket on his left thigh and snatched out a star-shaped security wrench. He fumbled to insert the tool into a small, plastic opening in the maintenance hatch in the ceiling, while balancing himself on the slippery porcelain tank. The bolt wouldn't budge.

"Damn it."

He grabbed the wrench with both hands and torqued on the bolt. It broke loose with a pop. Rust flakes cascaded down into his eyes. The square, four-tile hatch swung open with a creak. He stashed the bolt and wrench in his thigh pocket. He could hear the sound of approaching footsteps filtering in through the vent in the door.

"He's early."

The intruder adjusted the flashlight in his mouth, reached through the hatch opening with both arms, and jerked himself up into the attic. He then reached down with his left hand, fished his index finger into the hatch hole, and pulled the hatch shut just as the restroom door opened. He held himself perfectly still in a single-arm push-up position, while holding the hatch shut with his left hand. He wrinkled his nose against the musty smell of dust and insulation and fought the urge to sneeze.

The report of the footsteps stopped outside the last stall. Thunderous flatulence erupted directly below the hatch.

"Man, those burritos I had for lunch went through me like Turbolax," the security guard said.

Beads of sweat formed on the intruder's forehead; his pulse pounded in his ears. A disquieting thought occurred to him. The only thing separating him from the security guard was a perspiration-slick index finger in a plastic hole. If the guard looked up to the hatch, he would see the freckled finger jutting out, and the mission would come to an end before it started.

"Sweet fancy Moses," the guard said with a grunt. "That's some nasty stuff."

Come on dude, how about a courtesy flush.

The intruder's mouth went dry from clenching the flashlight between his teeth; his right arm quivered under the strain of supporting his body weight. Drops of sweat rolled down his left arm and into the plastic hole. The hatch slipped open a fraction of an inch.

Flush!

Thank God.

Footsteps headed toward the door. The hatch slipped down to the tip of his finger. The bathroom door slammed shut just as the hatch slipped and swung open. The intruder grabbed the flashlight from his mouth and licked his lips.

"Now that's a bad omen."

He tucked his nose into his shoulder and took a few deep breaths, then shoved his hand into his right front pocket and pulled out a small roll of wire. He reached down with his left hand and closed the maintenance hatch, then secured it with the wire. Shrouded in darkness, he switched on the flashlight and crawled methodically along the air conditioning duct. *If I follow this over two firewalls, I'll be over the target area.*

He snaked along the duct to the second firewall. He took off the backpack, unzipped the front compartment and grabbed a putty knife. Using the tool with the skill of a surgeon, he pried up the corner ceiling tile. The drop ceiling was held in place by a tongue-and-groove interlocking system. Once he removed the first tile, the other three simply slid out with little effort. He carefully stacked the tiles next to the opening.

He opened the large section of the backpack and pulled out a black nylon rope. He tied one end to the water main suspended above the opening, fished the other end down through the opening, then gave the rope a couple of firm tugs. He strapped on the empty backpack, then rappelled down the rope hand-over-hand until his feet touched the concrete floor. *The motion sensors should be focused on the door. Just don't make any sudden moves and everything will be hunky-dory.*

He crept along the rear wall, holding the flashlight against his right cheek, scanning the glass cases as he went.

"There it is," he whispered. "Pay dirt."

2

Tuesday, October 3
Steubenville, Ohio
Jefferson County Courthouse
9:00 A.M.

Danial Solomon sat beside his client at the defense table, drumming his fingertips on a manila folder. He looked over his shoulder at the capacity crowd in the gallery. A television crew and several reporter types lined the back wall.

A big-bellied bailiff wearing a rumpled, tan uniform, stepped into the courtroom from the judge's chamber and yelled, "All rise! Hear ye! Hear ye! Hear ye! This Court is now in session. The Honorable John T. Williams presiding."

The black-robed judge strutted through the door and climbed the three wooden steps to the bench. He clutched the arms of the high-backed chair and let his weight go with a groan. The old chair squeaked in protest.

"Please be seated."

Williams opened the manila file on top of the bench then adjusted the microphone.

"We're here for the purpose of sentencing Mr. Archie Kisner for his involvement in the August 4th burglary and assault on Mrs. Dorothy Bernhart and the death of her unborn child. Before I pronounce sentence, does the Defense have anything to say?"

"We do, Your Honor," Danial said.

"Very well. The Court will hear your statement."

"Thank you." Danial stood and addressed the bench. "Your Honor, I don't need to reiterate the bizarre nature of this case. When I first heard that someone broke into the Bernhart residence and savagely attacked a pregnant woman and her unborn baby, I felt sick to my stomach. Not a good feeling to have when a lawyer takes a case. And I'll be perfectly honest with you, I thought my client was probably guilty. However, just a few weeks ago in this very room, I discovered, along with everyone else, that everything we believed, everything the media beat into our heads, turned out to be wrong." He looked over his shoulder to the reporters lining the back wall.

"Now, I'll concede my client was illegally in Dorothy Bernhart's home with his brother Ralph. And Ralph's purpose for being there was less than honorable. But the bottom line is, Archie Kisner didn't assault Mrs. Bernhart in any way, shape or form. In fact, he stopped his brother's attack on her. You heard the testimony. Dorothy Bernhart herself said Archie saved her life. He even attempted first aid.

"Though the jury found my client guilty of burglary and assault, the verdict was in before the truth came out. In light of the mitigating circumstances and the late-breaking discoveries in this case, I respectfully ask this Court to throw out the assault conviction and reduce the burglary charge to the lesser included offense of illegal trespassing." Danial walked around behind the defense table and placed his hands on Archie's shoulders.

"My client isn't a threat to society, and a lengthy prison term would only prove debilitating. Therefore, I respectfully urge this Court to suspend my client's sentence and place him on probation. It's the only fair thing to do. Thank you for your time and consideration."

Danial Solomon sat down beside Archie and smiled at him.

"Thank you, Mr. Solomon," Judge Williams said without looking up from his notes. "Does the State have anything to add before I pronounce sentence?"

"Yes, Your Honor," Lori Franks said.

"Very well then, the State may proceed."

"I'll be brief." Lori stood behind the prosecutor's table and straightened her navy-blue skirt. "The State finds itself in the unusual position of agreeing with a great deal of what the Defense has offered. Nevertheless, the State objects to the Court modifying or reducing the jury's verdict, and instead requests leniency be reflected in the sentence. To that end the State recommends the minimum concurrent sentences allowable under law. Furthermore, the State does not oppose releasing the defendant on Judicial Release after he has served the required six months in the custody of the Ohio Department of Rehabilitation and Correction. Thank you, Your Honor."

Lori Franks sat down and glanced over at Danial. The corners of her mouth turned up into a faint smile.

"The defendant will rise for sentencing," Williams said in his deepest, most authoritative voice.

Archie Kisner stood ramrod straight to his full 6 feet 4 inches. He wore an orange smock, orange pants and orange slippers. Heavy shackles bit into his thick ankles. His head had been shaved following his conviction three weeks prior. The brown stubble did little to cover a jagged scar. It meandered along the crown of his head where it hooked sharply, slashed down his forehead and cut through an eyebrow. The flesh next to the scar sunk down a bit giving his head a lopsided appearance.

Danial stood and placed an arm around Archie's back, and whispered encouragement.

"There's no way we should get anything more than a few years. And with a little Providential blessing you could be eating dinner at my house tonight."

Archie smiled.

Judge Williams cleared his throat and read from a prepared statement written on a yellow legal pad. His hands trembled as he read.

"Having carefully considered the remarks just given by the Defense and the State and having further considered all the circumstances involved with the case, it is the ruling of this Court to uphold the jury's guilty verdict in both convictions. That being said I hereby sentence the defendant, Archie Kisner, for the crime of Aggravated Assault to serve a period of no less than 10 years and no more than 25 years in the custody of the Ohio Department of Rehabilitation and Correction."

Danial's jaw dropped.

"And for the crime of Aggravated Burglary, I hereby sentence the defendant to serve an additional period of no less than 10 years and no more than 25 years. The terms shall be served consecutively with no chance for parole until 20 actual years have been served." Williams slammed his ornate wooden gavel to the bench. "Court is adjourned."

A stunned silence filled the room.

"Your Honor!" Danial shouted. "I move for reconsideration."

Williams ignored him.

"The State concurs," Lori said.

Williams lumbered down the steps without looking back. He disappeared into his chambers and slammed the door shut behind him.

Downtown Steubenville
9:15 A.M.

Dr. Gaston Garvey sped his jet-black Lexus off Market Street into the parking lot in front of the Century School of Cosmetology. He slid to a stop next to a white Dodge minivan. He looked at himself in the rearview mirror. A bloodstained piece of toilet paper stuck to his Adam's apple, and a few dribbles of coffee dotted his freshly pressed, white shirt.

He climbed out of the car, as the minivan's side door slid open.

"It's about time," Dr. Gamble said.

"I forgot we changed the meeting spot."

"It was your idea."

"Don't start with me, Ed. This hasn't been a good morning."

Garvey climbed in and took a seat behind the driver. Two middle-aged doctors sat in the rear bench seat.

Dr. Gamble slid the door shut and said, "You look like death warmed over."

"I was up later than expected."

"Medical emergency?" Dr. Boone asked from the back seat.

"Bridge game."

They nodded heads while the security guard put the van in gear and pulled out into traffic. Five minutes later they arrived near the rear entrance to University Hospital and weaved through a mob of protesters. A group of students from the university carried bloodstained placards and jeered as the van pressed by. A small group prayed silently while holding hands. Another group wearing matching T-shirts with the slogan "Give Life a Chance" was huddled up on the left side of the road holding white candles.

"I'm glad this thing's got tinted windows," Dr. Pella said.

The van reached a string of Steubenville police officers enforcing the protest-free zone at the rear entrance.

Thwack!

Something smashed against the rear window. The projectile hit with such force the window splintered and showered the doctors with glass particles. The driver mashed the accelerator. They sped toward the ambulance entrance and screeched to a halt in front of the Emergency Room doors.

Garvey jogged around the rear of the van with the security guard to discover the remains of an enormous egg splattered across the rear window. What appeared to be the largest baby bird carcass he had ever seen... laid aborted and mangled and dead on the black pavement.

9:24 A.M.

Ian McKinney stood in front of a big, steel garbage dumpster admiring his handiwork plastered against the back of the van.

"Hey, you'd better beat it, man!" a male voice from the crowd shouted. "The cops saw you throw that thing."

"I wanted them to."

He spun around and tossed a red and white Playmate cooler into the dumpster.

"They're coming this way, dude," another voice said. "If you're not going to run, you'd better stick your chest out."

"Getting arrested is part of the plan," Ian said. "By the time this is over everyone will know who I am."

Two uniformed officers pressed through the crowd shouting for everyone to disburse. Ian stepped forward and stretched out his arms, wrists up.

"Go ahead and cuff me."

The officer reached down past the handcuffs dangling from his belt and snatched his nightstick. In one sweeping motion he slammed the wooden cylinder into Ian's ribs with a ghastly thud. Ian collapsed to his knees. The crowd pressed in.

"Get back!" the enraged officer shouted.

The second officer arrived on the scene with a taser in hand. He fired and struck Ian between the shoulder blades. Two metal probes pierced his skin; the electrical surge sent his body into wild convulsions. The two officers waited until the spasms stopped before handcuffing their unconscious prey and dragging him to their squad car, Ian's red hair fluttering in the wind.

The crowd closest to the scene turned and stampeded. In the midst of the chaos, two men dressed in black slipped into an open manhole in the middle of the parking lot. They could hear the muffled squawk of the squad car's siren as they strained to replace the manhole cover.

"I can't believe it!" shouted one man as he descended the wrought-iron ladder. "We're in!"

"Keep it down, bro," the other man whispered. "You're gonna get us busted before we get started."

3

Judge Williams sat behind his mahogany desk with his face in his hands. Loose folds of skin squirted between his fingers. He looked up at the young blond man sitting in the red leather chair across the desk from him.

"I can't believe I just did that."

"Screw him," Colin Casey said with an affected lisp. "He had it coming."

"I don't feel right about this at all. It's the first time I allowed politics to influence a sentence."

"What's the life of one retard compared to this election?"

"I feel sick."

"Look, Your Honor, this case has drawn incredible media attention, national attention - and you had to send a message to the voters of this county that you're tough on crime."

"I don't know..."

"You want to get re-elected, don't you?"

"Of course."

"Then do as I say, and you'll win by a landslide."

"But he won't get out of jail for 20 years."

"I don't mean to put this indelicately, but you've been on the bench for 18 years, and you're getting your butt wiped in the polls by a virtual unknown." Colin crossed his skinny legs and placed an exquisitely manicured hand on his knee. "The boys in Columbus sent me here because we can't afford to lose this seat."

"I know."

"Look at it this way. You're 66 now. If you get re-elected, this will be your last term before the mandatory retirement age. If you play ball now and win us this seat, I could easily see a federal appointment in your future."

"Are you serious?"

"For a good liberal judge like yourself, why not?"

9:46 A.M.

Dr. Gaston Garvey strolled into the operating room like he was walking onto the golf course. A 15-year-old girl lay anesthetized with her feet strapped into the stainless steel stirrups. He took a deep breath through his nose; he loved the smell of antiseptic. He walked over and picked up the chart. "How far along is she?"

"About 32 weeks," Nurse Martine said, looking up from the heart monitor.

"It seems I remember this name. Has she been here before?"

"This is her third abortion in two years," the nurse said. "Most teenagers these days see abortion as just another form of birth control. Tragic."

"Is she ready?"

"Yep," Martine said.

"Time to induce labor. Nurse, the Prostaglandin if you will."

Martine handed Garvey the syringe. He popped off the yellow safety cap and gently depressed the plunger. A small drop of yellow fluid beaded on the end of the needle. He flicked the shaft with his index finger, then grabbed the IV line and injected the port. He handed the empty syringe back to the nurse, then walked to the rear of the room. He motioned for Dr. Garland to join him. They leaned against the pale green wall.

"Now we stand and wait," Garvey said, "it could be hours. Is this your first late-term procedure, kid?"

"Yep."

"Nervous?"

"Yep."

"Don't be, there's nothing to it. You've observed one, haven't you?"

"A couple."

A MURDER OF INNOCENTS

"Good, I'll walk you through it." Garvey pulled down his mask a few inches and scratched his nose. "Too bad they don't allow coffee machines in the operating room. I could sure go for a cup after last night."

"Hey, what was all that commotion about this morning?"

"Couple of protesters got a little rowdy."

"Is that normal?"

"You interns got it sweet. You abort as many babies a week as I do, and no one's threatening to blow up your car."

"I'm not looking forward to my first death threat."

"It's no cup of tea," Garvey said.

"Was anyone hurt this morning?"

"Nothing serious. You play bridge?"

"Never."

"Great game. I played last night."

"Did you win?"

"Are you kidding? I got stomped. My partner's a moron. He bids a four no-trump on the last hand, and we don't have the count to say boo." Garvey shook his head. "Idiot."

"I have no idea what you just said."

"Doctors!" the astonished Nurse Martine said as she approached. "The patient is already dilated to eight centimeters."

"We'll be there in a minute." Garvey stretched out his arms and yawned. "Hey kid, what's 50 feet long and smells like urine?"

"I don't know, what?"

"The conga line at the old folks' home."

They chuckled.

"Let's go, kid."

They walked back to the patient, and Garvey checked the monitors. "Her blood pressure's a little high, but she'll be fine. It'll be a duck shoot."

"Just like a duck shoot," Martine echoed, frowning.

"What do you mean by that?" Garland asked.

"Nothing."

Garvey walked to the foot of the table and sat on the short

surgical stool. He flipped up the patient's gown.

"Forceps."

Martine handed him the instrument. Garvey inserted the forceps and probed around.

"Slippery little bugger. If I didn't know better, I'd say he's avoiding me."

Martine rolled her eyes.

"Ah, there it is." He gave a firm tug. "Okay, Garland, I've got the leg, and the fetus is in the birthing canal. You ready?"

"Yep."

"All right, here you go."

Garvey kept pressure on the forceps and stood up.

Garland slid in place and took the instrument.

"That-a-boy. Now extract the fetus until the feet come out using firm and constant pressure... good... good."

The baby's feet broke out.

"Now what?"

"Hand me the forceps and grab the feet with your hands."

The intern complied.

"Now pull him out to the neck." The legs broke out.

"He's kicking."

"Of course he is, what did you expect?"

"What now?"

"Keep pulling until you can hold the torso in the palm of your hand. Just be careful. If you deliver him all the way you've got to keep him."

"What?"

"Just a little gallows humor."

Nurse Martine shook her head.

Garland continued pulling until the infant's belly laid in the palm of his left hand. Only the head remained in the birth canal.

"Now what?"

Garvey handed him a pair of surgical scissors. "Trace your finger along the spine until you feel the base of the skull and bore yourself a nice little hole with the scissors. The fetus will go limp. Then you suck out the brains, the skull will collapse, and that's that."

"I'm not sure I can do this."

"Sure you can. Now do your job."

Garland traced his finger along the baby boy's spine and found the base of the skull. He firmly gripped the scissors and was about to draw them back when the baby's hand brushed against the index finger on his left hand.

The baby squeezed it.

"I can't do it."

"You've got to be kidding me."

"I'm sorry, sir."

"You have no idea how sorry you're going to be."

"I just can't. He's viable."

"Get the hell out of the way."

Garland stood. Garvey placed his left hand under the baby's torso and supported the weight while Garland slunk out of the way. Garvey jammed the scissors into the child's skull. The baby violently flailed his arms and legs. A stream of thick blood pulsated onto the baby's back.

"Is he supposed to be squirming like that?"

"Shut your trap, Garland, and help me hold him still." The intern reached in.

"Not like that you idiot, keep his head in the canal. Nurse, hand me the vacuum tube."

Gurgling blood oozed out of the wound and covered the baby.

Garvey let go to grab the suction device. The baby kicked with both legs and slipped out of Garland's grasp. The head slipped out of the birth canal. The baby took his first breath then filled the room with a bone-chilling scream.

"You idiot!" Garvey shouted in Garland's face.

"It's not my fault."

Martine lunged forward and pressed her right hand against the wound. Garland rushed toward the console at the head of the table.

"What are you doing?!" Garvey yelled.

"Calling a Code Blue!"

"You will not!"

"But sir—"

"I've got this under control."

"He's losing a lot of blood," Martine said.

"I said I've got this under control."

Garvey snatched the blood-covered baby from Nurse Martine like a rag doll. But it was a baby boy, and he looked at the doctor as if expecting help. He continued squirming, but more slowly. The doctor grabbed the infant by the forehead, twisted the head sharply to the right and snapped its neck.

The crying stopped.

He walked over to the biohazard disposal bin and tossed the lifeless body like yesterday's trash.

"What the hell did you just do?" Garland said.

"The girl and the hospital wanted the fetus terminated, and that's what they got. I solved the problem."

"But his head came out," Martine said. "We're required by law to provide first aid."

"What difference does it make whether the head is six inches inside or outside the vagina?"

"She's right," Garland said. "We'll lose our licenses. We'll go to jail."

"No one's going to jail. The surgical report will say it was a textbook procedure. No one else needs to know."

"We can't do that," Martine said. "We can't."

"We can, and we will," Garvey said. "Both of you are just as responsible as I am."

"No, we're not."

"Look, this is one of those unforeseen glitches that happen from time to time." Garvey pulled off his bloodstained gloves and jerked down his mask. "I did the merciful thing for him and for us. He wouldn't have survived anyway."

"That's it?" Garland asked.

"I don't want to hear about it again. Now get this mess cleaned up."

4

10:20 A.M.

Danial Solomon parked his granite-gray Dodge Charger in the reserved space just outside the two-story Victorian brownstone that housed his law office. He climbed the three concrete steps leading to the front door. Overhead a wooden placard, reading *Danial Solomon, Attorney at Law*, swayed in the gentle morning breeze. He pulled open the door and veered toward the kitchenette near his secretary's desk. He nodded a greeting, poured himself a cup of coffee, and headed for his office.

"I said, how'd sentencing go?"

"I'm sorry, Jennifer, I zoned out there for a minute. What did you say?"

"The sentencing?"

"Archie got 20 years."

"What?!"

"I'm afraid so."

"How is he?"

"Stunned... scared." Danial slumped down in the chair next to her desk. "I feel terrible."

"What're you going to do?"

"Appeal, I guess. But I really don't have a leg to stand on. Williams didn't break the law."

"I can't believe it."

"I've got a friend who might be able to help once Archie gets to the prison reception center." He took a sip of coffee.

"I've got a few phone messages for you. Do you want them now?"

"Sure, why not."

"Steve Foster called, he said you were supposed to probate a will or something?"

"Yeah, yeah. Next."

"Kathy April called; her son's in the Juvenile Detention Center."

"Can't help him. Have her call Luke Young."

"Lori Franks called."

His eyebrows elevated. "What did she want?"

"Said she needed to talk to you, and that she'd call back later."

"Hummm... interesting."

"Poor Archie."

"Yeah, I know. It's heartbreaking." He pushed open the door to his office. "I don't want to be disturbed."

"Gotcha."

He closed the door, kicked off his black loafers and paced across the floor. He watched his gold-tipped, navy-blue socks sink into the plush red carpet with each step. Now that sentencing was over, no official conflict stood between him and Lori Franks. They could date. That is, of course, if she agreed to go out with him. And that was a big *if*.

He mindlessly scanned the wall behind his desk where his bachelor's degree from Ohio University hung next to his Juris Doctorate in International Law from American University.

The next time I see her I'm asking her out.

He wandered past the wall of shelves filled with legal books of every description. He looked out the window. His eyes scanned the traffic racing along Route 7, then settled on a coal barge chugging north on the murky Ohio River.

Someone knocked on the door.

"Jennifer!" he shouted. "I said I didn't want to be disturbed."

The door crept open.

"Yeah, she told me." Lori Franks stuck her head in. "I'm sorry for intruding, but this is kind of important."

"Oh, it's you." He stood a little taller. "Come on in."

Lori pressed open the door and walked in. She appeared to be about 5 foot 2 and looked petite but curvaceous. The morning sun beaming through the window shimmered off her jet-black hair and sparkled in her violet blue eyes. Alabaster skin flowed over her narrow face and elegant neck. With a button nose and full lips, she could have been a supermodel if taller.

Danial held his breath then said, "What can I do for you?"

"There's a couple of things I wanted to discuss with you." She gracefully moved across the floor, then tripped over his shoes. He darted forward and caught her.

"What are your shoes doing over here?"

"Sorry about that." He sheepishly slid his feet into the loafers one at a time. "Please, sit down."

She took a seat in one of the leather chairs in front of his desk. He sat in the chair next to her.

"I want to help," she said.

"With?"

"Mr. Kisner."

"Oh."

"I can't believe Judge Williams threw the book at him like that."

"Probably a little revenge for his buddy Gus Gram getting indicted."

"You *are* going to appeal the sentence?"

"Of course, as much good as that will do."

"What about an appeal bond?"

"Not a chance, especially with Williams up for re-election."

"There must be something that can be done."

"By the way, I noticed your boss wasn't in court today. What gives?"

"I have no idea."

"I can't imagine him missing a free photo-op during an election year."

"Something must've come up."

An awkward silence filled the room for about ten seconds.

"Ms. Franks, is there—"

"Please." She reached over and touched his arm. "Call me Lori."

"All right, Lori, is there anything else on your mind?"

"I really don't know how to say this, so I'm just going to say it." She hugged her elbows. "Remember the other night, after the trial?"

"Yes."

"You know... at The Greenery?"

"Yes," he said with a smile.

"I really appreciate everything you told me about Jesus and salvation and going to Heaven and all, and I want you to know that I took it all to heart. I really did."

"That's great. I'm happy for you. 'The way is narrow that leads to life, and there are few who find it.'"

"I... uh..."

"What is it?" he asked.

"There is something else." She crossed her legs and allowed a shoe to dangle from her toes. "The hug thing."

"I've been giving that some thought myself." *Here's your chance. Ask her now.* "Lori, I would—"

"I hope I didn't give you the wrong impression."

"Wrong impression." His smile deflated. "What do you mean?"

"I didn't want you to think I was throwing myself at you."

"No, not at all."

"It was an emotional night for me."

"I understand completely."

"I always carry myself in a professional manner, and I have a great deal of respect for you professionally."

"Well, thanks."

"I just don't want things to get weird between us."

"Ms. Fra... Lori, consider it already forgotten."

"Thank you." She stood and stretched out her hand. "I knew you'd understand."

They shook hands.

"I've got to get back to the courthouse," she said. "I'll do all I can from my end to have Mr. Kisner's sentence reduced."

"Thanks."

"Sorry again for intruding." She headed for the door.

I'm sorry, too.

10:39 A.M.

Ian McKinney struggled to lift his eyelids; they wouldn't budge. The left side of his face felt cold and wet. He tried to roll off his belly. The muscles in his back and shoulders screamed in pain. He felt as if every inch of his body had been beaten with a baseball bat. He tried again to open his eyes. The lids pried apart. The world lay on its side. A pair of well-worn shoes was inches from his face. The feet were still in them. He flopped onto his side with a groan.

"Where am I?" His words sounded slurred in his own ears.

"Take it easy, my dude," a gravelly voice said. "You'ze all right?"

"I don't know."

"You'ze must be drinking to get that messed up."

"I'm not drunk." He staggered to one knee and took a deep breath. He felt a sharp pinch between his shoulders. "They got me with a taser."

"The laser thing must be one bad boy."

"Taser."

Ian tried to stand. Searing pain sent his body into spasms. He slumped to the floor.

"I think that cop broke my ribs."

"With the laser gun?"

"No, he clubbed me too."

"I didn't think cops beat white folks."

Ian reached for the stainless steel sink and pulled himself up. He examined the tiny cell with its vomit-green walls and rust-stained toilet.

"Sonny Dante." The black man offered his hand.

"McKinney... Ian McKinney." He stretched out his right arm, winced, and recoiled it to his side.

"Looks like they'ze did a number on you."

"They took care of business. I'll give them that."

"Been there, done that."

"I bet."

"Why come they whopped up on you?"

"Protesting down at the hospital."

"Protestin' what?"

"Abortion."

"Was it worth it?"

"I might have saved a life today. And who knows, maybe that kid'll be the next Frederick Douglass or Rosa Parks or Abraham Lincoln."

"Or maybe a garbage man."

"It doesn't matter. At least he'll have the chance to decide for himself." Ian wiped the dried drool from his cheek with the back of his hand. "Why are you here?"

"Violating my parole."

"What'd you do?"

"Got married."

"You're in jail for getting married?"

"I didn't ask my parole officer first."

"You're kidding."

"Straight up, dude. Was workin', keepin' my nose clean. Why'ze come I got to ask to get married? I'm a grown man."

"And people wonder why the prisons are overcrowded."

A deputy in a crisply pressed black uniform walked over and unlocked the door.

"McKinney, time for your phone call. You got a lawyer?"

"I think so."

"You're gonna need one."

The deputy led Ian to a row of phones mounted on the wall. He picked up a receiver and looked at the numbers scribbled on the palm of his hand. He punched the keys and waited while the phone rang in his ear. After a few rings a female voice came on the line.

"Good morning, Danial Solomon's office."

5

Archie Kisner stared out the window of the Jefferson County Sheriff's car. The handcuffs, secured to his waist by a belly chain, bit into his thick wrists. The car rocked to a halt at the rear gate of the Department of Rehabilitation and Correction Reception Center at Akron. Two parallel fences stood about eight feet apart, separated by row upon row of jagged ankle-breaker rocks. Sunlight glinted off the razor wire looping around the top of each fence. The gate opened electronically. A gray-uniformed officer emerged from a small brick building and shoved aside the mobile barricades.

The car drove in, and the gate closed behind it. The two deputies got out of the car and checked their weapons with the officer inside the guardhouse. One of the deputies returned and jerked Archie out of the backseat by the belly chain and forced him to the ground. The deputies stepped back behind Archie while a gray-shirted corrections officer checked under the hood, inside the trunk, and under the chassis.

"All clear."

"On your feet, Kisner," a deputy said.

Archie shuffled over and climbed back in the car. The inside gate of the sally port slid open, and the car motored along a single-lane road to the reception building. The deputies led him inside, removed the chains, and locked him in a holding cell. Twenty minutes later keys rattled in the lock, and the deadbolt released with a thud. A large, blond officer with a Neanderthal forehead stepped into the cell.

"So, you're the famous retard we've heard so much about."

Archie stared at the floor, afraid to speak.

"You will answer me, inmate!" The guard stepped forward and stood nose-to-nose with Archie. "When an officer asks you a question, you answer with 'Yes sir' or 'No sir.' Do I make myself clear?"

"Ya... ya... yessir." Archie looked up.

"Don't eyeball me, inmate!" Spit sprayed across Archie's face. "You never look an officer in the eye. Do I make myself clear?"

He averted his eyes. "Ya... ya... yessir."

"Very good, retard. My name is Officer Trouten, and I'll be conducting your cavity search. I'll give a command, and you do what I say. Understood?"

Archie nodded.

"I can't hear you."

"Yessir."

"Get naked."

Archie stripped off his shirt. Undressing in front of another man horrified him. If everyone was naked, maybe it wouldn't be so disturbing. He pulled off his pants. His underclothes were dirty; now everyone would see. He hesitated then peeled off his dingy socks; he felt ashamed. He disliked his feet. All his life he thought his big toes were strange. The one on the right had a coarse, crooked nail.

"All right, retard. Time to do your dance. Show me the top of your head."

Archie leaned forward.

"What the hell happened to you?"

"Mmm... mmm... my brother—"

"It was a rhetorical question, moron. Fold down your ears... open your mouth... stick out your tongue... run your fingers over your gums."

Archie's hands trembled as he obeyed. He felt less human with each command.

"Pick up your arms... lift your nuts... turn around and bend over... pull your cheeks apart... cough... show me the bottoms of your feet. Now put on your underwear and get into the barber's chair. Do it now!"

Archie raced to the chair. The inmate barber ran the clippers across his already hairless head. Moments later Archie found himself in the delousing shower being sprayed with pungent chemicals. The tan jumpsuit they gave him barely fit; the sleeves only reached midway down his forearms. They measured, weighed, and fingerprinted him. Each step along the way Officer Trouten barked commands and spewed profanity directly into his ear. Finally, an indifferent guard snapped his mug shot, and the transformation from human being to faceless number was complete.

Trouten unlocked the holding cell and snatched open the door.

"Get in there, maggot."

Archie stepped over the threshold, and Trouten tripped him. Archie flailed his arms, trying to catch his balance. Trouten kicked him in the butt and drove him face first into the stainless steel toilet. The door slammed shut. A muffled, sadistic laugh lingered beneath the door. Archie squatted in the corner of the empty, windowless cell and quivered like a dog that had just been kicked by a pair of muddy boots.

2:51 P.M.

Colin Casey sat behind County Prosecutor Anthony DiAngello's desk polishing his glasses with his pink silk tie. DiAngello was slow in returning from the restroom, so Casey took the opportunity to rifle through his desk. He slid out the top drawer and found an assortment of pens, business cards, and Post-it Notes neatly stacked in various compartments. He pushed it shut and pulled out the top drawer on the right-hand side. It felt heavy and turned out to be filled with overstuffed files and mini whiskey bottles. He thumbed through the top few folders and found nothing of interest. He dug a little deeper and discovered three files filled with old issues of *Playboy* magazine. Another ruinous addiction.

During his six weeks in Jefferson County, Colin Casey managed to rub just about everyone the wrong way. If it wasn't for his connections with the party bosses in Columbus, the locals would have run him out of town. But as much as the Jefferson County power brokers disliked him, they couldn't criticize his results. During his short tenure he raised more money for Judge Williams than the local party had managed all year. He also seemed to have an uncanny knack for keeping his finger on the pulse of public opinion.

Colin Casey had absolutely no respect for the good old boys in Jefferson County. Most of these blue-collar types were Democrats in name only, not realizing the national party had long ago abandoned *real* working-class values. Casey resented the fact that when it came to the major social issues of the day - abortion, gay rights, animal activism and environmentalism - these people were socially out of step with the ultraliberal national agenda. But he would endure these simpletons for awhile longer. These were the last dues he would have to pay before being appointed to the congressional seat soon to be vacated by the 10-term Democrat from Zanesville.

Colin heard footsteps approaching. He slammed the drawer shut and bolted for the couch. DiAngello walked in drying his hands on a brown paper towel.

"So tell me, Colin, what's your take on the McKinney kid?"

"It's a no-brainer. Transfer him to the nearest federal courthouse and be done with him."

"College kids are always acting up at the hospital." DiAngello sat on the corner of his desk. "A couple nights in jail and a restraining order usually knocks the sparks out of them."

"Have you read the police report?"

"Sure. The kid threw an egg at a hospital vehicle loaded with abortionists. What's the big deal?"

"He hit the van while it was inside the protest-free zone."

"So?"

"It's a felony, and you should have the Feds look into the matter."

"You're splitting hairs."

"A good politician knows how to split hairs. Besides, you need to make an example out of him."

"He's just a kid."

"He's the enemy."

"I've got this under control."

"You could've fooled me." Colin crossed his feet and locked his hands behind his head. "By the way, weren't you buddies with the coroner who just got indicted for drug trafficking and public corruption?"

"What's that got to—"

"Gram, wasn't it?"

"Gus Gram." DiAngello's face flushed.

"I'm just saying, a lot of people in Columbus are watching everything you do with a lot of interest, if you get my drift."

"I'm clean as a whistle."

"I hope you're right... for your sake."

"What are you trying to insinuate?"

"I'm just keeping my eyes open, that's all I'm saying."

"Your business here is finished." DiAngello's bushy, black eyebrows furrowed together. He spoke through tightly clenched teeth. "Get out of my office."

3:12 P.M.

"Get up, Kisner." Keys rattled in the lock. The door popped open with a bang. "You're being escorted to your housing unit."

No response.

Trouten stepped into the cell. "You've got to be kidding me. There's no crying in prison."

Archie stood and wiped his face on his sleeve.

"They'll rape you the first week. Now kneel down and put your hands behind your back."

Trouten slapped cuffs and shackles on him, then grabbed him by the armpit and dragged him toward the door.

"Move it you fat, worthless maggot. Pick up your feet."

The harder Archie tried to walk in the shackles, the more he staggered; he just couldn't find the rhythm of walking in chains. He stumbled and fell.

"Get up." Trouten kicked him in the ribs. "If you fall again, I'll drag you the rest of the way by your neck."

Archie staggered to his feet. The restraints cut into his ankles. He could feel blood trickle down into his shoes. He looked along the narrow, paved walkway from the reception building to the cellblock, and the distance looked infinite. Somehow, he managed to shorten his strides and keep moving. Towering light poles rose toward the sky and dominated the landscape. All the cinder block buildings looked identical: three-story rectangles with large green tubes running horizontally across the windows.

Archie staggered into the building marked A Block. A cacophony of voices echoed through the cavernous structure. Trouten unlocked the cuffs and shackles, then slapped Archie on the butt.

"Big Bubba's waiting for you. Make sure you get a kiss on the cheek first." Trouten walked away laughing.

Archie scanned the complex. Bars stretched from floor to ceiling and lined the front of the cells. A narrow, grated catwalk jutted out from each of the three levels. The sour smell of sweat, smoke, and dirty feet filled the air.

"Welcome to *Hotel California*," the gray-shirted officer said, as he pulled his feet off the wooden desk. "You're on Range 2, cell 42."

The officer swiveled around and pressed a button on the console built into the wall. A cell door near the end of the second tier rattled open. "Haul your big butt up there. Count starts in five minutes."

Archie climbed the metal steps.

"Look boys, fresh meat!" someone yelled.

"Shake it baby, shake it!" another voice shouted.

By the time Archie reached the top of the steps, the jeers

and chants turned into a continuous roar. He hustled down the catwalk through a shower of spit and obscenities. Tattooed arms reached out through the bars at him.

"Hey punk!" someone yelled. "I was savin' this for the roller, but you can have it."

A cup full of urine splashed into Archie's face just before he darted into his cell. The door rolled shut. He wiped the putrid mixture of bodily fluids on the back of his saturated sleeve.

"Dear God, help me."

6

In the steam tunnel below the University Hospital parking lot, Ron Kester watched a ribbon of light filter through a slit in the manhole cover and illuminate the side of Art Bently's face. A thick, musty stench permeated the damp chamber. Somewhere in the darkness Ron could hear the sound of water trickling. He leaned over and spoke in a confidential whisper.

"It's after three. The time is right. You ready to go?"

"I think so, Ronnie. I just hope my legs still work after being cooped up all day waiting."

"Your legs are fine."

"I still can't get over that break we caught this morning," Art said.

"Quite a distraction, wasn't it?"

"I wonder if he got away."

"I hope so. Those cops don't play."

"Haven't they heard of the right to assemble?"

"Watch your voice. If they beat protesters up there, what do you think they'd do if they caught us down here?"

"Sorry."

"Grab the duffel bag, it's—"

Beep! Beep! Beep!

Art's watch alarm went off.

"Turn that off!"

Art pressed every button on the watch until the noise stopped.

"Sorry, man."

"You trying to get us busted?"

"I said I'm sorry."

"Just grab the duffel bag and let's go. The tunnel to the left should take us directly into the hospital's basement."

They crawled through the cramped passageway, exposed pipes jutting out everywhere. Ron led the way carrying a small flashlight. Art inched along behind, dragging the canvas bag over the muddy cement.

Whump!

"Dammit," Ron said under his breath.

"What happened?"

"I hit my head on something."

"What'd you do that for?"

"Because I enjoy cranial pain."

They advanced another ten feet.

Thump!

"Dammit!"

Art snickered.

"You think it's funny?"

"I can't help it."

"You'd better help it."

"Don't bust your head anymore, and I won't laugh."

"Just shut up. We're almost there."

They made a right turn and crawled toward a block of light at the end of the tunnel. A steam grate marked the end of the passage.

"This is it," Ron whispered. "I hope my contact removed the screws like he promised." He laced his fingers through the grate and pushed. It didn't budge. "It's rusted shut."

"Need my help?"

"Let me try again." Ron shoved with all his might. The top of the grate broke loose.

"All right, Art. Help me gently push it through."

Art crawled forward and bumped the grate with his shoulder. It crashed to the floor. They froze.

"What do we do now?" Art whispered into Ron's ear.

"We wait."

The moments ticked away. Ten seconds. Thirty seconds. A

minute. Ron gathered his nerve and darted his head through the opening then quickly pulled it back.

"The coast is clear. We've got to move fast, just like we planned."

They dashed out of the tunnel and shucked off the black coveralls. Underneath, they both wore pale-green orderly outfits. They balled up the coveralls, tossed them back into the tunnel, then slipped on latex gloves.

Ron opened the duffel bag and pulled out a tool belt loaded with assorted screwdrivers, wire cutters, and rolls of black tape. He carefully slid out a khaki green ammunition canister and removed a large black box.

"Is everything all right?" Art asked.

"I think so." Ron gently shook the black box. "It sounds intact." He handed it to Art.

"How we doing on time?"

"We're running a little behind. Hand me the map."

Art reached into his back pocket and handed him a folded piece of paper.

"According to this, the incinerator is across from the freight elevator."

"And those disposal bins you talked about."

"Should be right there."

"Ronnie, I don't like the feel of this."

"Too late now. Let's do what we came to do."

3:45 P.M.

Dr. Gaston Garvey spent the better part of the afternoon lying on the couch in his 10th floor office worrying about the witnesses to his early morning antics. Somewhere between the three-martini lunch and afternoon rounds, he started thinking of his colleagues as potential informants.

He lumbered over to the corner of his office where a Dutch silver spirit-case sat on a glass table, with some siphons for club soda and some large cut-glass tumblers. He looked at his reflection in the polished silver. He was 35 but looked ten years older. He was almost completely bald with a few gray locks about his temples, his broad high forehead already beginning to furrow with wrinkles. Dark bags drooped from his wide-set dark gray eyes. He ran his thumb and forefinger over his thick brown mustache.

"What am I worried about? Those two aren't going to say anything." He poured three fingers of Scotch into a tumbler. "Besides, it wasn't my fault. They forced me to take extreme measures."

He carried the glass over to his desk and plopped down. He swiveled around and looked out the window at the protesters down in the parking lot.

"Yeah, Garland and Martine forced me to do it. But I'd still better cover my tracks."

He picked up the Dictaphone recorder and cleared his throat.

"Tuesday, October 3rd, Dr. Gaston Garvey's post-op report. A late-term D&X abortion procedure was conducted on a healthy, 15-year-old female. She was prepared for surgery by Nurse Martine with no pre-operative complications. Labor inducement proceeded with only a slight rise in the patient's blood pressure but not outside the normal parameters.

"Dr. Garland, my surgical resident, conducted the procedure. The fetus traveled through the birth canal in the breech position. Number four surgical scissors were inserted at the base of the skull just above the spine. A large perforation was made and the cerebral matter was extracted by suction per procedure. The skull collapsed, and the abortion was completed. I noticed a small leak in the extraction nozzle which resulted in an insignificant amount of plasma being displaced onto the specimen's back and torso. It should be noted that while on her way to the biohazard disposal bin, Nurse Martine slipped and dropped the fetus. While I cannot be certain, the fetus may have sustained post-operative trauma to the head and neck. Nurse Martine was not injured."

He turned off the Dictaphone and pulled out the top drawer of his desk. He grabbed a bottle of tranquilizers, tapped out three yellow pills into the palm of his hand, and tossed them into his mouth. He tipped back his head and washed them down with the remainder of the Scotch. In a couple of minutes everything would be all right.

7

Judge Williams struggled to keep his mind focused on the amicus brief sitting on the desk in front of him. His mind seemed to wander more these days. He rubbed his eyes and looked around his office. Memorabilia from his years on the bench lined the mahogany-paneled walls. A photo of him shaking hands with President Carter hung next to a string of commendations from governors Celeste, Voinovich and Taft.

The door swung open, and Colin Casey walked in.

"Ever hear of knocking?"

"Whatever." Casey rolled his eyes.

I can't believe the party threatened to cut off my money if I didn't let this punk run my campaign.

"I just came back from reviewing the surveillance footage from the hospital parking lot. I bumped into your opponent Steve Foster down there holding a press conference in front of the protesters."

"I don't know how he manages to get his face on TV every time I turn around."

"He wants your job." Casey sat down and crossed his legs.

"What was he talking about?"

"From what I gathered, he was ranting about the police using excessive force on the McKinney kid."

"McKinney who?"

"The kid who threw the egg at a hospital van this morning. DiAngello wanted to let him go until I talked some sense into him."

"Good."

"Foster may have done us a favor by siding with the protesters. I don't think it'll fly with the voters. Right now, everyone's on the tough-on-crime mantra."

"I'm tough on crime, but I'm still behind in the polls."

"I'm not a miracle worker."

I'd like to smack that smug little smirk off his face.

"Did you say something Judge?"

"Me... no... why?"

"Your lips were moving."

"I didn't say anything."

"You sure?"

"What was that about surveillance or something?"

"The hospital has cameras mounted on the light poles overlooking the parking lot. They caught the McKinney arrest on video." Casey chuckled. "The kid put his hands up, and the cops gave him a little thump therapy."

"They what?"

"They clubbed him a little, then shot him with a taser."

"For throwing an egg?"

"He deserved worse."

"It'll look bad for the authorities."

"No, it won't. The hospital is going to lose the video."

"Maybe I should preside over this egg-throwing case. It could generate some publicity."

"Surprisingly enough, that's not a bad idea." Casey winked at him with a malicious and mocking smile. "It does have some media potential. And with the right spin..."

"It can't hurt."

"Now that I think about it, I might have seen something on the video that just might give us an opportunity to turn this into a gold mine."

"Like what?"

"Leave that to me." Casey stood and headed for the door. "But I've got to move fast."

4:47 P.M.

Danial Solomon put down the phone feeling a little better about Archie's situation. At least someone would look in on him from time to time. Archie was big as a bear, but he had the mind of a child. Size would only take him so far in prison. As soon as the cons realized he was mentally defenseless, Archie would be an easy target.

Danial checked his monthly planner, then walked to the outer office.

"Jennifer, write a letter to Archie and let him know I'll be up to see him on October 21st."

"I'll get right on it. Anything else?"

"Not right now. I'm heading over to the jail to meet Mr. McKinney and see what he has to say for himself. I probably won't be back, so lock up when you leave."

"Very good, I'll see you in the morning."

Danial picked up his briefcase and strolled toward the door. Jennifer called after him.

"How did things go with Ms. Franks?"

"All right, I guess."

"Was it business or pleasure?"

"Why do you ask?"

"Just curious."

"Am I missing something here?"

"No."

"What's on your mind, Jennifer?"

"Well, I've noticed you've been mentioning her name a lot lately."

"So?"

"And I found it more than a little odd that she would come all the way over here to see you when she could just as easily pick up the phone."

"You've got me." He shrugged his shoulders. "I'll never figure out women."

Danial walked out the door, got in his car, drove over to the courthouse, and parked on the street. He gazed over at the Jefferson County Courthouse. A bronze statue of Edwin Stanton - Abraham Lincoln's famed Secretary of War - stood at the base of the steps. The statue always stirred feelings of community pride in Danial's heart. He passed up offers from some of the most prestigious law firms in the country in order to practice in the county where he grew up. He loved the Ohio River Valley and wouldn't live anywhere else. He thought back to the first time he saw that statue when he was a teenager. Despite being the most brilliant student to ever come out of the Steubenville City School District, he displayed a self-destructive personality at an early age. He began drinking at 14 and had a proclivity for exploding into sudden fits of rage. His teachers believed he would destroy himself before his intellect had the chance to bloom. The prediction probably would have come true had it not been for a chance meeting with a helpful Christian, Andy Lewis, on the campus of Ohio University.

Danial crossed the street and climbed the marble steps to the courthouse lobby. He stopped off at the vending machines and bought a Snickers bar, then walked downstairs to the jail. He waited at the booking desk where a female deputy sat with her back to him.

"Excuse me, ma'am. I'd like to see inmate Ian McKinney please."

"Family and friends visit on the weekends," she said, without turning around.

"I'm not family or friend, I—"

"Then you can't see him on the weekend either."

"I'm a lawyer."

"Oh." She spun around. "Could I see your credentials?" He flipped open his wallet.

"Go on back to the visiting room, and I'll have him brought over."

"Thank you very much, ma'am."

Danial's footsteps echoed through the narrow corridor leading to the interrogation rooms. The place reeked of sweaty feet, and the unmistakable stench of despair. He took a seat at the small table in the center of the tiny room. A single light bulb hung from the ceiling by a threadbare wire. Sky-blue paint covered the floor, walls and ceiling, producing the feeling of vertigo. While this may have been the desired effect for interrogations, it was nauseating for legal visits.

Danial rippled his fingertips on the table and couldn't get Lori Franks out of his head. He imagined spending an evening with her at the orchestra listening to a romantic rendition of *Brahms' Third Symphony*. He pictured them walking hand-in-hand at the park, kicking leaves as they went. He envisioned her sitting next to him at church on Sunday morning, maybe whispering something in his ear.

The door swung open.

"You've got 20 minutes!" the deputy shouted.

Ian McKinney gingerly stepped in. A young man of medium height and muscular build, he showed signs of considerable strength. His red hair was cropped short and combed forward on his temples. He was still young, but already wrinkled in brow and cheeks, with bright blue eyes and a smiling mouth.

Danial stood, and they shook hands. Ian bit his lip and grimaced. He pulled his arm back to his side.

"What happened to you?"

"We'll get to that later." Ian fumbled with the wooden folding chair and sat down. "So, you're T-H-E Danial Solomon?"

"What can I do for you?"

"I want you to be my lawyer."

"You haven't been charged with anything yet. They may hold you for a couple days and let you go."

"Oh, they aren't going to let me go. I can assure you of that."

"What makes you so sure?"

"Is this confidential?"

"Certainly."

"Well, you probably heard I threw an egg at a hospital van and broke the window."

"A fourth-degree misdemeanor at best."

"It won't be a misdemeanor when they find out what kind of egg it was."

"I don't follow you."

"It wasn't your everyday, garden-variety chicken egg."

"What was it?"

"A bald eagle's egg."

"Where did you get an eagle's egg?"

"I'm not prepared to say at this point." Ian looked Danial directly in the eye. "Are you willing to represent me?"

"I don't know."

"Why not?"

"I don't know anything about you. You might belong to some terrorist group."

"I can assure you, Mr. Solomon, I'm not a wacko. I have my reasons for doing what I did, and in time my reasons will become clear." He leaned back in his chair. "This is an easy case. I intend to plead guilty and take responsibility for my actions."

"So why do you need me?"

"I want my day in court."

"Why not have your day with a public defender?"

"Because I don't want to get screwed in the process."

"I'm listening."

"I'll give you $5000 to watch my back and protect my interests. It's that simple. What do you say?"

Danial steepled his fingers under his chin. "I'll tell you what I'll do. I'll agree to represent you under one condition."

"What's that?"

"If I find out you're lying to me, I'll withdraw from the case and keep the retainer. Understood?"

"Understood," Ian said with a beaming smile. "You won't regret this, Mr. Solomon. I can promise you that."

8

Lori Franks sorted through the mound of papers blanketing the top of her desk. Files jutted out of every crevice and drawer. Coffee-stained styrofoam cups dotted the clutter.

"I'm a disaster."

She boxed up all the related materials on the Kisner case to ship over to the Appellate Division. They could have some fun jousting with Danial Solomon for a while.

"Imbecile, I'm such an imbecile."

She jammed the last manila file into the overstuffed cardboard box and taped it shut. She yanked open the top drawer and rummaged around the chaos until her fingertips found a black marker. She pulled the cap off, scribbled an address on the box, then tossed the marker back in the drawer without replacing the cap.

"Why did I tell him the hug meant nothing? I'm so stupid. It meant everything."

Lori closed her eyes, and the image of Danial Solomon standing in front of her with his arms open popped into her mind. His athletic, muscular frame silhouetted in the streetlight. His brown and silver hair waved in the gentle breeze. He leaned his face so close to hers that she could see the structure of his ocean-blue irises, with the multitude of gray streaks and flecks, his pupils slightly enlarged and lustrous. Her heart took off at a gallop when she pictured his wide, full lips in a warm smile.

She opened her eyes and shook her head. Danial Solomon was the most attractive man she had ever seen, and she had already managed to alienate him.

"Who am I kidding? Why would he be interested in me?"

A knock at the door.

"Ms. Franks," her secretary said. "Mr. DiAngello wants to see all the assistant prosecutors in the main conference room immediately. He sounded upset."

"I'm on my way."

Lori walked down the hall past a row of cubicles and into the corner conference room. More than a dozen exhausted-looking men and women were crammed around the conference table; a few stood along the wall. DiAngello sat at the head of the table holding a remote control and facing the large-screen television mounted on the far wall.

"I want everyone to pay close attention to this."

DiAngello clicked on the television. A beautiful woman with shoulder-length blonde hair stood in front of the Steubenville Police Station holding a microphone. DiAngello bumped up the volume.

"Good evening, I'm Katie Welch, and this is the 5 o'clock news," her voice sounding raspy and seductive. "I'm standing near the spot where officers just found a newborn infant stuffed in some kind of ammunition container."

The camera panned down to a chalk circle on the pavement, then cut to the uniformed police chief holding a green container. He spoke directly into the lens.

"One of our patrolmen found a baby boy inside one of these." He held up the ammo canister. "It wasn't there long. Our surveillance camera indicates a blue VW Bug dropping off the ammo can." The TV screen showed an image of the car.

"Can you comment on the baby's condition?" Katie asked.

"Dead."

"How did he die?"

"We're not at liberty to release that information at this time. The remains have been sent to the county coroner's office for an official ruling."

"Are there any suspects?"

"Not at this time. We will search with the long arm of the law."

"Since the baby was found here at the station, is it possible a police officer is involved?"

"Absolutely not."

The camera flashed to a distance shot of Katie Welch strolling in front of a row of squad cars toward the chalk outline.

"Tragedy has once again struck our quiet community. The police have asked that anyone with information about this case call the police station anytime, day or night."

The camera zoomed in on her face.

"Again, the top story tonight, *Baby Ammo* found dead at the Steubenville Police Station."

The screen went black. DiAngello slammed the remote to the table. "Did you hear that?"

No one answered.

"They've already named him Baby Ammo. How cute. Does anyone here know how the baby was killed?"

"They didn't say, chief," a young assistant said.

"I'm not deaf. Of course they didn't say. I told them not to. Baby Ammo was stabbed in the back of the head." He squinted his red-veined eyes.

"What the hell is going on in this county?"

9

Midnight fast approached. The full Harvest Moon loomed large in the sky, its brilliance curbed by a passing cloud. As the eventful day of October 3rd wound to a close in the foothills of the Ohio Valley, a blue VW Bug drove out of the parking lot at University Hospital. It then crossed the street and parked in a secluded spot by the Subway restaurant. From this position the two men had an unobstructed view of the hospital.

The man behind the wheel pressed a tiny button on his watch, illuminating the digital face. Both men's eyes fastened on the bright light.

The driver broke the silence.

"Five... four... three... two... one..."

The watch chirped. They looked up and fixed their gaze on the hospital parking lot.

"Come on baby, it's time, it's time."

A brilliant light flashed. An instant later a savage, thunderous roar shook the car. A moment later a second explosion ripped through the parking lot, launching cars and SUVs through the air. The blast toppled light poles like falling dominoes. A massive, flaming crater swallowed cars and pickup trucks. An EV charging station burst into flames, torching electric cars. Fire spread to a building with propane tanks and oxygen cylinders, setting off a series of smaller explosions and a raging inferno. A glimpse of the apocalypse. Blaze-orange fire and smoke swirled and billowed up into the sky, lighting the darkness.

Then eerie silence... and then sirens.

The two men sat in motionless admiration of their

handiwork. Tiny pieces of debris cascaded through the dust-filled haze. The driver turned the ignition switch. The engine caught, and he shifted the car into gear.

"Never let a serious crisis go to waste."

10

Anthony DiAngello opened his eyes and felt sick. The room spun out of control. He slipped his right leg out of bed and anchored his foot to the floor. It didn't help. The phone on the nightstand continued to ring. He focused his eyes on the half-empty bottle of Jack Daniels mocking him from its perch next to the phone. Getting heavily inebriated had become his way of coping with life since his wife left him eight months earlier. He fumbled with the phone.

"Hello?"

"It's Colin Casey."

"What the hell do you want?"

"Sorry to call you so late, but this is big."

"It better be." DiAngello rubbed his eyes with his thumb and forefinger.

"There's been a bombing at the hospital. Looks like a war zone."

"What?!"

"You probably should get right down here."

"Are the Feds there?"

"Yeah, they've got yellow tape and chalk circles around everything."

"Then there's no need for me."

"But—"

"I'll deal with it in the morning."

"I really think you—"

DiAngello dropped the phone. He grabbed the bottle, tipped back his head, and chugged the bitter brown liquid.

7:35 A.M.

The sky glowed orange over the foothills of the Appalachian Mountains on the West Virginia side of the Ohio River. Spears of light darted through the tree line and illuminated the gutted parking lot at University Hospital. Anthony DiAngello squeezed through the crowds of gawking onlookers huddled around the blast sites, everyone trying to see who could best stretch his neck over his neighbor's shoulders.

Representatives from the FBI, the Secret Service, the County Sheriff's Office and the frantic Steubenville Police Department climbed all over each other, flashing badges and arguing over jurisdiction. Reporters from local, state and national news agencies took pictures, exchanged gossip and cussed the police for continually pushing them back. Rumors were heard, collected and embellished with astonishing speed.

The uptight throng swarmed around two overt explosion sites: the charred concrete where a big, steel garbage dumpster once stood, and the cratered area around the manhole in the middle of the parking lot where the pavement vanished, buckled and peeled back. Wrecked vehicles were strewn everywhere like wind-blown litter.

DiAngello spotted his administrative assistant, Bill Jenkins. He picked his way through the crowd and joined a small circle of men. County Sheriff Albert Rose stood next to a uniformed deputy, who stood next to Al Swift, director of the Emergency Management Agency. Colin Casey shifted from foot to foot across from DiAngello. Jenkins, standing to his left, handed him a styrofoam cup of coffee.

"Thanks Bill. All right, boys. Start from the beginning."

"I tried to tell you last—"

"Shut up, Casey. I want to hear it from my own people."

"The FBI is keeping it close to the vest," Sheriff Rose said. "All they're saying officially is the bomb in the steel dumpster shredded it instantly and showered shrapnel and debris all over the area. And according to their pyrotechnics expert, the explosion in the steam tunnel launched the manhole cover approximately 300 feet in the air before it landed on that Cadillac Escalade over there." He pointed to the crumpled mess of red-painted steel. "Cadaver dogs are searching the crater, the burnt building and all damaged vehicles for any human remains."

"Do they know who's responsible?"

"If they do, they aren't saying."

"It's the pro-lifers," Casey said. "I'm surprised it didn't happen sooner."

DiAngello scowled at him.

"He's probably right," Jenkins said. "This is where they congregate. Maybe it's retaliation for McKinney getting beat up."

"Could be."

"Hold on there." Sheriff Rose raised his hand. "Let's not rush to judgment like they did at the Olympic bombing in Atlanta."

"Who's rushing to judgment?" Casey said. "Have you seen the surveil... I mean, all I'm saying is we shouldn't overlook the obvious. They've crossed the line from peaceful protest to violent terrorism."

"The Feds will probably want to handle this thing all by themselves." DiAngello fixed his eyes on Al Swift. "You'll be our liaison with whoever leads the investigation. I want to know everything they know. Do I make myself clear?"

"Perfectly, sir."

"What's the latest on the murdered baby, Sheriff?" DiAngello sipped his coffee.

"The police chief said they've been over the closed-circuit footage a dozen times, and they're sure the televised VW Bug delivered the baby to the police station lot."

"Very good. Stay on them."

"Plus, we've been flooded with tips. Most are looking for reward money, but a few sound like they may have some merit."

"What about the autopsy?"

"It's on hold."

"Why?"

"Because our coroner, Gus Gram, is in federal custody, remember?"

"Have you called Belmont County?"

"Yep, no-can-do."

"What about Harrison County?"

"They haven't gotten back to me yet."

"Stay on them. We've got to show the people of Jefferson County we're still in control." He slammed his cup to the ground. The lukewarm coffee splashed on Casey's pants. "I want an arrest, and I want it now."

7:45 A.M.

Archie Kisner opened his eyes to the clatter of a nightstick rattling on steel bars. All of the cell doors rolled open simultaneously then banged to a stop.

"First call for chow," yelled the skinny officer with a crew cut. "Get off your racks and line up!"

Archie rolled out of bed and tugged on his jumpsuit. He looked in the steel mirror over the sink; he could barely make out the outline of his head through the rust. He twisted the sink handle, but no water came out.

"Last call for chow! Line up on the sidewalk!"

Archie filed out with the rest of the men and stood in line. He thought back over the life that led him to prison. His mother was killed by a drunk driver when he was 6. His father, overcome with grief, put a shotgun in his mouth and blew his brains out in the family garage. Archie found his body when he came home from school. After bouncing around foster homes, his older brother Ralph finally took custody. Ralph abused him in every conceivable way, and Archie wore on his head the mark of his brother's rage. The baseball bat had left an indelible scar and also left Archie mentally impaired. He knew Ralph did bad things, but he was afraid to resist him or turn him in. So here he stands, the accused accomplice to a heinous crime.

"You holdin' up okay, big man?"

Archie looked over his shoulder at the middle-aged black man. "Eyes front, cuz, or that roller will be on you like white on rice." Archie squared his shoulders.

"I'm Sonny, but you can call me Bones. What you name is slick?"

"Ar... Archie, you can call me Archie."

"I see you a new boy. Stay close to me, and I'll show ya da ropes."

Archie nodded and noticed a commotion at the front of the line. A young white inmate covered with tattoos endured a verbal onslaught from three gray-shirted officers. It appeared they were trying to provoke him.

Archie turned his head slightly over his left shoulder.

"What's going on?"

"Turn around. Don't let them see you talking." He hawked and spit. "That's Ossy up there. I did a nickel with him at the old Mansfield. He was young and stupid when he first got to the walls. You see that little Oriental-looking roller?"

Archie nodded.

"He and Ossy got into it on Ossy's last bit, and here they are again. I guess the Oriental's ready for round two."

The fracas died down, and the serpentine line of men slithered along the paved walkway to an enormous brick building. Archie walked into the chow hall and was greeted by the pungent stench of rotten vegetables and spoiled milk. An ocean of men in tan jumpsuits filled the cavernous room, four men per table. A makeshift handrail made of 3-inch galvanized pipe funneled the flow of humanity past the overworked, inmate food service workers. Sonny stayed closed to Archie in line.

"I usually don't kick it with the white man, but you off the hook."

Archie's mouth opened and confusion draped his face.

"Dig dude, if you want to avoid da drama in the joint, don't gamble, don't borrow, don't do dope, and don't mess with boys."

"But everyone is boys."

"Not that kind of boys. I'm talkin' punks, fags, you know, homosexuals."

"Oh."

"Sit over there with my homies."

Archie picked up his tray of two hard-boiled eggs, a ladle of grits and a cup of milk, and followed Sonny to a table where two other blacks were already eating.

"What it be like, Bones?" one man said with a mouthful of grits.

"I can't call it."

"You got the best hand up in here."

"If I had your hand I cuts mines off."

"You the big dog."

"What's with Frankenstein?" the second man asked.

"This here be Archie. He's cool."

A commotion started a few tables over. Two white inmates stood nose-to-nose. The place went silent except for the exchange.

"Did I say something wrong?" the taller man said.

"I said you did, and I meant it."

"How can I tell? My mouth ain't bleedin'. My back ain't dirty." He leaned in closer.

"Back up, punk."

"I ain't your punk. I'll slap the snot out of you."

"Your slapper broke?"

Silence.

"It's cool, it's cool." The taller man smiled and turned to walk away. "I'm just jerkin' your chain." He stopped, spun around, and blasted the shorter man square on the nose. Blood sprayed out of both nostrils. The impact knocked the man on his butt. Then the tall man pounced.

The cons cheered with every blow that landed.

The guard standing by the door pressed the alarm on his radio.

The shorter man kicked and flailed his arms and fought his

way to his feet. They locked onto each other and rolled over a table. When they separated the shorter man had a fork in his right hand. He swung it wildly. The tall man bobbed and weaved, then shot forward. The fork caught him in the middle of the forehead and ripped out a hunk of flesh. Blood gushed down his face.

The cons cheered louder.

Archie made a move toward the scene. Sonny grabbed his jumpsuit.

"Where you going?"

"Gonna stop the fight."

"A peacemaker? I'm Christian too, thanks to a street preacher, but the goon squad be ridin' down any minute. You don't want to be nowhere round when they do."

A few seconds later eight officers dressed in black riot gear poured into the chow hall. They shot pepper spray in the combatants' eyes, cuffed their hands behind their backs, and led them off to the hole.

"Wh... wh... what do we do now?" Archie asked.

"Eat fast before they lock us down."

9:35 A.M.

Colin Casey sat in the burgundy leather chair in the corner of Judge Williams' office, going over the latest poll data. Williams tapped a stem from his glasses against his teeth, waiting for the results. Casey glanced up and saw the judge hovering over him.

"It doesn't look good, Your Honor. We didn't get the bounce I expected after the Kisner sentencing."

"Why not?"

"Beats me. Maybe Foster's television campaign is striking a chord with the voters." He handed the papers to Williams.

"Maybe we should step up my TV spots."

"Bad idea."

"Why?"

"No offense, but you don't look too good on TV."

"We've got to do something."

"What we need is a nice, high-profile case to make you look in touch with the people and yet very judicial. Maybe something for *Court TV*."

"I've got the Robertson case scheduled for next week."

"Murder case?"

"Drugs."

"No good. We need something unusual, something flashy."

"What about the dead baby case?"

"You mean the fetus left at the police station?"

"Yeah."

"You've got to be kidding me. By the time these backwoods morons get around to solving that case, I'll be governor, and you'll be dead."

Williams shot a glare that wiped the cheesy grin off Casey's face.

"I think I've got just the ticket," Casey said. "I'll be right back."

"Where are you going?"

"To see the simpleton, DiAngello."

10:10 A.M.

Anthony DiAngello leaned back in his chair, feet propped up on his desk and the window blinds closed. The lights were dimmed, and the smell of strong coffee filled the room. Someone knocked at the door.

"Come in."

Bill Jenkins tiptoed in and took his customary position on the end of the green vinyl couch near DiAngello's desk. He spoke softly.

"Sorry to bother you, chief, but an arraignment has been scheduled for tomorrow morning in the McKinney case. We have to charge him or let him go."

"Let him go for all I care. I've got bigger fish to fry."

"But the lab report said the egg McKinney threw was from a bald eagle, which makes the case a misdemeanor of the first degree. The assault on van passengers makes it a felony."

"All right." DiAngello picked up his cup, his hand trembled, and he slopped coffee on his lap. "Give the case to Hartlieb. It'll be good experience and an easy win."

"I was thinking you may want to try this one yourself." Jenkins handed him the file, then headed toward the door. "It may be good for the people to see you in court. You know, show them you're involved hands-on."

"I don't think that's a good idea."

"You said it yourself, this is an easy win."

"I'll think about it."

"Let me know what you decide."

Jenkins closed the door behind him.

Anthony DiAngello stood and rubbed the small of his back. He was in remarkably good shape for a man in his early 50s. He dyed his hair black to match his bushy eyebrows. His brown eyes gave him an intense look, especially when he was angry. He had a large pointed nose covered with tiny black hairs, a narrow mouth with thin lips, and a prominent chin. He always wore a double-breasted suit. It was his trademark.

During his 13 years in public office, DiAngello earned the reputation of being a shrewd politician and a terrible lawyer. He never tried cases himself. His bold and brash personality withered when he stood in front of a jury. It was rumored in political circles that mafia connections alone kept him in office. He had developed political ambitions at an early age, after being elected class president in the 9th grade. He studied Political Science at West Liberty University and proved to be a poor student. His family pulled some strings and got him into the West Virginia University College of Law where he also floundered.

DiAngello paced around his office. A knock at the door froze him in his tracks. He could see the lanky silhouette of Colin Casey through the Venetian blinds hanging over his office door window. *That young punk is going to learn the hard way who runs the show in Jefferson County.* DiAngello walked over and plopped down behind his desk. He took a sip of coffee and scanned the contents of the file Jenkins left behind.

More banging on the door.

"Come in."

Casey entered looking agitated.

"What's on your mind? Can't you see I'm busy?"

"I came to discuss the McKinney case."

"I just happen to have that file right here in front of me."

"Good."

"Before you say another word, I've decided to try the case myself. I had my boys do some checking." He scanned the file with his index finger. "Here it is. It says in *State v. Saurman* that the State, within proper exercise of police power, may adopt appropriate means for the protection and preservation of wildlife."

"Hold on there, big guy," Casey said. "I came up here to tell you I've changed my mind. I think we should keep the case right here. Screw the Feds."

"I'm glad you're finally seeing things my way."

"It's got nothing to do with you. I need a nice, neat, high publicity case to get that old coot re-elected. And I think with a little help from my friends at the EPA and the Animal Rights League, I should be able to whip this thing up into a media extravaganza."

"The last thing I need is more media. Between the baby and the bombing—"

"Hear me out."

"Speak."

"I'm not talking about this local stuff, I'm talking about nationwide media that I can control. This is good for everybody; this is good for you."

"What do you need from me?"

"I need you to do exactly what I say, no questions asked."

"Who do you think you're talking to?"

"Listen, if you cooperate now, by the time I'm finished Williams will get re-elected, and you just may be poised for a run at Attorney General."

11

Danial Solomon pulled into the parking lot across the street from the courthouse and glanced at his antique gold watch - the one passed from his grandfather to his father and then to him. He stepped out of the car and buttoned both brass buttons on his navy-blue, Armani suit. The air felt cold against his head. He saw his reflection in the car window and made one last attempt to tame his unruly mop of hair.

Danial walked into the courtroom and looked around. The high vaulted ceiling was inlaid with hand-carved wooden reliefs. The oak-paneled walls were darkened with age. On the wall over the jury box hung an 8-foot tall portrait of Baron Friedrich von Steuben. As a boy, Danial had done a report on this Revolutionary War general who established an important fort on the bluffs above the Ohio River. The fort became the original settlement of what is now the city of Steubenville. On the opposite wall hung an identically sized portrait of Thomas Jefferson, for whom the county was named. A painting of the Seal of Ohio adorned the wall above the judge's bench. The pleasant scent of Murphy's Oil Soap lingered in the air.

Danial took his seat behind the defense table. A couple of clerk types milled around the judge's bench. The gallery was empty with the exception of a thin man with sandy blond hair sitting in the first row behind the prosecutor's table, typing away on a laptop computer. Danial wondered if Lori Franks would stop in for the hearing. *Then again, why would she? This case has nothing to do with her. But it would still be nice to see her. Maybe I can come up with a good excuse to wander up to her office after the hearing.*

A few minutes later Anthony DiAngello shoved open the large, double doors at the rear of the gallery. A young assistant walked in behind him carrying a small case of files. DiAngello stopped to talk with the thin man for a moment, then continued through the low swinging door. The man got up and followed him. He placed his briefcase on the table and sat down, never once looking over at the defense table. Danial walked over to the County Prosecutor.

"Greetings, Mr. DiAngello. And how are you this fine morning?"

"Good morning, Danial." DiAngello's face twisted into a confused expression. "I'm sure you know my other assistant, Doug Baker." Danial nodded, then shook the man's hand.

"Have you met Colin Casey?"

"I don't believe I have." Danial stretched out his hand. Casey offered a limp shake.

"Colin here has taken over as Judge Williams' campaign manager. He's going to show us hayseeds how they do it in the big city."

Casey rolled his eyes at DiAngello, then looked at Danial. "I'm guessing you're here to represent McKinney?"

"Yes I am."

"Really?" DiAngello said. "I wouldn't think a trivial case like this would be up your alley."

"The case doesn't seem so trivial to my client."

"Your client seems to have a blatant disregard for wildlife," Casey said. "I spent three months in the Amazon rainforest working to preserve the Resplendent Quetzal."

"Is that some sort of bird?"

"It's nearly threatened, officially."

"That's interesting," Danial said. "My client also spent a summer working in the rainforest."

"That's surprising. What did he do?"

"He worked on a slash and burn crew trying to open grazing land for the cattle ranchers."

"Really?" DiAngello asked.

"No, I'm just kidding."

Casey's face flushed.

"I'm sorry, sport." Danial slapped Casey on the shoulder. "Just having a little fun."

"I don't think killing a bald eagle is a laughing matter."

"Neither do I." Danial's face grew serious. "Personally, I'm against smashing eagles' eggs. They taste so much better when they're full grown."

DiAngello burst into laughter.

"You're quite the raconteur." Casey walked away with a devious grin on his face. He returned to his seat.

The creaking of the side door announced Ian McKinney's arrival. The young redhead was led by a female deputy. Danial turned back to DiAngello and said, "Please excuse me, I need to confer with my client."

"Certainly. Good to see you again, Danial."

The deputy removed Ian's handcuffs, and he took a seat next to Danial. A minute later a bailiff called them to order and made them stand. Judge Williams assumed his perch on the bench and rapped his gavel.

"Please be seated."

Danial focused on Williams' face. Something just looked different. His curly white hair combed straight back looked the same; it may have been a little shorter. Two pronounced wrinkles spanned the width of his forehead parallel to his thick white eyebrows. Deep lines ran from the sides of his nose down past the corners of his mouth. Large folds of skin now swallowed his once prominent chin.

"He's not wearing his glasses," Danial said.

"Who's not?" Ian asked.

"Never mind."

In a deep baritone voice, the old judge opened the session. "My notes tell me we're here for the purpose of arraigning one Mr. Ian McKinney. The defendant will rise, and the State may proceed."

"Thank you, Your Honor," DiAngello said. As he read from the document in his left hand, his voice trembled. "On Tuesday,

October 3rd, the defendant, Ian McKinney, did willfully and intentionally throw a viable egg of an endangered bird - to wit, an American bald eagle - and struck an inhabited vehicle belonging to the University Hospital. He smashed the egg, killed the fetus, and damaged the vehicle.

"The State of Ohio charges the defendant with destruction of the egg of a protected, non-game bird, a violation of the Ohio Revised Code, Section 1533.07, a misdemeanor of the first degree. However, there is an attached violence specification as the inhabitants of the vehicle suffered serious bodily injury which boosts the misdemeanor to a second-degree felony."

Danial shook his head. *Over-indictment. That's all they know.*

"Furthermore," DiAngello said a bit louder. "The State charges the defendant with violation of the state law prohibiting any abortion protester from entering a 35-foot protest-free zone outside a hospital or abortion clinic. Such violation constitutes a felony in the first degree. Additional charges may be forthcoming as soon as the State determines how the defendant procured the egg in question. Thank you, Your Honor."

"How does the defendant plead?"

"Not guilty, Your Honor," Danial said.

"Your plea has been accepted," Williams said. He looked at the stenographer. "Let the record reflect the defendant has entered a plea of Not Guilty. Trial will be set to begin October 24th. A schedule for discovery, pretrial, and motions is available through my bailiff."

"Your Honor," Danial said. "The defendant respectfully requests bond be set. And in light of the nature of the offenses and the fact that this is my client's first arrest, the Defense requests a personal surety bond."

"Your Honor, if I may interject." DiAngello stood and straightened his coat. "The State requests that no bond be set."

"What are you talking about, Tony?" Danial glanced over at DiAngello with an incredulous look on his face.

"For his own protection," DiAngello said. "The State has reason to believe this case will generate a great deal of interest among some radical groups. At times these factions have been known to be violent."

"Factious groups," Danial said. "Your Honor, the courtroom is empty. No one cares about this case."

"Bail will be set at One Hundred Thousand dollars," Williams said.

"That's outrageous! This is a petty vandalism case at best."

"I've heard enough," Williams said. "This hearing is over, and Court is adjourned."

Williams tapped his gavel then disappeared inside his chambers. Colin Casey stepped forward, whispered something in DiAngello's ear, then darted into the chambers.

10:45 A.M.

Dr. Harold Pella joined Dr. Gaston Garvey in his posh 10th floor corner office. The thick, mauve carpeting matched the drapes. Dusty rose textured wallpaper covered the walls and blended nicely with the light gray leather couch and chair. Garvey sat behind a marble and glass table he used for a desk, pecking away at his computer.

"What's your take on this bombing thing?" Dr. Pella asked as he opened the *Herald-Star.*

"It's probably some disgruntled protester."

"Probably not."

"Why do you say that?"

"They never try to hurt anyone."

"Well, I could care less about how cautious they are, they should all be shot. It'd be a good way to thin the herd."

"At least we won't have to worry about protesters for a while. It'll be nice to drive to work in my own car for a change."

Garvey swiveled his chair around and looked out the window. He had a beautiful view of the cable-stayed Veterans Memorial Bridge spanning the Ohio River.

"The newspaper says they are charging the nut who threw the

egg at us," Pella said. "I hope they throw the book at him, no pun intended." He chuckled at his little joke. "I heard the police beat him up pretty good."

"I hope they beat the stuffing out of him."

"Maybe they'll stop protesting now."

Garvey picked a baseball off its stand next to his computer. It was the ball Wille Stargel hit in the World Series against the Baltimore Orioles in Game Six. Garvey held the ball reverently.

"Those closed-minded bigots have nothing else to do but harass honest people like you and me. We're doing this country a service."

Silence.

"Hey, what do you think about that Baby Ammo case?" Pella asked.

"I think it's a sick world when some psycho jams a screwdriver into a baby's head and then stuffs him in an ammo box."

"Did the police say it was a screwdriver?"

"I don't know, but I'll tell you what." Garvey stood and stretched his back. "I hope they catch whoever did it and give 'em the electric chair."

11:10 A.M.

Anthony DiAngello knocked on the door of Judge Williams' chambers and waited to be summoned in. He was surprised to see Colin Casey sitting at the desk while the old judge stood peering over his shoulder.

"Excuse me, Your Honor," DiAngello said. "But I really need to talk to Mr. Casey."

"Go right ahead," Williams said.

"It has to do with a case presently before you. I wouldn't want to put you in a compromised position or create a conflict for you. He and I will step out into the hall."

"Nonsense," Casey said. "The judge isn't doing anything. He can step out."

Williams took a deep breath and blew it out through clenched teeth. He straightened and walked out. DiAngello couldn't believe his eyes. *The judge who struck fear into the hearts of all the lawyers who stood before him is now taking orders from this... this... little political lackey.*

"So, Mr. Prosecutor, what's on your mind?" Casey leaned back and put his feet up on Williams' desk.

"A monkey wrench seems to have fallen into your little plan. We have a complication."

"What're you talking about? Even you couldn't have screwed this up already."

"I'm not in the mood."

"All right, what's wrong?"

"The problem is Danial Solomon."

"You mean the comedian from this morning?"

"That's the one, and he's not to be underestimated."

"How sharp can he be? I mean he's practicing in the roaring metropolis of Steubenville."

"You'd be surprised."

"If he starts raking the mud too much, maybe I'll have a little chat with him. I'm sure he has a price to make him go away."

"Solomon is a bit different than most. He's not the type to back down."

"I'll make a few phone calls and see what kind of dirt I can dig up on him. In the meantime, concern yourself with those protesters down at the hospital."

"Why are you so concerned with those protesters? They've been here for years."

"Those hypocrites are the same people who keep this country in the dark ages. They oppose tolerance and social reform. Believe me, I've got something in store for those bigots. I'm just waiting for the right time."

12

11:15 A.M.

Danial Solomon waited in the tiny, blue room for the deputies to usher in Ian McKinney. He thought about the arraignment hearing and scribbled some notes on a yellow legal pad. And he thought about Archie Kisner, what a shame it was he sat in prison because of the sins of his brother. *Sure, he made some mistakes, but even in Ohio the punishment should fit the crime.*

His mind drifted to thoughts of Lori. The change in her over the past three weeks had been miraculous. Her tongue had once been so sharp and sarcastic. The Bible says, "For out of the overflow of the heart the mouth speaks." Now her words were salted with restraint and compassion. Even the hardness of her eyes had softened. The work of God in the soul is incredible once the heart surrenders to Him.

Danial thought back to the years before he committed his life to Jesus, and it made him cringe. He had attended church with his mom and dad *religiously*. Of course, he hadn't paid attention and daydreamed through the sermons. But in his own mind he figured he was doing right by God. After all, he at least showed up for church, and that's a lot more than most people do. What more could God expect?

His mind drifted through those early years of immaturity and insecurity and rationalization. Freshman year in high school introduced him to the world of being cool. It was hard work, learning how to drink beer with the older guys and pick on everyone else. Somebody had to, he thought. All the while he kept going to church. It didn't matter that his mom made him go, he went and that's all there was to it. Surely God would approve or at least overlook a few youthful indiscretions, wouldn't He?

Sophomore year brought notoriety as a track star; junior year he was elected class president and prom prince; and senior year ushered in statewide fame as a football star. Certainly, this was evidence that God was smiling on him. And then it happened. A well-placed helmet obliterated his right knee and his identity. Why, God? Why renege on Your part of the bargain? Six months later Danial's mother was diagnosed with cancer. Why, God? Eight months later his grandmother died while he held her hand. Why, God? Then the answer seemed clear: God hated him, so Danial hated Him back.

In college Danial chugged beer and did shots to assuage his pain and emptiness. His life spiraled out of control. But then he met Andy Lewis who introduced him to Jesus Christ. Things began to change.

The door swung open, and Ian stepped in looking surprisingly cheerful for a man who had spent the last 24 hours in jail.

"Sit down, Ian. We have some business to attend to."

"If this is about your retainer, I'm having the money wired to you this afternoon."

"It's not about the money."

Ian sat with a groan, holding his ribs.

"By now I guess you've heard about the bombing at the hospital?" Danial asked.

"Awesome, wasn't it?"

"Fearsome. It looked like the end of the world."

"Seriously?"

"I need you to be serious," Danial said. "Did you have anything to do with the bombing?"

"Who said I did?"

"No one said you—"

"If someone said I did, they were lying."

"I want you to look me in the eye and tell me you had nothing to do with it."

Ian's face grew serious, and he looked Danial in the eye. "I had nothing to do with it."

"All right, I'll take you at your word. Now, I want to go over a few things with you."

"What's up with my $100,000 bond? Who do they think I am, Jack the Ripper?"

"I really don't know what Williams was thinking. I don't know if he's going senile, or playing politics, but I'll ask for a bond-reduction hearing."

"Good, when?"

"I'll file the motion tomorrow. Hopefully he will give us a hearing on Monday or Tuesday."

"So, what happens now?"

"Well, the deputies handed me this on my way down here." Danial reached into his coat pocket and handed a folded document to Ian.

"What's this?"

"It's a copy of a search warrant."

"For what?"

"Your apartment."

Ian's shoulders slouched a bit. "When will they search it?"

"Probably sometime today."

"Oh."

"You look concerned," Danial said. "They're not going to find anything are they?"

"You never know," Ian said with a smirk. "Things could get interesting."

11:25 A.M.

Lori Franks picked up her phone. If she didn't do it now, she never would. She had to do it while the courage lasted. She called Danial Solomon's number. The phone rang twice then a female voice came on the line.

"Good morning, Danial Solomon's office, Jennifer speaking. May I help you?"

"This is Lori Franks, is Mr. Solomon in?"

"Hello, Ms. Franks. I'm sorry, but Danial isn't in right now."

"When do you expect him back?"

"I haven't seen him since he left for the courthouse this morning."

"He's over here?"

"At least he was earlier. I expected him back about an hour ago. Something must've come up."

"Please tell him I called."

"I most certainly will."

"Thank you very much."

Lori hung up feeling dejected. She picked up a file from her desk, when someone knocked on her door. Her pulse fluttered when she saw the outline of a man through the opaque glass.

"Come in."

The door crept open, and Anthony DiAngello stepped in. Lori's countenance fell.

"What can I do for you, Mr. DiAngello?"

"I've got a case I'd like you to handle."

"Which one?"

"The Baby Ammo case."

"Ah, sir. I just finished the Kisner case. Can't someone else take it?"

"I'm sorry, there must be some misunderstanding. I thought I was your boss."

"You are."

"Well, in that case, I'm ordering you to take the case." He walked out and slammed the door.

"I can't believe he just did that." Her mind turned back to Danial, and she bowed her head.

"Dear God, You know I've never been any good with relationships. I've done some terrible things and certainly don't deserve another chance. But if You see fit to allow Danial to take an interest in me, I promise I won't mess it up this time."

11:27 A.M.

Archie Kisner lay on his bunk staring at the battleship-gray paint peelings on the ceiling. The missing flakes revealed multiple layers of yellow, orange and blue. Graffiti covered the walls. The smell of stale cigarettes and sweat permeated the cellblock. Archie's feet dangled off the end of the metal bunk and pressed against the cinder block wall at the back of the cell.

Archie's first two days in prison etched a deep impression on his feeble mind. Most of the inmates griped about being locked down 22 hours a day, but that part didn't bother Archie. Being locked down kept the men from abusing him; he only had to deal with them while being herded to chow. He had not yet been allowed to take a shower. Sonny had explained that while he was in reception, he would only be permitted to shower every third day. There was nothing to read, but Archie really didn't care because he wasn't much of a reader. He did have the Children's Bible that ministry volunteer Andy Lewis had given him. If he couldn't make out the words, at least he could look at the pictures. Most inmates looked forward to mail call; but Archie was all alone in the world, so there would be no letters coming. Just the same, at mail call he found himself eager to see if someone had written. He may not have been a rocket scientist, but he knew life in prison was going to be a living hell. He wanted to go home.

11:29 A.M.

"So, what happens if they won't reduce my bond?" Ian McKinney asked.

"Then you sit in jail until the trial."

"Could I just pay the bond?"

"Do you have a Hundred Thousand Dollars?"

"Yeah."

"You do?! You can't be 19 years old."

"I'm 20."

"I don't even have that kind of money laying around, and I'm a lawyer. It's not drug money is it?"

"I recently inherited a considerable estate from my grandmother. She was a coal mine heiress."

Danial gave him a suspicious look.

"It's legit. You can check it yourself."

"I will."

"You can trust me, Mr. Solomon."

"All right then, let's move on. I have a buddy in the Prosecutor's Office. Oglebay Park reported an eagle's egg missing from their incubator on Monday after the park closed. You wouldn't know anything about that?"

Ian smirked.

"You don't need to answer that question," Danial said. "You can expect to be charged with aggravated burglary and any number of other things DiAngello can think up within the next few days. If that happens, you are looking at ten years or more at a minimum."

"That's pleasant news." The smirk disappeared from Ian's face. "They can't make the burglary charge stick. They need more than probable cause, don't they?"

"Yes, but juries are funny. I've seen them convict on circumstantial evidence plenty of times."

"What do they have on me so far?"

"Discovery won't officially start until Monday."

"Discovery?"

"By law the State has to make available every piece of evidence they collect on you, either good or bad. As soon as something hits your file, I'll bring it to you."

"Can we sue for police brutality?"

"On what grounds?"

Ian gingerly pulled up his shirt. The entire side of his body, from armpit to hip, was black and blue. The area over the ribs looked greenish purple.

"Oh my gosh, that's horrendous."

"If you can help me lift the back of my shirt, I believe there's some more marks back there. I've had a lot of pain between my shoulders."

Danial reached over and pulled up his orange shirt. A large, round bruise sat almost directly between his shoulder blades. The discoloration encircled a burn that oozed a yellow fluid. Danial's jaw tightened.

"Have you seen a doctor yet?"

"No."

"Good. I'll arrange to have you examined and photographed this afternoon."

13

Danial Solomon climbed the marble steps to the first-floor main lobby. He strolled over to the elevator, pressed the button, and watched the lights over the door. He really didn't have to see the probate judge; the Carney estate hearing wasn't for another month. But since his office just happened to be on the same floor as Lori's, maybe he would bump into her. That would be nice. But then again, what would he say to her? She might find it odd if he just happened to show up, or worse yet, she might think he was stalking her. Maybe this wasn't the best time for a fortuitous meeting. He turned to walk away when the elevator doors slid open, and out walked Lori Franks.

They stared at each other. The violet in her eyes stilled his breath. The world faded around them. That instant lasted a lifetime.

A man in a silk suit cleared his throat behind her and said, "Do you mind if I get off the elevator now?"

"Excuse me," she said, stepping toward Danial.

The man walked by.

They both started to speak but stopped short and gazed speechless with a strange smile, their eyes fastened on each other.

"You first," he said.

"No, you."

"I insist. Ladies first."

"Okay, I was going to comment on how funny it is to see you here." She looked at the ground. "I just called your office."

"You did?"

"I was just... um... I wanted to... um... talk to you about your private practice."

"Oh." His face deflated. "What about it?"

"Nothing specific. I've been considering a few things."

They looked at each other in silence.

"I'm a little busy at the moment," he said. "Maybe we could discuss it over dinner sometime." He bit his bottom lip. "I mean, it wouldn't be a date or anything."

"Sort of a professional dinner."

"Exactly."

"I'd like that very much." She looked into his eyes for a flash, then looked at the ground again.

"When would be a good time for you?"

"I'm free tonight."

His pulse quickened. "Sounds great to me. Where should I pick you up?"

"How about here in the lobby after work?"

"6-ish?"

"Perfect," she said.

12:35 P.M.

Detective Joshua Ross climbed out of his unmarked car in front of a new high-rise apartment building on Steubenville's upper east side. A drop of rain splattered against his forehead. He looked up at the overcast sky. A black-and-white squad car pulled up behind him and two uniformed officers stepped out.

"Now that the gang's all here, we can get this over with," Detective Ross said.

"Do you think we'll find anything?" the gray-haired officer asked as the trio walked toward the main entrance.

"Are you kidding? The kid threw an egg. How dangerous can he be?"

They found the manager's suite and knocked. A bald Italian man opened the door, surprised and gesticulating. "There's no trouble here," he said in broken English.

"We've got a warrant to search the apartment of Mr. Ian McKinney." Ross shoved the document in the manager's face. "Do you have a key to his apartment?"

"Sure, sure. I get it. Wait, wait." He waddled away and returned with a large ring of keys, sweat starting to glisten on his forehead. "He lives on the top floor. This way, this way."

He led them to the elevator at the end of the hall. The four men took a solemn ride upward.

"How does a young punk afford a place like this?" Ross asked.

"I don't know," the Italian said. "I don't know. I just collect the rent. Maybe he lives on pasta."

The elevator doors opened and the manager led them to the third door on the right. He fished through the ring of keys until he found the right one. He unlocked the door and pushed it open.

"Grazie," Ross said. "If we need anything else, we'll give you a call."

Ross and the officers walked in, while the manager nodded and sweated and nodded some more. Ross slammed the door in his face. The threesome found themselves in the living room and gave it the once-over. A large-screen television sat catty-corner on the far side of the room along with a Sega Genesis playstation. A Crestron stereo rack system sat in an oak entertainment center, complete with DVD/CD transport, Cerwin Vega concert speakers, and RCA satellite dish. A cherry-red beanbag chair sat on the floor in front of the television; there were no other pieces of furniture in the room.

Ross took a few steps along the wall and pushed open a door.

"It's his bedroom. We'll search it later."

The posse moved along and found the bathroom; it looked remarkably clean. Ross figured the kid must have a cleaning service. A few feet past the bathroom they discovered a second bedroom; it was completely empty. The kitchen was attached to the living room by a large, arched walkway.

"All right," Ross said. "This is all there is. Why don't you boys hit his bedroom. I'll search the kitchen, and we'll team up for the living room."

"How thorough a shakedown do you want?"

"Strap on some rubber gloves and tear the place up." Smiles curled up on both their lips.

"We aim to please."

The dynamic duo quickstepped it to the bedroom like kids on Christmas. Ross walked into the kitchen and jerked open the refrigerator door to see a 12 pack of Pepsi, several bottles of water, a large jar of grape jelly, and an industrial-sized container of crunchy peanut butter. He closed the door and looked in the freezer. Frigid steam rolled out then vaporized to reveal two empty ice cube trays and nothing else. He closed the door and moved on. The cupboards were empty. He pulled a pen out of his shirt pocket and poked around the garbage can. He pushed aside an empty Pizza Hut box and stirred around a few pop cans but didn't find anything except some junk mail and a losing lottery ticket.

At the far end of the kitchen a glass sliding door led to the balcony. Ross stepped out and admired the commanding view of the Ohio River Valley.

"I live in my mom's basement, and this punk lives up here." He shook his head and walked back inside. A breakfast nook sat off to his left. Newspaper clippings of various sizes papered the walls of the nook. He took a closer look, and his jaw dropped.

"These are abortion clinic bombings, all of them."

A few moments later a voice shouted from the bedroom, "Detective, you'd better get in here."

Ross jogged back to join the uniformed officers hovering over the computer center next to an unmade king sized bed. The gray-haired officer held in his hand diagrams for building a homemade bomb, downloaded off the Internet.

"Bingo," Ross said.

14

Danial Solomon sat in his car flipping through the photos taken of Ian McKinney. The doctor determined that two ribs on Ian's left side were broken. The area between his shoulder blades, where the taser darts had pierced his flesh, had sustained second-degree burns. Danial slid the photos back in the brown envelope and tucked it in his briefcase. His thoughts drifted to Lori as he opened the glove compartment and grabbed a brush. He looked in the rearview mirror and attempted to style his hair. The more he brushed the more the wiry strands rebelled; the gray ones were most uncooperative.

Danial climbed out of the car and squinted against the orange sun low on the western horizon. He nodded to the statue of Edwin Stanton as he walked by and trotted up the main steps to the courthouse lobby. Several media types milled around listening for the latest rumors on the bombing. Sheriff Rose had beefed up the deputy presence in the courthouse, and they all seemed to be obsessively drawn to the vending machines. Danial looked around, saw no sign of Lori Franks, and took a seat in a vinyl chair.

He checked his watch, then glanced at the clock on the wall over the receptionist's desk, then checked his watch again. He tapped his freshly polished wingtips on the floor. The elevator opened and Lori stepped out. When he had seen her earlier in the day, she had her hair pulled up neatly in clips. Now, her jet-black tresses spilled down over her shoulders. She wore an ivory silk blouse with a black cardigan tied around her shoulders. The ensemble nicely accentuated her curves. Her delicate profile paused and she scanned the room until she found him.

He stood. They smiled at one another.

"Shall we?" he said, sweeping his arm toward the door.

"I hope you didn't have to wait long."

"Not at all," he said. *I've been waiting all my life.*

They nodded and smiled, and then chatted as the car sped along the Ohio River on Route 7. The autumn hills on both sides of the river were speckled with every conceivable shade of red, yellow, orange and brown. They crossed the river at Bridgeport then drove through the Wheeling Tunnel. A few minutes later they parked outside Ernie's Esquire, then strolled into the dimly lit bistro. The maître d' met them just inside the door.

"Reservation, sir?"

"Solomon, party of two," Danial said.

The maître d' ran his finger down the list of names. "Oh, yes. Right this way, your table is ready."

He escorted them to a corner table near the grand piano where an old gentleman in a black tie softly played Beethoven's "Für Elise." They sat across the small round table from one another.

"So how are things down at the courthouse?" Danial asked.

"I'm so sick of all the politics. They wheel and deal with people's lives like it's all one big chess game."

"You're preaching to the choir."

"DiAngello gave me the so-called Baby Ammo case today."

"Any leads?"

"The police have eliminated all the cars that drove through the parking lot on the day the baby was found, except for a blue VW Bug."

"Sounds like a nasty case."

"I don't want it."

"I'm impressed with how fast they're moving on this one."

The waitress walked over and lit the candle centerpiece. She offered a wine list, but Danial declined. She handed them menus then walked away.

A busboy filled the water glasses and dropped off a basket of rolls.

"DiAngello's been pitching a fit since the bombing," Lori said.

"It's election time." Danial buttered a roll. "So, is this why you are interested in private practice?"

"Six months ago, a case like this wouldn't have phased me a bit. But after everything I've just gone through with the Lewis family - finding out about little Erin and all - this is too much. I mean they up and moved to Wyoming."

"They thought it best for everyone."

"I'm not saying it's not. Lord knows, with my attempted abortion, the baby rescue and my custody proceedings, I've put them through hell. It is just that everything is just so fresh. And I've only been a Christian for about a month now. My whole life has been turned upside down."

"I know it all seems so overwhelming," Danial said, wanting to reach across to hold her hands. "When you gave your heart to God, He gave you a new worldview. It's almost like you'd lived your life legally blind, and now all of a sudden, you've had corrective surgery. At first everything is going to seem overwhelming until you get used to it."

The waitress returned with two bowls of salad. She waited for a few moments, then said, "What will the lady be having tonight?"

"I'll have the French onion soup with a baked potato on the side, please."

"And for the gentleman?"

"I'll have the roast duck marinated in raspberry sauce, please."

"Very good." The waitress gathered the menus and hurried toward the kitchen.

"I've started reading the Bible daily," Lori said. "There's so much I don't understand, and I've got so many questions."

"Like what?"

"Oh, I don't want to keep bothering you. Someone said I should get a study Bible and a Bible dictionary. I've already twisted your ear enough. And I'm tired of hearing my own voice."

The reflection of the flickering candle danced in her eyes. She seemed like a soulmate. And she looked beautiful. And Danial's stomach tightened.

"Lori, I... uh..."

"What is it?"

The waitress approached and placed their orders on the table. The delectable aroma of raspberry and duck filtered through the air. They ate quietly, occasionally making eye contact and smiling. When they finished, the waitress cleared the table and offered a dessert menu. Lori declined; Danial ordered a piece of New York Cheesecake.

"You started to say something before dinner," Lori said.

"I did." He took a deep breath, and his stomach tightened again. "I've got to be honest with you, Lori, I find you incredibly interesting and attractive, and I'd like to be more than friends."

A dimple appeared suddenly in her left cheek.

"And, it's all right if you don't feel the same way, but—"

"I do, I do!"

"You do?"

She nodded and looked as if she'd burst. "Yes."

"But Tuesday you said—"

"I know, I was stupid and scared of my feelings."

The waitress delivered the cheesecake. They playfully took alternating bites until it was gone. They said little, but their eyes spoke volumes.

8:15 P.M.

Dr. Gaston Garvey felt the effects of the alcohol as he staggered toward the bathroom. A few minutes later he stumbled back to the card table set up in the middle of his fashionably appointed living room. The interior design work was the only thing his ex-wife left behind after the divorce.

Garvey grew up in Lakewood, a suburb of Cleveland, and did his undergraduate work at Baldwin-Wallace College. After graduating near the top of his class he got accepted to Case Western Reserve University's School of Medicine. Following graduation, he was repeatedly turned down for residencies at the Cleveland Clinic. Finally, he took a position at Steubenville's University Hospital. Garvey married right out of medical school but after eight years, multiple ulcers, and a vicious divorce, Garvey found himself a bachelor once again.

"I dealt and bid one club," said the doctor sitting to Garvey's right. "My lawyer was down at the courthouse and heard some rumors about the bombing."

"I double one club." Garvey fanned out his cards. "What'd he hear?"

"Something about the kid who threw the egg may have also been involved."

"I pass," said the doctor to Garvey's left.

The conversation ground to a halt as all eyes turned to Garvey's partner.

"Oh, it's on me? I bid one no-trump."

"Dealer bids two spades." He folded up his cards and looked at Garvey. "Have you heard anything new on the Baby Ammo thing?"

"Game in hearts," Garvey said. "No, but the whole thing pisses me off. I ought to write a letter to the editor and get it out of my system." He gulped a mouthful of beer. "I pass."

Again, all eyes focused on Garvey's partner.

"Sorry, I pass."

"Dealer doubles four hearts." He picked up his cards. "If you write a letter, you can mention my name too. Anyone who could do that to a baby needs to be locked away."

"Your sock," Garvey said to the man to his left. He guzzled some more beer. It drowned his conscience.

15

Detective Buck Demus drummed his fingers on the steering wheel of his unmarked cruiser. A thin veil of fog slightly obstructed his view of the duplex on Clinton Avenue. He double-checked the address he acquired from the Bureau of Motor Vehicles.

"This is the place," he said.

"I don't see any VW Bug," the uniformed officer said, sitting in the passenger seat.

Demus picked up the radio microphone. "All listening units, stay in position until we acquire the target." He hung up the microphone and said, "It looks like our arrest has turned into a stakeout."

The early morning sun struggled to burn off the haze. Demus nursed his *Super Cup* of black coffee with his eyes fixed on the house. The side-by-side duplex sat about 50 feet back from the sidewalk. The yellow siding looked new. The tall grass in the front yard effectively captured the leaves falling from the knotty oak tree near the driveway.

"Unit 1, this is car 74. Be advised I've got a visual on a blue VW Bug license number Alpha... Bravo... Tango... six... niner... four."

"Copy that," Demus said into the microphone. "It's show time."

A few minutes later the VW Bug came to a rolling stop at the intersection at the end of Clinton Avenue. A black-and-white patrol car followed at a distance. The blue Bug continued down the street and turned into the driveway.

"Move, move!" Demus shouted into the radio.

The black-and-white accelerated and then screeched in behind the Bug. Demus pulled in behind him. A young girl stepped out of the Bug and walked toward the patrol car. The officer kicked open his door and pointed a shotgun at the girl's face.

"Freeze or I'll shoot!"

He pumped the weapon.

She screamed and staggered back.

Demus jerked his 9mm out of his shoulder holster and stalked toward her. Uniformed officers brandishing an assortment of weapons crawled out from behind neighboring houses and trees and surrounded the trembling teenager.

"Are you Norma Fitzpatrick?" Demus asked.

She nodded with a look of terror in her eyes.

"You're under arrest for the murder of John Doe."

"But... but... I don't know any John Doe."

"Oh, you don't?" Demus said. "Maybe you know him by the name Baby Ammo."

9:15 A.M.

Danial Solomon walked from the elevator through the corridor to Anthony DiAngello's office wondering what in the world the prosecutor could want the day after the arraignment. *Surely he wouldn't offer a plea bargain. Discovery hasn't even started yet. He might want to drop the charges, but that's highly unlikely.* Danial knocked on DiAngello's office door.

"Come in."

"My secretary said you wanted to see me," Danial said and closed the door behind him.

"Have a seat Danny boy."

"What can I do for you, Tony?"

"I've got something I want you to see."

"What is it?"

"You'll see." DiAngello pressed the intercom button on his

desk. "Send in the file."

The door opened and in walked Colin Casey who took a seat right next to Danial. He proffered the file, saying, "I think you'll enjoy this."

Danial took the file, opened it and began reading. The file contained a report of the findings from Ian McKinney's apartment.

"Devastating," Casey said. "Isn't it?"

"I'm sure I don't know what you mean. This has nothing to do with the charges against my client."

"It will in about four hours when this file is presented to the grand jury," DiAngello said. "Along with some additional things."

"Like what?"

"You'll see. Watch the 5 o'clock news."

"Then why show this to me now?"

"Just trying to be helpful," DiAngello said.

Danial handed the file back to Casey and stood up. "It's circumstantial at best, it proves nothing. Is there anything else?"

"No," DiAngello said. "Just a little courtesy. You know, early Discovery and all."

"I see." Danial took long strides toward the door. "Good day, gentlemen."

Danial made a beeline for the elevator. He felt so angry at Ian for lying to him, the urge to choke welled up inside his chest. He kicked the elevator wall, then fought to regain his composure as the elevator doors opened in the basement jail. He bellied up to the booking desk with credentials in hand.

"I'd like to see Ian McKinney."

"I'll have him brought right over," the deputy said. "You can go on back and wait for him."

Danial walked down the corridor, with its familiar nauseating scent, toward the interrogation rooms. He turned the corner and saw three uniformed officers standing guard outside one of the rooms. Angry muffled voices drifted through the soundproof door. One of the deputies nodded to Danial. He nodded back and stepped inside the opposite room to await his client. A couple minutes later a groggy-looking Ian walked in, his hair matted to his head and something crusty stuck in the corners of his eyes.

"Sit down," Danial said with uncharacteristic firmness.

Ian obeyed.

"You lied to me."

"No I didn't."

"You lied to me."

"I don't know what—"

Danial slammed his fist on the table. "I saw the diagrams of a bomb, Ian. Deputies and a detective found them in your apartment with your fingerprints all over them. Now deny it and I'll walk."

"I can explain."

"And you had a memorial of clippings to abortion clinic bombings."

"I really can explain."

"This ought to be good."

"Please, give me a chance."

"I think we've come to the point where you tell me everything."

"I'll tell you anything you want to know."

"Start at the beginning."

"All right." He took a deep breath. "I'll start at the beginning. My mother - my biological mother that is - had some problems when she was younger."

"Problems?"

"Emotional problems, mental problems."

"Go on."

"Well, anyways, she got pregnant when she was 16 and her parents wanted her to go get an abortion. My mom may not have been the sharpest tool in the shed, but she knew she didn't want to murder her kid. But what could she do? She was completely dependent on her parents; she couldn't even drive. So, she broke down and agreed to go."

"But you didn't die."

"I'm getting to that. They put her on a bus to Wheeling - they didn't even have the guts to take her to the clinic themselves. Fortunately for me, Operation Rescue was out in force, picketing out in front of the clinic. A young couple listened to her story and urged her not to go through with it. They invited her into their home until I was born, and even helped her get me placed with a Christian family. If my dismissive grandparents would have had their way, I wouldn't be here right now. My body would have been incinerated and my brain tissue used for research."

"It's a moving story, and I don't doubt it's true, but—"

"But what's it got to do with the price of eggs in China?"

"Exactly."

"Well, knowing how I almost didn't make it into the world, every time I see a pregnant woman going into a hospital to get the brains sucked out of her baby it makes my blood boil. And when those butchers ride into work all high and mighty, I just, just have to do something."

"So, you bombed the place?"

"Haven't you been listening?"

"Of course."

"If I was involved in a bombing, I'd be no better than those butchers."

"So why the diagrams and newspaper articles?"

"I'm trying to figure out what's really going on, I'm trying to find a connection, who and how—"

"What are you talking about?"

"I can't prove anything yet, so..."

"You're not helping me here."

"You've got to trust me."

"I've got to know more," Danial said. "but I've got to go."

"Please believe me, I'm not a bomber."

"Whether you are or not, I can guarantee you'll be charged before the end of the day—"

"Will you defend me?"

"Ian, this case is getting more complicated by the minute. It's going to require a lot of time and effort."

"Don't worry about the money, Mr. Solomon. You'll run out of breath before I run out of money."

9:40 A.M.

Norma Fitzpatrick cried uncontrollably in the interrogation room. A detective and a deputy stood behind her. Detective Demus ranted and raved and spewed questions and his raunchy coffee breath right in her face. Demus was an odd-looking man with a big head and wide body. His eyes seemed too big and were unusually far apart.

"So, you didn't do it," Demus said. "Then how come your classmates and teachers said you were looking pregnant when you came to school Tuesday morning and by Wednesday your girlish figure returned. Was it a crash diet?"

"I... didn't... do... it," she said between sobs.

"Norma, all you have to do is tell the truth, and we'll help you sort this thing out," said a voice behind her.

"I'm telling you the truth." She pulled a few tear-saturated strands of her chestnut hair out of her eyes.

"We checked every abortion clinic in Ohio," Demus said. "And lo and behold, nobody's heard of you. And your parents are conveniently out of town this week. No witnesses, huh, Norma?" He paused. "We notified them of your arrest."

She made eye contact with Demus.

He leaned closer. "That's right, we tracked them all the way to Miami. I'm sure they'll be pleased with you when they get back."

Her crying intensified.

"We know you're scared," said the friendly voice from behind. "People make mistakes when they get scared. We all do."

"We found your diary, Norma," Demus said.

"No!" she screamed.

"We know all about what you were going to do." Demus produced the pink, lace-covered book from a box by the door. "Here's the entry from last Sunday night: 'Carl is going to help me get rid of this shame. I can't wait to get it over with.'"

Norma covered her face with her hands.

Demus grinned at her. "As soon as we find this Carl person, things are really going to get interesting. Why don't you make it easy on all of us and tell us the truth?"

She felt trapped, like a badger caught in a trap. She would gladly chew her own arm off to get free. She screamed at the top of her lungs, "Somebody help me!!"

"Save your breath. This ain't the movies. Nobody can hear you. So why don't you—"

The door blew open and struck Demus in the back. A good-looking man in a gray suit pressed in.

"Get out!" Demus yelled in the man's face. "This is official business."

"Don't say another word," the man said to Norma, then turned back to Demus. "From this second forward, I'm representing this girl."

"Solomon, you seem to have a habit of sticking your nose in my business."

"Would you rather have a boot up..."

16

Danial Solomon returned to his office a weary man. He trudged over to Jennifer's desk and slouched down into a chair. Jennifer stopped typing and looked up from her computer.

"You look like they just cancelled Christmas. Rough day?" she asked.

"You wouldn't believe it."

"Try me."

"DiAngello dug up some dirt on McKinney, tying him to the bombing."

"Are you serious?"

"As a heart attack. He told me to watch the 5 o'clock news."

"Probably explosive," she said.

"That's not the half of it. While I'm down giving McKinney the third degree, I hear this commotion coming from the interrogation room across the hall. As it turns out they arrested a teenage girl in the Baby Ammo murder, and good old Detective Demus is over there shoving bamboo shoots under her nails."

"That name sounds familiar."

"He's the piece of work that beat up Archie the night he was arrested."

"What did you do next?"

"I took her case and cleared the room and threatened to sue Demus."

"Man, you did have a rough day."

"Now I've got to call Lori and give her the news."

"You mean Ms. Franks? Why do you have to call her?"

"It's a long story, I'd rather not get into it."

"Come on now, Danial, I've been a very sympathetic ear

through several of your relationships, haven't I?"

"So?"

"Sympathy is what a woman gives in exchange for details. Now spill it."

"Lori and I went to dinner last night."

"What?! And you didn't tell me?"

"It wasn't a planned thing. Well, anyway, one thing led to another, and we told each other about our feelings for one another."

"What feelings?"

"We like each other."

"Exact words, give me exact words."

"I will not."

Jennifer pouted her bottom lip in a feigned expression of hurt.

"But now do you see my dilemma?" he asked.

"No."

"Lori is prosecuting the Baby Ammo case."

"And?"

"We have a legal conflict."

"Oooohhhh, now I see. She's going to think you don't like her."

"You did it again."

"I did what again?"

"One of those feminine leaps of logic that leave us men clueless."

"What are you talking about?"

"What in the world does me taking this case have to do with whether or not I like Lori?"

"She's going to think it does."

"You can explain that to me later." He looked at his watch. "It's almost time for the news. You want to watch it with me?"

"Sure." She stood up. "I'll get the coffee."

Danial went into his office and flipped on the television. Talking raisins danced across the screen, so he pressed the mute button on the remote control. He set the DVR just in case. Jennifer tiptoed in with a cup of coffee in each hand. She handed him one, and they took their seats. The lead-in for the news filled the screen. Danial turned on the volume.

Anthony DiAngello stood on a platform behind a podium banked with microphones. The camera zoomed in on a man in a black suit to DiAngello's left. The breaking news ticker indicated he was the FBI director out of Youngstown. Sheriff Rose stood to DiAngello's right, and Colin Casey stood next to him. The camera cut to a pretty blonde in the foreground.

"This is Katie Welch, live at the Jefferson County Courthouse where Prosecutor DiAngello has just stepped to the podium and is about to give a statement."

DiAngello's face filled the screen. "The grand jury, at about 2 o'clock this afternoon, issued the first of three indictments in the University Hospital bombing to Mr. Ian McKinney. He's already in custody on related charges. The names of the other two suspects will not be released at this time as we have not yet apprehended them. We have some surveillance footage to show."

The camera zoomed in on a TV sitting atop a metal stand in the corner where a deputy stood by waiting for the cue. DiAngello nodded and black-and-white images came to life on the screen. A crowd of protesters marched around the buffer zone. A yellow arrow pointed to a man in the corner.

"This footage was shot from the top of a light pole in the parking lot of the hospital. If I can direct your attention to the lower left-hand corner. The arrow is pointing to Mr. McKinney."

The throng parted as a white van pressed through. As soon as it broke free of the crowd, a figure stepped forward and threw something at the van.

"That object you've just seen McKinney throw was a bald eagle egg," DiAngello said. "Now watch closely."

Ian scampered back to the crowd, picked up a square object and tossed it into the steel garbage dumpster a few feet away. The screen froze with the object in midair.

"This next shot is from the camera over the Emergency Room Ambulance Bay. You can see that the protesters scurried in all directions like cockroaches when the lights come on. In the midst of the chaos, two men in black dashed into a manhole and quickly pulled the lid closed. The next footage was taken before midnight, before detonation...."

A VW Bug drove out of the parking lot. The manhole and the big dumpster were in plain view. All quiet. A clock in the upper right-hand corner showed the time to be a few minutes before midnight. Fast-forward and a brilliant flash filled the screen. The dumpster vaporized and flaming debris rained down on the area. A moment later an eruption of fire poured out of the manhole and an enormous explosion stopped the footage.

"In conjunction with the FBI and ATF, we've initiated a nationwide manhunt for the two individuals you saw crawling into the manhole."

The reporters launched a flurry of questions.

"We're not prepared to answer any questions at this time."

"What about Baby Ammo?" a female voice asked. "Is it true you have somebody in custody?"

"An arrest was made this morning, but no charges have officially been brought at this time."

"Who's the suspect?"

"I cannot release her name at this time."

"But it is a female?" a man asked.

"That's what I said."

"Why can't you give us her name?" another voice asked. "Is she a minor?"

"I've said all I'm prepared to say at this time."

DiAngello walked off the stage followed by his entourage.

"What do you think of that?" Jennifer asked.

Danial held up his index finger. "Hold on a minute."

The screen flashed to a pretty brunette reporter holding a microphone up to Judge Williams.

"Your Honor, I'm Victoria Heitman with the 5 o'clock news. What can you tell us about the restraining order you issued?"

"In light of the recent activities at University Hospital," Williams said, "I've taken it upon myself to issue a temporary restraining order against all abortion protesters at the hospital."

"How long will the order last?"

"Until I say otherwise."

The camera zoomed in on the reporter's face. "There you have it, another late-breaking development. Back to you at the studio."

Danial turned off the television and stared at the blank screen for a few moments.

"What do you think?" Jennifer asked.

"To tell you the truth, I don't know what to think."

17

Ron Kester parked his brown Toyota pickup near the side entrance of the Bob Evans Restaurant on Sunset Boulevard. He could see Art Bently through the window at the prearranged booth. Art stood 5 foot 10 and weighed about 210. His skinny arms and legs looked odd on a man his size; he carried the bulk of his weight in his belly. His black hair had grayed at the temples. One continuous black eyebrow ran the width of his face above hazel eyes, a pug nose and an oversized mouth. His stubbly beard came in salt and pepper.

Ron calmly walked in and joined Art in the corner booth near the restrooms. A waitress delivered two piping hot cups of coffee then took their orders. Art fidgeted nervously, his denim pants squeaking on the blue Naugahyde seat.

"Jeez, Ron, I'm really scared about this stuff we got started."

"We just shed some light on an evil thing is all."

"Jeez, this is big. You saw the news."

"But they didn't show our faces. If they knew who we were we'd already be in jail."

A sleepy-eyed waitress walked over balancing a platter of food. She placed a steaming tray of scrambled eggs and bacon in front of Art and a heaping mound of blueberry pancakes in front of Ron. The aroma brought a smile to Ron's face.

"Anything else?" she asked.

"Not right now, thanks," Ron said.

She walked away.

"Believe me, Art, this is all going to be worth it as soon as Birch does his thing. He said the people in D.C. are pretty excited."

"You talked to Birch?"

"This afternoon." Ron jammed a bite of pancakes into his mouth. "He said we need to lay low for a while until this blows over."

They ate quietly for several minutes. Art kept looking out into the parking lot. A Steubenville police car pulled in between Ron's truck and Art's VW Bug.

"Hey Ron, look. Maybe he's following us."

The officer got out of the car and headed for the side door.

"What do we do?" Art asked, in a whisper.

"Stay calm and keep eating your toast."

The cop pulled open the door, walked over and took a seat on a stool at the counter, and ordered a cup of coffee. Ron and Art ate slowly and watched him out of the corners of their eyes. The waitress poured the coffee into a large styrofoam cup. The cop picked it up and headed for the same door he came in. They waited till he drove away before resuming their talk.

"Man, that was close," Art said. "What do we do now?"

"My uncle's got an old hunting cabin he hasn't used in years. We could hide out there."

"Where is it?"

"Near Moundsville, West Virginia. No one would ever find us."

"When do we leave?"

"Tonight."

"Jeez, tonight?"

"You heard the news, there's a manhunt out for us. The Feds and the police work 24/7. We need to get while the gettin's good."

"But tonight?"

"I've got the truck packed, and I'm leaving with or without you. Now, you coming?"

"Yeah, I'm coming. What do I need?"

"Grab some clothes and your guns, and we'll be ready to roll."

They finished eating, paid the bill and tipped the waitress. Ron followed Art's car to his home in Yorkville. Ron waited in his truck, drumming his fingers on the steering wheel in time with the music. Twenty minutes later Art hustled out the back door with two gun cases and a large cardboard box. Ron leaned over and opened the door. Art placed the box on the seat and slid his weapons behind it.

"How long will it take us to get there?" Art asked.

"We'll make some detours to shake any followers and stick to the back roads. I've intentionally picked a roundabout way, so we should get there by three."

"How long you expect we'll be gone?"

"When it's safe to resurface."

"I hope it's worth it."

"It is, and it will be. Now close the door, and let's get going."

They backed out and nearly bumped into the blue VW Bug parked in the driveway.

11:20 P.M.

Archie Kisner lay in bed staring at the dingy ceiling. His door buzzed and rattled open.

"Kisner, front and center," the guard yelled over the chaos.

Archie slipped on his jumpsuit and ran out onto the catwalk. He looked down at the guard's desk. An enormous black officer wearing a white shirt with brass captain's bars on the shoulders stood next to the gray-shirted officer. Even though it was nearly midnight, the captain wore mirrored sunglasses and repeatedly slapped his baton into his left palm.

Archie marched down the range, slowing when he reached Sonny's cell near the top of the stairs.

"Not good, Arch. Either someone died or you going to the hole."

Archie lumbered down the steps. It couldn't be a death notice, because everyone in his family was already dead. He thought back over the day, and for the life of him he couldn't think of any rules he had broken. He apprehensively approached the captain.

"You Kisner?"

Archie looked down at the captain's patent leather shoes.

"Yessir."

"Come with me."

"You want me to cuff him, Cap?" the guard asked.

"Naw, if he gets uppity on me, I'll split his skull." He shoved open the heavy steel door. "Let's go Kisner."

They walked out onto the yard under the flood of lights. Archie's hands trembled; he trembled all over. He wanted to ask where they were going, but he was too scared to speak. The captain led him through the front door of the Administration Building, down a long hallway, and into a windowless corner office.

"Sit down," the captain said.

Archie obeyed. The captain strolled around behind the desk and unhooked the radio from his belt; he turned it off and set it on the desk. He unsheathed the baton and laid it on the desk next to the radio, then sat down and took off his sunglasses.

"You're probably wondering what you're doing here?"

Archie nodded; his hands still trembled.

"I'm Captain Jackson. A friend of mine gave me a call a few days ago and asked me to do him a favor. You know a man named Danial Solomon?"

"Yessir, he's... he's my lawyer."

"You got a good one then. He asked me to look in on you from time to time and make sure you're holding up all right. You okay?"

Archie's lip quivered. "Yessir."

"Good. I know that sign out front says this is the Department of Rehabilitation and Correction, but believe me, we're lean on the rehab and such. Most young kids come here with penny-ante stuff, and we turn them into hardened criminals. The old cons call this gladiator school. But in every joint, there's a flicker of light. You know what that light is?"

Archie shook his head.

"That light is Jesus Christ."

For the first time in three days, Archie Kisner smiled.

"We got a couple of good chaplains here who love the Lord.

You make sure you're at the chapel as much as possible. God can do wonders in a man's life in pits like this. Old Joseph did about 13 years in slavery and prison while God was preparing him for big things. Let God have His way. You understand me son?"

"Yessir."

"Now if you get into any trouble, you tell the nearest officer to notify me immediately. But it won't do you much good to be dropping my name around. The cons will think you're a snitch. So, the things I tell you, keep between you and me. Understand?"

"Uh huh."

"Now give me your hands."

Archie leaned forward and the two men joined hands. Captain Jackson led Archie through a powerfully moving prayer. A prison officer and a convicted felon stood at God's throne of grace as brothers.

Monday, October 9
8:35 A.M.

Colin Casey reveled gleefully in his self-constructed media extravaganza. Over the weekend and at his request, representatives from several activist groups descended upon the normally quiet Ohio Valley. Animal rights groups villainized Ian McKinney for his atrocity against the unborn eagle. Pro-choice groups condemned him as a radical hypocrite who resorted to bombing. Pro-life groups were up in arms over the death of Baby Ammo. The hotels and motels within 30 miles of Steubenville flashed "No Vacancy" notices. Signs, banners, and T-shirts touting one group or another could be seen almost everywhere.

Colin Casey grew up the son of a small-town politician. His father served four terms as mayor for a town whose population never exceeded a thousand. Yet, political fervor struck young Casey at an early age, and his ambition knew no limits. He was active with the Young Democrats at *the* Ohio State University and following graduation his rise within the state party could only be described as meteoric. He had only one brother, a shiftless youth, whom the family had lost track of years ago.

Casey strolled into Judge Williams' office like he'd just won the lottery. His sandy blond hair looked a little unkempt, and dried toothpaste ringed his lips. He carried a copy of the Sunday *Herald-Star* under his left arm, and a stack of survey printouts.

"Smile, Your Honor, I've just orchestrated the greatest comeback in political history. You and Foster are running at a statistical dead heat."

"Excellent! What gave us the push?"

"A combination of things. The injunction we filed on Friday played well. It stayed in the news all weekend. And I think the activism I brought you on the McKinney case went a long way."

"I see you brought in some heavy hitters: the Animal Rights League, the EPA, the Audubon Society, Defenders of Wildlife."

"I pulled out all the stops." He opened the Sunday paper and laid it on the desk. A picture of Williams adorned the front page along with a short article. "Did you see this?"

"Yeah, I saw it. Impressive, but in the future, if you're going to attribute a quote to me, I'd appreciate knowing if you're going to put words in my mouth."

"I didn't have a chance to get ahold of you in time to make the front-page deadline."

"So, what do we do now?"

"We continue drawing distinctions between you and Foster. He's still preaching his social conservatism every chance he gets. So, what we do now is tie him to those picketing lunatics down at the hospital, and he'll go down in flames."

"Sounds like a plan."

"Now we need to press those buffoons upstairs to nail McKinney. Between the eagle egg and the bombing, the free press will be worth a mint. And I might be able to get the trial on *Court TV.*"

"I'll make a few calls and grease the skids." Williams picked up the phone with a smile. "This old dog can still do a few tricks."

8:50 A.M.

Danial Solomon sat in the tiny blue visiting room waiting for his first meeting with Norma Fitzpatrick. The thought of a young woman brutally murdering her own child totally repulsed him, and this was certainly not the kind of case he would usually take. But God brought Norma into his life for a reason. While she obviously needed his legal help she also needed the Gospel. She needed a new life.

The door opened and a female deputy escorted Danial's newest client. Norma Fitzpatrick was about 5 foot 4, and looked slightly overweight. A thin mop of stringy auburn hair crowned her round face. She had very thin eyebrows, dark brown eyes, a pudgy nose and full lips. The blaze orange jail garb didn't agree with her pale complexion. She appeared nervous and exhausted.

Danial stood and shook her hand. "I've got to be honest with you, Norma, right now it doesn't look good. The circumstantial evidence is overwhelming."

"I didn't do it."

"I know you said you didn't do it, but if we're going to put a defense together, we need a plausible explanation for the evidence they have against you."

"Like what?" She sucked in her right cheek and chewed on the skin.

"Well, for starters, how do you explain that the car caught on camera, dropping off the baby at the police station, matches your VW Bug?"

"It must be a coincidence."

"Coincidence won't carry the day in court. You've got to do better than that."

Norma shrugged her shoulders.

"Of course, the most critical issue we have to address is the fact that you were pregnant the day before the baby was found, then all of a sudden you're no longer pregnant the day after."

"I can explain that."

"Go ahead."

"Not now."

"What do you mean not now?"

"I'm not ready to talk about it yet." Tears welled up in her eyes, then bubbled over and ran down her cheeks. She wiped them away with the back of her hand.

"I know this is hard on you, but I need to know what happened in order to provide you with an adequate defense." He handed her his handkerchief. "I spoke to your parents last night."

"This should be good."

"I wish I had better news for you. But they said they told you they were completely against you having an abortion, and if you did this to your own child, then you deserve the consequences."

"My parents don't understand me at all." Her lip quivered. "They don't care about me. They just don't want their friends to talk bad about them." She paused for a moment. "I don't have any money to pay you."

Danial grinned. "I kind of figured as much. That's all right, I've taken cases pro bono before - that means free of charge. And if you're telling me the truth you won't even be indicted. I filed a motion requesting a DNA test. If it comes back negative, they probably won't charge you. But then again, the public wants a conviction, and Prosecutor DiAngello is anxious to give them one. Frankly, I don't think he cares who he convicts, just as long as he gets a conviction."

"But I didn't do it."

"Then you have nothing to worry about."

"I was home with a friend that afternoon. I certainly didn't drop my baby off at the police station."

"You have an alibi, good, what's your friend's name?"

"I can't tell you."

"I'm trying to believe you, but you're not helping me."

"You don't understand, I can't get him involved." She sucked in her cheek and began gnawing again.

"What happened to your baby?"

She dropped her eyes and took several deep breaths. She looked up and opened her mouth, then dropped her eyes again.

"Whatever you say is confidential. I'm your lawyer, you can trust me."

"I had an abortion."

"But your name didn't show up on the records of any abortion facilities in Ohio."

"I don't want to get my friend in trouble."

"This friend of yours, was he the father?"

Norma nodded.

"Did he kill the baby?"

She shook her head.

"All right, you don't have to answer any more questions for now. The nurse will be in this afternoon to draw some blood. I'll let you know when the results come back."

9:10 A.M.

Lori Franks sat quietly in Anthony DiAngello's office waiting for him to get off the phone. From listening to his side of the conversation she gathered he was either talking to his ex-wife or her lawyer, and he wasn't doing well for himself. He stopped mid-sentence, his face soured, and he ended the call. He ran both his hands through his curly black hair. "Sorry for the delay, now, where were we?"

"Baby Ammo," she said.

"That's right. What's the status of that case?"

"The Harrison County Coroner's Office faxed us the official pathology report this morning."

"It's about time."

"I found it rather surprising. They ruled the baby died from a broken neck."

"I thought there was a puncture wound in the back of the head."

"There is."

"Maybe one wound was supposed to mask the other?"

"The puncture happened first."

"Has the girl made a statement yet?"

"No, but we've got enough to go to the grand jury when the time comes."

"I've got a thousand irons in the fire here, so forgive me if I'm being redundant, but what exactly do we have?"

"A couple dozen classmates and three teachers have given statements verifying she was pregnant on Monday when she left school." Lori dug through the bulging file on her lap. "We also have her diary. She chronicles the day she got pregnant, and her parents' reaction when they found out. In the final entry she discusses getting rid of her shame."

"Anything else?"

"The make and model of her car matches the one the police say was used to drop off the baby at the police station. I'm pretty sure that'll be enough to bring back an indictment."

"Let's go to the grand jury this afternoon."

"One glitch there, Chief. We have to petition the Juvenile Court for jurisdiction to try her as an adult."

He smacked himself on the forehead. "That's right."

"First thing this morning her lawyer filed a motion requesting a DNA test. If it comes back negative, we could be setting ourselves up for a big embarrassment."

"The legendary Mr. Solomon." DiAngello leaned back in his chair with a scowl on his face. "Of the hundreds of attorneys practicing law in Jefferson County, every time I turn around Solomon's got his foot on my neck."

"Maybe we should wait until the lab results come back. If the DNA is a match, she's in trouble."

"That makes sense." He dabbed at his nose. "You know I'm handling the McKinney case personally."

She nodded.

"You just tried the Kisner case against Solomon; how does he think?"

"Danial doesn't think the way most people do. It seems that his mind operates on a higher level of logic. He can simultaneously process multiple divergent concepts, make them dovetail into a cohesive point, then explain it all to a jury in such a way a 3-year-old could understand." Lori smiled; her pulse quickened. She wanted to mention his dreamy blue eyes. "From a strictly professional standpoint, I'd say he has the keenest mind I've ever encountered."

"Hum."

A rapid knock on the door. Before DiAngello could open his mouth, the door popped open and Colin Casey stuck his head in.

"Sorry to bother you, Tony. I just got word the FBI is investigating a break-in at the Fort Henry Arsenal in Wheeling. They believe the amount of explosives missing roughly coincides with the damage at the hospital."

Casey withdrew his head and closed the door.

"That punk knows more about what's going on in my jurisdiction - my office - than I do." DiAngello shook his head in disgust. "He really burns me up."

"He gives me the creeps," Lori said.

9:30 A.M.

"Good morning, counselor," Ian McKinney said as he shuffled into the visiting cube. "What's new?"

"The Discovery process officially began today, Ian."

Danial reached into his brown leather briefcase and grabbed a manila file, then slammed it on the table. His eyes glistened with anger and betrayal. "You swore you were leveling with me, you promised you weren't part of some terrorist group."

"I'm not."

"Have you watched any TV over the past three days? You and your buddies are national news."

"I don't know those men."

"Give it a break, Ian. First, a detective found articles from every abortion clinic bombing since the 1970s plastered all over your kitchen like some sick shrine—"

"I told you I can explain."

"I'm tired of your explanations." Danial slapped the palm of his hand against the table. "What about the dozen schematics in your apartment for do-it-yourself bombs?"

"But—"

"What kind of madness did you rope me into? And you can forget about bond, it was revoked this morning."

"Mr. Solomon, I know it looks bad, but I really can explain."

"Save it, I'm not finished yet. We haven't discussed the video footage of you tossing a bomb into the big dumpster."

"It wasn't a bomb."

"I suppose a steel dumpster exploded by some fluke of spontaneous combustion?"

"It was—"

"I don't want to hear it, not right now." Danial bent over to get nose-to-nose with his visibly shaken client. "The video also shows two men going into the manhole where the second explosion took place. Right now, the police and the FBI are moving heaven and earth to find them. Now I'm going to explain this very carefully, and I want you to think about this long and hard before you give me an answer, because this bombing is a million times worse than your egg-throwing fiasco."

"I don't—"

"Before you say another word, let me say this, someone could go to prison for life for this bombing. The first person to become valuable to the prosecutor is the only one who will ever see the light of day again. Having said that, I ask you again, who are those men?"

Ian shook his head and mumbled, "I don't know."

"How did I know you were going to say that?" Danial grabbed the file and his briefcase and stormed toward the door.

"Mr. Solomon, wait!"

Danial looked over his shoulder.

"Why would I go through all the trouble to plan and execute my egg throw, if I was going to bomb the same hospital later in the day?"

18

Archie Kisner returned to his cell after lunch still feeling hungry. A few minutes later the cell door rolled shut. A guard picked up a mesh bag of mail and began making his rounds. Mail call in prison *usually* brings a touch of love and a touch of freedom. Letters are more than written words on a page; they are paper touched by the hands of a loved one, something tangible to hold onto when the lights go out. Some letters smell of perfume, others contain smudges of lipstick. Others are sprinkled with tears from a girlfriend or wife who could wait no longer. Some letters bring disappointing news from the courts. For most men, even a bad letter is better than no letter at all. Some men would rather not hear about life on the streets. They serve their time detached from it. But for the most part, mail from home brings great anticipation and joy to those behind bars. One letter in a million brings news of an early release.

The guard stopped at the first cell at the end of Archie's range and yelled, "Jimmson, number."

"Two-five-two-seven-three-eight."

"You got two letters from Michigan." The guard handed the mail through the bars without looking up from his stack. He walked past two disheartened men then stopped at the fourth cell.

"Wang."

"Two-five-two-nine-nine-five."

"One letter, from China."

Archie could hear the guard's footsteps approach.

"Olson."

"Two-five-two-seven-seven-six."

"Two letters from Minnesota."

"Lopez."

"Dos-cinco-dos-siete-siete-seis."

"You must have a fan club, five letters from Mexico and New Mexico."

Archie hated mail call; no one ever wrote. In fact, he had only received one letter and that was from Danial Solomon's office. But then again, it was probably best that nobody wrote since he couldn't spell well enough to write back. Still, a letter would be nice. Archie lay with his face buried in his pillow. He didn't want to see the officer walk by again without stopping. He listened as the guard took a couple steps, then stopped directly in front of his cell.

"Kisner."

Archie lifted his lopsided head, his face plastered with a broad, beaming smile. "Tttwooo... ffiivve..."

"Save it Kisner, I'm just messin' with you. Nobody loves you."

Archie drove his face into the pillow to muffle the sound of his crying. *If my mother was still alive, she'd love me, and probably write to me too.*

The hours ticked by and the tears stopped. The cellblock settled into its afternoon lull. Archie flipped through his Bible to the Gospel of John. He traced his enormous finger under the first line and phonetically sounded out the words.

"Inn theee beeginnninng... whuz... theee... Whoord... and theee... Whoord... whuz width... God—"

Someone pounded on the steel wall to his left.

"Shut up over there, I trying to sleep."

The young man in the cell to the right joined in.

"Yeah, why don't you keep ya Frankenstein zipper-head lookin', slow-talkin', retarded self quiet over there. Some of us non-ignoramuses be tryin' to catch some winks."

"Word," said the first voice. "Dude tore up from the floor up."

A few dispersed chuckles fluttered along the range.

"Sorry," Archie said timidly.

He returned to his reading. His lips moved as he whispered

the syllables. It took nearly 45 minutes to read the first chapter. He didn't retain much, but what did sink in blew his mind. *Wow, God came down here and walked with us. That's awesome!*

3:30 P.M.

Danial Solomon climbed the steps to his office and pressed open the door.

"Good afternoon, Jennifer."

"Good afternoon, Danial. Nice of you to stop by today."

"I spent the morning at the courthouse." He walked over to the coffee machine.

"Did you happen to see Ms. Franks while you were there?"

"No."

"Did you call her over the weekend?"

"No."

"Danial!"

"I'll call her this afternoon."

"You'd better." She shot him a glance that singed his eyebrows. "By the way, the private investigator, Mr. Stedman is waiting for you in your office."

"How long's he been here?"

"Not long, maybe ten minutes."

"Hold my calls."

He stepped into his office and closed the door behind him. Eugene Stedman stood to greet him. A former policeman, he was tall and thin and commanded respect. He had thick hair for a man in his 60s, but his face was wrinkled like a Bull Pug dog. He looked old enough to be one of the original Pinkerton detectives, but he made an excellent witness on the stand. He wore an XX-Large suit and well-worn wing-tip shoes. They shook hands, then Danial walked behind the desk and sat down. Stedman sat in one of the two chairs across the desk from Danial.

"I appreciate you coming on such short notice," Danial said. "And thanks again for all your help with the Kisner case. If it wasn't for you the kid probably would have gotten the chair."

"No problem, Mr. Solomon. But I'm a little surprised to be here. I thought you weren't going to be taking any complicated cases for a while."

"Things have a way of getting complicated all by themselves."

"So, what can I do for you?"

"I need you to do some work on two separate cases."

"Which ones?"

"Have you been following the Baby Ammo case on the news?"

"Yep."

"Well, that's one of them."

"You sure have a way of getting those high-profile cases." He cleared his throat and crossed his legs. "For a minute there I thought you were going to say you wanted me to work on the bombing down at the hospital." He chuckled.

Danial didn't smile.

"You're representing McKinney?"

"I'm afraid so. In fact, that case is top priority right now."

"Do you think the kid did it?" Stedman asked.

"He says he didn't."

"They all say that."

"Yeah, I know. But I gave him the third degree this morning like he was on the stand, and he didn't break. I want to believe him." Danial swiveled around and lifted a cardboard box from the floor. He slid it across the desk to Stedman.

"What's this?"

"It's everything I've got so far on the McKinney case. There's even video footage from the parking lot before and at the moment of the blasts."

"What exactly do you want me to do?" Stedman leafed through the mound of documents and DVDs in the box.

"First, go over everything in there and make some exciting discoveries."

"Gotcha. What else?"

"Have you seen the recent news footage of the two men climbing into the manhole the morning of the bombing?"

"Sure."

"I want you to find them."

"Do you want me to find Jimmy Hoffa while I'm at it?"

"I'm not looking for him... yet."

"Every law enforcement agency in the country is after them."

"Exactly, which is why I need you to find them first. Those two are the key to this case. Without them, we're sunk."

"You might be sunk with them too."

"That's a chance I've got to take." Danial stood and offered his hand.

"When you find them, I'll have a nice bonus waiting for you."

"Bonus or not, you're still asking for a miracle."

"You bet I am." They shook hands firmly. "And I expect to get one too."

4:10 P.M.

Lori Franks kicked off her shoes and sat Indian style on her chair. She rubbed her feet and reviewed Detective Demus' arrest report from the Norma Fitzpatrick case. It said a lot of nothing. She tossed the report onto her disaster area of a desk, rubbed her eyes and thought of Danial.

"Why in the world would he take a case he knew would cause a conflict?" She locked her fingers and hugged her knees. "Unless that's why he took it. It's a lot more tactful to conveniently allow duty to stand in the way of a relationship you really don't want to be in."

Lori picked a few loose papers from her desk and filed them away in their proper place. She organized a few things, and then launched into a full-blown cleaning session. Lori didn't clean often, and then only when she had something eating at her mind. Her mother joked that Lori only rested when the world was about to collapse. The mindless work provided enough of a distraction to allow her subconscious mind to kick in.

The phone rang.

"Hello."

"Lori, how are you?"

"It's been one of those days."

"I'm sorry I didn't call over the weekend. I really wanted to. I just didn't know what to say. I had a wonderful time on Friday night."

"Me too."

"FYI, I've got some bad news. I took the Fitzpatrick case."

"Yeah, I know. I saw your motion for the DNA test. I'm not going to oppose it."

"Good, because she says she didn't do it, and the test should clear everything up."

"I hope so," Lori said. "I'd like to drop the charges and the case."

"You're not mad?"

"Why would I be mad?"

"I don't know. My secretary said something crazy like you'd think I didn't like you because I took the case."

"No, no."

"I knew you'd understand. During interrogation Norma literally cried out for help. It was a rescue."

"So, what do we do in the meantime?" she asked.

"We pray for the DNA results to come back quickly."

"I'll press the hospital."

"You really looked beautiful Friday night."

She blushed. "I was a mess."

"I'm sure you'd look great in a burlap sack."

"Well, if you say so. But it wouldn't be much fun shopping for burlap sacks."

19

Darkness. Utter darkness. The thundering cadence of a heartbeat resounds through aquatic sloshing. Warm fluid passes rhythmically in-and-out of lungs, but it doesn't suffocate. Not long ago the tiny enclosure seemed as big as the universe, but now there's barely enough room to twist a smidgen. A restrictive cord attached to the waist is secured to a rubbery wall. Off in the distance, intermittently between the rapid pounding, the sounds of a second beat slow down.

Mommy must be taking a nap. She needs her rest, you know. I love her and she loves me. I can't wait to meet her. It won't be long now. I'm getting pretty big for this place. At first, I never wanted to leave the safety and warmth of my mommy. I thought I'd be satisfied listening to her muffled voice and laughter - I can recognize her voice anywhere - but now I want to see her face. Lately it's been getting a little cramped in here. It won't be long now.

The liquid atmosphere drains; the tiny chamber collapses.

What's going on? This never happened before. But I don't sense any fear from my mommy so this must be a good thing. I could use a little more time though, maybe four more weeks. My lungs need more time to develop, and my ears aren't quite ready yet. But mother knows best. I love her and she loves me.

Cold metal tongs invade the sanctuary and slip along the legs and torso. They jam into the soft ribs and snap closed, pinching the fatty skin.

Hey! Watch it, that's gonna leave a mark. I may be little, but I have feelings too. When my mom finds out you hurt me, she's going to be really mad. She loves me you know, and I love her too. You don't need to force me out. If the fluid didn't drain out, I would have flipped over on my head - the way God designed me to in a week or so. But maybe my mommy couldn't wait to see me. I know I can't wait to see her.

The slippery metal tongs thrust again and clamp down on his left leg just below the knee. Searing pain explodes. The tiny leg frantically recoils, desperately kicking the collapsed chamber.

Let go of me! You're hurting me! Stop pulling, don't you think I want out? I've got big plans you know. God has tucked away in my brain the future cure for cancer. All I need is a chance, and I'm going to make my mommy proud. I love her so very much.

A sliding rush and both feet break out. The first sensation of air flutters over moist skin. The forceps relinquish their death grip; two latex-clad hands grasp the feet and pull.

Wow, that breeze feels funny and a bit chilly I must say. I've never felt air before but I kinda like it. Yeah, I could get used to this.

Powerful hands pull; the entire body is exposed and wiggling, all except the head. A deep bruise is already forming where the forceps crushed the fragile leg.

Hey, don't stop now, I'm just about free. The air blowing over my wet body is getting pretty cold now. If you'd let go I'm sure I could squirm my way out. I'm only a few inches from seeing my mommy. I've waited such a long time to see her. Please, won't you let me go so I can see my wonderful mother? I like a good joke as much as the next guy, but enough is enough already. I've waited over eight months to feel the touch of her cheek against mine. I want to snuggle in her loving embrace. It's awfully dark in here, and I'm ready to see the light.

Sharp scissors puncture the base of his skull. The arms and legs wince and flail from the pain. A stream of dark crimson blood gurgles out of the wound. The tiny mouth opens in the birthing canal and expels a silent scream loud enough to shake the foundations of Heaven. Somehow the will to live overcomes the pain and a final kick and wiggle bring freedom. A rush of oxygen touches the face, and a cry of agony fills the room.

Somebody help me! I can't take the pain! Will somebody stop the pain!

Unfocused eyes latch onto a nurse.

Are you my mommy? Will you kiss it and make it better? I'm feeling weak and cold and the pain...

A doctor grabs the baby from the nurse, and for a moment the baby looks directly into his eyes.

Now I'll be all right, I'm in the hands of a healer. I don't know what the poke in the head was about, but I'm sure he can fix it. All those years of study to save lives, and the oath to do no harm. I know he can stop the bleeding. My little wound shouldn't be hard to fix. I want to look my best when I meet my mommy for the first time. I love her so very much, and I want her to see me. But I'm feeling very cold; my vision is growing dim. Doc, maybe you should do something kinda fast. I can feel my life fading. Put those healing hands to work!

The doctor looks away, grabs the baby by the forehead, and snaps the tiny neck.

The crying stops.

Dr. Gaston Garvey bolts upright in bed, drenched in sweat. His chest heaves; his pulse races out of control. He glances over at the large red numbers on the nightstand - 2:49 a.m.

"It was only a dream, a nightmare," Garvey said out loud to chase the demons away. "Third time this week. Thank goodness it was only a dream... or was it?"

20

Tuesday, October 10
9:15 A.M.

Colin Casey secured reluctant approval from Prosecutor DiAngello to tour Ian McKinney's infamous apartment, with the stipulation a uniformed officer accompany him at all times. DiAngello instructed the officer to see to it Casey touch nothing and never be left alone anywhere in the apartment at any time. The County investigators had already swept the place and bagged and tagged everything, but DiAngello wasn't taking any chances; he didn't trust Casey one bit.

Casey, the rookie officer, and the building manager made their way to the top floor of the apartment building. The officer peeled back the yellow police tape from across the door.

"Are you going to remove that tape when you leave?" the manager asked in a heavy Italian accent.

"Yes, why?"

"The tenants have been complaining. They say it ruins the atmosphere."

"Sorry about that," Casey said. "Life's a beach."

"What do I know?" The manager stepped forward and unlocked the door.

"We'll let you know when we're finished," Casey said and closed the door behind him. He and his shadow gave the place the once-over. They started in the kitchen. Chalk outlines on the wall showed where the newspaper articles once hung. Casey lingered for several seconds in the doorway to the bathroom; it looked pristine. They paced down to the bedroom. Casey carefully scrutinized the computer workstation, while the rookie officer scrutinized him. After a few more minutes in the living room, they headed for the door.

Casey grabbed the doorknob, let go and turned to the officer. "I'm going to use the toilet before we go. Nature's calling."

"Take care of your business."

"I believe it was back by the kitchen."

"I've got all day."

Casey double-timed it back to the bathroom, the rookie following close behind. Casey stepped in and closed the door, pinning the rookie in the doorjamb.

"What are you doing?"

"I've been ordered not to let you out of my sight, and I'm not going to."

"Use your head, man. Do you really think DiAngello wanted you to watch me take a dump?"

"I'd rather err on the side of caution."

"A minute of privacy, that's all I'm asking."

The rookie wiggled out. Casey closed the door, walked over to the toilet and sat down. The small room reeked of disinfectant. He could see that the officer was looking under the door.

He'll only be able to see my feet.

He shucked down his trousers but left his underwear up. His eyes darted around the room and settled on a green plastic hairbrush. He quietly pulled a plastic glove from his shirt pocket and wiggled his left hand into it. He then shoved his right hand into his underpants and pulled out a Ziploc baggie. He reached over with his left hand and grabbed the brush by the handle and gingerly placed it into the baggie. He pulled out the waistband of his underwear and stuffed the brush down into the crotch. *Just in case that gung-ho nut decides to pat me down.*

Casey flushed the toilet and ripped off the plastic glove while a gallon of water slurped down the drain. He snatched the toilet paper, tugged off a generous wad, then wrapped it around the plastic glove and flushed it down the toilet. He pulled up his pants and looked in the mirror. A renegade nasal hair jutted out his left nostril. He plucked it out, watering his eyes. He patted the stash between his legs to make sure it laid firmly in place.

He noisily washed his hands then walked out whistling the "Star Spangled Banner."

Jefferson County Jail
1:25 P.M.

Danial handed Ian McKinney the newest indictment. Ian settled down into the chair. His lips moved as he read. Danial could see the strain taking its toll on his client. Dark puffy circles under Ian's eyes evidenced sleepless nights. Gnarled fingernails were chewed to the quick.

"I guess I don't need to tell you the stakes just went up," Danial said.

"They've charged me with terrorism?"

"And about a dozen other things."

"Mr. Solomon, you've got to believe—"

"Calm down, Ian, I believe you."

"You do?" Ian leaned back with a sigh of relief.

"The trial is only two weeks away. I'll ask for a continuance, but he'll deny it. He obviously wants the trial to start before the election."

"Politics."

"They're going to try the case through the media, but that's all right. I've got a few tricks up my sleeve. But first we've got to focus on your defense. I need some information."

"I'll tell you anything you want to know."

"The State has requested a hair sample. Are you willing to submit one?"

"What if I refuse?"

"DiAngello will get a court order, and they'll force you to comply." Danial shifted his weight. "If you refuse it'll look like you're hiding something. You don't have anything to hide, do you?"

"No. But why do they want a hair sample?"

"Investigators must have found some hair at the crime scene

in Oglebay Park."

"I'll give 'em as much hair as they want."

"Good. Next, I want you to make a list of everyone who saw you throw the egg, and especially anyone who saw the police beat you up."

"Man, that's going to be tough. The only one I know for sure who saw it is a guy named Michael Andrew. He was standing right there."

Danial scribbled down the name. "Does he belong to any protest groups?"

"Not that I know of."

"Would he be able to give us the names of some of the others who might have seen what happened?"

"Probably, he knows everybody."

"Good. I'll get right on him. Is he from Steubenville?"

"Wintersville."

"More news. I've hired a private detective to work on your case."

"How much will it cost?"

"It'll come out of my retainer."

"Not that it matters or anything."

"I've got him searching for your two co-defendants."

"I told the detectives already, I was solo. An egger, not a bomber."

"If you have any information I can use as leverage, it would be very helpful right now."

"Mr. Solomon, if I could help myself I would. I'm not trying to do life in prison."

"If you don't know, you don't know. But make me a list of people who might know something about the bombing, maybe some of the other protesters."

"I'll make a list, but it may surprise you."

"Very good. Now I want you to think about pleading no contest to the charges related to the egg throwing. A no contest plea is not an admission of guilt, but close enough that it could bolster your credibility when you deny the other charges. We need to add credibility to your testimony, and right now we don't have squat."

"Okay, I'll plead no contest. Actually, it will serve my whole purpose."

Mingo Junction, Ohio
2:05 P.M.

Eugene Stedman sat on the couch in his double-wide trailer watching the videos from Danial's evidence box. Thick, blue-gray smoke from his Camel non-filtered cigarettes filled the room. Several photos of Norma Fitzpatrick's VW Bug lay on the pressboard coffee table. He leaned forward and reversed the footage and played it again in slow motion. The blue car weaved through the police station parking lot. The view was mostly obstructed by several parked patrol cars. He studied the video closely. He found the exact image he wanted and pressed the pause button.

"That's it!"

He grabbed the photo showing the rear of Norma's car and compared it to the image on the screen.

"That's what I thought I saw."

He jotted down a few notes, then viewed the next video. It contained the footage of the McKinney arrest and the two men climbing into the manhole. He watched it at regular speed three or four times, and then again in slow motion. Nothing. The images were too grainy to make out facial features or distinguishing marks. He pressed the pause button, then jammed his bony fists into his eye sockets.

"These old peepers ain't what they used to be."

He stood, took a full drag, and barked out a series of deep, productive coughs.

"I really need to quit."

He sat back down to another video. The clock in the corner of the screen showed the time as near midnight. The hospital parking lot featured the cars, SUVs and pickup trucks of late shift and night shift employees. A VW Bug drove away. In minutes a brilliant flash filled the screen. The second explosion launched the manhole cover into the air like an Estes rocket, then ended the footage. He reversed it and watched it again in slow motion.

"I'm missing something. It's right in front of my face, and I can't see it."

Jefferson County Jail
3:17 P.M.

Danial stood to shake Norma Fitzpatrick's hand; she had not stopped crying since the female deputy escorted her into the visiting room.

"Could... I... have... a hug?" she asked between sobs.

His heart melted. "Sure."

She squeezed him so tight he feared his back would crack. He patted her shoulder and waited for her to stop crying. He felt a dampness on his chest where her face rested, her tears saturating his shirt. He handed her his handkerchief. She sniffled and wiped her tears. As soon as she composed herself somewhat, she began chewing on the inside of her cheek.

"Please don't do that, Norma. You're going to hurt yourself."

"Sorry, it's a habit I have when I'm stressed." Tears continued to run down her cheeks.

"I stopped to let you know the hospital said the DNA test results will be in tomorrow morning. Ms. Franks, the prosecutor, and I will be going over there first thing in the morning."

"You mean it's almost over?"

"Almost. Ms. Franks made a verbal commitment to drop the charges if the results come back negative."

"Do you trust her?"

"A lot more now than I did a month ago."

"Will they let me go right away?"

"I don't see why not."

"What time? What time will they let me go?"

"Well, if the results are in by nine, I don't see any reason why they wouldn't let you go by noon."

"I hope so. I can't spend another night in this place."

"Just hang in there a little longer. Tomorrow will be here before you know it."

21

4:30 P.M.

"I'll never be ready in two weeks," DiAngello said, shuffling through a pile of papers on his desk. "You should have talked to me before you had that senile old man schedule a trial like this so soon."

"Relax counselor," Colin Casey said, holding up his hands.

"You know I'm handling this case myself. What're you trying to do? Make me look like a fool?"

"We had to schedule the trial before the election. We shot up in the polls five points today. I've got to keep the momentum rolling."

"You seem to think you call the shots around here."

"I'm not trying to step on your toes, I just need to keep the pressure on from now until the end of the month."

"I don't care what you need."

"Look, if you're not ready, then ask for a continuance. But at least ask for it after the trial begins. We need the media blitz."

"You've stepped on my last nerve, Casey."

"Work with me, Tony. You've got nothing to worry about. The press is demanding this guy's blood, and you've got him on video for crying out loud. I could even prosecute this case."

DiAngello stood up, his bushy brows squinted together. He poked his finger into Casey's chest. "You listen to me and you listen good. If you screw this up, I'll—"

"You'll what?"

"I'll... I'll..."

"You'll do nothing. I know all about you and Gus Gram."

DiAngello's face turned from red to purple. A pulsating vein popped out over his forehead.

"You're lucky you're not sitting in jail with him right now," Casey said. "But we'll keep that just between the two of us... for now."

"Get the hell out of my office! Now!"

4:57 P.M.

Dr. Gaston Garvey nursed his fourth Alabama Slammer and looked around the dimly lit Top Hat Lounge. A few businessmen laughed a little too loud in the far corner. A couple of silver-haired men perched themselves on the stools beside him at the bar. He turned his attention back to his drink and stirred the ice cubes with his chubby fingers.

"I used to think making a lot of money was the key to happiness," Garvey said to the young bartender who seemed more interested in the wad of cash in his pocket than the incoherent gibberish spilling out of his mouth. "I'm in my 30s and make more money than I could spend in a lifetime, and I'm miserable."

"I don't have that problem."

"Then I thought if I married a really beautiful woman, I'd be happy. But my miserable wife left me." He took a sip of his drink. "I guess you hear this kind of stuff a lot, huh?"

"Yeah, but I've got nothing better to do, so feel free to spill your guts."

Garvey felt slighted, but it didn't matter. He polished off his drink then noticed the news coming on the television suspended from the wall behind the bar.

"Could you turn that up?" Garvey's words slurred over his lips.

"Sure." The bartender wiped his hands on the white apron tied around his waist and turned up the volume.

"I'm about due for a refill here too, buddy."

Garvey watched through blurry red eyes as the 5 o'clock news re-aired the press conference on the steps of the Jefferson County Courthouse. He squinted and tried to focus on Anthony

DiAngello, who spoke through a forest of microphones. He announced the bombing charges leveled against Ian McKinney, wanting swift and fierce justice. Colin Casey came to his side and occasionally leaned over to offer advice. The focus of the conference shifted to Baby Ammo.

Garvey shook his head as a fresh drink slid into place on the bar in front of him. "What kind of world do we live in when teenage girls stick ice picks into the skulls of their own babies?"

"Beats me."

"No wonder I can't find peace in this life. There's none to find."

"Do you really think she did it?"

"As sure as I'm sitting here, she did." Garvey tipped back his head and chugged down the sweet liquor. He wiped his mustache with the back of his hand and gestured for a refill.

"I'm sorry, Doc, I've got to cut you off. You've had too many already."

"I'll be the judge of that."

"How about some coffee or something to eat?"

"No." He looked at his watch. "I'm supposed to meet a friend in a few minutes." He left a $20 tip and staggered for the door.

The sun slowly lowered toward the western horizon; a pinkish-orange tint trailed behind it. The chilly October air felt good on Garvey's face. It seemed to revive him. He wandered around the parking lot searching for his car. He stumbled past it three times before he did a double take, then reeled toward the jet-black Lexus. He fumbled with his keys, then tried to shove his house key into the door lock.

"That's not it."

He tried a few more keys before he managed to get in and start the engine. His head gyrated and swirled wildly; a strong vertigo sensation ran through his body. He flipped on the air conditioning and turned the stereo on high; the Red Hot Chili Peppers roared out of the speakers. He dropped the car in reverse and punched the accelerator. The rear wheels screeched and smoked over the asphalt.

BAM!

He slammed the rear end of his car into the side of a police cruiser.

"Where did that come from?"

A uniformed officer approached the driver's side window. He took off his mirrored sunglasses and attempted to dry the hot coffee dripping from his pants with a napkin. He motioned for Garvey to open the window.

"What problem seems... no. What problem is... no. What seems to be the problem, officer?"

"You must be drunk."

"You betcha. I'm ripped out of my mind."

"Step out of the car, sir."

"Why? Don't you believe I'm drunk?" Garvey chuckled.

"Get out of the car."

Garvey stepped out and tried to stand up straight. He locked his knees and handed the officer his driver's license. He wobbled in place while the officer inspected the license.

"Well, Doctor Garvey, we're going to do a little field sobriety test. Think of it as a physical examination." The officer chuckled. "Now that's funny."

Garvey tried to follow the commands but failed each test miserably. The officer pronounced him under arrest. Garvey reached inside his coat. The officer grabbed his wrist.

"What are you reaching for?"

"I can save us both a lot of trouble if you'll let me make a phone call."

"It doesn't matter to me if you do it here or at the station."

Garvey hit the speed dial. "Hello... yeah... hi Tony. I'm not doing too good... I need a little help... sure."

Garvey nodded his head then handed the phone to the puzzled officer and said, "It's for you."

"You've got to be kidding me."

"Nope."

"Hello, who is this?... Mr. DiAngello!"

22

Wednesday, October 11
University Hospital
8:43 A.M.

Lori Franks parked her candy-apple-red BMW on the street in front of University Hospital. A light drizzle beaded on the windshield. She fished around on the floor underneath the seat for her collapsible umbrella; she found it. She checked her watch.

"I don't want to appear too eager."

She sat still and thought about where Danial might take her for their first official date. Maybe it would be the predictable dinner and a movie, but then again Danial wasn't a predictable kind of guy. Perhaps he would invite her over for a home-cooked meal; that would be nice and cozy. The possibilities were endless and fun to think about.

She stepped out of her car; the raindrops felt cold against her face. She pressed the button on the umbrella handle and snapped open the canopy. She walked across the street and into the lobby. Danial stood waiting in front of the reception desk wearing a gray herringbone, two-button suit and tile blue tie, his tan overcoat draped over his left arm.

"Good morning, Ms. Franks," a hint of formality in his voice.

"Good morning, Dan... ah, Mr. Solomon."

They shook hands rigidly. A disarming smile spread across his face. "The moment of truth has arrived."

"Where are we supposed to go?"

"The receptionist told me to wait right here. She said the lab technician would deliver the DNA report shortly."

Lori looked around the waiting room. An elderly man sat off

in the corner looking emotionally numb. A ball of something dripped off the end of his nose.

"What do you think about Colin Casey?" she asked.

"You mean the skinny LGBTQ guy who's got his nose in everyone's business?"

"That's the one."

"I don't like him."

"Isn't that being judgmental?"

"Call it discernment."

"What makes you say that?"

"I smell a rat. He's got an agenda and he's got Judge Williams jumping through hoops like some kind of sideshow pony."

"He's doing the same with DiAngello."

A middle-aged couple brushed past walking rapidly and mumbling to one another.

"Lori, I've got something I need to say to you."

Oh, no. That doesn't sound good. She mustered a smile. "All right."

"I want to apologize for getting us into this mess."

"You don't have to."

"But I want to." He shoved his hands into his pockets. "Things went so well last week, and now we're stuck in this drama."

"It'll all be over in a minute."

"I still feel bad."

"If you feel that strongly about it, I'll let you make it up to me." She smiled.

"I promise."

"So, where're you going to take me?"

"I thought we'd split a burrito at Taco Bell then head off to the library for some reading."

"Are you serious?"

"Of course... not."

She laughed and touched his arm; it felt knotty with muscles.

"I've got big plans," he said. "But it's a surprise."

"When?"

"This weekend. Friday night, if you're free."

"I'm free."

They stared deeply into one another's eyes.

"Excuse me," said a technician in a white lab coat. "Are you the lawyers here for the Fitzpatrick test results?"

"Yes," they said in unison.

"I've never seen such warmth between a prosecutor and a defense attorney."

They stepped back from one another.

"Well, out with it," Lori said.

"Which one of you is from the Prosecutor's Office?"

"I am."

The technician shuffled through a stack of papers on his clipboard. He detached a form and put it on top. "I need your signature before I can release the results."

"Very well, give me your pen."

The young technician searched his pockets and came up empty. Danial reached into his shirt pocket and handed Lori a gold pen with the acronym WWJD engraved on the shaft. She signed her name and smiled.

"You need to sign and date here as well." He pointed to a line on the back of the form. Lori jotted her initials next to his finger.

"What did the test say?" she asked.

9:05 A.M.

Archie Kisner's stomach rumbled as he paced the short length of his cell waiting for breakfast. His cellblock would eat last because of a disturbance at the previous evening's chow. The smell of stale breath and cigarettes mixed with the shouts of men yelling from cell to cell. How much Archie wished he could get somewhere by himself.

Archie discovered that one of the biggest misconceptions about prison is the belief that it is an isolated existence. Nothing could be further from the truth; in prison no one is ever alone. No privacy. No place to get away. Communal showers. Hundreds of men climbing over each other to use the toilet, the phone, to be first in the chow line. Prison is an amalgamated sea of humanity that its denizens detest. Life in prison *is* lonely, but it's the loneliness of being lost in a crowd.

The clatter of cell doors rolling open brought a momentary silence, all the doors except one. Archie walked to his door and shook it. It didn't budge.

"Hey, C.O.!" Archie yelled down to the officer at the desk. "My door is closed."

"It must be jammed, Kisner. I'll call the locksmith as soon as I get the rest of the guys ready for chow. Then I'll tell food service to send you a tray."

The men filed out of the building. Five minutes later Archie found himself in the rare position of being completely alone. At first, he wasn't sure what to do. He wanted to go to chow. Prison cuisine was bad, but at least it filled the belly. He looked along the empty range, then turned and knelt down by his bed.

"God, it's me again. I hope I'm not bothering You. It's early I know. But I just want to thank You for wakin' me up to see another day. You didn't have to do it, but You did. I ask You to forgive me for all the things I done wrong. Thanks for lettin' me go to the chapel for the first time today. I don't read the Bible too good, but I'm tryin'."

He could hear the exterior door open then close, then the light tapping of leather shoes strolling across the concrete floor. Then a metallic shuffle as the soles slid across the iron steps.

"God, the locksmith is here to let me out, so I'll talk to You later today if You aren't too busy and all. In Jesus' name. Amen."

Archie started to get off his knees when he felt a bucketful of something cold douse his body. It ran off his hair and into his eyes, instantly burning. He looked through blurry eyes at the outline of a man standing at the bars.

"What'd you do that for? That stuff's burning my eyes."

No reply.

"I don't want no trouble. I just want out."

He swallowed some of the fluid and wretched it back up.

University Hospital
9:20 A.M.

The lab technician handed Lori and Danial each a copy of the report.

"The results of the test, with a 99.99 percent accuracy, is that Norma Fitzpatrick is the mother of the baby in question."

Their mouths dropped open.

"Have a nice day," the technician walked away.

"It can't be," Danial said.

"Unbelievable."

"She was so convincing."

"This changes everything, Danial, you know I've got a job to do."

"I know."

"And with the DNA confirming that she killed her baby, DiAngello could push for the death penalty."

"I know."

"She isn't showing remorse, Danial. Or any willingness to accept responsibility. A jury will slam her hard."

"I know. Take a life, lose your life."

"What are we going to do about us?"

He loosened his tie. "It's nothing personal."

9:22 A.M.

Archie Kisner frantically wiped the burning liquid from his swollen eyes. The odor of strong chemicals stung his nostrils. He rubbed his saturated sleeve over his face, and layers of skin peeled off with each stroke. He inadvertently swallowed another mouthful. His tongue swelled. His throat constricted. He tried to cry out for help, but no sound came out. *I can't see! I can't breathe!*

He struggled to stand. His bare feet slipped in a puddle of the cold, slippery fluid. He gasped for breath, both hands on his throat. He staggered to his feet, a look of terror in his eyes. The figure at the door struck a match, held it for a moment, then tossed it into the pool on the steel floor at Archie's feet.

Archie ignited into a ball of flames.

No, no! It burns, it burns!

He forced out a guttural moan as he flopped around the cell trying to extinguish the flames. The pungent stench of burning flesh and hair filled the room. He thrashed around as fire engulfed his body. He ran headfirst into the cell door and knocked himself to the floor. Flaming scalp stuck to the bars. His skin blistered and broiled. His arms and legs flailed then stopped and contracted into a quivering, smoldering mound in the fetal position.

The man at the cell door casually walked down the range as if nothing happened. He trotted down the steps and disappeared out the back door of the building.

The pain shrieked then screamed then wailed then whimpered then moaned then murmured then mumbled then...

Thank you, God, the pain has stopped. Hey, that looks like Jesus standing there with His arms open. I'm coming, Lord, I'm coming.

23

Near Moundsville, West Virginia
9:30 A.M.

Art Bently split firewood on a stump in front of the old hunting cabin nestled back in the woods of the Appalachian Mountains. The one-room shack had a sagging roof and it listed slightly to the right, the gray logs weather-beaten. The wind whistled through gaps in the old chinking. Art buried the blade of his axe into the stump and glanced over at Ron Kester. Ron looked powerful and imposing with an axe as he hewed a beam from a fresh-cut maple log. He stood 6 feet tall and weighed over 230 pounds. His thick black hair tousled in the breeze. A jagged scar jutted out from under his widow's peak. His new beard came in black and thick. His hazel eyes were sharp and alert.

Art wrested his axe loose and split a few more logs. Physical exertion didn't come easy to him. He stood up straight and arched his aching back. He peered at the stream snaking its way down the canyon about 20 yards from the side of the cabin. A camouflage tarp covered the truck parked off to the left of the cabin near a narrow, overgrown path cut through the dense trees. The scenic spot was a good choice, defensible against antagonists. For Art it was a beautiful place to visit, but he sure didn't want to live there for too long.

"Stop your gawking and get back to work!" Ron yelled.

"I feel like lonely Moses on top of the mountain."

"It's not that bad and you like the view. No wonder they say it's almost Heaven."

"If this is Heaven, I don't want to see Hell."

A twig snapped. They froze. Something rustled in the trees. A deer appeared then disappeared back into the undergrowth.

Ron exhaled and returned to his work.

"Ron, can we turn the radio on now? I'm getting bored."

"How many times do I have to tell you; we only turn it on at noon and 5 o'clock for the news."

"Jeez, man."

"We have to conserve the batteries, and I don't want some high-tech FBI agent or anyone else for that matter getting an electronic fix on us."

"Don't you think you're overdoing it? We're so far from civilization the mosquitoes can't even find us."

"It's not the mosquitoes I'm worried about. And besides, I've got something for you to do to keep from getting bored."

"What's that, Ron?"

"You know how you've been complaining about the leaky roof?"

"Yeah."

"Well, I'm going to teach you how to make wooden shingles."

"C'mon, man."

"Stop your whining. There's no telling how long we could be up here, so we might as well make the place livable."

Jefferson County Jail
9:50 A.M.

Danial Solomon sat in the tiny blue visiting room stewing in his own juices. He was mad about the test results, but more so, he felt disappointed in himself for being deceived. Over the years he had developed a sort of sixth sense for detecting when a client was lying. Only on rare occasions did he get deceived, and then only by extreme pathological liars. Norma didn't seem to fit into the sociopathic category, but at this point he didn't know what to believe. The evidence was mounting up.

Norma entered the room with a spring in her step. She bounced down into her chair with a big smile on her face.

"So, what time will I be out of here?"

"That's up to the jury."

Her smile vanished. "Jury?"

"At best, I'd say 15 years or plea for less."

"What're you talking about?" She started chewing the inside of her cheek. "You're scaring me."

"Cut the crap, Norma. The baby's yours."

"No, it's not."

"Oh yes, it is."

"Nooo." Her hands trembled.

"I want answers."

"I swear to God, I didn't do it!"

"You don't have to convince me, you have to convince a jury of your peers."

"I didn't do it!" she shouted and pounded on the table.

"Norma, the DNA test is conclusive. Your baby ended up at the police station with a broken neck and a puncture wound in the skull."

"No, no, noooo!" she shrieked, sounding like she was upside down in a roller coaster.

"The police have video of your car at the scene. Now I'm a reasonable man, but I've got to tell you, it's not looking good."

She sobbed out of control.

"Save your tears. It's time we start talking about a plea bargain."

"I can't go to prison."

"You can and you will."

"No... please... help me."

"Help me to help you." Danial stood and leaned against the wall opposite her. "Tell me what happened."

"I can't."

"Who's the father, Norma?"

No answer.

"If you didn't do it, the father must have. Who is he?"

She shook her head. "He didn't do it."

"If he was in jail, would you come forward to help him?"

"Yeah."

"Then how come he hasn't come forward to help you?"

"It's complicated."

"I'll tell you why, because he's giving you up to save himself."

"That's not true," she said. "He loves me."

"Then why not give me his name, and we'll see how much he loves you."

Someone knocked on the door. A deputy stuck his head in and said, "Sorry to bother you. I know it's not protocol to disturb attorneys when they're with clients, but Mr. DiAngello sent me down to tell you the hair sample they took from McKinney is back from the lab. He wanted to make sure you got the results as soon as possible."

"Thank you very much," Danial said. "I'm just about finished here."

The deputy left. Danial reached into his briefcase and handed her a copy of the DNA report.

"I'm going to be honest with you, I've got a big case that's getting ready to go to trial in a couple of weeks. Until that case is over, I'm not going to be able to spend much time with you or on your case. Do you understand?"

She nodded.

"Think about what I said. You have my phone number if you need to reach me."

"Can't you just stay and talk awhile?"

"I've got to go." Danial picked up his briefcase and yanked open the door.

"Carl Vance," she said in a faint voice.

He stopped and looked over his shoulder. "Who's Carl Vance?"

"He's the father."

10:10 A.M.

Danial felt an ominous twisting in his stomach as he walked toward Anthony DiAngello's 3rd floor, corner office. Only one thing could bring a defense attorney into DiAngello's private inner sanctum - bad news. Danial knocked on the door; its Venetian blinds rattled and scratched against its glass window.

DiAngello met him at the door with a plastic smile plastered across his face. "Good morning, Mr. Solomon."

"Good morning."

"Please forgive me for interrupting while you were in conference with a client. But I felt certain you would want this information as soon as possible."

Colin Casey sat behind DiAngello's desk with a beaming grin. DiAngello escorted Danial over to a chair across from the oak desk.

"Mr. Solomon, you remember meeting Colin Casey?"

"Vaguely." They shook hands. Danial remembered the limp shake and the pink tie. "So, what exactly do you do, Mr. Casey?"

"I'm on assignment in Jefferson County as a political advisor and liaison from Democratic Party headquarters in Columbus."

"Fascinating," Danial said. "And does your role as political advisor allow you access to confidential evidence in my client's case?"

"Excuse me?"

Danial nodded toward the open report on the desk in front of him.

"He was just leaving, weren't you Colin?"

"As a matter of fact, I was." He patted Danial's shoulder as he walked out.

DiAngello walked around the desk and handed him the hair sample report. "Young Mr. Casey often oversteps his bounds," DiAngello said.

"So I see."

"The FBI and the Bureau of Criminal Investigation matched your client's hair sample to those found at the Oglebay Park crime scene as well as those found at the Fort Henry Arsenal. It seems Mr. McKinney was a busy little boy."

"Maybe he was, maybe he wasn't."

"I'm prepared to offer a plea bargain."

"What do you have in mind?"

"Your client pleads guilty to one of the bombing charges, I really don't care which one. He agrees to give a full statement and agrees to testify against the other two whenever we arrest them, and I'll drop everything else."

"What about time?"

"Fifteen years." DiAngello crossed his legs and locked his hands behind his head. "Maybe ten."

"I'd like a couple of days to consider it."

"Take all the time you need. My door is always open to you."

"I appreciate that, sir." Danial's cell phone chirped from his inside coat pocket. He pulled it out and looked at the screen - Eugene Stedman was calling.

"Excuse me, Mr. DiAngello, but I've got to take this call."

"By all means. You can use the conference room just outside my door. It's to the left."

"Thanks."

Danial hustled to the conference room and raised the phone to his ear.

"What is it, Mr. Stedman?"

"I've been going over the videos you gave me, and I've found something interesting."

"Is it good news?"

"Yes. The car that was seen at the Steubenville Police Station - the blue VW Bug - doesn't belong to Norma Fitzpatrick."

"How do you know?" Danial shifted mental gears from Ian to Norma. "Did you make out the license number?"

"No, but the car in the video has normal tail lights, and the police photos of Fitzpatrick's car show a broken tail light."

"Good work. That is good news. She also gave me the name of the baby's father - Carl Vance."

"Do you want me to run him down?"

"No. Stay on the hunt for the bombing guys. I'll go pay Vance a visit myself. He's probably a student over at Steubenville High."

24

10:25 A.M.

Captain Jackson ran across the prison yard holding his radio and nightstick against his hips, responding to the medical emergency. He was first to arrive at Cellblock A. Inmates lining the sidewalk in front of the building stepped aside to let him through. A gray-shirted officer stood with his back pressed against the exterior door, his eyes wide open and his face clammy with sweat.

"What's this about, Miller?"

"Terrible, Cap, terrible. The smell could make a billy goat puke."

"Calm down and tell me what happened."

"Aw man, we came back from chow. And... aw man... I unlocked the door and - bam - the stink liked to knock me down."

"What stink?"

"Burnt flesh. Man, someone got torched in there."

"Who?"

"I don't know, some inmate got stuck in his cell this morning. The door jammed or something."

"Who?"

The emergency squad arrived in a silver golf cart with a flashing red light attached to the front. Two nurses wearing green scrubs jumped off the cart, each carrying a box of first-aid equipment.

"Open the door," the first nurse said.

Miller didn't move.

"Open the door!" Jackson shouted.

Miller snapped out of it and rattled the large brass key in the lock; the door popped open. The stench of singed hair and

137

charred flesh and fecal matter poured through the opening. Officer Miller doubled over with dry heaves. The inmates near the door scattered.

"Whoa!" Jackson said, covering his nose and mouth with a handkerchief. "That's foul."

The nurses ran back to the cart and strapped on respirator masks, then raced back and into the building.

"Miller, send a couple of inmates in there to open some windows."

A few minutes later the nurses returned looking horrified.

"Bottom line," Jackson said.

"We couldn't get to him."

"The cell door is still locked," the second nurse said.

"But he's definitely dead," the first nurse said, pulling off the respirator mask. "A crispy pile of goo on the floor."

"Who's the inmate?" Jackson asked Miller again.

"Fisher maybe, I don't know for sure."

"It be Kisner, Boss," a voice near the door said.

Jackson turned around. "Who said that?"

"Me, Sonny Dante."

"Are you sure it was Kisner?"

"Yessir."

A couple minutes later the doctor arrived. They handcuffed and shackled the corpse per procedure before placing him in a body bag. They carted him off to the infirmary to await transfer to the morgue.

"We have a volunteer to clean up the mess," Officer Miller said.

"We can't touch anything in that cell. It's a crime scene."

"The Major radioed over and says get the place cleaned up and get the inmates back inside."

"We'll see about that. Don't do anything until I get back."

Captain Jackson stormed across the yard, then returned 20 minutes later with his tail between his legs.

"All right, Miller, who's the volunteer?"

"We're going to clean it up?"

"The Major said the investigator is off post, and we have to have everybody locked in the building before count. He says it was a suicide."

"What do you think?"

"I said it's a crime scene. Now where's your volunteer?"

"Standing over there," he pointed toward the door.

"You," Jackson said. "What's your name again?"

"Dante, sir."

"All right, come with me."

Sonny Dante gathered up the cleaning supplies and struggled to carry them to the second range. Jackson stood in front of the cell along with a few officers. They stepped back to allow Dante access. The nauseating stench of burnt flesh was so pungent, he had to tuck his nose inside his shirt and take short breaths in order to remain in the cell. Starting at the far end, he swept the mop over the soot and debris. Scraps of burnt cloth and skin stuck to the mop.

Dante dashed out of the cell, uncovered his nose, and took several deep breaths. Jackson looked over at him and said, "Pretty nasty in there."

"It don't smell none too good." Dante bent over the railing and retched.

"You all right there, partner?"

"Yeah, I just need some air."

"Take as much time as you need."

Dante tucked his nose in his shirt once again and went back in. Fire and smoke damage touched everything in the cell. The sheets were completely burned through, and the plastic mattress had melted away. The only thing that remained unharmed was the Children's Bible under the bed. Sonny tucked the Bible under his arm. He gave the cell another rinse with the mop.

"That's the best I can do."

"You did fine," Jackson said. "I appreciate the help."

"Do you mind if I keep this Bible?"

"Go right ahead," Jackson said as he stepped in to inspect the cell.

12:35 P.M.

Eugene Stedman had spent the better part of the previous two days glued to his screen watching the bombing videos. The monotonous hours paid off as he made a magnificent discovery: awhile before the explosions a VW Bug drove into the parking lot and parked. The silhouette of two figures could be seen in the front seat. The black-and-white footage didn't reveal the color of the car. But it looked an awful lot like the one caught on video at the police station earlier that day. And it was the same car that left the hospital lot just prior to the explosions. These could be the two mystery men.

Stedman took out a notebook and jotted down a profile of his prey. These two evidently wanted to inspect the bombing scene before the explosions to make sure no one would be hurt. They were careful and probably educated. Such men wouldn't go through all the trouble of planning a mission and then use their own car. Therefore, they must have rented one.

Stedman did his vehicle search the old-fashioned way; he called around to all the car rental companies within a 50-mile radius. He found one strong lead - a Hertz dealer just across the bridge from Steubenville, in Weirton, West Virginia.

Stedman trudged down the plywood steps outside his trailer and climbed into his rusted-out truck. He kicked aside some empty soda pop cans and twisted two bare wires together from under the dashboard. The engine sputtered to life. His heart raced for the first time since the Kisner trial ended; he lived for adventure and the thrill of the hunt.

Stedman drove north along the Ohio River and parked his truck in front of the Hertz office. He disconnected the wires; the truck bucked and backfired before shuddering down. A salesman burst through the door with a toothy smile.

"I can see by your truck you made it here just in time. Are you interested in a Buick rental until you can buy a new car?"

"What?"

"If you'd like me to call Triple-A, we could get your heap towed away at no cost."

"I'm not here for a rental. My truck's running just fine."

"Oh, sorry."

"I spoke to your manager this morning. He has a record for me from a car rented last Tuesday."

"Right this way, sir."

The salesman led Stedman to the waiting room just to the right of the manager's office. He helped himself to the complimentary coffee. A few moments later the salesman returned with a computer printout.

"Here you go, sir. I hope this is what you're looking for."

"Thank you very much," Stedman said as he snatched the report from the salesman's hand. He ran his finger down the long list of models that were rented on October 3rd. He stopped when he reached the VW Bug.

"Here it is."

He reached in his shirt pocket and grabbed a yellow highlighter, then traced it across the transaction. His hands trembled as he examined the report a bit more closely, and noticed the time of the rental - 5:56 p.m.

"It's too late."

"What's too late?" the salesman asked.

"The car was rented on Tuesday evening," he said. "They needed to rent it first thing in the morning."

"What are you talking about?"

"Nothing," Stedman said. "Nothing at all."

Steubenville High School
1:38 P.M.

Danial wanted some time to consider DiAngello's plea bargain before discussing it with Ian McKinney. The media was comparing this case to the abortion clinic bombings in Atlanta and Boston, and some of the more zealous reporters were even trying to tie Ian to those cases as well.

Danial had stopped by his office and had Jennifer make a call to run down Carl Vance. The principal's office confirmed that Vance was indeed at Steubenville High School, and he had a free period right after lunch. The principal agreed to arrange a meeting. Danial decided to stop at Wendy's for a bite to eat, and then made his way over to the high school.

It had been a number of years since Danial set foot inside his alma mater, but he remembered the route to the principal's office very well. Being in the building brought back a flood of memories. Photos of championship football teams from years gone by lined the main hall. Steubenville Big Red had a long tradition of state athletic supremacy, and Danial felt proud to be a part of that glorious past.

He strolled through the hall examining the trophy cases and team photos as if looking for something in particular. About midway down the hall he found what he was looking for: the 1985 Ohio Valley Athletic Conference Championship team photo. He had been the star tailback and team captain. He admired the photo and recalled the names of his teammates when a high-pitched voice startled him.

"Can I help you, mister?" asked a young girl.

"I'm here to see the principal," Danial said.

"You must be Mr. Solomon."

"Yes."

"The principal sent me out here to keep a lookout for you. Please follow me."

They walked down the hallway past the School Records board. Danial glanced up to see if his mark in the 100-meter dash had been eclipsed... *10.4 - that's almost a full second faster than my time. Now I really feel old.*

The young girl escorted Danial through the busy office. It looked almost exactly as he remembered it. She knocked on the principal's door.

"Mr. Solomon is here to see you."

"Send him right in."

Danial walked past a middle-aged, balding man sitting near the door, and then into the office. The principal stood, and they shook hands.

"I'm Principal Barrows."

"Danial Solomon, thanks for seeing me on such short notice."

"No trouble at all. Now what can I do for you?"

"I'm representing one of your students - Norma Fitzpatrick. I'm sure you've heard about the case."

"Yes, of course. How is she?"

"She's a scared young woman who is in serious trouble."

"I've been following the case pretty closely," Barrows said with a look of sincere compassion in his eyes. "If there is anything I can do to help, please let me know."

"That's why I'm here. I do want to talk to a student here named Carl Vance. I understand he's free this period."

"I'm afraid you're somewhat confused, Mr. Solomon. Carl Vance is not a student here."

"I'm certain my secretary said you were going to arrange for me to speak to him."

"I did arrange for you to speak to him." Barrows leaned forward and spoke into his intercom: "Missy, please send in Carl Vance."

"Now I'm really confused. First you say he's not a student, and now you're sending him in."

"Carl Vance isn't a student here, he's a teacher."

The door opened and in walked the balding, middle-aged man Danial had just walked past.

"What can I do for you, Mr..."

"Solomon, Danial Solomon."

Principal Barrows stepped out, closing the door behind him.

"Good to meet you, Mr. Solomon. What can I do for you?"

"I'm representing a student named Norma Fitzpatrick. I'm assuming you're familiar with the case."

"I am. I personally don't think she did it."

"Oh really, why's that?"

"Norma is a good student, very dependable and a sweet kid. She just isn't the type of person to do such a thing."

"It's good to hear you say that. But I've got to tell you, I didn't come here to get a character reference from you. This may be uncomfortable for you, but I've got to ask you a very personal question."

"Please feel free," Vance said.

"Are you the father of her child?" Danial asked, his voice a little strained. "She said so."

"She what?!" His eyes flew wide open. "Is this some sort of joke?"

"I'm afraid not."

"I've been happily married for 16 years. I've got a daughter who's almost Norma's age. I don't know what kind of game you think you're playing here, but I resent it." His face flushed. "I've taught here at Big Red ever since I graduated from college, and I can assure you that fooling around with my students is not an activity I indulge in. I've been named *Teacher of the Year* four times, I'll have you know!"

"I can see you're upset. I didn't come here to insult you."

"Do you realize if a wild accusation like this gets out, I'll lose my job fast enough to make your head spin?"

"Mr. Vance, I understand the delicacy of your position. And it certainly isn't my intent to disgrace you or cause your family any public hardship."

"I can't tell."

"But you have to understand that my client's life may be at stake, and I must know who the father is."

"I am not him!"

"If you'll agree to a DNA test, we'll quietly put this behind us."

"I'll gladly submit to a DNA test."

"My office will be getting in touch with you to make the necessary arrangements. I'm grateful for your cooperation."

"You're welcome, but please tell that client of yours to stop slandering me."

25

Lori Franks must have pulled her hair back too tightly in the morning, because as soon as she let her hair down her headache subsided. She hated to wear her hair down while at work. She went to great lengths to look as plain as possible, but her efforts were in vain.

Lori never enjoyed being called into Anthony DiAngello's office. And lately, each time she left one of these impromptu meetings, she felt like she needed a shower. She had been diligently working on the Fitzpatrick case, even though it was uncomfortable for her and Danial. She organized the case summary DiAngello requested and all the related documents. She felt frazzled and bowed her head for a quick prayer.

"Heavenly Father, You know I'm new at this, but I need help. My life is a complete mess. I hate my job, and I don't know what to do. My heart is aching over little Erin. I know I forfeited my right to be a mother when I went in for the abortion, but she's my daughter. I know the Lewises are good parents and love her. And I know they are really happy living in Jackson Hole. I just don't know how to feel or what to do. Please give me some guidance towards seeing her. I need it. In Jesus' name. Amen!"

She picked up the armful of legal materials and headed out the door. Even though she wasn't ready to admit it to anyone, the once battle-hardened, stoic feminist was beginning to soften from the inside out. The transformation began a month earlier when God removed her heart of stone and replaced it with a heart of flesh, and the metamorphosis was only beginning.

Lori walked down the hall, took a deep breath and knocked.

"Come right in, Ms. Franks. I'd like to have a word with you."

She took a seat on the couch near his desk and caught his gaze lingering a bit too long on her chest.

"How're things going with the Baby Ammo case?" he asked.

"All right."

"I imagine with the DNA test coming back positive, you have old Solomon right where you want him?"

"I've actually not spoken to him since the results came in."

"Good. With all the evidence so strongly in our favor, I don't want you to offer any plea bargain with less than 30 actual."

"Thirty actual! There's no way in the world Danial would advise his client to accept an offer like that."

"Well, if he won't accept the offer, take him to trial and bury him in paperwork." He shifted his weight in the chair. "Push to have the Juvenile Court bind her over as soon as possible. There's more than one way to skin a cat."

She shook her head.

"Do you have a problem with that?"

Lori took a breath to speak; DiAngello cut her off.

"Before you answer, let me say your job is on the line here." DiAngello leaned back in his chair with his hands behind his head. "Now, do you have a problem with that?"

Lori's concerned eyebrows squinted down over her violet blue eyes, and her lips thinned as she formulated her thoughts and converted them into words.

"Yes, I do have a problem with that... so... I quit!"

2:30 P.M.

Danial Solomon wasn't thrilled to see the eyesore Eugene Stedman called a truck parked on the street in front of his office. The morning didn't turn out the way he had hoped. Now he kicked himself for taking his attention off the McKinney case to run a wild goose chase for Norma.

Most good attorneys keep several irons in the fire, and Danial had a nagging feeling he was forgetting something. He stopped on the first step leading to his brownstone office to check his daily planner.

"Great, I forgot all about the Arnold probate hearing this afternoon." He shook his head. "Archie's brief is due tomorrow, and I still haven't finished Discovery in the Tabor case. It looks like it's going to be a long night."

Jennifer met Danial at the door with a smile and a cup of cinnamon coffee. "Mr. Stedman is waiting for you in your office. How did it go down at the school?"

"Don't ask."

"That bad, huh?"

"Worse." Danial handed Jennifer his briefcase. "I'll need all the Arnold files. I've got a 3 o'clock probate hearing."

She nodded and handed him a pile of messages. "There's nothing earth-shattering in there. I'll get the files together. Do you want me to buzz you when it's twenty to three?"

"Sure."

He took a sip of coffee then walked into his office and said, "What've you got for me?"

"Unfortunately, not much. I spent the morning running down a lead on the VW Bug I believed our boys used. But it turned out to be nothing."

"Why's that?"

"The car wasn't rented until 5:56 p.m. Our boys needed it first thing that morning."

"Next. Ian wrote down a list of people who could be helpful." Danial slid the paper across the desk. "One of these people could know something about the bombing."

"Knowing about it is one thing," Stedman said. "But talking about it is another."

"Well, somehow you always manage to get hard-to-get information."

Stedman looked away and burst into a coughing fit. He held up his index finger until it passed.

"Sounds like you could use another cigarette," Danial said.

"Very funny. What's with the circled one here?"

"That's Pastor Stone. Don't worry about him. I'll visit him myself."

"He may be more willing to talk to me than you."

"Whatever you say. You're running the show." Stedman tucked the list in his shirt pocket and scratched his leathery, wrinkled forehead. "The other reason I stopped by was to pick up any additional video from the day of the bombing."

"What do you mean?"

"Well, you gave me the video that ran from 8:00 a.m. till 10:00 a.m. which covered the McKinney arrest and the two men climbing down into the manhole. And I've seen the footage of the VW Bug in the police station parking lot. I've also seen the video covering the hour prior to the explosions. I'd like to see anything that happened throughout the rest of the day."

"That shouldn't be a problem. I've got to go over to the courthouse later this afternoon. I'll get any available footage."

"Very good," Stedman said. "I'll get right on this list."

The red light on the intercom lit up. Danial pressed the button. "What is it Jennifer?"

"Phone call on line 1."

"Take a message. I'm just finishing up with Mr. Stedman."

"I really think you should take this call," Jennifer said, her voice trembling with emotion.

"Sorry about the interruption," Danial said to Stedman. "Danial Solomon here. What can I do for you?"

"My name is Sonny Dante, and I an inmate."

"How did you get my number?"

"I'm a friend of Archie Kisner. I got your number from a letter he left in his Bible."

"What're you doing with his Bible?"

"That's why I calling. Archie Kisner is dead."

"Archie's dead?!"

"Yessir, burned to death."

"Is this a prank call?"

"No sir."

"Are you sure it was Archie?" Danial's heart raced as the reality of the news struck him like a body blow.

"I know cause I'm the one who cleaned up his cell. That's where I got his Bible."

"Wait a minute. They had you clean up the cell? Was the State Patrol present?"

"No. Just the shift captain and a few guards. Inmates were out for chow."

"This is bad, this is real bad. Don't say anything else over the phone. I'll be up to see you as soon as I can get away."

"What should I do till then?"

"Keep your mouth shut. Don't talk about this to anyone. Do you understand me?"

"Understood."

University Hospital
3:30 P.M.

Dr. Gaston Garvey had been manipulating the surgical schedule to avoid being teamed with Nurse Martine and the intern Garland. However, today he made a point to get them on his squad. He wanted to see how they were holding up.

While Garvey scrubbed his hands, Martine and Garland attended to an anesthetized young woman.

"Has Garvey said anything to you since... since... you know?" Martine asked.

"I've avoided him like the plague."

"Why? Has he said something to you?"

"Yeah."

"He did? What'd he say?"

"He called me to his office a few days after it happened. He asked me if I had said anything to anyone. When I told him I hadn't, he said good, because if I did, he'd make sure I never get another internship."

Martine shook her head as she pressed her stethoscope

against the patient's chest. "What are you going to do?"

"Keep my mouth shut, I guess. What else can I do?"

"I don't know." Martine checked the girl's pulse. "This job is really getting to me. We've had preemies survive that were less developed than some of these aborted babies. I'm not trying to be religious or anything, but I became a nurse because I wanted to save lives, not take them."

They stopped talking as Garvey approached.

"Garland, are you familiar with the Dilation and Curettage procedure?"

"Sure."

"Since I'm responsible to certify you, why don't we have a little oral exam? Explain the D and C."

"Are you serious?"

"I most certainly am."

"All right." Garland spoke in a condescending monotone. "The uterus is approached through the vagina. The cervix is dilated to permit the insertion of a curette, a tiny spoon or hoe-like instrument. I then scrape the wall of the uterus, cutting the baby's body to pieces and scraping the placenta from its attachments on the uterine wall. Bleeding is considerable."

"Good. Now the Saline injection method."

"Saline abortion is usually carried out after the 16th week of pregnancy, when enough amniotic fluid has accumulated in the sac around the baby. A long needle is inserted through the mother's abdomen directly into the sac, and a concentrated saline solution is injected into the amniotic fluid. This salt solution is absorbed both through the lungs and the gastrointestinal tract, producing changes in the osmotic pressure. The outer layer of the baby's skin is burned off by the high concentration of salt. It takes about an hour to dehydrate and kill the infant. The mother goes into labor, or is induced to deliver a dead, shriveled baby."

"Very good." Garvey walked over to the patient. "For this one, I think we'll go with the suction abortion procedure. The D and C would be too messy. Martine, wheel the suction machine over."

"Yes, Doctor."

"As a matter of fact, I think we'll make it easy on ourselves and use suction on all eligible patients this afternoon. How many do we have waiting?"

"Ten."

"Not many, a light day. All right, Garland. Let's hear the suction procedure."

Nurse Martine rolled her eyes.

"Suction abortion, also known as vacuum aspiration, is similar in principle to the Dilation and Curettage. Whether manual or electric, a thin but powerful suction tube is inserted through the dilated cervix into the uterus. This tears apart the body of the developing baby and the placenta, sucking the pieces into a container. The smaller parts of the body are recognizable as arms, legs, head, and so on."

4:42 P.M.

Danial went through the motions during his afternoon appointment, but his mind was on Archie. After the probate hearing he ran to the Clerk's Office and picked up the videos Stedman requested. Now he backed through his office door, balancing his briefcase on top of a cardboard box.

Jennifer saw him struggling with the door and raced over to grab the briefcase as it toppled off the box.

"Thanks."

"What's all this?"

"Video footage that Stedman wanted, so please give him a call and tell him to pick it up." Danial set the box down on the chair next to Jennifer's desk. "Boy, bad news travels fast. Those media vultures are swarming all over the courthouse wanting comments on Archie's death."

"They make me sick," Jennifer said.

"They applauded when he got sentenced to forever and a day. But now that he's dead, it's all of a sudden a human-interest story."

"There's someone waiting for you in your office."

"Who is it?"

"I promised I wouldn't say."

Her smile hastened him toward the door. He walked in to find Lori Franks sitting behind his desk, her hair spilling down over her shoulders, her shoeless feet propped up on an open drawer.

"Hello," he said, surprised and confused.

She jumped up, ran around the desk and flung herself in his arms.

He dropped his briefcase. "Wow! So much for keeping our relationship professional."

"It's over," she said.

"What do you mean it's over?"

"I quit."

Danial leaned back to get a good look at her face. Their eyes met. Tears brimmed on her eyelashes. She pressed her cheek against his chest.

"You're serious?"

"I couldn't take it anymore. I tried. I really did, but if I hadn't gotten out of there I would've lost my mind."

"It's all right, Lori. God's in control, and He will work this out."

She clung tightly to his chest.

"Have you thought about what you want to do?"

"I thought I'd work for you, if you'll have me."

"You're hired."

She squeezed a bit tighter.

26

Judge John Williams sat at his desk trying to focus on the Post-Conviction opinion his clerk had written earlier in the week. It had been over ten years since Williams had done any of his own writing on legal matters. And now he didn't even do much proofreading; he found it difficult to concentrate for long periods of time. At first he struggled to remember the Latin phrases. Now even the fundamental premises of the Ohio Constitution and Ohio Revised Code eluded him. As much as he wanted to deny it, the words of his longtime friend and doctor resounded loudly in his ears: "John, you have Alzheimer's."

Could it be true? Am I losing my memory? I still feel fine. I do get confused and frustrated... but so does everyone else.

Colin Casey burst through the door and slammed the newspaper down on the desk. "Did you see this?"

"Yes, I did."

"Would someone please explain to me how the suicide of a convicted felon is somehow front-page news?"

"Beats me."

"I can't believe the media is cramming this stuff down our throats. It's been everywhere." He paced back and forth in front of the desk. "It was the lead story on the 5 and 11 o'clock news last night, and now this."

"They sure made me out to be the bad guy," Williams said, "with that talk of a long sentence driving him over the edge."

"He did the taxpayers a favor."

"Maybe it *was* my fault."

"Well, I can tell you this much - this hurts us bad. I'm afraid to see this evening's polls. If we don't do something fast to stop this bloodletting, we're going to slide right out of contention."

Casey stormed around the room. He kicked the desk, then the wastebasket. Williams sat quietly, not wanting to say something that might add fuel to the fire.

"This is exactly why I hate working in small towns," Casey said. "The people are fickle. In the city, if some retarded criminal set himself on fire it wouldn't make the metro section of the paper. I can't wait to get out of this rat hole."

"What should we do?"

"I don't know."

"Maybe we should issue a statement."

"Nothing we could say would clean up this mess." Casey ran his fingers through his sandy blond hair. "No, the bombing trial is our ticket at this point. I've got a special prosecutor coming in to assist DiAngello."

"What did he say to that?"

"Nothing yet, he doesn't know. I'm not taking any chances. We cannot afford any more glitches."

9:15 A.M.

Danial had suggested that Lori take a few days off to collect her thoughts before coming to work, but she would hear none of it. She was eager to do something to feel useful. So, after a breakfast at Danial's favorite restaurant, Chick-fil-A, the two were heading northwest on routes 45 and 14 for a meeting with the warden of the Akron Correctional Reception Center.

"Now that you've had 24 hours to think about it," Danial said, "how do you feel?"

"I did the right thing. I can't tell you how much better it feels to be out of there."

"For what it's worth, I think you did the right thing too." Danial looked over at her. The bright morning sun brought the violet out in her eyes. "I look forward to seeing what the Lord has in store for us."

"Why do you think God allowed Archie to die?" she asked.

"God sometimes allows suffering and tragedy to bring about some greater good or to stop a greater evil. Sometimes both."

"What greater good?"

"It's case by case. It's always something new and special."

"That's not very comforting for Archie. Or is it?"

"Think of it this way, God created us as free moral beings. Apparently, someone exercised their free will to kill Archie—"

"But you said God may have allowed this to happen."

"In the sense that Archie is in a much better place and his killer will be stopped."

"I'm still a little confused."

"It's all a matter of perspective. As humans we think death is the absolute worst thing that can happen. But as Christians, we know that death is the doorway to Heaven."

"Now what about Erin?" she asked.

"What about her?"

"I've been thinking about her a lot lately, and I can't believe I almost killed her - my own child - I almost killed my own child."

"But you didn't," Danial said. "God intervened in Erin's situation and saved her life. He used a compassionate doctor to stop an evil procedure for Erin's greater good. It could also be said that your suffering led to your moral and spiritual repentance and salvation."

"Believe me, I know God saved her, God and that good old doctor. But now those maternal feelings I thought were dead are streaming back.

"I'm sure that's normal. Telling others could save more babies."

"For seven years I was absorbed with thoughts of my aborted child, what he or she might look like, hair and eye color. And I had flashbacks. I can still feel my feet up in those stirrups." She shuddered. "I can't tell you how many nightmares I had and all the haunting visitations..."

"It sounds like you went through Post-Abortion Stress Syndrome."

"I must've had it bad. But now that I've found out Erin is still alive, it seems like my mind doesn't know how to sort out how I'm supposed to feel."

"Do you think it would help if we arranged for a visit?"

"I don't know."

"I call Andy and Marianne Lewis at least once a week."

"I may not be ready yet, but I want to be."

"Lori, I wish I had the right words to say to wipe away all the pain, but I don't. I do know this, God is sovereignly in control."

After a long drive, Danial pulled off the highway and weaved along back roads following directions from the GPS. The autumn trees looked beautiful with their orange, red, yellow and brown leaves falling to the ground.

The car broke into a clearing. Behind a huge parking lot, and behind miles of fencing and razor wire, sat the prison. They walked to the entrance building, both carrying briefcases. The over-weight guard working the front desk refused to allow them in to see Sonny Dante.

Danial insisted on his appointment with the warden. After what seemed to be an eternity, a second officer escorted Lori and Danial up a winding staircase that led to the office complex overlooking the prison. A large man in a blue suit stepped out of the main office.

"I'm Warden Erdman. I understand you had some difficulty seeing an inmate."

Warden Arnold Erdman stood 6 foot 3 and weighed over 240 pounds. Prematurely gray hair lined his temples, which made him look older than his 42 years.

"I spoke to the visitation officer on the phone, and according to him you were denied access because neither of you are listed as the attorney of record for the inmate you want to see."

"That's because neither of us are representing Mr. Dante," Danial answered with a smile.

"Well, state policy prohibits unauthorized visits of any kind, but I can make exceptions if there's a good reason."

"It has to do with Archie Kisner."

"Archie Kisner?"

"The inmate who died yesterday."

"Whoa, hold on a minute. What have you got to do with Kisner?"

"I am... or I should say, I was his attorney."

"You can't talk to Dante or any other inmate or, as far as that goes, any staff in this prison concerning Archie Kisner."

"I was told the official cause of death was suicide. So, what's with all the secrecy?"

"Do you have something to hide?" Lori chimed in.

"I have nothing to hide, and I don't like your tone young lady." Erdman looked over at Danial. "I expect you to control your secretary while she is in this institution."

"Secretary!" Lori shouted. "I'll have you know I was the prosecuting attorney who convicted Kisner!"

"Calm down," Erdman said.

"Isn't it prison policy to seal off the scene of any death until the State Patrol has a chance to investigate?" Danial asked.

"What are you getting at?"

"You had an inmate clean up the cell before any outside official could examine it."

"An oversight by the Major. He was concerned about getting the maximum-security inmates back in their housing unit. He is being reprimanded."

"Reprimanded! The man tampered with a murder scene."

"Who said anything about murder?" Erdman's face turned red.

"A man gets incinerated while locked in his cell in a vacated building, then the scene gets wiped clean. That sounds like a cover-up to me."

"This meeting is over." The warden slung his glasses to the floor; spittle shot from his mouth. "You will leave the premises at once, or I'll have you physically removed!"

The escort officer tugged at Danial's arm.

"I'll make it my life's work to find out what happened here and to see justice."

27

Lori Franks found herself in the unfamiliar role of visiting a client at the county jail. Over the past seven years she had spent countless hours in the jail interrogating and coaching witnesses, but now she felt inadequate and nervous.

"Norma, I know we've never actually met, but I've been working on your case from the very beginning."

"Mr. Solomon never mentioned having a partner."

"I just started working with him yesterday."

"Then how have you been working on my case from the beginning?"

"The truth of the matter is, I was the prosecutor working on the case for the state."

"But now you're working with Mr. Solomon?"

"Correct. So, here's the scoop. From the State's perspective, the case against you is airtight."

"But I didn't do it!"

"That's almost irrelevant. The evidence is overwhelming, and the most damaging is the DNA test. You can come up with alibis until you're blue in the face, but the scientific evidence says the baby's yours."

Norma dropped her head.

"Second, there's the police video showing what appears to be your car dropping off the baby and then speeding away. We know otherwise, but the State has the DNA match. Third, the person you said was the father - a Mr. Vance I believe - has emphatically denied any involvement and is willing to take a

DNA test to prove his innocence."

"He what?" Norma said. "Carl would never say something like that. He loves me. As soon as I graduate, he's going to divorce his wife, and we're going to get married."

"Is that what he told you?"

"He's been sayin' that all along."

"Well, it's time for a reality check, Norma. It's likely there isn't going to be any wedding following graduation, because there isn't going to be any graduation. The truth of the matter is, if you lose at trial the best you could hope for is 15 to 30 years in prison."

"Thirty years!" Norma screamed as tears filled her eyes. Lori slid over and put her arm around Norma's convulsing shoulders.

"Norma, I know this is going to be hard for you to swallow, but it's time to start thinking about a plea bargain. With my connections in the Prosecutor's Office, if we wait things out till after the election, I could arrange for a manslaughter plea."

"Manslaughter."

"A maximum sentence of five years."

"Five years! Carl won't wait five years."

8:50 A.M.

"Ian, I know this sounds crazy," Danial said, "but it's our best shot."

"A press conference?"

"You only get one chance to tell your story and this is it. You said the reason you threw the egg was to get the world's attention. Well, now you've got it. NBC, ABC, CBS, FOX, CNN, NPR, NEWSMAX, the AP, I've got them all."

"You really think this is best?"

"It's a win-win. You get your bully pulpit, and I get witness credibility. Plus, it's Friday. The story will run all weekend."

"Maximum exposure."

"Now you get it."

A smile stretched out across Ian's face. "I sure do. What time?"

"Ten o'clock, plenty of time to make the noon news."

"So, what do you want me to do?"

"Just tell your story. You must have been thinking of what you'd say?"

"Of course, I've already got it written down."

"Good. Just don't get carried away, and whatever you do, don't laugh."

"I'm too nervous to laugh."

"Keep it short, don't answer any questions, and I close the conference with a zinger."

"What zinger?"

"You'll see."

9:10 A.M.

Anthony DiAngello breezed into his courthouse office an hour late. Alcohol reeked out of his pores. He gave his secretary stern orders to hold all calls and let nobody into his office, not even if the future of the free world depended on it. He shut the door, closed the blinds and buried himself in his leather couch. A cold sweat broke out on his forehead.

"I overdid it."

The couch felt like a tiny boat being tossed about by the sea. His knuckles turned white as his fingers gripped the cushions. Slowly he drifted off to sleep. At 9:40 the sound of a commotion outside his door startled him awake. Colin Casey barged in. DiAngello spewed a stream of obscenities.

"This better be important, Casey, or I'll have you on the next bus smokin' back to Columbus."

"Take it easy counselor, I'm here to brighten your day. Judge Williams just received a phone call from the TV station inviting him to a post-press conference interview."

"What press conference?"

"Danial Solomon scheduled a press conference for 10 o'clock

this morning on the 2nd floor. Apparently, Ian McKinney has a prepared statement."

"Sounds like he's going to plead guilty to the bombing."

"The invincible Mr. Solomon is throwing in the towel."

DiAngello got to his feet, walked over to his desk and grabbed his double-breasted suit coat; he straightened himself in the mirror. His brain started firing on all cylinders, and the implications of the press conference began taking shape in his mind.

"On second thought, Solomon isn't throwing in the towel. He's positioning himself for trial."

"That's crazy."

"Crazy like a fox."

"I don't get it."

"He's conceding the stuff he can't defend. It's a pretty sharp trial tactic. He can tell the jury his client has taken responsibility for what he *has* done."

"I guess that makes sense," Casey mumbled.

"What's the matter? All this legal maneuvering over your head?"

9:45 A.M.

Danial went over last-minute instructions with Ian before the press conference. Ian handed him his speech and he read it.

"This is good, very good actually," Danial said. "Are you ready?"

"You're sure this is the right thing to do?"

"Listen, Ian, you want to take responsibility for your actions and send a message to the world."

"Yeah."

"Then we're doing the right thing. That's why you're paying me the big bucks."

"Maybe I'm getting more than I paid for."

"I'll be sitting right next to you. As soon as you finish your speech, I'm going to end the press conference."

"What's this zinger you talked about?"

"You'll see. Now, before we go out there, would you like for me to pray with you?"

"Thanks for the offer, Mr. Solomon, but I don't need that kind of crutch to get through life. Like others, I'm pro-life but I'm not a Christian. If it works for you, more power to you."

The two walked out of the small room and down the hall to the elevator. Two deputies walked behind Ian. The elevator opened on the 2nd floor and the entourage filed toward the conference room filled with representatives from every branch of the media. Bright camera lights focused on the opened door. Danial pressed into the crowd, making a path for his client. A chorus of questions filled the air. A small, solitary table banked with microphones stood at one end of the room. Once they took their seats at the table, Danial motioned for silence and addressed the radio, TV and newspaper reporters.

"I'd first of all like to thank you all for coming on such short notice. I know this case is of great public interest, and my client wants to be as forthcoming as his present position allows. As for the ground rules for this conference, my client has a prepared statement. He will not be fielding questions from the media today."

Grumbling swept the room.

"I'm sorry, ladies and gentlemen, but we have a trial to prepare for, and I've got to protect my client's rights. So, without further ado, I present Ian McKinney."

TV cameras zoomed in on Ian.

"Thank you for giving me this opportunity to address the public. I'm quite certain that by now most people look at me as some sort of Unabomber nut or something, but let me assure you I am not. It is quite unfortunate the bombing happened to take place on the day of my arrest, because that dastardly act has overshadowed the message I am trying to send. Before I get into the specifics of what I did, I'd like to spend a few minutes explaining why I did it. I think it is obvious that I support the pro-life position. Sadly, the sequence of events that transpired has tainted the messenger, but I hope you won't let it taint the message.

"Abortion is a crime that kills the child and the conscience of those involved. Abortion on demand is legal in this country. We have walked away from the words Thomas Jefferson wrote that gave birth to this great nation: 'We hold these truths to be self-evident, that all men are created equal, that they are endowed by their Creator with certain unalienable rights, that among these are *LIFE*, liberty and the pursuit of happiness.'

"Abraham Lincoln, as he struggled with the issue of human slavery, said, '... this old Declaration of Independence... declares that all men are equal... If one man says it does not mean a negro, why cannot another man say it does not mean some other man?' Or in the case at hand, some other baby?

"The congressman who drafted the Fourteenth Amendment was from Ohio. His name was John A. Bingham, and in writing that famous amendment, he declared that 'All are entitled to the protection of American law, because its divine spirit of equality declares that all men are created equal.' But here we stand over one hundred years later, and we've allowed one of the fundamental rights in our Constitution - the right to life - to be chiseled away. We as a nation are standing on a slippery slope. It won't be long until the rights of liberty and the pursuit of happiness are also stripped by the black-robed activists we call judges."

Ian's voice strengthened as the weight and force of the subject matter bolstered his fortitude. He swallowed, licked his lips, and took a breath.

"Someone once said, 'The cultural environment for a human holocaust is present whenever any society can be misled into defining any individual as less than human and therefore devoid of value and respect.' The Holocaust by Nazi Germany didn't *begin* with the gas chambers that slaughtered millions of Jews. No, that was the end result of a desensitized nation. In the 1930s, racist eugenics led to legalization of abortion.

Nazi "purification" of Germany and Austria included lethal gas euthanasia of 200,000 young and old people with mental and physical infirmities. Other unwanted people groups were decimated too. But no one stopped to ask the unwanted what they thought about being designated for destruction.

"Professor John Hunt, Ph.D. wrote about 'The Abortion and Eugenics Policies of Nazi Germany.' After World War II at the Nuremberg war crimes trials, there was a case involving abortion titled *United States of America v. Ulrich Greifelt Et Al.* It led to 25-year prison sentences for abortionists who encouraged and compelled abortions. The prosecutor called abortion an inhumane act, an act of extermination. And he said that a woman's voluntary abortion was also a crime against humanity.

"So what we Americans condemned as a war crime just 55 years ago has now become a right protected by our Constitution, though I defy you to find it written there. *This* murder of innocents is becoming one of the worst genocides in history. If America continues on its present course, we may owe Adolf Hitler an apology!" He slammed his hand on the table.

"In Ronald Reagan's powerful book, *Abortion and the Conscience of the Nation*, he said, 'The abortionist who reassembles the arms and legs of a tiny baby to make sure all its parts have been torn from its mother's body can hardly doubt whether it is a human being. The real question for him and all of us is whether that tiny human life has a God-given right to be protected by the law - the same right we have.'

"President Reagan also quoted a young pregnant woman named Victoria who said, 'In this society we save whales, we save timber wolves and bald eagles and Coke bottles. Yet, everyone wanted me to throw away my baby.' How does this make sense? Since when does the life of an animal become more important than the life of a human baby?" Ian's voice trembled with emotion. "I am standing here today because in the United States of America, it's against the law to kill an unborn bird, but it's perfectly legal to kill an unborn human being.

"I threw the egg to expose the cold, brutal hypocrisy of the law, and I sincerely hope my action will not be in vain. But while I'm a man of passion, I'm also a man of conviction. Therefore, I'm declaring today I'll plead No Contest to the charges concerning the bald eagle egg. However, I once again emphatically deny any involvement in the explosions that took place at University Hospital the night after my arrest. I condemn such things and hope those responsible are captured and brought to justice. Having said that, I have nothing further to say."

Flashes erupted.

Reporters shouted questions and jeered.

Danial stood and motioned for silence. The crowd reluctantly quieted down. He pulled a large envelope out of his briefcase, opened it and slid out a stack of glossy photos of the injuries Ian sustained during his arrest. He passed them around.

"I would also like to announce that following this press conference, I'll be filing a multi-million dollar lawsuit against the Steubenville Police Department for police brutality and violations of my client's Eighth Amendment rights against cruel and unusual punishment."

28

6:30 P.M.

Danial Solomon carefully followed the directions Lori gave him to her condo on Lovers Lane. He parked his granite-gray Dodge Charger on the street, stepped out and looked over the roof of the car. It looked like a scene out of a Norman Rockwell painting. A waist-high, white picket fence surrounded the property. A cobblestone walk led from the gate to the porch. Red leaves from the elm trees littered the yard. The white condo looked like a house, picturesque with green shutters and trim around all the windows.

Danial climbed the steps feeling like a teenager on prom night. He knocked on the door and stood with his hands behind his back. A few moments later the door swung open, and he held his breath.

Lori wore a blue cocktail dress with a sweetheart neckline and fitted waist. A delicate gold necklace dangled from her neck. As she stepped back to let him in, the light sparkled off her diamond earrings.

"Come on in," she said. "I have to get my coat."

He pulled his right hand from behind his back and handed her a single pink rose. "For you."

"Thank you. It's so beautiful, and you're so sweet. I'll put it in water."

She hurried off to the kitchen and returned with the rose in a crystal vase. She set it on a table in the living room. Danial helped her on with her coat.

"So where are you taking me?"

"It's a surprise."

"How about a hint?"

"Ahhh... no."

She pouted her pretty bottom lip.

"You look adorable, but it's not going to work."

They walked to the car in silence. Danial opened the door for her then trotted around to the driver's side. They drove past the Fort Steuben Mall and onto Route 7 listening to the *Focus on the Family* broadcast; Dr. James Dobson discussed raising children with loving discipline. The sun hovered just above the horizon, its beams shimmering off the murky Ohio River.

"We're heading south," Lori said. "So that means..."

"We're not going north."

She punched him in the arm.

They drove past the enormous cooling towers of Brilliant's power plant, past the hulking steel mill in Tiltonsville and crossed the river at Bridgeport. Danial maneuvered the car through Wheeling Island, crossed the Wheeling Suspension Bridge, and pulled into the parking garage next to the Capitol Theatre.

"Are we going to a concert?"

"I'm not saying."

"Awe, come on."

"All right, you beat it out of me, it's a concert." Danial reached into his coat pocket and produced two theatre box tickets to the Wheeling Symphony Orchestra. A tuxedo-clad usher escorted them to their seats as the concertmaster struck a note and the tuning began.

"What are they performing?" Lori asked as the usher exited the box.

"An orchestral suite by Handel from *The Water Music*."

"This is such a wonderful surprise."

"The night is still young."

The lights dimmed. The conductor tapped his baton on the podium. A hush fell over the crowd. He raised the baton, glanced around the orchestra, dipped the baton and sweet music filled the hall. About a half hour later the music stopped, with an instant of silence followed by rapturous applause. Lori and

Danial rose to their feet, gazing tenderly into one another's eyes. When the clapping died down, they returned to their seats. Danial took her hand; it felt soft and delicate.

The conductor lifted his baton, and the orchestra lit into a moving rendition of Mozart's *Symphony No. 40 in G minor, K.550.* The concert ended about 40 minutes later. They drove down to the Wheeling Wharf, then boarded a restored paddlewheel riverboat. It had been converted into a four-star restaurant and was decorated in a pre-Civil War motif, complete with a Dixieland band. They were seated at a table near the front of the boat, next to a window that offered a panoramic view of the waterfront.

"This is spectacular," Lori said. "I didn't know this existed."

"It's the Valley's best-kept secret. The food is exquisite."

The waiter came and took their orders. Danial and Lori talked about their childhoods, law school, the weather - everything but work. The waiter placed a plate of tenderloin filet in front of Lori, and Danial's favorite, New Orleans stuffed shrimp, in front of him. They ate for a few minutes, chatting and enjoying the atmosphere.

The waiter pushed the dessert cart to the table. Lori chose a small piece of cheesecake. Danial selected pecan pie and they both ordered French vanilla coffee. In the background, over the dinner noise, the band played a waltz.

"Would you like to dance?" he asked.

"I'd love to."

He led her by the hand to the small, hardwood dance floor in the center of the boat. A white-haired couple had beaten them to the floor and gracefully floated around with the ease of 50 years practice.

"I'm not very good at this," she said with a smile.

"That's all right, neither am I."

He held out his right hand. She took it, and they awkwardly moved around in a circle. They looked around the restaurant, then at the elderly couple moving elegantly across the floor, and then into each other's eyes. Her violet-blues twinkled in the light reflecting off the mirrored ball overhead. Her eyes were warm and inviting, and for a moment Danial thought if he looked deep enough he could see the faces of his future children in them.

The music stopped, and they stepped back to clap. The heel of Lori's blue pump caught a seam in the floor, and she stumbled. Her shoe fell off, revealing bright red toenails. She slid her foot back in, her face flushed with embarrassment.

"Graceful, huh?" she said.

"Like a ballerina."

The music resumed with "The Blue Danube Waltz." Danial offered his hand, and she took it. They danced slowly, drawing ever nearer. The world disappeared as Danial looked into her eyes once again. She radiated complete and utter beauty. He tried to tell her, but the words stuck in his throat. Their bodies moved closer together. She closed her eyes and tipped her head back. His heart fluttered. He closed his eyes and leaned forward. Their lips met; electricity seemed to shoot through his body. The music stopped. The sound of applause erupted and startled them apart. They looked around.

"For a minute there, I thought they were clapping for us," she said.

Danial smiled. *That kiss deserved a standing ovation.*

29

Stealthy Art Bently knelt down on the forest floor shrouded by a layer of dawn fog. He slowly turned his head to look over at Ron Kester who lay a few feet to the left. Both men wore camouflage fatigues, faces painted black and green like commandos.

Ron nodded almost imperceptibly toward Art, and then darted his eyes to the right. Art followed the direction of Ron's gaze and slowly raised the Remington compound bow. Since the dawn of civilization, men have used the bow and arrow for hunting animals and killing enemies. Modern high-tech bows and razor-sharp arrows are far more lethal. Art peered through the forest and saw the silhouette of the target. Ron nodded once again as if to ask, "Can you see him?"

Art answered with a nod of affirmation. Ron's early morning pep talk echoed through his head: "Desperate times call for desperate measures. We aren't the bad guys here, and we've got to do whatever it takes to survive. Whatever it takes."

Art shook off the thought and reacquired the target. He may not have been as tough as Ron, but he was a better archer. He slowly drew back the bowstring to the corner of his mouth and intentionally slowed his breathing.

Ron mouthed the word: "Now."

A sharp-edged broadhead arrow whistled across the Appalachian mountainside. Thud!

Both men leapt to their feet and ran toward the intruder's last position. "You got him!" Ron shouted. "I can't believe you got him."

"This is my first kill."

But that wasn't exactly true. As a boy, Art had shot a sparrow with his 760 Powermaster BB Rifle and cried as the bird flailed on the ground and finally died. Art vowed from that day forward never to kill again. But now, 40 years later, he had killed for the second time.

They slowed to a trot and then to a walk as they cleared a grassy knoll where they believed they would find the carcass. He was gone. They found a thick blood trail. The stream of crimson led through a briar patch and into the woods. Ron bent over and poked the tip of his index finger into a pool of warm, watery blood.

"It's dark. You must've got him in the liver. He won't last long."

Art felt sick. Not only did he cause death, but intense suffering in the process.

The sun broke over the treetops and turned the sky apple green. Ron led the way through the briars, through the trees, and down over a slight grade into a clearing. From that vantage point, the two men had a clear view of the area.

"There he is!" Ron shouted, pointing towards a stream about 50 yards straight ahead.

"Sure enough."

On the bank of the stream, with life ebbing out from the wound in his side, lay a full-grown whitetail deer. Before the men could reach the prey, the steaming breath stopped.

"An 8-point buck. Looks like venison steak tonight," Ron said as he slapped Art on the back.

2:30 P.M.

Danial Solomon tapped the eraser end of a pencil on his desk blotter while listening to elevator music blare through the phone. He watched Lori arrange her workstation at the opposite end of the office. They had decided that they would face each other. She wiped off the card table and neatly arranged her stackable trays and files. It would have to do until they could find her a big office desk.

"Warden Erdman," the voice said over the phone. "May I help you?"

"Mr. Erdman, this is Danial Solomon."

"Oh, it's you."

"I'm calling about Archie Kisner's body."

"He was cremated yesterday morning."

"Cremated!"

"Yeah, you know, when you incinerate a body."

"Was there an autopsy?"

"It was pretty obvious the cause of death was fire," Erdman said in a sarcastic tone.

"I see you have an astute grasp of the obvious."

"Now see here—"

"Did you at least determine the accelerant used in the fire? I mean, you don't sell gasoline in the commissary, do you?"

"I'm not at liberty to discuss the investigation."

"Maybe the Attorney General will."

"Listen, Solomon, we can play verbal gymnastics all day. What do you want?"

"I'd like custody of the body."

"Are you the next of kin?"

"No. He has no next of kin."

"ODRC policy states that only family can claim the body of a deceased inmate. If no family comes forward to claim the body, then the remains are interred at the prison cemetery in Columbus."

"But—"

"Now if there's nothing else I can do for you—"

"As a matter of fact, there is. I have an attorney-of-record form in front of me for Sonny Dante. I'd like to fax it to you."

"Fax me anything you'd like, but you still can't see Dante."

"Why not?"

"He's presently in segregation under investigation."

"Investigation? For what?"

"That's confidential. Now if there's nothing further, I've got a lot to do."

"How long do you suppose this investigation will last?"

"It'll last as long as we need it to."

"Well, let's just make sure inmate Dante doesn't have any accidents with matches while he's in segregation."

The phone went dead.

Danial looked over at Lori, sitting behind her table focused intently on a file. She looked up; their eyes met. A warm sensation swept over his body. He smiled. Lori was truly the most beautiful woman he had ever seen.

"If we continue in practice together," Danial said, "we're going to need a bigger office."

"I think this is kind of cozy." She blew a lock of hair off her forehead. "You know, after talking to Norma last Friday, I think she's telling the truth about Vance."

"He was awfully convincing."

"I'm guessing he's going to balk, so let's at least subpoena the DNA test. It'll either eliminate him as the father or verify Norma's claim. I'll get right on it. Now that's settled, what's on your mind?"

"I'm thinking about poor Archie. I can't imagine any worse way to go than by fire." Danial scratched the side of his head. "There's no way Archie killed himself."

"He didn't seem like the suicidal type to me either."

"I'm also afraid we may have put Dante's life in jeopardy by going to the prison like we did."

"We had no way of knowing the warden was going to react like he did. Think of it this way, we may have saved Dante's life by letting them know we're watching every move they make."

"You're probably right," he said. "Now a big question for you... what are we going to do next for Ian McKinney?"

9:15 P.M.

Eugene Stedman made little progress interviewing the list of possible informants Danial had given him. He spent about an hour talking to Jim Wilson, president of the Greater Ohio Valley Pro-Life Association. If Wilson knew anything, he wasn't saying. However, Stedman noticed the secretary seemed rattled when the questioning turned to the bombing. He made a mental note of it.

He returned home and watched the surveillance videos for hours.

"Since no one is willing to talk to me, maybe a little after-hours visit will yield better dividends."

Stedman sat on the edge of his bed and slipped a black turtleneck over his head. He pulled on a pair of black pants, then laced up his police issue boots. He gazed in the full-length mirror behind the bedroom door; he looked as ridiculous as he felt.

"But you've got to dress the part."

He pulled out his sock drawer, picked up his snub-nosed .357, and jammed it in the back waistband of his pants. He grabbed his cigarettes and his black ski mask, and out the door he went. Surprisingly, the truck started as soon as he twisted the wires together. He lit a Camel non-filter and pointed his old truck toward Steubenville.

He drove down Lawson Avenue and parked across the street from the converted storefront that now served as the headquarters for the Greater Ohio Valley Pro-Life Association. The streetlight illuminated two oversized picture windows: the left side proclaimed the organization's name, stenciled in red letters; on the right pane was a picture of a smiling baby in a large bassinet.

Stedman climbed out of the truck and walked in front of the building. It was dark inside with no sign of movement. He continued to the end of the block and turned the corner, into a narrow alley he had seen a delivery truck drive down earlier in the day. It provided access to the rear of the buildings. Stedman slithered along, avoiding sparse pools of light. He found the rear of the Pro-Life building and gave a sigh of relief - no security light. He crouched down in the shadow of the building, pulled on the ski mask, and trotted toward the rear door. His boots tapped lightly on the concrete. He tried the knob. *A deadbolt.*

He gave the back of the building a once-over. He analyzed a rusted fire escape ladder suspended a few feet above his head. It led to a dilapidated, 2nd floor balcony and exterior door. Judging from the decay, the ladder hadn't been used in years. He squatted down and jumped as high as his arthritic legs would allow. He stretched his right arm toward the bottom rung but missed. He lost his balance and stumbled to the ground. The awkward landing jarred his gun free; it clanked and clattered on the cement. *I'm getting too old for this.*

Stedman stashed the gun back in his pants, took a few steps back and made a running start at the ladder. His left hand gripped the bottom rung. *Got it!*

The ladder broke free from its rusted slumber with a loud metallic clang. Stedman froze for a moment and looked around. He shimmied up the ladder and stepped onto the balcony. He was about to pull the ladder back up. He weighed the options of leaving it down and taking the chance someone could report it to the police... or pulling it back up and making that wretched noise again. He decided to leave it down.

He crept over to the door, reached into a pocket, and pulled out a small flashlight and lock-pick set. He clenched the light in his teeth and made short work of the ancient Russwin lock. He slipped into the building and gently closed the door behind him.

Stedman found a stairway and gingerly descended. His heart raced as adrenalin surged into his circulatory system. All his senses were heightened, and the rush felt exhilarating. He hadn't felt so alive in years.

Having been here earlier in the day, he knew exactly where to find the office area. Unfortunately, the office back door faced the two large windows in the front of the building, giving anyone who happened to walk by an uninterrupted view.

Stedman squatted down; his knees made the grinding sound of gravel pressed over bubble wrap. He examined the lock, and his stomach knotted. *Why would anyone bother to put a keyless entry system in a dump like this?*

He scanned the window on the door. A wooden frame secured by brass screws bordered the glass window. Stedman reached into his pocket and pulled out a multi-tool. Using one of the screwdrivers, he removed the screws and placed them in his front pocket. He goosenecked around to make sure no one had seen him. He carefully removed the pane of glass, then reached through and opened the door from the inside.

Into the office area, he searched the desk and found nothing. He rooted through the filing cabinet. Sweat filled the ski mask, causing the double-knit material to droop over his eyes. He ripped off the mask and took a deep breath. He pulled out the bottom drawer and found a file marked "Meeting Minutes." He ran the flashlight over the file contents: a membership roster and meeting minutes. He picked up the file and was about to leave when he spotted a ledger on top of the cabinet. *Jackpot! It's the financial records.* He reviewed the figures.

The sound of keys fumbling at the front door rattled through the building. Stedman looked at the door. Two shadows walked in.

No place to hide. No time to reassemble the back door. Stedman gripped the ledger and file and ran as fast as his old legs would carry him. Out of the office, he crouched at the bottom of the back stairway. The office lights flipped on.

"Hey, what happened to the door?"

"It's not just open. Someone took it apart."

Stedman's heart thumped erratically. His chest heaved; he struggled to catch his breath. He figured his would-be pursuers must be at the desk, and if he was going to make a break for it, now was the time. He spurred his legs on. His boots thundered up the steps.

"Someone's running upstairs!" he heard someone yell.

Stedman slid down the outside ladder and then dashed for

the alley. He staggered and fell, clutching his chest. He took a few wheezing breaths and struggled to his feet. He reeled down the alley like a drunken sailor, grasping his booty firmly in his hands.

30

Tuesday, October 17
Jefferson County Courthouse
8:50 A.M.

Ever since entering the political arena several years earlier, no candidate Colin Casey worked for had ever lost an election. But as he sat behind Judge Williams' desk reviewing the morning data, it looked like this could be the first. Casey glanced over at the old judge buttoning his black robe. *That bumbling idiot could put a smudge on my record. He's probably too senile to judge a pie-eating contest.*

Casey finished reading the report and said, "It's still nearly a dead heat. The latest numbers show you both at about 40 percent with about 20 percent undecided. It's time for us to make our last push for voters sitting on the fence."

"Maybe I should hit the stump again," Williams said. "When I first ran for Probate Judge 30 years ago, I spent the week before the election speaking at card parties and kissing babies. I could pour on the charm one more time."

"You must be kidding."

"Well, no."

"One slip of the tongue and the press will crucify us."

"I don't know about that."

"No, it's time for attack ads."

"I never believed in such tactics."

"Nonsense. Now, I couldn't find any dirt on Foster, so we'll need to invent some."

"That's slander."

"So what? We need to do something, and smearing his name is all we've got left."

"He'll sue."

"He can't touch us. I'll run the ads through one of the political action committees."

Casey droned on about the science of mudslinging, but his words faded into the background as Williams found his mind drifting back to his first election. He was young, sharp as a tack, wanting to change the world - with his wife, still alive, standing by his side. Those were the days.

"Earth to Williams, come in Williams!" Casey shouted.

"I'm sorry, you were saying?"

"I was saying I intend to use the remainder of the campaign funds on the television attack ads. We have three weeks left, and there's no use letting the money go to waste."

Williams fumbled with the top button on his robe. "Do whatever you've got to do."

9:15 A.M.

Danial pecked away at his computer, putting the finishing touches on a Summary Judgment motion he needed to file in a wrongful death suit. He clicked save, then looked over at Lori's empty table; he missed her. She was off securing the DNA subpoena for Carl Vance. She said she wanted to deliver it herself. Danial maneuvered the cursor to the print icon and clicked the mouse. The printer whirred to life.

Jennifer's voice came over the intercom: "Eugene Stedman is here to see you."

"Send him right in."

The door opened, and the lanky frame of Eugene Stedman filled the door. His skin was pale, almost jaundiced. The puffy bags under his eyes looked as if they were filled with coffee grounds.

"Good to see you, Mr. Stedman," Danial said and stretched out his hand. "I certainly hope you've got something for me. Jury selection starts next week."

"I've got a few leads."

"Good, did you see Bert Hankes?"

"Yeah, I saw him."

"What'd you think?"

"Man, what a nose picker, about the best I've ever seen. And he didn't do it like a woman, you know, like she ain't really doing it but scratching her nose, then flicking it away before you can see it."

"Mr. Stedman, focus please."

"Oh yeah, where was I?"

"You were telling me about Mr. Hankes."

"That's right, the nose picker. He said he didn't know anything about Ian McKinney or the others, and didn't see anything that day down at the hospital. Then the next thing you know he's at his nose again. He must be a coal miner or something because he worked them nostrils straight, buried his finger to the knuckle."

"I get the picture."

"He looked like a busy little groundhog kicking up dirt. And when he dug out what he was looking for he held it out in front of him to admire his handiwork."

"Mr. Stedman."

"And when he thumbed it away you had to be fast on your feet, because he really didn't care what or who it stuck to."

"Mr. Stedman," Danial knocked on the desk. "Are you feeling all right?"

"Oh, sorry. I didn't get much sleep last night."

"The leads."

"I managed to get a copy of the membership roster for the Greater Ohio Valley Pro-Life Association."

"And?"

"According to the minutes from the week after the bombing, only five people were absent. When I ran down the whereabouts of those five, I discovered two of them had disappeared." Stedman pulled a notebook from his front pocket. He flipped through a few pages. "Here it is, the two men are Ron Kester and Art Bently. Both men took a leave of absence from the mill, and no one has seen them since the bombing."

"Unbelievable... could be the perpetrators."

"Could be."

"Now all you have to do is find them."

"I've got a lead on that as well."

"Tell me more."

"I happened across the Pro-Life Association's financial ledger. Everything was pretty standard stuff, except for one account entitled Special Disbursements."

"What's that about?"

"I don't know, but the money's being sent to a post office box in a small town in West Virginia."

"Which town?"

Stedman thumbed through the notebook again but couldn't seem to find what he was looking for. "I must have written it down someplace else. So, if you don't have any objections, I'd like to drive down there and have a look around."

"By all means, go. If you'll need some money for the trip, I'll have Jennifer cut you a check."

"Thanks, but I should be able to manage. I'll keep track of my expenses and turn them in to you." Stedman got up to leave.

"Mr. Stedman, you wouldn't happen to know anything about the back door break-in over at the Pro-Life Association's headquarters, would you?"

"Why do you ask?"

"There was a small write-up in the metro section of the paper. And by chance, they happened to report their financial ledger missing."

"Coincidence," Stedman said with a grin.

"Well, they also found a black ski mask that had a few strands of gray hair entangled in the fibers."

"Imagine that."

"I'm pretty sure if the ledger somehow gets returned, they wouldn't pursue the matter."

Stedman smiled. "I'll make sure the ledger finds its way home."

Akron Correctional Reception Center
9:40 A.M.

Sonny Dante woke up to a banging on the door. The food slot slid open, and someone yelled, "Pack your stuff, you're being released from the hole!"

Sonny was born and raised in the Hough area of inner-city Cleveland. He had been in and out of prison for most of his adult life, but this was his first incarceration for a parole violation. Who'd of thought they'd throw someone in jail for getting married without permission? He had been on parole for two years, moved to Steubenville and was working steady. Now this.

"Turn around and put your hands in the slot." The handcuff port on the door slid open.

"You said I was being released."

"Inmates are cuffed at all times in segregation."

Sonny complied.

The door opened and the gray-shirted officer led Sonny down the underground range of cells. A plexiglass room sat off to the left. Inside, a young black man lay spread-eagled on a metal slab, naked, his arms and legs secured with leather straps.

"What's up with that dude?" Sonny asked.

"Swallowed some dope. We're waiting for it to come out."

The guard led Sonny to the Sergeant's office.

"You are being released per the Major. Report to the Quartermaster to get your pack-up and return to your housing unit. Turn the white jumpsuit in at the QM."

"Yessir."

"Get out of here."

The guard escorted him to the door and unlocked it. Sonny stepped inside a 4-foot-square chamber. A slot in the door opened.

"Put your hands through here, and I'll take the cuffs off."

The officer radioed the control room and the exterior door buzzed open. Sonny walked outside, took a deep breath of fresh air, and rubbed his wrists.

"Only three more weeks, and I outta here. I never comin' back."

The Quartermaster was located in the rear of the institution near the maintenance building. Sonny made his way across the prison yard. The segregation unit was a prison within a prison, and after a few days of isolation, being able to walk across the yard felt like getting a parole.

The Quartermaster door was unlocked, but all the lights were off. He hesitantly opened the door and stepped inside.

"Hello! Is there anybody here?"

From the rear corner of the building a faint voice said, "Who's there?"

"Dante."

"Come back here and get your pack-up."

Sonny weaved his way through the maze of shelves and cardboard boxes.

"Where you be?!" he yelled.

"Over here."

Wham!

A crushing blow on the back of Sonny's neck drove him down to one knee. A swarm of fists and kicks rained down on him. He tried desperately to cover his face. He teetered on the brink of losing consciousness.

"That's enough!" one of the assailants shouted.

"Not yet!" yelled another.

Through the flurry of arms and legs, Sonny could see a flash of steel. Before he could move, the shank plunged deep into his midsection.

"Now you did it!"

"Let's get out of here!"

31

A young doctor ran to meet the gurney being unloaded from the helicopter.

"He's lost a lot of blood doctor," a nurse said.

"Get me two units of plasma, stat!"

The EMTs transferred him to another gurney, and the trauma team sprang into action. A nurse cut away the blood-soaked jumpsuit. The hilt of the shank protruded from the torso. Another nurse changed IV bags and hooked up the plasma. The doctor wired leads to his chest; the heart monitor blinked to life.

The guard who accompanied Sonny on the flight bumped into the doctor.

"Sorry."

"What the hell are you doing here?"

"Guarding the inmate."

"Get out of my way."

The guard stepped back as the doctor increased the plasma flow. Both men watched the heart monitor. The pulse strengthened, and the bleeding increased.

"The blade must have hit an artery," the doctor said to the nurse to his right. "We have to operate. Call the OR and tell them we're on our way."

"Yes doctor."

The trauma team shoved the gurney toward the nearest elevator. The guard tagged along.

"Where do you think you're going?" the doctor asked.

"With you."

"The hell you are."

185

"Sorry, Doc. It's the law."

"You can't take a gun into the operating room. Do you have any idea how volatile an oxygen-enriched atmosphere is? You could blow the entire wing off the hospital."

"I've got standing orders not to relinquish my weapon."

"That's ridiculous. The inmate's practically dead."

"Yeah, but what if he came to during the operation and tried to overpower you? You'd be glad I was there with my weapon."

"He's already handcuffed and shackled."

"Standing orders."

The doctor shook his head.

The surgery lasted five hours. The surgeon removed the 7-inch steel shank, which had punctured the spleen and nicked the splenic artery. He repaired the artery but decided to give Sonny a night to recover before going back in to remove the spleen.

Sonny opened his heavy eyelids at 6:10 p.m., his right arm handcuffed to the bed, his feet shackled together, and his body wracked with pain. He looked over at the relief officer sitting beside the bed reading *TIME* magazine.

"What happened?"

"You got stuck."

6:35 P.M.

Eugene Stedman's rust-stained truck didn't attract much attention as he pulled into Benwood, West Virginia. In fact, by local standards the truck was in pretty good shape. He managed to secure a room at a motel on the edge of town, a good spot to lay low.

The bare wooden floor creaked under the weight of his steps; his outstretched hand touched a wall with faded wallpaper. He sat on the edge of the overstuffed feather bed and lit a cigarette. He inhaled deeply on the first drag, held his breath, then exhaled. His lungs rattled and coughed.

"I really should quit."

He took a second puff and began plotting out his strategy. He didn't want to attract attention to himself, so he thought it best not to waltz around town asking the locals if they had seen two strangers. And besides, he didn't have any photos to show them. He scribbled a note to get Bently and Kester's driver's license photos.

He flipped through the ledger he lifted from the Pro-Life office. He found the Post Office box number where the special disbursements were being sent.

"Looks like I'm in for a stakeout."

He stretched out on the bed and opened up his latest issue of *Commando* magazine.

7:40 P.M.

Lori Franks stopped by Moffo's Pizza Shop on her way to Danial's apartment and picked up a large pepperoni pizza with extra cheese. He said he planned on spending the evening reading bombing cases, so she decided to drop by to surprise him with a snack. She had never been to his apartment on the north end of Steubenville, so Jennifer had given her the address and directions.

She parked her BMW on the brick street in front of his apartment; he lived on the top floor of a well appointed over-and-under duplex. She climbed the steps and rang the doorbell. Danial came down and opened the door.

"Pizza girl," she said.

"What a pleasant surprise! Come on in."

Danial wore gray sweatpants and a white T-shirt with *Ohio University* emblazoned across the front in green letters. She had never seen him without a sport coat, and the sight of his muscular, well-defined arms took her by surprise.

"Do you work out?"

"Yep."

"I can tell."

"Here. Put the pizza on the kitchen table." He cleared a stack of law books off the round oak table. "This is wonderfully unexpected."

"I thought you could use a break." She lifted the lid, and the aroma of melted Romano cheese and garlic wafted up with the steam. "How's it going?"

"Not good. I must've read 30 cases, and so far, nothing."

"How many more do you have to read?"

"A billion."

"Can I help? Just tell me what to look for?"

"I'd hate to torture you like that."

"Don't be silly. I work for you now."

They ate pizza and chatted about Ian and Norma and Archie. When they finished eating, Danial threw the box away and grabbed a couple more cans of Pepsi from the fridge. He handed one to Lori and sat down beside her at the table. They read cases for about 40 minutes without a word passing between them.

"Where's the bathroom?"

"It's down the hall," he said, pointing past the living room. "It's the first door on the left."

She found it. After she finished, she washed her hands and dried them on the towel hanging to the left of the sink. She noticed a manual water pick that looked like a large plastic syringe. A mischievous grin spread across her face as she pulled out the plunger and filled the tube with cold water. She replaced the plunger, concealed the apparatus in the palm of her hand and walked back to the kitchen fighting back a smirk.

Luckily Danial didn't look up from his book.

She flipped through one of the books with her right hand, while slowly lifting the water pick with her left so the tip would clear the edge of the table. She pressed the plunger and snickered as a stream of water arched into the air and hit Danial in the face.

"What the—"

He attempted to block the flow with his right hand. She playfully diverted the water and continued soaking him, giggling like a child.

"So now you want to play, huh?"

He snatched his can of Pepsi, put his thumb over the opening and shook it. Carbonated soda sprayed her in the face. She screamed and raced back to the bathroom to reload.

She turned the water on high, and it knocked the water pick out of her hand. She picked it up in time to see Danial slide in the door holding a pitcher of water.

"No!"

Splash!

"That's freezing!" she screamed.

"It should be, I got it out of the icebox. Have you had enough?"

"Yeah," she said.

He handed her a towel, and she patted her face dry. She looked at herself in the mirror; her knit sweater sagged off her shoulders. She filled a cup with water, took a sip, then threw the rest in his face.

He raced for the kitchen. She frantically looked around the bathroom for a bigger weapon. She threw open the door under the sink and found a gray plastic bucket.

"Perfect."

She swung the door closed just in time to deflect a wall of water.

"Missed me!"

She filled the bucket in the tub, then hurried out of the bathroom, her feet slipping on the wet linoleum. She scampered into the kitchen, caught Danial at the sink and soaked him from head to toe. She laughed and pointed, then bolted down the hall with him in hot pursuit. She tried to turn the corner into the bathroom but slipped on the wet floor. He drenched her back.

She screamed.

"Truce," he said.

"Truce."

"Put your bucket down."

"You first," she said.

"Same time."

"Okay."

They slowly bent down, neither taking their eyes off the other. Danial's water pitcher touched the floor first. She watched his grip. As soon as his knuckles flinched, she launched the rest of her water into his face. He stumbled and kicked over his pitcher. She dashed past him. He stuck out his left arm and hooked her around the waist. She tried to pry herself free, but his grip was too strong. He regained his footing, scooped her up and flung her over his shoulder.

"Put me down!" she shouted and pounded her fists on his back.

"I'll put you down all right."

He carried her to the bathroom, plopped her down in the bathtub, and flipped on the shower. She tried to squirm free, but powerful arms pinned her under the stream of pulsating water. She reached up, gripped his shirt and pulled. He lost his footing on the wet floor and tumbled into the tub.

They giggled and laughed. Danial reached back and turned off the water. He collapsed next to her. He wiped a strand of wet hair out of her eye.

They kissed.

32

Sonny Dante watched ceiling tiles flicker by as the orderly pushed his gurney into the operating room. The sterile scent reminded him of a dentist's office. The anesthesiologist came in and seemed to have trouble finding a good vein for the IV port. After the third attempt the harpoon-like needle found its mark. A nurse came over and lifted his hospital gown.

"Mr. Dante, I'm going to prep you for surgery, so I'll have to shave a large part of your upper abdomen. It's going to feel a little cold."

A few minutes later the anesthesiologist returned and placed a mask over Sonny's nose and mouth. "I need you to breathe naturally."

Sonny nodded. *If I don't wake up, I ready to come see you Lord.*

He drifted off to a dreamless sleep.

Consciousness gradually returned in stages. He heard indistinguishable sounds and tried to open his eyes but couldn't. His mouth felt dry and his throat hurt. He wanted to ask for water, but his lips wouldn't move. He wasn't sure how long this limbo would last. He felt water sprinkle his face. He strained to open his eyelids. The blurry image of a guard dressed in gray came into focus.

"Time to go, we're running late."

Sonny tried to speak; a moan slipped out.

The guard unlocked the handcuffs and shackles and stripped off the hospital gown. The slight jostling sent waves of pain through Sonny's body. He looked down to see a gauze pad,

191

stained yellow, taped to his torso. The guard produced orange pants from somewhere and fished them up Sonny's legs, causing him to wince and writhe in agony. The guard slapped on the shackles. He was in the process of fishing a belly chain around Sonny's waist when the PACU post-op nurse came in.

"What do you think you're doing?"

"I'm preparing this inmate for transfer back to prison."

"He came out of surgery 20 minutes ago."

"So?"

"You can't put chains around his waist. He's had two abdominal operations."

"I don't give a rat's—"

"You've contaminated this sterile environment. This unit is full of patients in very delicate conditions. You've placed all of their lives in danger!"

"That's all fine and good, but I've got a job to do, lady, and I'm already runnin' late. Why don't you make yourself useful and give me a hand getting him off the table and into this wheelchair."

"I'll do no such thing."

"Suit yourself."

The officer grabbed the waist chain. Sonny howled.

"Stop it," she said. "I'll help."

"Push the chair closer."

"At least let me give him something for pain."

"No narcotics or he can't be discharged."

She found some aspirins and a cup of water.

"Thanks," Sonny said weakly.

"Let's go, let's go."

"This is going in my report," she said.

"Yeah, whatever." He grabbed Sonny by the cuffs.

"No, don't pull at him like that. Let's get him in an upright seated position. Yes, that's it. All right, now gently swing his legs over the edge of the table."

Sonny groaned, and the nurse helped him put on an orange shirt.

"See how I'm holding him in the armpit area. Now gently lift up and slide him down into the chair."

Sonny collapsed into the wheelchair. The officer grabbed the handles and shoved it toward the door.

"I can take it from here."

The guard weaved the wheelchair through the halls; Sonny curled to one side, doubled over with pain. They reached the door. The prison van waited outside.

"All right get out of the chair," the guard ordered.

Sonny tried to comply but his abdominal muscles, first punctured by the shank, then lacerated by the surgeon's scalpels, refused to obey. The guard seized him by the arm and jerked him out of the chair.

"Hurry up inmate, we've got to be in the joint in 20 minutes."

Sonny shuffled toward the van; each step shot pain through his abdomen. The rear doors of the cargo van were opened. It was about a 3-foot distance from the ground to the top of the bumper. The seats had been removed, and a wooden bench had been installed along a wall. No seat belts.

"Get in."

Sonny lifted one leg and moaned loudly. He tried the other but realized that the chain between the shackles wasn't long enough to allow him to step up into the van.

"For cryin' out loud, get in the van."

Sonny fumbled in on his back. Despite having an unusually high threshold for pain, tears trickled out of his eyes as he sat on the wooden bench. His torso convulsed and throbbed with pain; he tried to hold himself upright as the van began to move. *They don't even treat animals this way.*

Every time the van hit a pothole or came to a sudden stop, Sonny slid along the bench and cried out in agony. With each passing minute the effects of the sedation wore off further, freeing his nervous system to experience the full weight of his injuries. By the time they arrived at the Norton Prison Hospital inside the Cleveland House of Corrections, blood covered Sonny's shirt from the seeping incision. The guards pushed him inside.

The interior walls had been painted over so many times that multi-colored paint chips lined the floor along the baseboards like confetti. The ceiling tiles that hadn't collapsed were stained from water damage. The stench of death and despair lingered in the air.

"Lord, let me die."

2:25 P.M.

Danial Solomon's law office looked like a disaster area with books, briefs and witness lists piled everywhere. Danial hunched over a pile of papers on his desk, poring over abortion clinic cases in search of something - anything - to use in Ian's defense. A box of documents and surveillance videos sat on the desk where Stedman had put it before heading south into West Virginia. Danial yawned and looked up to see Lori sorting through the mail at her table.

She was no stranger to pretrial madness, but this was her first time working on the shoestring budget and manpower of a private practice defense team. It had been a number of years since she actually went to the law library on her own to do research and the menial legwork of photocopying cases. But she didn't mind. Even though she would only have a supporting role at the trial, the case meant more to her than any other she could remember. She felt like a star athlete who had been traded to a rival team and relished the chance to go head-to-head with her former coach.

She opened an envelope, read the contents and looked up to see Danial watching her.

"Uh oh," she said.

"What is it?"

"It's a notice of the competency hearing in Juvenile Court for Norma Fitzpatrick."

"For when?"

"Tomorrow morning."

"What?"

"I'm afraid so," she said.

"Jury selection starts on Monday for Ian."

"I'm sorry Danial, I should have seen this coming. DiAngello wants to bury you in paperwork."

"It's working. Now I've got to drop everything and get ready for this hearing."

"Is there anything I can do to help?"

"I've been working on a profile for the juror most likely to be sympathetic to the defense."

"What've you got so far?"

"Not much, just leaning toward picking men."

"That's a bit chauvinistic, don't you think?"

"I don't mean any offense." He steepled his fingers under his chin. "More often than not, women are pro-choice. Since I can't ask them straight out, I don't feel comfortable loading the jury box with women who may have an axe to grind."

"Do you want me to work on the jury profile?"

"Better yet, you could run over and see Ian."

"For what?"

"To review the State's witness list."

"Sure."

"And before you go, I want to make one thing perfectly clear."

"Yeah?" she said.

"I won the water fight."

4:10 P.M.

Judge John Williams sat at his private booth in the rear of the exclusive Twilight Lounge. The place was almost empty; the regulars wouldn't pile in for another two hours. A waitress delivered the drinks. Williams looked over at the man who was about to get him reelected. *Maybe I was wrong about the young Mr. Casey; you can't argue with success.*

Williams tipped his glass of rum and Coke and nearly downed the entire contents with one gulp. He set the glass down and rubbed his bushy white eyebrows.

"This has certainly been an interesting week."

"We've had some setbacks." Casey lifted his glass of wine in a toasting gesture. "But the 30-second TV spots should start running tomorrow."

"How bad are they?"

"Let me put it this way, these ads will make those responsible for the Willie Horton ads look like amateurs."

"For example?"

Casey snickered through his nose. "One hints that Foster accepted campaign contributions from the North American Man/Boy Love Association."

Williams laughed. "What else?"

"Another hints he stole money from his clients' trust funds. Nothing too blatant, everything's veiled."

Williams belted down the remainder of his drink and motioned for the waitress to bring another. He looked around the dark room. Little dots of red glowed from the candles on the other tables.

"So. I'm guessing you won't be sticking around for much longer," Williams said.

"I'll be gone by noon on Wednesday following the election. This isn't my kind of town. Too small." Casey took another sip of wine. "Too many uneducated holy rollers."

"The McKinney trial starts next week."

"I know."

"What about *Court TV?*"

"In the bag."

"Excellent," Williams said. "I love it when a plan comes together."

The waitress brought another rum and Coke, and the two men toasted to their imminent success.

33

Wearing his red flannel shirt, Ron Kester filled a plastic bucket from the stream that ran near the cabin. He had the strangest sensation that he was being watched. He listened closely. Nothing but the sound of water trickling over rocks. *My mind is playing tricks on me.*

He carried the bucket through the knee-high grass still wet from the dew. He looked up with pride at the newly repaired and re-shingled roof, and actually hoped it would rain so he could see if it leaked. The deer carcass hung from a hook in the roof. He pushed on the door; it scraped across the floorboards.

"You got the fire started yet?" he asked.

"Yep."

"Good. I need my coffee."

Ron set the bucket on a small square table while Art tossed another log into the wood-burning stove.

"You know, I was thinking," Ron said. "Since this cabin doesn't have any windows, maybe we should cut some slots in the walls."

"It would give us some light."

"And gun ports."

Ron poured some water in the coffeepot and handed it to Art. Soon the rich aroma of fresh coffee filled the cabin. Art carried two plates of pancakes and the pot of coffee to the table. The floor creaked under his weight. Ron chuckled.

"What's so funny?"

"Do you remember Mr. Thompson?"

"Our middle school shop teacher?"

197

"Yeah."

"Jeez, what made you think of him?"

"Search me. His face just popped into my head, and I can't get him out."

Art laughed then snorted. "How about those eyebrows?"

"They looked like two mustaches, and the way he wiggled them..." Ron laughed so hard he held his belly.

"And what about that thing he did with his little finger in his ear?"

"Oh man... and remember how he'd always blow his nose then look in his handkerchief like he was expecting to find some gold or something?"

Food fragments shot out of Art's mouth; spittle ran down his chin. Tears filled Ron's eyes; he tried to catch his breath.

"What ever happened to him?" Art asked, wiping his chin.

"He married Mrs. Hill."

"You mean the hill-sized home economics teacher?"

"Yeah."

"No way. Why would she marry him?"

"I don't know, too lazy to commit suicide I guess."

They broke up laughing again, then finally settled down enough to finish the meal.

"How long do we have to stay up here?" Art asked.

"Until it's over."

"Do you think anyone knows we're here?"

"Birch knows, but nobody else."

"Any chance he'd tell somebody?"

"Not a chance."

Ron stood, then walked over to the front door constructed of four rough-hewn boards with one diagonal cross support. He pulled it open; it scuffed across the old floorboards.

"We need to replace this door." He stomped his right foot. "And this floor too. We need to make this cabin into a Ming fortress."

"What are you worried about, Ron?"

"Just in case."

"Sounds like paranoia to me."

8:58 A.M.

Danial Solomon strolled down the center aisle of Judge Robert Peterson's courtroom. Lori sat at the defense table next to Norma Fitzpatrick. Two men in blue suits sat at the prosecutor's table. Danial pushed through the swinging doors separating the gallery from the court proper and took a seat next to Norma. He put his hand on her shoulder.

"Sorry I'm late. The power went off in my apartment."

"I've brought her up to speed," Lori said.

"Who are they?" Danial thumbed over at the prosecution.

"Reed and Keller."

"Are they any good?"

"I don't know. We'll find out."

Danial gave Norma the once-over. Her chestnut hair was pulled back in a ponytail, and without make-up she looked about 12 years old. The orange jumpsuit looked harsh on her.

"Do I need to do anything?" Norma asked.

"Yeah, look young and innocent."

She smiled.

A brown-uniformed bailiff stepped into the courtroom from the judge's chambers and ordered everyone to stand. The judge entered with his customary rigid dignity and perched himself behind the bench. He pinched a pair of round reading glasses onto the end of his nose, read something, then said, "We're here to decide whether or not Miss Norma Fitzpatrick is competent to stand trial as an adult. Is that correct?"

"Yes, Your Honor," Danial and Lori and the two suits said in unison.

"Very good. The State may proceed."

"Thank you, sir, the State will be brief."

Lori leaned over and whispered, "That one's Reed."

Danial nodded.

The short, stocky man stood in front of his seat.

"Your Honor, Norma Fitzpatrick is 15 years old, but she is mature beyond her years. Prior to killing her baby—"

"Objection," Danial said, half-standing.

"I'll rephrase," Reed said. "Prior to her arrest for the death of her baby, Ms. Fitzpatrick had at least two prior abortions that we know of. Her behavior displays a pattern of adult conduct that leads to adult consequences. Surely someone with this much sexual experience is well aware that intercourse leads to babies, and that killing babies is wrong."

"Objection," Danial said. "My client is currently accused of killing one baby."

"Overruled," Judge Peterson said. "This Court is aware of the defendant's status."

"Thank you, sir," Reed said. "I could stand here and waste this Court's valuable time by reciting a litany of cases in Ohio and across the country... that show near universal consistency in ruling teenage girls competent to stand trial as an adult in cases like this. The bottom line is this..." He slapped the back of his right hand into his left palm. "She's had sex, she's had abortions, and she knows right from wrong. She's engaged in adult behavior; she should be held responsible as an adult for capital murder. I have nothing further, Your Honor."

He sat down.

Danial patted Norma on the back. She sucked in her cheek and started gnawing. He whispered in her ear. "Stop it, it makes you look guilty."

She stopped.

Danial stood and straightened his coat. "Your Honor, I've read the case law Mr. Reed referred to, and he's correct. The courts almost unanimously hold teenage girls competent to stand trial as adults in cases like this. But as I read these cases well into the night last night, I found a startling coincidence. The courts also almost always find that men over 18 years of age who have sex with young teenage girls are guilty of statutory rape." He cleared his throat and looked over at the prosecutors.

"I'm sure my colleagues find nothing wrong with my observation, and don't get me wrong, I agree minors should be protected from those who would seek to take advantage of their innocence."

"What's your point?" Judge Peterson asked.

"Just that this is the first time where these two universal rulings come into conflict."

"Speak English, Mr. Solomon."

"Your Honor, my client contends that one of her teachers, a 45-year-old man, is the father of her baby. We have issued a subpoena for a DNA—"

"Objection!" Reed shouted.

"Overruled. Continue, Mr. Solomon."

"Thank you, Your Honor. The State cannot have its cake and eat it too. If the DNA test confirms the teacher to be the father, the State will charge him with unlawful sexual contact with a minor - as well they should. But that puts them in a quandary. On the one hand they'll say Mr. Teacher has taken advantage of a young girl, a minor, who doesn't have the capacity to make consenting adult decisions regarding sexual matters. And on the other hand, the State wants this Court to rule that this same young woman, a minor, has the capacity to make adult decisions and stand trial in a capital murder case." He stepped over behind Norma and put his hands on her shoulders.

"Your Honor, if you rule Norma is competent to stand trial as an adult, you'll practically be granting Mr. Sexually Deviant Teacher immunity from prosecution. After all, if she's competent to face the death penalty as an adult, she must've been competent to consent to sex with a 45-year-old married man. And the deviant teacher skates. So let's let a minor be a minor. Thank you."

Judge Peterson sat still for a moment then removed his glasses; he had pink spots on each side of his nose. "The Court will not render a decision at this time."

Reed stood. "But Your Honor—"

"Silence."

Reed sat down and sulked while Keller flipped through his notes.

"The Court further orders a trial brief to be submitted by both the Prosecution and the Defense." He reviewed his calendar. "Have the briefs on my desk by November 5th. There'll be no extensions." He rapped his gavel and stood. "Court stands in recess."

34

Tuesday, October 24
Jefferson County Courthouse
8:45 A.M.

Colin Casey reclined in Judge Willams' chair, his feet propped up on the desk. He flipped through a report and said, "Great news, we've surged in the polls. We're up seven points. This late in the campaign, that's almost insurmountable."

"Yeah, and my office is being swamped with complaints from Foster's people."

"Screw 'em."

"This is getting messy."

"Now remember, today's trial is being carried live on *Court TV*. It's important that you never look directly into the camera, or people will think you're flippant or showy like Judge Ito. And never sit up straight; slouch back to one side and rest your chin on your fist. We're shooting for the disinterested power look."

Williams nodded his head as he checked his look in the full-length mirror inside his private bathroom door. The new robe looked phony and it itched.

"I don't see why you had to get me a new robe. I wore the other one for 20 years."

"It looked like it had been worn for 20 years, and it was way too short."

"It was comfortable."

"You looked like a flasher."

"Well, after the election I'm going back to my old robe."

"After the election you can preside over your cases naked for all I care. But for right now, I want you to at least appear sharp."

The door opened, and the din of the packed courtroom filtered in.

"Are you ready, sir?" the bailiff asked.

"In a minute."

"One last thing," Casey said. "Whatever you do, please don't show any sympathy to the Defense. To Joe Citizen out there in TV land, the prosecutor doesn't represent the state, the judge does. People don't want impartiality, they want toughness."

8:55 A.M.

Danial Solomon had spent the previous hour going over all the likely trial events with Ian McKinney, and now the two of them sat quietly at the defendant's table. Ian looked more like a busboy than a bombing suspect. He combed his red, curly hair neatly to the side. His blue eyes exhibited just enough fear and uncertainty to draw sympathy. His fresh-shaven face accentuated his smattering of freckles.

Lori Franks pushed through the crowd and sat down beside Danial. She looked professional with her black hair pulled back in a French twist. She wore a navy-blue business suit that hugged her petite frame. The V-neck blouse highlighted her long elegant neck.

"You look great," he whispered.

She smiled. "I've never seen it this crazy."

Danial glanced around the gallery. A camera crew made adjustments to their equipment along the back wall. A second crew set up near the jury box. Uniformed deputies lined the walls, while spectators and media types shoved towards coveted seats. The brass sparkled, the wood shined, and the scent of lemon fresh Pledge hung in the air.

The bailiff checked his watch and strolled to the front of the courtroom.

"All rise! Hear ye! Hear ye! Hear ye! This Court is now in session. The Honorable Judge John Williams presiding."

The heavy oak door swung open and the black-robed

Williams climbed the three steps to his bench. In his patented single motion, he smote the gavel and plopped down in his high-backed chair.

"You may be seated."

Williams opened the file on the bench in front of him and instinctively reached for the reading glasses that usually hung on the string around his neck. He patted his chest twice. *Yeah, that's right, contacts.* He majestically scanned the capacity-filled gallery. He then inspected the jury before looking at Anthony DiAngello, sitting behind the prosecutor's table.

"At this time the matter of *The State of Ohio versus Ian McKinney*, Case Number 00-CR-A-00152, will come to order. The State may proceed with opening remarks."

DiAngello stood and said, "Special Prosecutor Schaeffer will be delivering the opening remarks for the State."

"Very well," Williams said. "Mr. Schaeffer, you may begin."

"Thank you, sir." Schaeffer stood, then walked toward the jury box.

Danial scrutinized his rival. Randall Schaeffer stood a little over 6 feet tall and looked rather thin. He had a thick mat of fawn-colored hair combed straight back. A large pair of glasses covered his green eyes. He had an oversized Adam's apple that disappeared when he swallowed. His charcoal, herringbone suit hung loosely on his lanky body.

"Ladies and gentlemen of the jury, I'd like to begin by thanking you for taking this time out of your busy schedules to fulfill your civic duty. The justice system depends on your open-mindedness." He leaned against the wooden banister in front of the jury box.

"Civic duty is something not much discussed these days. We live in a world that encourages isolation by its technological advances. We no longer walk to the local grocery store and chat with our neighbors along the way. Now we can even get on the Internet and electronically place our orders, and they arrive on our doorsteps - without ever being in contact with another living soul. Regrettable, don't you think?

"Nevertheless, civic duty is what this case is all about. You see, in order for a society like ours to function, a certain amount of liberty is delegated to each individual. We call it freedom. But the price tag of freedom is responsibility, and it's mutual responsibility that allows us to drive along an undivided highway without living in constant fear of a head-on collision. We trust the other drivers will be responsible enough to stay on their side of the road. But what would happen if American drivers decided to disregard the rules of the road? I'll tell you what would happen - fear and panic would rule the roadways and render them useless to the citizens of this great country." Schaeffer paused, cleared his throat. "You see, ladies and gentlemen, without laws and rules and common civic responsibility, society and the democratic form of government crumble.

"This case is about one man, the defendant, Ian McKinney, who decided he didn't agree with the laws of this great state. And instead of working through the democratic process like every other American, Mr. McKinney decided to help himself to explosives from the Fort Henry Armory and blow up some public property." Schaeffer paced along the jury box.

"This case is very simple, really, and the evidence is clear and compelling. Mr. McKinney broke into the Fort Henry Armory and was kind enough to leave behind strands of his hair. The State will call an FBI forensic expert who'll confirm with 100% certainty that the hair found at the scene of the crime belonged to the defendant, Ian McKinney. Next, the State will present detailed schematics found at the defendant's apartment that outline a step-by-step procedure for constructing and detonating a bomb."

A hushed murmur rippled through the gallery.

"The State will present surveillance videos from the University Hospital parking lot. You will see with your own eyes the defendant planting a bomb in a garbage dumpster that later exploded around midnight. A camera also captured his accomplices planting a second bomb in the manhole in the center of the parking lot. These two accomplices are still at large, but you can rest assured, we will bring them to justice." Schaeffer stepped back and folded his hands at his waist.

"There's another element of this case that we must explore. In an attempt to create a diversion from his more sinister actions, Mr. McKinney broke into a zoo building and stole an endangered eagle's egg. And what did he do with this egg? He threw it at a hospital vehicle carrying several doctors. While this offense pales in comparison to the bombing, it is yet another part of this heinous crime. The State will call Dr. Gaston Garvey to the stand, a passenger in the van at the time of the senseless assault. His life was placed in jeopardy, not only by the projectile, but also by a ticking time bomb.

"You see, ladies and gentlemen of the jury, this case is really rather simple. It doesn't matter which side of the abortion debate you find yourself on, some things are inherently wrong - things such as vigilantism and anarchy. Such things undermine and threaten our very way of life and make a mockery of our Constitution. Terrorist behavior strikes at the core of all things American."

Danial rubbed his chin. *This guy is good.*

"I said earlier that this case is about civic duty, and it is. It's your civic duty to find the defendant guilty on all charges. In so doing, you will remove one psychopath from the streets of Ohio. And you'll be sending a powerful message to all the would-be bombers out there that this county and country will not tolerate such unconscionable behavior. Thank you."

Schaeffer returned to his seat. Judge Williams glanced over at Colin Casey who sat in the front row of the gallery. Casey gave an affirming nod.

Williams looked over at the defense table.

"Mr. Solomon, you may proceed with your opening remarks."

"Thank you, Your Honor."

Lori patted Danial on the hand and mouthed the words, "You've got this."

Danial stood, buttoned his suit coat and slowly walked toward the jury; the sound of his wingtips on the hardwood floor echoed off the vaulted ceiling and through the cavernous room.

"Good morning, ladies and gentlemen," Danial said with a confident smile. "My name is Danial Solomon, and that lady over there is my colleague Lori Franks. We'll be representing the defendant in this case, Ian McKinney.

"I imagine at this point you're not feeling too kindly toward my client. Let's be honest, if everything Mr. Schaeffer said is true, then my client must be some sort of animal who deserves to be executed. But the State has a job to do; they must paint Ian McKinney as a maniac, to make you feel that with such a man loose on the street, all of us are in danger. I have a job to do too, to help you see through all the smoke and mirrors the State will give you, and boil this case down to its most basic question: Did Ian McKinney plant a bomb in the University Hospital parking lot on October 3rd?

"There are certain things I'll concede to you and to the State. I'll concede that my client did in fact throw an eagle's egg at a hospital van. He pled No Contest to that offense and is willing to take responsibility for his actions. But let's be honest, throwing an egg is nothing more than a statement, and certainly does not make him a vigilante, nor an anarchist, nor a terrorist. And please keep this in mind. Just because Ian McKinney threw an egg doesn't mean he planted a bomb; the one has nothing to do with the other."

Danial paced along the jury railing, carefully making eye contact with each member.

"Mr. Schaeffer spoke of civic duty. He painted the laws and rules of this country as a panacea for the social ills we face today. But he's trying to sell you a pipe dream; don't buy it. We live in an immoral society, where the line between absolute right and wrong has been erased and replaced with social relativism."

The jury foreman shook his head. Danial stopped directly in front of him.

"So, you don't agree with me? Well that's all right. But if you don't think we live in an immoral, dysfunctional society, then explain why pediatricians in one part of a hospital work feverishly to resuscitate and give maximum supportive care to prematurely born infants only six months developed, while in another part of the same hospital obstetricians butcher full-term babies. The ironic thing is that the babies being killed are larger and healthier than those premature babies others are trying to save.

"We live in a society where minors are deemed too immature to make decisions about smoking and drinking, but are allowed to make abortion-on-demand decisions without parental knowledge or consent. We live in a society where we cheer the Special Olympics and athletes with Down Syndrome and Spina Bifida competing with beaming smiles, and then say that unborn babies suffering from the same afflictions aren't fit to live. We live in a society where it's considered child abuse for a pregnant mother to use drugs because of potential harm to her unborn child, but it's perfectly legal for the same mother to murder the same child and call it abortion. We live in a society where some accuse others of a war on women, but demand that "trans" men go into women's restrooms and locker rooms and sports competitions. This is the immoral, schizophrenic nature of the society we live in. But allow me to get back to the abortion exposure case at hand.

"The State would have you believe that my client is guilty of attempted assault. For what? For throwing an egg at a vehicle? Doesn't that seem a bit excessive? My client didn't assault anyone, and he didn't plant a ticking bomb. I'm asking you to be patient. There is a Proverb that says, 'He who states his case first seems right, until the other comes and examines him.' So, please do not rush to judgment until you have heard both sides of the story. Thank you."

Danial walked back to his seat.

All eyes turned to Judge Williams who froze for a moment as if his mind had drifted somewhere else.

Colin Casey cleared his throat. Williams blinked.

"The State may call its first witness."

"Thank you, Your Honor," Schaeffer said as he stood. "The State calls forensic expert Barbara Centers to the stand."

Judge Williams rapped the gavel, started to speak, then paused for several seconds. "One hour recess...."

35

Eugene Stedman parked his truck across the street from the Benwood Post Office. He lit a cigarette, then realized he already had one burning in the ashtray. He looked across the street; the sun glinted off the glass wall near the door. He put on a cheap pair of sunglasses and walked over to locate the box number 717 - the one from the Pro-Life Association's ledger. Then he loitered.

A few minutes later a blue pickup pulled into the parking lot next to the Post Office. A large, bearded man in a flannel shirt looked over his shoulders as he hustled inside. He went straight to box 717. He looked around and jogged back to his idling truck. He climbed in and pulled out.

Stedman returned to his truck and twisted the wires under the dash together. The engine sputtered and whined and churned.

"Damn it."

He tossed the spent cigarette out the window and tried again; the arthritic engine groaned to life. He jammed the truck into gear and followed after his prey, careful not to get too close. The two trucks weaved through Benwood, past the lumberyard and onto Route 250. Stedman drifted back; his truck couldn't keep up. Thankfully, the suspect's truck turned at the Moundsville exit, and Stedman closed the gap.

The bearded man's truck drove through the center of town and turned left at the ancient Moundsville Penitentiary. The gray-stone walls towered above the street. It looked like a medieval castle with battlements and towers. They drove past it, then back into the hills on a two-lane country road that soon dwindled to a single-lane road. Stedman faded back and followed at a distance. He checked the fuel gauge - a quarter tank left.

The target truck turned off the road onto a two-track dirt road. Stedman stopped and waited until the dust plume from the target's tires advanced a couple hundred yards.

"I gotta be careful. If something happens out here, no one will ever find me."

Stedman bent over and grabbed his service revolver from under the seat. He tucked the gun into the waist of his pants. The two-track weaved around enormous boulders, deep ravines, and into a narrow clearing in the dense forest. Stedman veered off the path and coaxed his vehicle into a thick patch of undergrowth. He camouflaged the old jalopy with pine boughs, then stealthily crept through the forest.

10:10 A.M.

"I'm telling you, Art, there's movement out in the bushes."

"You're paranoid. You said yourself nobody knows we're out here."

"If you're being hunted by unknown hunters, paranoia can save your life."

"What do you want me to do?"

"Get down and don't move."

Art squatted down by the wood stove; Ron laid flat on the wooden floor and peered out through one of the new slots he had cut in the wall.

"I see movement out on the tree line."

"What do we do?" Art asked, his voice trembling.

"We dig in and defend ourselves if they start shooting."

Ron crawled toward the back of the cabin where the guns leaned against the wall in leather cases.

"I don't know if I could shoot somebody," Art said.

"I don't want to shoot anybody either." Ron unzipped the gun cases.

"Maybe we should just go out and talk to whoever it is. Maybe it's just the game warden."

"If it's any law officer, he'll say he is. Obviously, we don't shoot. But if it's some guy saying he's some backwoods Avon lady or something, we're going to defend ourselves. You can believe if someone comes all the way out here to find us, they mean us no good. For self-defense, take a position at that front corner slot." Ron handed one of the rifles to Art, then crawled back to his slot near the door. A rustling in the bushes on the edge of the clearing caught his attention. He slowly slid the barrel of his rifle through the 6-inch slot and placed the crosshairs of the scope on the vague outline of a figure crouching behind a bush.

"Your call," Ron whispered as he lightly touched the soft pad of his index finger against the trigger.

Jefferson County Courthouse
10:15 A.M.

Barbara Centers took a seat on the witness stand, and the bailiff administered the oath. She appeared to Danial to be in her early 50s, a stern woman who looked as though her mouth should always be full of pins.

"The State may proceed to examine the witness," Judge Williams said as he leaned back in his chair the way Casey had coached him.

"Thank you, sir," Schaeffer said as he picked up a stack of reports and stepped up to the podium in front of the witness stand. "Ms. Centers, would you please state for the record your present occupation?"

"I'm a forensic scientist with the Federal Bureau of Investigation."

"And how long have you been in that position?"

"Just over eight years now."

"And could you please explain your area of expertise?"

"I specialize in crime scene analysis and DNA evidence."

Schaeffer looked over at the jury with an expression that seemed to say, *Impressive, huh?!* While still looking at the jury he asked, "During your eight years of service, how many cases have you worked on that dealt with DNA evidence?"

"Dozens, perhaps a hundred or more."

"So, this case is nothing new for you?"

"No, I'd say rather routine."

"Okay, then let's cut to the chase. I understand you had the opportunity to examine the incubator room at Oglebay Park, as well as the Fort Henry Armory. Could you please tell the jury what you found?"

"I found reddish-colored strands of hair."

"At both scenes?"

"That's correct."

Several members of the jury glanced over at the defendant's red hair. Ian offered a wry smile and shrugged his shoulders.

"Was DNA testing conducted on the hair?"

"Yes."

"And would you please share with the jury the results of your testing?"

"The strands of hair found at both crime scenes match the hair sample from the defendant."

"How certain are you these tests are accurate?"

"One hundred percent."

A chorus of whispers swept the courtroom.

Schaeffer triumphantly nodded to the jury and said, "No further questions, Your Honor."

"Mr. Solomon, you may cross-examine the witness," Williams said.

"Thank you, Your Honor."

Danial stood and looked up at the portrait of Baron von Steuben that hung above the jury box, as if to gather his thoughts.

"Ms. Centers, in all your years working with the FBI, have you ever encountered a case where you suspected the evidence had been planted?"

"No."

"Come on now, in all the cases you've studied, there hasn't been one single instance where you suspected the slightest inkling of foul play?"

"Objection!" Schaeffer shouted. "The witness has answered the question."

"Sustained," Judge Williams said. "Defense counsel will proceed with another question."

"Is it possible that someone accessed the crime scene and planted the hairs you found?"

"Anything is possible, hypothetically. But with the authorities cordoning off the area and keeping an around-the-clock watch on each scene, I'd say the chances of that happening were exceptionally slim if not impossible."

"Not probable, but possible?"

"Not likely."

"Ms. Centers, when was your FBI office contacted in connection with the break-in at Oglebay Park?"

"You'll have to give me a moment. I'll need to consult my notebook." She dug through her satchel.

"Take all the time you need," Danial said.

She rifled through the bag. "Here it is, now what was the question?"

Judge Williams looked over at the stenographer who read back the question.

"According to my notes, the break-in at Oglebay Park occurred on a Monday night, October 2nd, and it was reported to my office by the local authorities later that week. I arrived on the scene on Friday, October 6th."

"And when was your office notified of the break-in at the Armory?"

Ms. Centers glanced through her notes. "The break-in occurred on Monday night, and I was notified later that week. I collected the hairs the following Tuesday."

"So, in each case, several days elapsed from the time of the crime and the time the hairs were collected?"

"Yes, that's correct."

"So conceivably, someone had ample time and opportunity to sprinkle a few hairs around the crime scenes?"

"Objection!" Schaeffer shouted. "Arguendo!"

"Overruled!" Williams shouted back.

Danial continued with calm, cool, steely resolve. "The break-in at the Armory was discovered the evening of Monday, October 2nd. My client has confessed to stealing an eagle egg at Oglebay Park at the same time. So how could one person be in two places at the same time - leaving strands of his hair in two places at the same time? He couldn't. It certainly appears that his confessed crime has become his alibi. So could someone please tell us why a Tuesday morning egg-thrower has been framed as a bomb-thrower?"

"Objection!" Schaeffer yelled.

"Sustained."

Danial walked back to the defense table, saying, "We're all wasting our time here. No further questions."

The muffled sound of whispers elevated into a near roar. Colin Casey frantically motioned for Williams to do something.

"Order in the court!" Williams yelled as he beat the gavel against the top of the bench. "This courtroom will come to order at once!"

The noise subsided. Williams looked back over at the prosecution table. "Would the State like to re-direct?"

Schaeffer stood up. "Yes, we would, sir."

"Proceed."

Schaeffer walked back up to the witness stand and softly spoke to the visibly agitated witness. "Is there any way of determining how long a hair could have been at the crime scene?"

"No."

"So, in the case at hand, the hairs you found could have been there for days or even weeks before the most recent break-in at the Armory?"

"The hairs could have been there for months or even years."

"Is it possible that the break-in occurred earlier and wasn't discovered until the evening of Monday the 2nd?"

"Possible."

"So, in your expert opinion, was the defendant involved in some break-in at the Armory?"

"In my expert opinion, the evidence indicates Mr. McKinney was involved in at least one break-in at the armory and one at Oglebay Park."

"No further questions, Your Honor."

Schaeffer strutted back to his seat looking confident that the fire was out.

10:30 A.M.

Eugene Stedman had the odd feeling that he was being watched. *I need to backtrack and come up from behind the cabin. I'm a sitting duck out here in the open.*

He drifted back into the cover of the trees, and moving in a wide arc, slowly found his way towards the windowless rear of the cabin. His knees creaked as he squatted down behind a tree 20 feet away from the back wall. His chest heaved; he gasped for breath. Despite a slight October chill in the air his shirt was soaked with sweat. His body craved another dose of nicotine; he fought the urge to cough. *Lord, if You get me through this alive, I promise to quit smokin' for good.*

He crawled toward the rear of the cabin. He pulled the revolver from his pants and held it up near his face. His heart thundered so hard against his chest he feared he was having a heart attack. *It's now or never.*

Stedman crept along the side of the cabin and stopped at the front corner. He darted his head around and pulled it back. The door was only a few feet away. *It looks clear.*

He paused, took a few deep breaths, dashed around the corner and kicked open the door.

10:45 A.M.

Ron Kester had grown edgy as the minutes ticked by. He knew it was the calm before the storm. He checked his watch, about a half hour since he'd seen the movement near the tree line.

"Maybe it was just some animal," Art said. "Or a shadow or something. But whatever it was, I'm glad it's—"

Crash!

Six men in black fatigues crashed through the door, each with HK MP5 automatic weapons.

"ATF! Freeze! - if you move you die!"

Ron and Art were pinned to the floor and handcuffed. Outside, the rhythmic whirl of helicopter blades descended upon the clearing. The squad leader unclipped a small radio from his belt.

"This is Big Dog. The marbles are in the bag."

10:55 A.M.

Private Investigator Eugene Stedman stood in the doorway completely dumbfounded by the aroma of Starbucks coffee and the sound of classical music.

Inside the large log cabin, a half-dozen people diligently worked at computers and video equipment. Others stood at a big screen TV. And others sat on couches talking or tapping on their phones. In the far corner, a satellite dish pointed through a skylight in the cathedral ceiling. A surprised young lady looked up from her computer.

"May I help you?"

36

Danial and Lori stopped at the Arby's drive-thru before returning to the office. As far as Danial could tell, the first day of trial ended in a draw. But a lot of work remained. He called Jennifer on his cell phone and asked her to set up the TV and DVD player. He also asked her to find some midnight oil because they would doubtlessly need to burn it.

Danial parked the car in his reserved space next to his office. He grabbed the sandwich bag, Lori picked up the drinks, and they tramped up the steps to the office. Lori pushed open the door and bumped a balding man standing in the doorway. Danial recognized him.

"Mr. Vance, funny seeing you here."

"I need to talk to you."

"I've got to be honest with you. Now is not a good time. I'm in the middle of a trial, and I've got a lot of work to do."

"This can't wait."

"All right, step into my office, but we'll have to keep this short."

Danial escorted the middle-aged man into his office and offered him a chair. Vance looked over his shoulder at Lori who sorted through a stack of files on her desk.

"Can we talk in private?"

"Nope, this is as private as it gets."

"What about attorney-client privilege?"

"You're not my client."

Vance paused; his lips moved before he spoke. "I'm here to talk about Norma."

"Go on."

Vance stared down at his hands. "I've decided I won't be taking the DNA test."

"It's a little too late for that," Danial said, sifting through a file. "The court issued a subpoena. If you don't take the test, you'll go to jail for contempt."

"You didn't let me finish. The reason I won't be taking the test is because I know I'm the father of Norma's baby."

"What?!"

Lori dropped the file she held. "You admit it?"

"Please let me explain. We didn't mean for any of this to happen."

"You were having sex with a student - a child," Danial said.

"But we love each other."

Lori stomped around her table and looked like she would attack him. Danial motioned for her to hold her peace.

"Go ahead, Mr. Vance. Please continue."

"It all started so innocently..."

11:14 A.M.

Sonny Dante had a perfect view of the duct work through the missing ceiling tiles above his dilapidated bed. In fact, all 12 beds in the maximum-security ward were pre-World War II vintage. They were the kind with the two hand cranks: one for raising the top half of the bed, and the other for adjusting the leg section. Each bed was broken and frozen into a different configuration. Only two beds resembled flatness, and these were always snagged by the able-bodied.

A game developed among the men to try and match the bed configuration to the particular ailment. The man to Sonny's left had his legs operated on, so he had the bed with the lower portion locked in an elevated position. Sonny's bed, stuck in a gentle V, was not particularly affliction-friendly for a man with his abdominal muscles shredded by shank and scalpel.

Sonny lifted his head and gazed around the ward. Fly strips

dangled from the ceiling; roach traps dotted the floor; and in the corner nearest the restroom, a rat lay motionless with his head caught in a spring-loaded trap. The place reeked of disinfectant, sweat and urine; the stench would have staggered a goat. In the bed to Sonny's right lay a hollow shell of a human in the final stages of AIDS. His skin was jaundiced. A tube, inserted through his ribs, drained a putrid greenish fluid into a cast iron bedpan on the floor. A feeding tube swung freely as the man coughed and gurgled. Sonny looked down at his own problems - two sets of stitches, the wounds still seeping. *Here I is laying with my belly cut to shreds and it ain't healing, and here's this dude launching who knows what into the air with every breath. Lord, please keep me safe and deliver me from this demonic pit. I know I not supposed to feel sorry for myself, but this is more than I can stand. Please—*

The sound of plastic sliding over the floor and the shuffling of feet interrupted his prayer. He looked over to see the source of the sound. Two inmates dragged a body bag by the feet into a tiny room just off the entrance to the ward. The expressionless look on the pallbearers' faces showed this was a routine part of the job; it probably fell under the classification "Other duties as assigned."

As the two inmates finished their unpleasant task and walked away, the gravity of the situation set in. *Dudes be goin' toes up round here. They spend the last hours of their lives staring at busted ceiling tiles, their bodies achin', then they die and wake up in Hell.*

11:19 A.M.

"Let me get this straight." Danial spoke through clenched teeth. "You got Norma pregnant. You took her across state lines into West Virginia to get an abortion so you could evade Ohio's parental consent laws. But the abortion clinic in Wheeling was not equipped to do partial-birth abortions. So you drove her back to Ohio to be an outpatient at University Hospital, but she was actually registered in Wheeling."

"That explains why her name didn't show up in any abortion clinic in Ohio," Lori said.

"So, let me ask you something, Mr. Vance," Danial said. "Have you ever given any of your students aspirin when they've had a headache?"

"No."

"Why not?"

"It's against the law without parental consent."

"But you didn't hesitate to take a student in for an abortion - major surgery - without the knowledge or consent of the parents?"

"Yeah."

"You don't get it do you?"

"What?"

"You got a 15-year-old girl pregnant, commonly known as statutory rape, a felony that carries up to five years in prison. Next, you take her through an elaborate cross-state journey to have an abortion without being detected. Which makes me wonder how many other students over the years made the same trip."

"Hey, that's not fair."

"Then when Norma gets arrested and is facing prison or the death penalty, you bare-faced lied to me to protect yourself." Danial leaned over his desk.

Vance slouched back in his chair. "It sounds bad when you put it that way. My bad."

"Now you get it. You're bad. I could call you worse. You should thank God I'm now a Christian, because five years ago I would have dragged you out of my office."

A large vein protruded over Danial's right temple. As he rose, fists clenched, he spoke slowly and deliberately. "Vance, I advise you to get out of my sight right now. I sense my self-control slipping."

Vance jumped out of his chair and bolted for the door.

"I'm warning you, Vance, stay where I can find you. Don't make me hunt you down!"

Vance bumped into Jennifer as he ran past and knocked a handful of mail out of her hands.

Danial dropped into his seat taking deep breaths. Lori stood frozen. She had never seen this fiery side.

"So, the gentleman is also a fierce warrior."

"Only when I have to be."

"I'm guessing this isn't a good time, but a letter came I thought you would be interested in. I put it on top." Jennifer handed the mail to Danial.

He examined the plain-white envelope with the postage embossed in the corner. He pulled out the letter and read aloud.

"I know who killed Archie Kisner."

"And whoever wrote it didn't even sign their name," Jennifer said.

Danial leaned back in his chair, rubbed his eyes and said, "Poor Archie will have to wait until later. I just can't deal with this right now."

Jefferson County Courthouse
11:30 A.M.

Colin Casey leaned back into the overstuffed leather couch in the corner of Judge Williams' office and sipped a glass of wine. He felt content with himself and was pleased with the first day of trial. He imagined himself on his first day as a member of Congress, maybe the Senate a few years later, then... who knows?

"Well, what do you think?" Williams asked.

"I'm having a phone poll conducted right now to get viewer reactions."

"I got a little worried when Solomon got on that roll."

"Worried?" Casey said with a laugh. "You panicked. It's a good thing the cameras were on Solomon, because you looked like a caged rat."

"I don't know what got into me."

"Well, don't space out again, or we'll both be looking for

another job."

"I won't."

"What'd you think of Schaeffer? We went to Ohio State together."

"He's good. I think the jury likes him."

"He's not the only surprise I've got for Mr. Solomon. The next one should be hitting the news soon."

1:30 P.M.

Lori and Danial were into the third agonizingly boring video from the University Hospital parking lot when the intercom buzzed to life on Danial's desk. Lori hit the pause button on the DVD player. Danial walked over and pressed the glowing red button.

"What is it, Jennifer?"

"You have a phone call."

"Take a message."

"It's Eugene Stedman on his cell, near Moundsville."

"Put him through." Danial motioned for Lori to come closer.

"Mr. Stedman, I've got you on speaker. Ms. Franks is here with me. What do you have for us?"

"Well, I've got good news, bad news, and other news. What do you want first?"

"Give us the good news."

"The good news is the two men we've been looking for have been found."

"Good work, Stedman."

"Well, not really. The bad news is my bad. The ATF beat me to them."

"What's the other news?"

"I found something that will reveal more about Ron Kester and Art Bently."

"What?"

"I'd rather not say over the phone. This is sensitive stuff to a lot of people."

"When can you get here?"

"I'm coming back to Steubenville right now."

"I hope whatever you found is big."

"It's huge, Mr. Solomon, it's huge!"

Eugene Stedman said goodbye and kissed goodbye the promised cash bonus for finding Kester and Bently. He spewed a stream of obscenities that would make the most profane sailor blush. He slammed his fist against the hood of his old truck.

The return trip to Steubenville went smoothly until he put the pedal to the metal. The truck shuddered, the RPMs dropped, the engine knocked, and finally the road-weary truck groaned and died. Stedman managed to coast the vehicle to the side of the road. Streams of antifreeze and what appeared to be engine oil flooded from under the chassis.

He tried to flag down cars but no one stopped. So he stripped the vehicle of all valuables and stashed them in an old duffel bag he found behind the seat. He crushed out his last cigarette. He walked as fast as his arthritic knees would allow, dragging the duffel bag behind, cursing all the way. In a little over an hour he covered about two miles. With every step along the way, the duffel bag felt like it was gaining weight. He sat on the guardrail to rest, drenched in sweat and feeling lightheaded. A car approached but didn't even slow down as Stedman waved his arms. *They probably think I'm some kind of psychopath waiting to kill my next victim. I guess I can't blame them. When was the last time I stopped to help a stranger in need?*

Stedman checked his watch and started moving again. But this time his journey would be brief. After pressing forward for another few yards, Eugene Stedman collapsed on the side of the road and rolled into a ditch. A stream of blood flowed out of his nostrils.

37

Danial pulled into the courthouse parking lot and looked up at the sunrise over the West Virginia hills, a dazzling display of pinks and reds. He marveled at God's creation and said a silent prayer. And then rapid-fire thoughts raced through his mind. He felt uneasy about sending Lori to run down Vance's story, but couldn't put his finger on why. He certainly trusted her ability and intellect; that wasn't it. Maybe when she was gone he found himself feeling somehow less complete. He had never felt this way before, and the new feeling in his heart left him unsettled.

The whole Stedman thing concerned him as well. Stedman said he'd be back to Steubenville, but when Danial phoned for the tenth time by 6:00 a.m., no one answered. Eugene Stedman was compulsive, impetuous and overzealous, but he certainly wasn't irresponsible. And all that talk of a huge discovery. Danial had spent his few precious hours in bed tossing and turning and trying to figure out what Stedman had found. And now with his inexplicable disappearance, Danial feared the discovery may have cost him his life.

Before meeting with Ian, Danial dropped by to see a sleepy Norma Fitzpatrick. He told her about Vance's confession, and she confirmed the story and even added some details that Vance left out. Danial explained they were not out of the woods yet. Vance might not agree to testify and would more than likely invoke his Fifth Amendment rights. And still, no one managed to explain how the baby ended up in an ammunition canister at the Steubenville Police Station.

Norma begged Danial to stay a little longer just to visit; no one had come to see her since being arrested. The long hours of isolation wore her down, and teenage insecurities ate her up inside. It broke Danial's heart to leave her in such a condition, but he had business to attend to.

The second day of trial began with the State showing edited versions of surveillance videos to the jury on a large screen television. Special Prosecutor Schaeffer carefully pointed out the image of Ian throwing the egg at the van, then tossing some sort of container into the garbage dumpster that later vaporized in the brilliant explosion. Schaeffer also took great pains to point out the two hazy figures climbing down into the manhole.

Judge Williams ordered a short recess before allowing the State to call its next witness.

"The State calls Detective Joshua Ross to the stand."

In the back of the courtroom, a tall and confident looking officer rose to his feet. His black uniform looked striking with a chest full of commendations. He made his way down the center aisle and took a seat on the witness stand. The bailiff administered the oath, and Schaeffer began the questioning.

"For the record, please state your name and present occupation."

"My name is Joshua Ross, and I'm a detective with the Jefferson County Sheriff's Office."

"And how long have you held that position?"

"Six years."

"And what is your capacity with the Sheriff's Office?"

"I'm in the Detective Division."

"And in your duties as a detective, were you assigned to work on the Ian McKinney case?"

"I was."

"As you investigated this case, did you have the opportunity to inspect the defendant's apartment?"

"I did."

"Would you explain to the court, in your own words, what you found when you examined the defendant's residence?"

"I arrived at the McKinney apartment with two uniformed

officers. We got the building manager to let us in and did a walk-through of the place."

"What do you mean by a walk-through?"

"I mean we did an overall inspection of the premises before sifting through everything with a fine-toothed comb."

"And did you see anything in plain view?"

"Well, first I sent the uniformed officers to search the bedroom, and I went to the kitchen. We did see things in plain view."

"And what did you find?"

"I found what appeared to be some kind of sick shrine to terrorist bombings—"

"Objection!" Danial shouted over the murmuring gallery. "Conjecture!"

"Sustained," Williams said looking over at the witness. "Just tell us what you saw and leave the interpretation to the jury."

"Yes, Your Honor."

"Please describe what you saw," Schaeffer said.

"In the kitchen's breakfast nook, on the walls, I saw newspaper articles of abortion clinic bombings plastered all over the place."

"What happened next?"

"About that time one of the officers shouted for me to come to the bedroom."

"What did they find?"

"They found a stack of diagrams and instructions on how to build a bomb."

The gallery erupted. Colin Casey motioned for Williams to let the outburst continue for a few seconds.

"Order! Order in the court!"

Schaeffer walked back to the prosecutor's table and picked up a stack of papers mounted in plastic and labeled with large red letters.

"The State would like to enter into evidence the diagrams found in Ian McKinney's apartment as State's exhibits A through M."

"Let the record so reflect," Williams said.

Schaeffer passed the diagrams around the jury. He waited until they were enthralled by the exhibits before turning his attention back to Ross.

"What did you do once you found the bomb-making instructions?"

"I called the Sheriff's Office and requested a forensic team be called in."

"I have no further questions, Your Honor." Schaeffer sat down.

Williams looked over at Danial and asked, "Does the Defense wish to cross-examine the witness?"

"Yes I would, Your Honor."

"The witness is yours, Mr. Solomon."

Danial stood, walked to the jury box and leaned on the railing.

"Mr. Ross, did you happen to find any dynamite or gun powder at my client's apartment?"

"No, I didn't."

"Did the forensic team find any dynamite or gun powder at my client's apartment?"

"Not as far as I know."

"Did any of you find any other bomb-making components at my client's apartment?"

"No."

"You found the diagrams and instructions to make a bomb, but you didn't find any of the ingredients necessary to make a bomb. Don't you find that odd?"

"He could've assembled a bomb anywhere."

"I don't recall you mentioning exactly where it was that you found these bomb-making instructions."

"Some were in the computer's printer; some were in the trash can under some other papers."

"In the trash can," Danial said, raising his eyebrows. "Now why do you suppose they were in the trash?"

"Objection!" Schaeffer yelled, jumping up to his feet. "Speculation."

"Sustained," Williams said, leaning back in his chair as

rehearsed.

"Well, let me ask you this, did you attempt to verify where these bomb plans came from?"

"Of course I did. He downloaded them off the Internet."

"Did you consult with an engineer to verify these instructions actually worked?"

"No."

"Detective Ross, do you know how to read an electronics schematic?"

"No."

"Then how did you conclude the plans you discovered were instructions for a bomb?"

"Because the title across the top of one page said, *Instructions For Making a Bomb.*"

Snickers and laughs fluttered from the gallery. Danial walked to the defense table and picked up two diagrams mounted to green matting. He held them up for the jury to see, then showed them to Ross.

"I have in my hands two sets of diagrams; one is for a transistor radio, and the other for an explosive device. They're both labeled as instructions for building a radio. If I placed both in front of you, could you tell me with 100% certainty which plan is for the bomb?"

"Objection!" Schaeffer yelled once again. "Relevance."

"The relevance should be quite clear," Danial said. "If some of the alleged bomb plans found in my client's apartment won't produce a functioning explosive device, then—"

"Sustained," Judge Williams said.

"But Your Honor—"

"What part of sustained don't you understand, Mr. Solomon?"

"I've got just one more question," Danial said. "Can you say beyond a shadow of a doubt that all of the plans found in my client's apartment will produce a functioning explosive device?"

"No, I cannot."

"No further questions, Your Honor."

Williams looked over at Schaeffer who whispered something

into DiAngello's ear.

"Would the State like to redirect?"

"I would, sir."

"Proceed."

Schaeffer stood behind the table. "Detective Ross, do you know how an internal combustion engine works?"

"No, I do not."

"Do you know how to drive a car?"

"Yes, I do."

Schaeffer looked at the jury and said, "Don't sweat the small stuff."

"Objection," Danial said, half-standing.

"I withdraw the statement, Your Honor. I have no further questions."

"Very good," Williams said. "Mr. Ross, you may step down."

Ross climbed down, put on his mirrored sunglasses and walked out of the courtroom. As soon as the doors closed behind him, Williams said, "This is a good place to break for a long lunch. When we come back the State will call its next witness."

"What time will we resume?" Schaeffer asked.

"One o'clock," Williams answered. "Will the State be ready?"

"The State intends to call Dr. Gaston Garvey, but he may be in surgery."

1:10 P.M.

"The State calls Dr. Gaston Garvey to the stand," Schaeffer announced.

Gaston Garvey stepped forward wearing his most expensive silk Armani suit, his thinning gray hair meticulously gelled in place across his balding scalp. He made his way to the front of the courtroom and tripped up the two wooden steps leading to the witness stand. He nervously stroked his mustache as the bailiff administered the oath. Schaeffer began the questioning.

"Please state your name and occupation for the record."

"My name is Dr. Gaston Garvey, and I am Chief of Obstetrics at University Hospital."

"Chief of Obstetrics," Schaeffer said. "Is it common for a man of your age to hold such a position?"

"At 35, I'm one of the youngest departmental chiefs in the state."

"You must be awfully good at what you do."

"I do all right."

"In your capacity at University Hospital, are you ever required to perform abortions?"

"On rare occasions."

"And I understand there are usually groups of protesters down at the hospital who are opposed to such procedures?"

"There's never a shortage of wackos down there."

"Objection!" Danial shouted.

"Sustained." Williams leaned over. "Answer the question and refrain from interjecting personal opinions."

"And over the years you've worked at University Hospital, have you ever received any threats from these protesters?"

"Yeah, I've had animal blood thrown on me, car bomb threats, that sort of thing."

"And has the hospital taken any precautions to ensure the safety of the doctors?"

"Yeah, hospital security picks me and the other doctors up at various locations around the city and drives us to work each morning."

"And on the day of October 3rd, were you in the hospital van when the defendant savagely attacked it with the eagle egg?"

"Yes, I was."

"Could you explain to the jury what actually took place that morning?"

"As I recall, the pick-up van was at the cosmetology school early that morning. And I believe the driver said the hospital parking lot was swarming with lunatics."

"Objection! Hearsay," Danial said without standing.

"Sustained," Williams said. He looked over at Garvey. "Please refrain from offering the statements of others."

Schaeffer paced in front of the judge's bench. "So, you were in the van, and what happened next?"

"We drove over to the hospital. The van slowed down as the protesters pressed in tightly. Over the years, you learn to ignore such ignorance. Anyway, the van pushed through the crowd, and just as we were approaching the rear entrance something crashed against the van. It splintered the window and showered shards of glass all over us."

"Excuse me for interrupting," Schaeffer said as he walked up next to the witness stand. "You mean to tell us the projectile hit with such force it actually splintered the window?"

"Yes, it did."

"Was anyone injured?"

"All of us had to have shards of glass removed from the back of our necks, and I believe Dr. Gamble had to have a shard removed from his scalp. Luckily, no one was hit in the face."

"So, theoretically, had a piece of glass hit one of the passengers in the face, it could have caused blindness?"

Danial rolled his eyes. "Objection, argumentative."

"Sustained. Ask another question, counselor."

"At any time during the incident, did you feel your life was in danger?"

"I most certainly did. I had no way of knowing what hit the vehicle. For all I knew, we were being shot at."

"No further questions, Your Honor."

Lori slipped in and joined Danial and Ian at the defense table.

"Mr. Solomon," Williams said. "You may cross-examine the witness."

Danial got up and walked over to the jury box. He leaned on the railing, then looked directly at Garvey. The two locked eyes for a few moments. Danial waited until Garvey looked away to begin his questioning.

"So, tell us, Dr. Garvey, how many years have you been in the baby slaughtering business?"

"Objection!" screamed Schaeffer.

"Sustained."

"Okay, I will rephrase the question. How long have you been stabbing babies in the back of the neck with scissors sharper than shards of glass?"

"Objection!"

"Sustained! Mr. Solomon, you are skating on thin ice here."

Danial turned his back on Garvey and stared at the portrait of Baron von Steuben, until he heard Garvey's butt squirm in the leather seat.

"How long have you been performing abortions?"

"Ever since medical school."

"And how long would that be in years?"

"About eight years."

"And about how many abortions do you perform each year?"

"I couldn't even venture a guess. I don't keep track of such things."

"Is it hundreds or thousands?"

"Objection," Schaeffer said. "Relevance."

"Sustained. Mr. Solomon, please ask a question that pertains to this case."

Danial walked up to the witness stand and smiled at Garvey.

"Dr. Garvey, this case is about abortion. What time do the mothers and victims usually arrive at the hospital before the killings commence?"

"Objection!" Schaeffer screamed. "Censor him."

"Mr. Solomon, approach the bench - now!"

The judge turned off the microphone as Danial walked up. Williams leaned over the bench, his face beet-red. He pointed his crooked index finger in Danial's face.

"I don't know who you think you are, coming in here and attempting to mock me on nationwide television, but I'm not going to have it. If you so much as smirk the wrong way, I'll throw you in jail for contempt, and we'll continue this trial without you. Do I make myself clear?"

"Yes, Your Honor."

"Now return to your seat."

Williams looked at his Rolex watch and turned on the microphone. "There is no use in continuing at this point. The Court stands in recess until tomorrow morning."

Williams rapped the gavel on the wooden block next to the engraved name plate on the bench and then disappeared into his chambers; Colin Casey was right on his heels.

38

1:35 P.M.

Colin Casey looked out the window behind Williams' desk. A circuslike atmosphere engulfed the entire block surrounding the courthouse. TV crews staked out every conceivable entrance to the building with huge black cables snaking through the crowds to nearby broadcast vans. Pro-choice activists cheered for the conviction of the man who dared to challenge their choices. Small pockets of pro-life supporters milled around carrying placards. Animal rights activists protested the deliberate killing of the unborn eagle. One particularly clever protester carried a poster depicting the embryonic development stages of a baby eagle.

In the midst of the chaos three unmarked federal vehicles pushed through the crowds and crawled toward the sheriff's entrance to the underground jail. The media pounced. Several armed officers poured out of the courthouse dressed in full riot gear, surrounded the black SUVs, and pushed the converging throng back.

The driver of the first SUV stepped out and looked around. He pressed his right hand over his tiny radio receiver earpiece. He unlocked the rear door. Out stepped a second agent who in turn helped a prisoner out of the car. The burly black-haired man wore a bulletproof vest over a blaze orange jumpsuit, his wrists handcuffed and linked to a belly chain wrapped around his waist. His feet were shackled. A stoic expression shrouded his face.

The second SUV carried a second prisoner, with salt and pepper hair. When he climbed out of the car the squad of officers collapsed around the two prisoners and whisked them into the building through a cacophony of jeers from the angry crowd.

"I see my second surprise has just arrived," Casey said.

Williams peered out the window at the crowd below.

"It's really coming unglued down there."

"Free press, that's what this is." He rubbed his hands together. "I'd like to see the look on Solomon's face right about now."

1:45 P.M.

Sonny Dante had watched the AIDS patient to his right rally throughout the morning. By this time the man had propped himself up on a pillow and appeared lucid. The gravity of this man's situation pressed on Sonny's heart. *This dude could die any minute.*

Sonny wanted to help the man but didn't know what to do. He decided to find a Bible. He swung his feet over the edge of his bed; a pinching abdominal pain reminded him to go slow. He pulled open the nightstand drawer - nothing. He gingerly shuffled toward a steel picnic table bolted to the floor in front of the television - nothing. He searched through piles of year-old magazines and newspapers strewn around the ward - nothing. He gave up the search and limped back to bed. He eased himself to his knees.

"Dear Heavenly Father, I come to You today in the name of Jesus. I thank You for allowing me to see another day, and for the blessings You've given me, in spite of these prison walls. Lord, I lift up this man in the bed next to me in prayer. I don't know his name, but You do. And Lord, I would really like a Bible. I don't know what to say to him, and a Bible would help. Amen."

Sonny stayed on his knees for a few moments to listen to the Holy Spirit speak to his heart. He could almost hear a quiet voice speak softly to his soul.

"Look up."

Sonny looked up. In the corner of the restroom door, a coverless book was wedged in the hinges to prop the door open.

Sonny struggled to his feet and made his way to the book. It had obviously been jammed in the door for years. Rust from the hinges streaked across the bound edge of the book and had fused the paper to the door.

He reached up and winced. He fought through the pain and applied pressure to the door with his left hand. He wriggled the book free. The door swung closed.

"Hey, put that back!" someone yelled. "Some of us can't open that door."

Sonny glanced over to see a man with one arm and an angry expression looking right at him.

"Sorry about that. I'll put another book in there right away."

His answer seemed to calm the man who went back to watching the television mounted in a cage on the wall.

Sonny turned his attention back to his newly discovered treasure. The book smelled musty. The pages fell open to the book of Psalms, and Sonny smiled from ear to ear.

"Thank you Jesus!"

But his dying neighbor had fallen asleep again.

2:06 P.M.

Colin Casey, Special Prosecutor Schaeffer, and Anthony DiAngello met in the prosecutor's 3rd floor corner office. DiAngello looked out the window on the crowd assembled below.

"How did the world get so crazy?"

One of the secretaries carried in a platter of cold cuts, set it down on the conference table, then hurried away. Schaeffer made himself a bologna sandwich and said, "Obviously, we're going to ask for a continuance so we can interrogate the new suspects."

"The agent in charge downstairs said they aren't talking," DiAngello said, then turned his attention back to his multilayered Dagwood sandwich.

"It doesn't matter if they're talking or not," Schaeffer said. "I still want to question them. A little pressure goes a long way."

"Nothing better than a confession to seal up a conviction," DiAngello said.

Casey paced near the door. "I really don't care who you talk to or what kind of pressure you apply. But I'll say this, we can't afford to have this trial stopped for too long. We're 10 points up in the polls, but the election is in two weeks."

Schaeffer took another bite of his sandwich. He washed it down with a cold can of root beer.

"I need 48 hours. If Williams will give me just two days, I don't see why we couldn't continue the trial Monday."

"Forty-eight hours works for me," Casey said pompously. "I can guarantee you a continuance for that exact amount of time."

4:15 P.M.

After picking up chicken dinner at KFC, Lori and Danial returned to the office, reviewed the events of the day, and had a strategic brainstorming session. On a legal pad they listed all the possibilities of what may have happened at University Hospital on October 3rd. They worked over the facts like pieces of a jigsaw puzzle. At times the pieces seemed to make sense, but without talking to Ron Kester or Art Bently, they could neither confirm nor deny their hunches.

While Lori reviewed a surveillance video yet again, Danial worked the phone trying to run down the whereabouts of one Eugene Stedman. He had already driven to Stedman's trailer; no sign of him there. Several calls to various law enforcement agencies were also unfruitful.

"Danial, I've got to ask you. What were you trying to do with Dr. Garvey? You could've been thrown out of court."

"I was just stalling for time. I didn't want to go much further without knowing what Stedman found."

"Why didn't you just ask for a continuance?"

"Williams hates me. I had to upset him to stop the trial."

"I thought he was going to have a stroke."

"At least it worked." He loosened his tie. "I'm concerned about Stedman. It's not like him to just disappear."

"Something must have come up, I'm sure he's fine."

Lori turned her attention back to the surveillance images. Her face lit up.

"Come here, Danial, I think I've found something."

"What is it?"

She grabbed the remote control off the top of the television and pressed the rewind button. She played the video in slow motion and pointed her finger at the clock in the upper right-hand corner.

"Did I just see what I think I saw?" Danial said. "Rewind that."

She pressed the button, and the two stood inches from the TV with their eyes glued on the tiny digital numbers in the corner of the screen.

Jennifer dashed in.

"Danial, pick up the phone. I've been buzzing you. Pick up the phone!"

Danial hustled over to his desk and picked up the phone. He listened intently, said thank you, then hung up. He dropped his head and rubbed his eyes.

"What is it?" Lori asked.

"That was the West Virginia State Patrol. They found Stedman's truck abandoned along Route 2. The vehicle was stripped with no sign of Stedman anywhere. They suspect foul play but can't file a missing person report until he is gone for at least 24hours."

"What do we do now?"

"We pray," Danial said.

39

Sonny Dante carried the coverless Gideons Bible over to his neighbor's bed.

"Sorry to bother you, but I couldn't help but notice you awake and feelin' a little better so's I thought I introduce myself. My name is Sonny Dante."

"I'm John." He stretched out his skeleton-like hand.

Sonny hesitated at first, then carefully grasped the frail hand. "Good to meet ya John. I couldn't help but notice you had a pretty tough way to go, and it looks like you could use some good news."

"I sure could."

"Well, the good news is... eternal life in Heaven is a gift that God wants to give you."

"Hold on there. I didn't think you were going to preach to me."

"I not preaching. I just trying to offer you something I know you need."

"Since when did you become my personal self-help guru?"

"I didn't mean to offend ya, John. But I don't know if ya noticed it, yesterday they drug a body bag into that room over there, and it wasn't empty. And I going to be straight with ya here. People are dying around here everyday, and they're going straight to Hell. I'm no doctor or nothin', but you ain't lookin' too good. So, I figured you at least like to consider what happens after you die."

Sonny stood up and started walking away.

"Wait a minute. Maybe we could start over." He reached out his hand.

"Hi, my name is John."

241

Sonny shook his hand and sat back down on the foot of the bed.

"I'm sorry for being so defensive. I guess I'm not used to people trying to be friendly to me for no reason. I've been down for about 12 years, and it's been my experience that everyone's got an angle. I figured you were just jerking my chain or something."

"I not playing with you. I take my faith serious."

"I can respect that," John said. "Now what were you saying?"

"I was startin' to tell you about the gift God is offering you right now."

"Why would God offer a gift to me?"

"Because He loves you."

"I can't believe that."

"Well, He does."

"You don't know the things I've done." John's lip quivered. "I've been involved in homosexuality ever since my older brother molested me when I was 13. I got into drugs and by the time I first got arrested, I was even stealing from my mother. I actually stole her wedding ring to buy a rock of crack. I've been in and out of reform schools and prisons all my life, and the things I've done since I've been down are worse than the stuff I did on the line." Tears trickled down both of his cheeks. He wiped his nose against the shoulder of the hospital gown. "When I got sick I figured that God was getting even with me for the things I did."

"God doesn't love us because we're so loveable," Sonny said. "And we just suffer the consequences of our own actions."

"Don't I know it."

"It's impossible for you to be too bad to be forgiven. Have you ever read about the Apostle Paul?"

John shook his head.

"He was one bad dude. Before he got saved he went around jailin' and killin' Christians. Can you imagine that?"

"No kidding?"

"He called himself the chief of all sinners."

"I've never heard that before, but then again, I've never heard too much of anything that's in that book."

"Want me to show you that story about Paul?"

"Sure."

Sonny flipped through the tattered Gideons Bible to the ninth chapter of Acts and began to read about Saul, whose name was changed to Paul:

"Meanwhile, Saul was still breathing out murderous threats against the Lord's disciples. He went to the high priest and asked him for letters to the synagogues in Damascus, so that if he found any there who belonged to the Way, whether men or women, he might take them as prisoners to Jerusalem. As he neared Damascus on his journey, suddenly a light from Heaven flashed around him. He fell to the ground and heard a voice say to him, 'Saul, Saul, why do you persecute Me?'"

Sonny read the entire chapter. He explained how Saul, through his encounter with the Lord Jesus Christ, was born again; and from that day forward Paul became a powerful Christian who spread the Gospel everywhere he went.

"Ya see, John, there's no such thing as being too bad to be forgiven by God. If God was able to forgive Paul, He is certainly able to forgive you."

John smiled.

"Behind bars or free, most people are prisoners of Satan's spiritual deceptions and sin. But there's a way out, through biblical faith in Jesus Christ and real repentance of sin. He will set you free - for a new life and eternal life. That's true freedom."

John smiled again.

"So now ya know God's willing and able to forgive you; are you willing to repent and receive that forgiveness?"

"I don't know how."

Sonny put his arm around the emaciated man. "First, you have to see that you're a sinner and turn from sin. From what you said before, I can see ya don't have a problem with that. But it takes more than that, it takes trusting Jesus Christ. He came to earth for a special purpose. Most people know He did miracles, and He led a perfect life, and He was a great moral teacher. But they don't understand the main reason He left Heaven, came to earth, and took on the form of a man."

"I don't."

"He came here as Savior to die on the cross to pay the penalty for our sins, and to purchase a place for us in Heaven. He offers this to us as a gift." Sonny flipped to the book of Isaiah and read from Chapter 53:

"He was pierced for our transgressions, He was crushed for our iniquities; the punishment that brought us peace was upon Him, and by His wounds we are healed. We all, like sheep, have gone astray; each of us has turned to his own way; and the Lord has laid on Him the iniquity of us all."

John slid down in his bed.

"Do you see what these verses are saying? Jesus, who lived a sinless life, became a sin offering and our substitute on the cross. We receive forgiveness and the gift of eternal life by repenting and placing our faith in Him."

John looked pale.

"So, John, are you ready to turn from your sins and receive the Lord Jesus as your Lord and Savior?"

John's body heaved. He adjusted one of the tubes protruding from his chest. "Yes, I would love to receive Jesus as my Lord and Savior."

"Could I lead you in prayer?"

"Please," John said.

They bowed their heads.

"Dear God, I thank You for Your love and forgiveness, because I know I ain't worthy. I thank You for offering me the gift of eternal life. I know I'm a sinner and can't save myself. I know You're a loving and merciful God, but I know You must punish sins. So I thank You for sending Jesus Christ to die on the cross for my sins. And I believe in my heart that You raised Him from the dead. I ask Jesus to come into my heart as Savior and Lord. I repent and surrender my life to You. From this day forward I'll seek to obey You and serve You now and forever. Amen!"

"Amen," John echoed as tears streamed down his face. "Thank you."

"You don't need to thank me," Sonny said. "I just one hungry beggar telling another beggar where to find bread."

Sonny leaned over and gave John a gentle hug.

"No one's hugged me since I got diagnosed with AIDS three years ago."

"Well, I just picture Jesus hugging you, and lepers too."

"Is it all right if we pray for my brother - you know, the one who molested me?"

"Sure we can," Sonny said with a smile. "What's his name?"

"Colin Casey."

40

Danial showed up in the attorneys visiting room wearing a pair of stonewashed jeans and an Ohio University sweatshirt. Ian McKinney arrived a few minutes later, escorted by an old deputy in a crumpled uniform. Ian held up his wrists; they were cuffed.

"What's with that?" Danial asked.

"Sheriff's orders," the deputy said.

"Well, take them off him."

"I can't."

Danial stood up. "You can and you will."

The deputy shrugged and uncuffed him. Ian rubbed his wrists and sat down. The deputy closed the door behind him.

"Ever since the FBI brought in those two guys yesterday, they've been giving me the maximum-security treatment."

"There's not much I can do about that."

"Have you talked to them?" Ian asked.

"Who?"

"Kesley and Bentler?"

"You mean Kester and Bently?"

"Yeah."

"No. I can't talk to either of them unless they ask to speak with me."

"Any new developments?" Ian asked.

"We've run into a snag."

"What snag?"

"The private investigator I hired is missing."

"You've got to be kidding me. Maybe the guy took the money

246

and ran."

"I don't think so."

"How can you be so sure?"

"Because I haven't paid him yet."

Ian dropped his face into his hands. "I'm screwed... what about the two bombing guys?"

"What about them?"

"They know I wasn't involved."

"That's all well and good, but unless they volunteer that little tidbit, it won't do any good."

9:45 A.M.

A salesman driving from Wheeling to Weirton, West Virginia checked his watch; he was running late. He flipped the switch on the radar detector to its highway setting and punched the accelerator. He was cruising along Route 2 at upwards of 80 miles an hour when the detector went crazy. He stepped on the brakes and the nose of his car dipped. He looked around and couldn't see any patrol cars. He looked up, and in the corner of the windshield he spotted a police helicopter. He shook his head. Around the next bend a West Virginia trooper stood next to his car, red light flashing.

The salesman pulled over, opened his window and waited for the inevitable. The trooper swaggered up with his right hand on the butt of his pistol.

"License and registration please."

The salesman handed the items to the trooper.

"This is a driver's license," the trooper said.

"That's what you asked for."

"When I said license, I thought you'd have a pilot's license because you were flying back there."

"A real comedian."

A scowl twisted the trooper's face. "If you think that's funny, you'll love this. Step out of the car."

"But off—"

"I said, get out of the car."

The salesman obeyed.

"Put your hands on the hood and spread 'em."

The salesman complied. The trooper kicked his legs further apart; he fell face first onto the hood. He turned his head to the right and looked into the weeds.

"Hey, there's somebody laying in the ditch over there."

"Don't try to be slick," the trooper said, patting him down.

"I'm not, look."

The trooper turned and looked. "I'll be damned. There is someone over there."

The trooper marched over the berm and into the ditch, the salesman following right behind. A long, lanky man lay face down. The trooper rolled him over and felt for a pulse.

"Is he alive?" the salesman asked.

"Barely. Stay with him. I'm going to radio for a helicopter."

The trooper ran toward his patrol car and yelled over his shoulder. "Check for ID!"

The salesman examined the old man's face. His skin looked gray. His lips were cracked and chapped. Blood had coagulated around his nose and mouth.

"Hang on buddy. Help is on the way."

He reached into the old man's back pocket and pulled out a well-worn leather wallet. He found his driver's license. He cupped his hands around his mouth and shouted toward the squad car.

"His name is Eugene Stedman!"

1:35 P.M.

Sonny Dante's eyes flung open to the piercing blare of an alarm. He rolled toward the sound. A searing pain in his abdomen drove him onto his back again. He turned his head toward the noise. The heart monitor connected to John Casey flatlined.

"Somebody help!" Sonny screamed at the top of his lungs.

Nobody came.

Other inmates in the ward gathered around.

Still nobody came.

Sonny bit his bottom lip and rolled onto his side with a groan. The gawkers pressed in.

"Get back!" Sonny shouted. "Give him some air."

"It's a little late for air," a heavily tattooed man said. "Dude's dead."

Sonny pressed his way to John's bedside. John's eyes were open, and his vacant gaze aimed up and to the left.

"Somebody help!" Sonny yelled.

A gray-shirted officer unlocked the gate to the ward, and two nurses sauntered in like they were going to lunch.

"All right, boys, step aside," one of the nurses said. "The show's over."

The second nurse turned off the alarm then felt for a pulse. She looked at her watch and picked up the clipboard at the head of the bed.

"Ain't you going to do nothin'?" Sonny asked.

"I just did," she said. "I pronounced him dead."

41

Monday, October 30
12:57 P.M.

Danial Solomon pressed his way through the corridors of the Jefferson County Courthouse, teeming with all manner of humanity. The media camped out near available power outlets. Armed deputies manned the metal detectors at every entrance. Tension charged the air like electricity. Just outside the two oak doors of the courtroom, Danial checked his watch and gave Lori a smile.

"It's three minutes till one right now," he said. "Williams will call the room to order at precisely one o'clock, so wait five minutes before you bring them in."

"I've got reserved signs on the two seats directly behind our table like you asked me."

"Very good. I think that covers everything. Can you think of anything we might have left out?"

Lori smiled; a gleam twinkled in her violet blue eyes.

"Just that I love you."

Danial's heart leapt.

"I love you too."

They kissed.

"I've got to go," he said looking at his watch. "We'll talk more about this later."

He pulled open the heavy wooden doors and squirmed through the crowd to the defense table where Ian sat fidgeting. A large-bellied bailiff entered the room, tugged up his pants by the belt loops and announced: "All rise! Hear ye! Hear ye! Hear ye! This Court is now in session. The Honorable Judge John Williams presiding."

Judge Williams took his seat, and reviewed the file sitting open in front of him.

"The trial of Mr. Ian McKinney will now resume. I trust the State has had adequate opportunity to question the federal detainees."

"Yes, Your Honor," Schaeffer answered.

"Very good," Williams said and closed the file. "If my memory serves me correctly, Mr. Solomon was cross-examining Dr. Garvey when we broke for recess. We'll pick up where we left off. Bailiff, escort Dr. Garvey to the stand."

The bailiff waddled to the jury deliberation room and returned with the balding doctor. The bailiff escorted him to the witness stand. In spite of the cool courtroom temperature, a thin layer of sweat glistened across his brow.

"Dr. Garvey, you're still under oath," Williams said, then looked over at Danial. "The witness is yours."

"Thank you, Your Honor."

Danial stood and strolled in front of the jury box and casually greeted the members. When he reached the foreman, near the witness stand, he turned to face the doctor.

"Dr. Garvey, in your testimony from last Wednesday you admitted to performing abortions, is that correct?"

"Yes."

"That includes partial-birth abortions."

"The proper term is late-term abortion, and yes I have performed them."

"And on the day in question, October 3rd, did you perform a partial-birth, excuse me, a late-term abortion?"

"I don't remember."

"I was afraid your recollection might be a little faulty, so I subpoenaed the surgical schedule and medical reports from October 3rd. So, if it wouldn't be too much of a strain on your memory, would you like another stab at the question?"

"What question?"

"Did you perform a late-term abortion on Tuesday, October 3rd?"

"Now that I think about it, yes, I think I did."

Danial leaned against the railing in front of the jury box and quietly stared at the double doors in the rear of the courtroom. And as if on cue, the doors swung open and in walked Lori Franks with Nurse Martine and Surgical Resident Garland. They strutted down the center aisle; Lori went to the defense table, Martine and Garland to the reserved chairs. Danial and Lori met eyes, and they both smiled. Danial turned back toward the witness stand. Dr. Garvey's face turned ashen. His eyes fastened on Nurse Martine.

"Dr. Garvey, when you performed this partial-birth abortion, did everything go according to plan?"

"Objection!" Schaeffer yelled. "Relevance!"

"Your Honor," Danial said. "If you'll give me the chance to pursue this line of questioning, the relevance will become exceptionally clear."

Williams looked over at Colin Casey who sat behind Anthony DiAngello. He nodded.

"Objection overruled. I'll give you a little latitude here, Mr. Solomon, but the relevance had better become crystal clear."

"Thank you, Your Honor." Danial turned back to Garvey. "So, tell us, doctor, did everything go according to plan?"

"It did."

"Are you absolutely certain? No mishaps during the procedure?"

Garvey glanced at Martine, then twisted his tie. "Oh, now that you mention it, following the procedure Nurse Martine slipped and fell on her way to the biohazard container. It appeared to me that the birthing material may have suffered some post-procedural trauma. It's all in my report."

"By birthing material, you're referring to the baby, are you not?"

"The fetus, that's correct."

"So let me get this straight. Your testimony is that nothing unusual happened other than that the nurse, while carrying the baby, slipped and fell."

"That's it. It's all in my report."

"So you said. But I was over at the hospital on Saturday, and I analyzed your report. It sounded a little fishy."

"I'm sure I don't know what you mean."

"I took the liberty of interviewing both Nurse Martine and your surgical resident, and they told me a somewhat different story. I will ask you one more time, did anything unusual happen during the abortion procedure?"

"I stand by my surgical report, and I don't recall anything further."

Danial walked right up to the edge of the witness stand; only a few feet separated the two men. Danial peered into Garvey's eyes. "You don't recall that blood-covered baby in your hands?"

"Objection!" Schaeffer shouted.

"You don't recall the baby squirming and writhing in pain?"

"Objection!"

"You don't recall that innocent baby taking his first breath of air and then shrieking from the pain as the blood pulsed from your stab wound in the base of his skull?"

"Objection!" Schaeffer yelled.

Williams stared blankly ahead.

"No!"

"You don't recall snatching the baby from the nurse's hands and then snapping his fragile neck?"

"Objection!" Schaeffer rushed around his table and charged the bench. "Don't just sit there, Your Honor, do something!"

Williams blinked deeply then slammed his gavel to the bench. "Order! Order in the court!"

Schaeffer sat down in front of a livid Colin Casey. Casey motioned toward Danial who still stood nose-to-nose with Garvey.

Williams looked confused. "Mr. Solomon, would you repeat the last question?"

Casey stood, flailing his arms. Danial stepped back from the witness stand stunned by the instruction. He expected to be thrown out of court.

"Dr. Garvey, it's a crime to commit perjury in this state, so before you answer my question, allow me to state for the record that I have two affidavits from eyewitnesses to what happened in that operating room on October 3rd." He paused. "Did you snap the neck of the baby delivered during the botched abortion?"

"Objection!" Schaeffer shouted yet again, his voice filled with exasperation. "Dr. Garvey isn't on trial for murder here."

"Objection sustained," Williams said. "Mr. Solomon, I've already warned you. Your cross-examination is over, and I'll see you in chambers following today's proceedings. Do I make myself clear?"

"Yes, sir," Danial said as he returned to the defense table to collect himself.

"Would the State like to redirect the witness?"

"No, Your Honor. I really don't see how any of this tomfoolery has done anything to diminish the State's case. As a matter of fact, the State rests."

Williams looked down at Colin Casey who motioned with his hand to keep the trial moving.

A deputy tapped Danial on the shoulder and handed him a note. Danial unfolded it and read it. He smiled and handed it to Lori. She read it, nodded and pumped her fist.

"Your Honor, could the Defense have a short recess?"

"Mr. Solomon, we've only been in session for 20 minutes."

"Your Honor, the first witness is not presently in the courtroom. I only need 15 minutes or—"

"You can have ten."

"Thank you sir."

"Ten-minute recess."

Williams rapped the gavel. Danial bolted for the rear exit; Casey shot to the bench.

1:30 P.M.

Danial returned, and everyone took their seats.

Judge Williams called the Court to session. "Is the Defense ready to call its first witness?"

"We are, Your Honor," Danial said. "The Defense calls Ronald Kester."

"Objection," Schaeffer said, jumping to his feet.

"He can't object to a Defense witness."

"Overruled."

The courtroom doors swung open, and an outburst erupted in the gallery as the spectators got their first look at the elusive suspect. Two armed federal agents escorted Ron Kester down the center aisle. He wore a blaze orange jumpsuit, a bulletproof Kevlar® vest, handcuffs and shackles, and a defiant look in his eyes.

"Order!" Williams shouted. "I will not tolerate another outburst like this. If it happens again, I will clear the gallery."

Schaeffer whispered in DiAngello's ear.

The witness took the stand and the bailiff swore him in. Danial walked over to question the man making national headlines.

"Would you please state for the jury your name and occupation?"

"My name is Ronald Kester. I work at Wheeling-Pittsburgh Steel."

"And how long have you worked there?"

"Just over a year."

"What did you do before working at Wheeling-Pittsburgh Steel?"

"I was the general manager of a chain of abortion clinics."

"That's ironic," Danial said. "How long did you manage these abortion clinics?"

"For over 15 years."

"Did you make a lot of money?"

"Quite lucrative," Kester said. "We took in an average of

$15,000 dollars a day. It worked out to a little over $4 million a year before taxes and expenses."

Mumbles rippled through the gallery.

"Did you say $4 million a year?"

"Yes sir."

"How did you get started in the abortion business?"

"I got involved in the abortion industry a few years after the Supreme Court legalized *abortion-on-demand* back in 1973. My decision to start an abortion clinic had nothing to do with ideals or women's rights; it had everything to do with greed. A few fraternity brothers and I were sitting around the frat house talking about different business ideas and someone mentioned abortion clinics. I pulled out a calculator and did some math. It didn't take a rocket scientist to figure out this was a recession-proof business. After graduation a group of us did some research, consulted Planned Parenthood and started making money."

"But why did you quit?"

"I'm getting to that."

"Please continue."

"Shortly after we opened our clinic doors, I got myself appointed to the board of directors for several pro-abortion organizations. They gave us invaluable advice."

"What kind of advice did they give you?" Danial walked over to the jury box.

"They advised us on how to grow our business. It's tougher than you think. We couldn't advertise on radio or TV, at least not directly. I mean, can you imagine a radio spot saying, 'Go out and have unprotected sex and leave the abortions to us'? So, they showed us how to lobby our local school boards to get sex education into the schools at the earliest possible grades. The more kids talk about sex, the more they'll have sex."

"What else did they advise you?"

"They advised us to pass out low-quality condoms and low-grade birth control pills free to anyone who came to our clinics. Our goal was to increase our teenage business by 400% during our first ten years."

"That's disgusting."

"I'm not proud of it."

"Did you reach this goal?"

"We actually shattered it. As soon as Planned Parenthood got Washington to legislate sex education and condom distribution in public schools nationwide, business shot through the roof. Due to rampant fornication we had to open five additional clinics just to keep up with the demand."

"So why did you walk away from such a lucrative career?"

"I know this is going to sound insane, but I never thought about the babies until my girlfriend got pregnant. I wanted her to have the baby, she refused, and the next thing I knew, my baby was one of the countless victims murdered in my own abortuaries. Then it hit me. I couldn't stop thinking about the thousands of other babies who would never laugh or play or grow up because of the procedures we provided.

"Then one snowy white day in January when I was leaving work, I saw this little old man holding a sign in front of my door. I had seen this guy probably a thousand times. I always treated him with utter disdain, and he always returned my disgust with kindness. It infuriated me. But this day it was different. I don't know why I did it, but I offered to buy him a cup of coffee. And in that coffee shop, he told me about Jesus Christ and judgment or salvation. I never went back to the abortion clinic again."

Danial turned and paused for a moment of silence, allowing time for the jury, gallery and TV viewers to ponder those words. Then he slowly approached the witness stand. "Now allow me to direct your attention to the events of October 3rd. Were you at University Hospital on that day?"

"I was."

"I know you weren't here earlier, but the State showed a video of two men climbing down into a manhole in the hospital parking lot. Would you happen to know who those men were?"

"I do."

"Who were they?"

"Me and Art Bently."

Whispers filled the courtroom. Williams lightly rapped the gavel against the bench without saying a word.

"What were you doing in the manhole?"

As Ron described crawling through the underground tunnel to the hospital, he drifted back to the day that changed his life forever....

The hospital's freight elevator doors were midway across its cluttered basement. Ron checked the map and pointed.

"According to this, the incinerator is across from the freight elevator."

Art carefully set the black box on the floor, and under Ron's watchful eye, he unsnapped the latches and lifted the exterior casing. The video camera appeared to be unharmed by the unusual trip into the bowels of the hospital. Art lifted the camera and flipped the power switch. To the relief of both men, the red indicator light lit up.

"Thank God for small miracles," Art said with a sigh of relief. "Now, let's find the right disposal bins and get out of here."

Ron walked up to the first bin marked "Biohazard" and pulled up on the lid. It didn't budge. He gave it a second tug and noticed a metal pin holding the latch closed. He slid it out and lifted up on the handle, raising the lid. Ron looked inside then staggered back, fighting the urge to vomit.

"What is it?" Art asked, rushing forward with the camera.

"Someone's leg is in there."

"Do you want me to get a shot of it?"

Ron doubled over covering his mouth with his hand.

"No, man. You really don't want to get that on film."

Ron regained his composure, slammed the lid shut and replaced the pin. They moved on to the next disposal bin. Ron pulled the pin and lifted the lid to see blood-soaked surgical scrubs. He repeated the process two more times, then found his objective - the lifeless corpse of a baby girl. The body, approximately seven pounds, looked completely developed. The face was disfigured; the soft skull had collapsed upon itself like a deflated balloon.

Ron's face contorted with pain and disgust. He held the lid open so that Art could get a shot of the dreadful sight with the video camera.

"Zoom in on the face," Ron said.

"I am."

"Now fade to black."

"We got what we came for, now let's get out of here."

"Let's look at a couple more bins first. It would be good to show a couple of different children, so we don't get accused of manufacturing the whole thing."

"Let's get to it. I'm feeling sick."

"Just a couple more minutes."

"If the mother didn't want her, then why not give her up for adoption?"

"You're preaching to the choir, Art."

Three unexplored biohazard disposal bins remained. On the other side of the huge steel furnace stood a line of empty bins that had already given up their contents to the flames. It looked like Auschwitz, where Nazis disposed of their victims through ovens and chimneys. Ron opened the next two bins and found only soiled surgical clothing. Then he opened the third container.

"Oh no."

"What is it, Ron?"

"It's another baby!"

Art rushed over with the camera to get a look.

Ron held the lid open, and there he was. A fully developed, little baby boy lay with his head slumped to one side, a tuft of blond hair matted to his head with dark crimson blood. *He should be sleeping in a bassinet or in the loving arms of his mother, not alone in a hospital basement waiting to be incinerated like garbage.*

"I got the pictures, Ron. Let's get out of here."

"We can't just leave them here. At the least they deserve a proper burial."

"No way can we get them out of here without getting caught."

"The boy looks worse than the girl, even more disfigured in this house of horrors. We need hard evidence, so we have to take him. Let me figure out how to do it, while you start crawling back to the car."

"I don't like the sound of this, Ronnie."

"Don't worry, I've got an idea that will put this sick hospital in the headlines nationwide."

Ron's eyes misted over as his story came to a close. The courtroom remained silent; so much so that Danial felt hesitant to speak.

"And would you please explain to the Court what your idea was?" Danial asked.

"My idea was to take the dead baby to the police. I'm not a doctor or anything, but that baby's neck didn't look normal at all."

"Then what happened?"

"I put the baby into my toolbox - an ammunition canister - and then carried him through the tunnel and up to Art's VW Bug. Then we dropped him off at the Steubenville Police Station."

The gallery came unglued.

"Order! Order!" Williams pounded his gavel.

Danial waited until the noise died down.

"What was the purpose of making the video?"

"We made it for a national pro-life group in Washington, D.C. Its executive director, Mr. Birch, plans to include the footage in a documentary. You know, show the politicians and the people what really happens to babies during these late-term, partial-birth abortions. Expecting demand for the video, our Pro-Life Association has produced countless copies."

"So just to make this perfectly clear," Danial said, "you did not plant a bomb at University Hospital?"

"No."

"And you did not have any contact with, or plan to plant any bombs with, the defendant Ian McKinney?"

"No, sir. I had never seen him before the day he was arrested at the hospital."

Danial stepped back from the witness stand and glanced at the jury.

"No further questions, Your Honor."

42

Eugene Stedman opened his eyes. A television was mounted on the wall across from him. Some sort of tube snaked out of his nostrils. He tugged and it popped out. The place smelled clean. He turned his head to the left. A man lay in a bed with his mouth wired shut.

"This must be a hospital," he said. "Which one?"

He was thirsty, and he felt weak. He examined his body. Someone had removed his clothes and put one of those stupid hospital gowns on him. An IV line ran from his left hand to a clear plastic bag on a stand next to his bed. He rested his head on the pillow and willed his mind to focus. The last thing he could remember was his truck breaking down.

"I must have passed out."

He looked around his bed and found the call button for the nurse and pressed it. A few moments later a crotchety old nurse lumbered in on bad feet.

"You're awake," she said.

"Where am I?"

"Weirton Medical Center."

"What happened?"

"You were severely dehydrated. You about died."

"What day is it?"

"Monday, October 30th."

He sat up. "I've got to get out of here."

"You're not going anywhere until the doctor releases you."

"I don't have any health insurance," he lied.

"Oh... I'll get your things."

"I need to make a phone call."

262

"Just dial 9 and give the switchboard the number you want."

The nurse waddled away. He picked up the landline phone on his roommate's stand and pressed 9. The switchboard operator put him on hold. The nurse returned with the discharge papers already signed.

"Your duffel bag is in the closet over there." She pointed to the door next to the bathroom.

He nodded and she waddled away again. The phone's elevator music stopped, and an operator came on the line.

"Number please."

"Jefferson County Courthouse."

"One moment."

2:05 P.M.

"Would the State like to cross-examine the witness?" Judge Williams asked.

"You bet I would," Schaeffer said.

"You may proceed."

Schaeffer stood and clapped his hands. "That was quite a self-serving performance you shared with us, very moving oratory. But let me ask you, do you have in your possession the video camera used during that underground excursion?"

"No."

"Why not?"

"I threw it in the incinerator before I left the hospital."

"No video camera," Schaeffer said with a smirk. "That's convenient. Do you have a copy of the video?"

"No, we took it to—"

"Oh," Schaeffer said. "No video either."

The main doors swung open, and two men in dark suits jogged down the center aisle and up to the bench. Williams leaned forward, and they whispered for a few moments. One turned and walked to the side door, the other headed back to the main entrance.

Williams struck the gavel, "Court stands in recess. Everyone will evacuate the building in a quiet and orderly fashion."

2:42 P.M.

Danial stood next to Lori amidst a throng of people in the parking lot down the block from the courthouse, waiting for the FBI task force to do a bomb sweep of the building. Sheriff Rose pulled up in his cruiser and opened the window.

"All clear. False alarm. You can return to the courthouse."

A collective sigh went up, followed by copious complaints and expletives. The crowd herded past the parking booth. A yellow taxi drove up near the parking lot exit. Danial and Lori looked stunned; the back door opened, and Eugene Stedman climbed out.

"Where've you been?" Danial asked.

"It's a long story, based on that Pro-Life post office box, in Benwood. I've got something to give you." He reached back inside the cab and produced a DVD.

"What's this?"

"It's my discovery. From Benwood I thought I was tailing Kester or Bently to the Moundsville area. But it was a Pro-Life staffer. So I inadvertently barged into the Pro-Life Association's video production lab. They were mass-producing copies of a video Kester and Bently made and gave to the Pro-Life office in Steubenville. The office phoned the lab when I was there, saying Kester reported they were in ATF custody."

"Amazing," Lori said, smiling and shaking her head.

"It's all there in the DVD, Baby Ammo case and everything."

"Praise God!" Danial said. "And thank God for the bomb threat or this would have been too late."

"I thought so," Stedman said.

"What do you mean?" Lori asked.

"I called it in."

3:10 P.M.

Everyone reassembled in the courtroom. The crowd took their seats, and Judge Williams rapped his gavel.

"Court will resume session with the State cross-examining Mr. Kester."

"Thank you, sir," Schaeffer said. "Could you please have the stenographer read back the last exchange."

Williams nodded to the stenographer.

"The State asked: 'Do you have a copy of the video?'"

"The witness said: 'No, we took it to—'"

"Thank you," Schaeffer said. "Mr. Kester, you expect the jury to believe your story with no corroboration, no tangible evidence?"

"Your Honor," Danial said. "The Defense now has a copy of the video."

Williams looked dazed. "Will Colin Casey please approach the bench?"

Danial looked at Schaeffer, who shrugged then glanced at DiAngello who mouthed back, "You've got me."

Casey approached the bench.

"What should I do?" Williams asked.

"As much as I hate to think McKinney might be slipping off the hook, the bomb threat and this video must have the viewers at home going wild. I say play the video; the outcome of the case is really of no concern to us, as long as it plays well on television."

"Good idea."

"When I get back to my seat, instruct the Court you had to admonish me for making inappropriate gestures to the jury, and that such behavior will not be tolerated."

Casey returned to his seat. Williams did as he was told. He next ordered the bailiff to bring in the large-screen TV and DVD player, and the entire courtroom watched in stunned silence as the details of Kester's testimony played out in living color. When the video ended, Schaeffer resumed cross-examination.

"The video proves nothing. Just because you took footage of aborted babies doesn't prove that you didn't plant a bomb as well. Your Honor, I have no further questions for the witness."

"The federal agents may escort Mr. Kester from the stand," Williams said. "The Defense may call its next witness."

"Thank you, Your Honor," Danial said. "The Defense calls Colin Casey."

Casey's face flushed beet red. "May I approach the bench?"

"Approach."

Danial and Schaeffer approached the bench as well. "Your Honor," Danial said. "I must say, and I'm certain Mr. Schaeffer would agree, that allowing a civilian to approach the bench in the midst of a trial is highly irregular, and an abuse of discretion. And before you entertain anything Mr. Casey may have to say, allow me to add that the disposition of his testimony could have a profound effect on your career. It behooves you to put him on the stand."

Williams looked at Casey then at Danial, then back to Casey, then to Schaeffer. He mopped his brow with a handkerchief.

"Bailiff, swear in Mr. Casey."

Casey locked his eyes on Williams as he made his way to the stand. Once he took a seat on the witness stand and was sworn in, he placed his hand over the thin microphone and whispered to Williams, "I'll ruin you for this."

Danial ignored the exchange and began his questioning.

"Would you please state your name and explain for the jury your present occupation?"

"My name is Colin Casey. I'm a political consultant."

"Are you presently working on anyone's campaign?"

"I am."

"And would you please tell the jury who it is you're working for?"

Casey looked over at Williams and flashed a venomous smile. "I'm presently working on Judge Williams' campaign."

Mumbling filled the courtroom.

"And in this capacity, have you advised the judge on the *politically correct* stances he should take on some of the issues in this campaign?"

"Generally, political consultants advise their clients on political issues."

"Was abortion one of those issues?"

"One of many."

"And I understand that you're pro-abortion."

"Pro-choice."

"Pro-abortion, pro-choice, pro-death, it doesn't matter what label you put on it, death is death. The point is, you have an interest in such things. And naturally, you had reason to watch the events down at University Hospital rather closely."

"Yes." The jaw muscles at the base of Casey's cheeks flared out; he gnashed his teeth together.

Danial turned to Judge Williams. "Your Honor, earlier in the proceedings, the State entered into evidence and showed surveillance videos from the University Hospital parking lot. The Defense would like to have video number..."

"Sixteen," Lori said.

"Thank you," Danial said. "The Defense would like to show video number 16 once again and question the witness on some of its aspects."

"Bailiff," Williams said, "retrieve video 16 from the evidence table and play it for the Court."

The bailiff complied, and video images flashed across the screen. Danial walked over, stood next to the television, and pointed to the numbers in the upper right-hand corner.

"Please pay special attention to the clock." He pointed to the numbers. Minutes later he pointed again.

"There! Did you see that?"

A few members of the jury nodded; others looked confused.

"Bailiff, rewind the DVD and show that again," Williams ordered. "I didn't see anything."

The bailiff played it again in slow motion. Danial stood by, pointing at the numbers once again.

"There it is, did you see how the minutes instantly change from 11:41 p.m. to 11:52 p.m.?"

Danial looked over at Casey who sat frozen in the witness seat.

"You wouldn't happen to know why ten minutes of surveillance footage somehow came up missing?"

"I haven't a clue."

"But you agree the video has been altered?"

"I didn't say that."

"According to the hospital security logs, you were the first person to take possession of the video after the bombing."

"I have no way of knowing that I was the first."

"Bailiff, play the video again," Danial said. "This time pay special attention to the car that pulls into the parking lot before the explosions." Danial waited until the VW Bug drove into the parking lot and parked. "Stop the video right there."

Danial stepped away from the television and Lori handed him a photograph of what appeared to be an identical car. He walked over to the jury box.

"The car on the screen is a VW Bug." He held up the photograph. "This car is also a VW Bug. This photo was generated from the surveillance camera at the Steubenville Police Station and shows the car Ron Kester and Art Bently drove when they dropped off Baby Ammo. Looks identical doesn't it?"

Danial walked back over to the defense table and picked up yet another photograph of a VW Bug. Holding the photo above his head, he said, "This is a photograph of the car Norma Fitzpatrick was driving the morning of her arrest for the murder of Baby Ammo. All three cars look identical, don't they?"

The heads in the jury box nodded in agreement.

"Coincidence? I don't think so."

"What's that got to do with me?" Casey asked.

"Quite a bit. But we'll get to that. Lori, could you give me a hand here?"

Lori got up from behind the defense table. Danial handed her the two photographs; she held them above her head.

"Notice the left tail light on the Fitzpatrick car. Do you see how it's broken?"

The jury nodded.

"Now look at the photo from the police station and the video image from the hospital before the explosions. Those cars have tail lights that are intact. Since the car with the broken tail light doesn't match the other two, we can eliminate it off the top. Which means Norma Fitzpatrick had nothing to do with either case. Lori, why don't you drop that picture on the floor."

She did.

"Now, ladies and gentlemen, please take another look at the car in the hospital parking lot. Notice the insignia on the bumper, the logo of a rental car company. Now look again at the back of the car in the police station picture Lori is holding. Do you see an insignia or logo on the bumper?" The jury members shook their heads.

"You don't see one do you. That's because these two cars are different. However, that's not what the bombers wanted you to think. Isn't that right, Mr. Casey?"

"You're out of your mind, Solomon."

Danial turned to the jury. "Do you see what happened? Mr. Casey noted the make of the Baby Ammo car on the Tuesday evening news. And he decided to set up its driver or occupants as the bombers."

"I don't know what you're talking about."

"I have a few questions I'd like to ask you, Mr. Casey. Where were you on the night of October 3rd between the hours of 11 o'clock and midnight?"

Casey looked over at Schaeffer; he attempted to stand to object but DiAngello grabbed him by the shoulder and forced him back down. DiAngello leaned over and whispered in Schaeffer's ear: "Don't make me stop you from getting out of that chair again."

"Where were you, Mr. Casey?" Danial asked.

"I was at home watching TV."

"Was anyone with you?"

"No."

"Home alone, huh. That's convenient." Danial's eyebrows furrowed as he crossed his arms. "Do you know a man named James Barq?"

"Never heard of him."

"You don't know him? He knows you, and he has been arrested by the FBI."

"What?"

"I'm afraid so. He says you hired him."

"Really? Seriously?"

"Would it surprise you to learn he confessed to breaking into the Fort Henry Armory for explosives?"

Casey's eyes darted around the room.

"He also confessed to renting a blue VW Bug in Weirton on Tuesday evening at 5:56, and to driving you to the University Hospital parking lot between 11 o'clock and midnight."

"I don't know what you're talking about."

"He admitted to planting one of the bombs at the hospital. And you know what else he said? He said you planted the other bomb, then drove the Bug to Subway so you two could watch the fireworks."

Shouts and jeers filled the courtroom.

Williams beat the gavel against the bench. "Order!"

The courtroom came to order, and Danial continued his questions.

"Now we know why you cut 10 minutes from the surveillance video of the hospital parking lot. I know this may sound like a question from an old Perry Mason movie, but why did you do it? I'm sure an intelligent young man like you must have had a good reason for doing something so monumentally stupid. At least explain why Armory cameras show you picking at a hairbrush a week later."

Casey pressed his lips together tightly; his eyes darted around the room again.

"Come on. Here's your chance to explain yourself. We're on national television." Danial pointed at the cable and network news cameras in the back of the courtroom. "Don't you think you owe your dear family an explanation for your embarrassing idiocy?"

A wild look radiated from Casey's eyes. His gaze settled on Danial. "You want to know why I did it? I'll tell you why I did it.

Because I like to expose smug little hypocritical bigots like you. And admit it, Solomon, as soon as you heard that bombs went off at the hospital, you secretly felt elation, didn't you? You pro-life extremists are all the same. You all make me sick. Surely an intelligent man like you can understand a pro-choicer bombing an abortion clinic so pro-lifers take the blame."

Danial shook his head.

"Oh, come on now. I didn't invent this concept. Who do you think planted the bombs down in Atlanta?"

"I have no further questions, Your Honor," Danial said, "now that we know Ian was innocently studying bomb diagrams and clinic clippings to determine the perpetrators."

"Make no mistake about it, Solomon, we're in a culture war." A sinister expression draped Casey's face. "And in every war, there are casualties. What's the harm of collateral damage as long as the blame falls on someone else?"

Williams slammed the gavel. "I've heard enough. Bailiff, place Mr. Casey under arrest."

The bailiff approached the witness stand and seized Casey by the arm. Danial walked over and whispered in Casey's ear.

"Your buddy Barq is *very* talkative. We were worried that we would have to gag him to get him to stop talking. You're awfully talkative too, and I'd like to thank you for confessing on national television... under oath. I'll ask your judge to put you in prison for 20 years, like Archie."

Casey went berserk. He punched the bailiff and throttled Danial by the neck. The two men tumbled to the floor. Danial shoved against his chest. Casey released his grip. Three bailiffs pounced on him and wrestled him to the ground. They cuffed him and led him out.

When the courtroom came back to order, Schaeffer stood up and said, "Your Honor, in light of this truly bizarre soap opera, it's the State's contention to drop the charges against Ian McKinney, and I'm certain Mr. DiAngello will be dropping the charges against Norma Fitzpatrick as well. Isn't that right, Anthony?"

DiAngello stood up. "That's correct, Your Honor."

Williams pondered the announcement for a moment. "It is the will of this Court to accept the recommendations by the State, and I hereby decree all charges stemming from the bombing at University Hospital be dropped against Mr. McKinney. Court is adjourned." He struck the gavel then disappeared into his chambers.

The bailiff cleared the room. Anthony DiAngello walked over to the defense table carrying his briefcase. He stretched out his hand. Danial stood and shook it.

"Congratulations, Mr. Solomon."

"Thank you, sir."

"I have a proposition to offer you."

"What's that?"

"I'll dismiss your client's plea and all the charges related to the egg-throwing incident."

"In exchange for what?"

"You drop the police brutality lawsuit."

"Done deal," Ian said, "but ask them to lighten up."

"In that case," DiAngello said, "you're free to go."

"Right now?"

"Right now."

"Thank you, Mr. DiAngello, thanks Mr. Solomon." Ian slapped Danial on the back. "I'll call you later. I've got a lot to do." He jogged for the door. "I need a new cooler, but I'll never carry another egg!"

Danial stood and picked up his briefcase. Lori stood beside him. "If you'll excuse us, Mr. DiAngello. This has been a long day."

43

Steubenville is always a blur of excitement on election day. With the former coroner Gus Gram's seat open, both parties eagerly awaited the outcome of that race. And just before the polls opened, Judge Williams withdrew from the election. He cited health problems, but in reality, the FBI had given him a clear ultimatum: step down or be indicted along with Colin Casey for public corruption. The old judge chose to slip away quietly.

In the week following the Ian McKinney trial, Danial refused to take on any new cases. He and Lori decided to make the partnership official. They found a new suite of offices in the center of town, perhaps the first of Franks & Solomon law offices from Cleveland to London to Singapore.

Danial, Lori and Jennifer were busily packing boxes in preparation for the move when Eugene Stedman stopped by with a box of donuts. He coughed and assured them he was feeling better, picked up his paycheck, and went to buy another old truck.

Shortly after Stedman left, Norma Fitzpatrick stopped by to express her gratitude. Lori took Norma aside and said that the disgraced and divorced Carl Vance would be charged for the rape of a minor, and it was in her best interest to stay away from him. After much persuasion, Norma agreed to visit a Christian pastor to help her deal with everything she had been through over the past few months.

Then Danial's jaw dropped as he watched Ian McKinney park and step out of a battleship gray Rolls-Royce.

"My grandmother left it to me," Ian said. "The coal magnate's daughter."

"I see you weren't kidding," Danial replied.

"I stopped by to tell you about something that happened in jail. Can we speak privately?"

They sat down in Danial's office as Ian described meeting a bright-eyed happy inmate.

"He told me this rather entertaining story... 'A Christian lady goes to the grocery store carrying her Bible. A couple of teenage kids notice the Bible and start mocking her. One of them said, 'You don't believe in Noah's Ark, do you?' And she said, 'Yes I do. It's in the Bible, so I believe it.' The teenagers laughed. A little while later another kid put his two cents in and said, 'You don't believe that Jesus walked on water, do you?' Again, the lady replied, 'It's in the Bible, so I believe it.' The boys laughed and laughed.

'Just as the lady was about to check out, one of the boys said, 'Surely you don't believe in Jonah and the whale, do you?' With her faith undaunted, she answered again, 'It's in the Bible, so I believe it.' The boys laughed again, and one of them said, 'Why don't you explain to us how a man can live three days and three nights in a big fish without dying.' To which she replied, 'I don't know, but when I get to Heaven, I'll ask him.' The boy shot back with great amusement, 'What if Jonah's not in Heaven?' She paused for a moment, looked the boy in the eye and said, 'Well, if Jonah's not in Heaven, then you can ask him.'"

Ian added, "If Jonah's not in Heaven that would mean he was in Hell, and the lady was saying the boys would see him in Hell."

"What did you think of the story?" Danial asked.

"Well, it made me think. And I began reading the Bible. I learned about real repentance and biblical faith, and I'm here to tell you that I'm a new Christian."

Danial's jaw dropped again, and then he smiled. "I'm so happy for you, brother. Jesus said, 'If you abide in My word, you are My disciples indeed. And you shall know the truth, and the truth shall make you free.' Now you have true freedom. Welcome to the family."

Around noon Jennifer went to Pizza Hut to pick up some take-out for lunch. An unfamiliar black man walked into the outer office. Danial set down a box of *Federal Reporters* and shook the man's hand.

"I looking for Mr. Solomon."

"I'm Danial Solomon, but presently I'm not taking any new cases. As you can see, we're in the process of moving."

"Oh, I not lookin' for no lawyer. I just got out of the joint. I here to talk about Archie Kisner."

"What about Archie Kisner?"

"We've talked on the phone and I sent you a letter a couple weeks ago. It had no return address."

"Are you Mr. Dante?"

"Do you want to hear about Archie or not?"

"By all means," Danial said.

"I was there when Archie got killed."

"The warden told me the building was empty."

"That's cause, I didn't tell nobody. I was there. Believe me, I know what happens to guys who sees too much. Anyway, like I said, I was livin' in the same building as ole Archie. I used to look out for him. Well, the day he got killed, something really fishy happened. His cell door wouldn't open. And I says to myself, 'Sonny, these ole cell doors shouldn't be gettin' stuck for no reason.' So I skipped chow and stayed real quiet. A couple minutes later, here comes this guard with some kind of bucket in his hand. And in front of God Almighty he walks up as bold as you please to Archie's cell and douses him with it. He strikes a match and says somethin' about snitchin' on someone named Gam or somethin' and lights him up." Sonny shook his head. "It took everything I had to keep my peace."

"Gam," Danial said quietly. "Are you sure he said Gam?"

"I not exactly sure. But it sounded like Gam."

"Could it have been Gram?"

"That's it!" Dante clapped his hands. "It was Gram. Does that mean anything to you?"

"It certainly does," Danial looked over at Lori who bobbed her head.

He looked back at Sonny.

"Have you told anyone about this?"

"Are you kiddin'?"

"Are you willing to identify this killer and repeat what you just told me to the Ohio State Highway Patrol? They have jurisdiction over crimes in the state prisons. I can guarantee nothing will happen to you."

"Will that roller get arrested?"

"Most definitely."

"I'll do it."

Danial left the packing to Lori and drove Sonny Dante to the Ohio State Patrol post in Wintersville. Six hours after Sonny repeated his story to the chief investigation officer, the guard in question was walked out of the Akron Correctional Reception Center in handcuffs. He was trembling, and others were trembling too.

44

A damp cold permeated the air as Danial Solomon stepped out of his car in front of Lori's condo on Lovers Lane. His breath billowed in front of his face. He adjusted his maroon cashmere scarf to keep the cold off his neck. He strolled along the cobblestone path to Lori's front door. White lights twinkled and traced the outline of the elm trees in the front yard. He thought about how much fun they had putting those lights up. Then he recalled their wrestling matches in all those red leaves. He smiled as he thought about letting her win on occasion so she wouldn't quit.

He climbed the steps and rang the bell. Lori opened the door and threw her arms around his neck.

"Merry Christmas," she said.

"Don't you have any mistletoe around here?"

"We can pretend."

They kissed.

He helped her on with her coat, then hugged her from behind. They walked hand-in-hand toward his car as large fluffy snowflakes cascaded down around them.

"Looks like we'll have a white Christmas," he said.

"I hope so. I'm looking forward to hitting the slopes. Do you ski, Danial?"

"Never a day in my life."

"Oglebay Resort is 45 minutes away."

"I'm more the inner-tubing type."

"I'll teach you," she said.

He opened the door for her, then jogged around the front of

the car. He started the engine, and the voice of Nat King Cole singing "O Holy Night" fluttered from the speakers. As they drove along Route 7 toward Wheeling, the snowflakes glanced off the windshield, and they talked about the new office and the need to hire a paralegal or two or three.

They crossed the Ohio River into Wheeling and parked at the Capitol Theatre. Danial produced theatre box tickets to the Wheeling Symphony Orchestra's rendition of *The Nutcracker Suite;* the same seats as their first date. The concert was marvelous. The audience showed their gratitude with thunderous applause.

Following the concert, they drove down to the wharf and the Riverboat Restaurant. The old paddlewheeler had altered its Dixieland motif. Crushed-velvet maroon and green tablecloths adorned every table. A four-piece chamber group played sounds of the season. Huge pine wreaths lined the walls and offered a faint scent of Christmas trees. The maître d' escorted them to the same table they had on their first date.

"This is absolutely gorgeous," Lori said.

"They outdid themselves."

"This Christmas is the best one I've ever had, and it's not even here yet." She laid her hands on the table palms up. He held them. "And I have you to thank, Danial."

"So, you found out about the Liver of the Month Club membership I bought you?"

"Liver of the what? You serious?"

"No."

"Danial!"

"I'm just playing."

"I'm being serious. This is the first time the birth of Jesus actually means something to me."

"He *is* the reason for the season."

The waitress came over and took their orders. They both decided on the Lobster Bisque and veal cutlets. Danial ran his index finger around the rim of his water glass.

"What are you thinking about?" she asked.

"Archie popped into my head. You know, he doesn't even have a headstone, just a brick in the ground with his number on it."

"That's sad."

"I think I'll take a ride over to see him after the holidays."

"I'd like to go with you." She reached over and touched his arm. "One after another, we've seen a murder of innocents."

The waitress came over and dropped off a small basket of dinner rolls. "Dinner will be ready in about 20 minutes."

"Very good," Danial said with a nod.

Lori buttered a roll and handed it to him.

"Bread in a basket always reminds me of Jesus multiplying the loaves and feeding thousands of people. He is still doing miracles today, and we are living proof of His grace and love and guidance." Danial put his hand over his water glass and slid it in front of Lori. "Water always reminds me of the water of life, and of life with you."

She picked up the glass and saw a gold glimmer at the bottom. She used her spoon to fish out a 1 carat princess-cut diamond ring. When she looked up, Danial was kneeling beside her chair.

"Lori, I've looked around for ten years for that special woman God made to complete me. I began thinking that woman didn't exist... until I met you. I would rather die than live another day apart from you. Will you marry me?"

Her hands trembled as she reached down to wipe a tear from his eye. Her lips quivered. She nodded her head.

"Yes."

She flung her arms around his neck.

They embraced.

Lori pressed her cheek against his and whispered, "I thought you'd never ask."

He whispered back, "Let's take a honeymoon to Yellowstone Park, so you can see Erin and she can see her uncle."

The people in the surrounding tables burst into applause. Danial stood and slid the sparkling ring on her finger. She admired it in the candlelight.

"This time they really are clapping for us," she said with a loving smile.

Danial reached over, lifted her hand to his lips, and kissed it. "Every love story deserves applause."

THE END

Please Enjoy The Following Excerpt From:

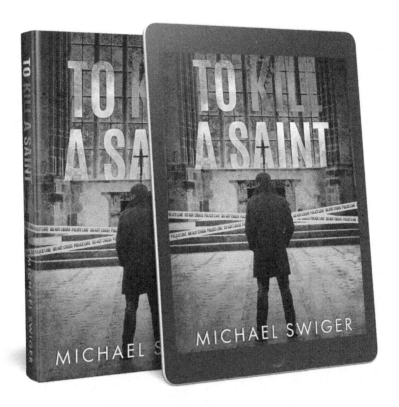

1

Saturday, October 14
Clifton Park, 6 miles west of Cleveland
Lakewood, Ohio
2:04 A.M.

Cuyahoga County Prosecutor, Peter Saul, fumbled for the phone on the nightstand beside his bed.

"Who is this?"

"April Denholm. Sorry to wake you, sir, but we've stumbled onto a pretty gruesome scene a few blocks from your house."

Peter Saul looked over at his sleeping wife, Marilyn, her red hair draped across her face. He spoke in a hushed whisper.

"What'd you find?"

"A women called the station a few hours ago to report a peeping Tom over at St. Andrew's Church. We didn't get here until a few minutes ago."

"Why the delay?"

"She's notorious for false alarms, so the local police didn't take her seriously."

"Go on."

"When the patrolmen arrived, the front door was open, so they walked in and found a corpse stabbed to death on the altar. It's pretty messy."

"Did you call Jimmy Graham?"

"He's already here snapping pictures."

"I'll be right over."

"There's more."

"What?"

"The pastor is all scratched up, and he isn't talking."

"I'll be there in ten minutes."

Saul hung up the phone then turned on the lamp on the nightstand. He slung his legs over the side of the bed and fished his feet around for his slippers. He shuffled over to the closet and pulled a pair of jeans over his pajama bottoms. He tugged on an Ohio State sweatshirt, a pair of wingtips, and grabbed his tan overcoat. He walked around the other side of the bed, leaned over, then kissed his wife on the cheek. She opened her eyes.

"What time is it?"

"It's very late."

"Where are you going?"

"They found someone murdered over at St. Andrew's."

"That's just down the street."

"Don't worry, everything is fine."

"Check on Jason before you go."

"I'm sure he's okay."

"Just look in on him."

"I will. Go back to sleep."

He kissed her on the forehead; she closed her eyes. He walked down the hall and noticed light reflecting on the hardwood floor under his stepson's bedroom door.

That kid will be the ruin of me.

He trudged down the arched stairway, across the great room with its vaulted ceiling, and into the attached garage. A few minutes later he parked his black BMW on the street outside St. Andrew's Church. Yellow police tape, strung from tree to tree, fluttered in the breeze and surrounded the white-sided building. The steeple's silhouette reached into the moonlit sky. Lights blazed through the windows. Saul walked up the uneven sidewalk and nodded to the uniformed patrolman standing near the front door.

Lieutenant April Denholm met him inside the vestibule, her bright blue eyes looking surprisingly alert for this time of the night. Wheat-gold ringlets dangled around her oval face and partially covered her milk-white neck and narrow shoulders.

"Give me the scoop," Saul said.

"The deceased is a blonde female approximately 25 years old.

No ID. She was stabbed repeatedly, dozens of times actually."

"Does the pastor know her?" Saul asked.

"If he does, he's not saying. You want to talk to him? We've got him in the office."

"Not yet, I want to look around first."

They walked down the center aisle; the sound of their shoes echoed through the cavernous room and mingled with the rapid clicking of a camera shutter. As they approached the sanctuary, a sickish-sweet scent of blood mingled with a tinge of sage permeated the air. The victim came into full view, tied to the altar. She lay with her arms and head hanging off one end of the altar, her blonde hair spilling back toward the floor. The pink blouse was ripped open and saturated with blood. Her bra was hiked up around her throat. Ample breasts were cut to ribbons. Punctures and slashes riddled a taut abdomen. White lace panties hung from her left ankle. Coagulated blood blanketed the stone altar, and puddled on the floor in an irregular, black pool. A gray skirt lay crumpled on the floor.

Jimmy Graham stopped snapping close-ups and turned toward Saul.

"Howdy, Pete. How's this for a little late-night excitement?"

"I could do without it, Jimmy. What's your take?"

"Well, it looks to me like one of the first blows must've hit a lung. You see how this fine mist of blood covers everything like red spray paint?"

"Uh huh."

"If you look close you can see it emanates from this one diagonal wound here to the right of her sternum, right here, between the ribs." He pointed with his finger. "Blood in the lung must've mixed with air and sprayed everywhere."

"You're a regular Sherlock Holmes," Denholm said.

"You got any better explanations?"

"Lose the attitude people," Saul said. "We all have a long night ahead of us. Jimmy, I want pictures of everything."

"I'm on it."

"Any sign of rape?"

"It's hard to tell."

"We'll probably have to wait on the autopsy for that one."

Saul turned toward Lt. Denholm. "What about this peeping Tom?"

"Detective Myles is talking to the neighbor right now."

"Good."

"We found some footprints near that window over there."

"What?" Saul's eyes flew open wide. "What are you talking about?"

"We found footprints."

"Why didn't you say so?"

"We found them since I called you."

Saul's forehead wrinkled. "Let's go have a look."

They walked toward the side door to the right of the sanctuary. A uniformed officer stood in the doorway, his crystal blue eyes blazing; he stepped aside. Around the side of the building, two lights mounted on tripods illuminated a large patch of ground.

"What did you find?" Saul asked.

"We've got a pretty good set of impressions," Lt. Denholm said. "They look fresh but a little indistinct."

"What do you mean, indistinct?"

"Whoever stood here didn't stand still, almost like he was dancing in place."

"Can you lift the impressions?"

"I'll be able to get a couple good casts. There may be more footprints around here. I'm keeping everyone off the grounds until daylight."

"Good, good."

"You think the perp staked out the scene before he went in and took care of his business?" Graham asked.

"Maybe."

"Or a lookout," Denholm said.

"Or maybe a witness." Saul patted her on the back. "Take your time, these prints are critical."

"Now do you want to see the good pastor?"

"Yeah, I guess it's time."

The group walked back around the church. Crickets chirped in the cool air.

"You know," Saul said, "it's been my experience that most homicides that get solved are done so within the first 48 hours."

"Why's that?" Denholm asked.

"Any witnesses who haven't stepped forward within the first couple days probably won't appear at all. And usually new clues don't surface after the initial investigation."

"That makes sense."

"So, we need to take our time and make these first hours count. The Chinese general Sun Tzu says, 'That which depends on me, I can do; that which depends on the enemy cannot be certain.'"

"That's interesting."

"What's this guy's name?"

"Jamison. Pastor Howard Jamison."

They walked back in the side door then crossed the front of the church. A uniformed officer tied a plastic bag over the victim's left hand. On the left-hand side of the sanctuary two uniformed officers stood with their backs against a door; they stepped aside. Saul and Denholm walked in and closed the door behind them. Off in the corner of the small, rectangular office sat a chubby, bloody, middle-aged man with his face buried in his hands. Thin hair lay plastered to his balding scalp by a layer of sweat, like strands of brown seaweed. He wore a light blue shirt with the sleeves rolled up to the elbows and a pair of pleated, tan Dockers.

"Pastor... Jamison," Saul said.

The man looked up. Three deep gouges ran from the center of his high forehead and down his left cheek. Dry, crusted blood ringed the nostrils of his beak-like nose. His puckered eyelids quivered as a pair of vacant gray eyes darted around the room.

"Pastor Jamison." Saul threw a leg over the edge of the desk and bumped a book – a Satanic Bible. "I need you to tell me what happened."

Jamison started to say something, checked himself, then dropped his head.

"What did you do?"

Silence.

"Pastor Jamison, it would really be helpful to tell us what happened here tonight."

No response.

"Do you know who that girl is?"

Jamison looked up; his face went white to the lips.

"Pastor, it's quite late," Saul said, his voice rising at each word. "And there's a dead girl in that room over there, on the altar for Christ's sake, and I want to know how she ended up with a chest full of holes."

Tears welled up in Jamison's eyes, brimmed over his lashes, then ran down his cheeks. His thin lips trembled; he spoke in a breaking voice.

"I'd like to talk to an attorney."

Saul didn't speak for a long moment, then a wolfish smile spread across his face.

"In that case, you have the right to remain silent..."

Don't Miss These Best Sellers By

MICHAEL SWIGER

In *A Trial of Innocents*, a pregnant woman is savagely beaten, leaving her unborn baby dead, and the would-be mother clinging to life in a coma. A special-needs man, who can't or won't talk, is arrested. The sensational crime draws national media to a quiet Ohio Valley community crying for vengeance.

Prosecuting Attorney Lori Franks, beautiful and ruthless, will stop at nothing to advance her career. Having sought an abortion years before, she now seeks the death penalty against a handicapped man accused of killing an unborn baby. When a chance meeting followed by a DNA test confirms her baby was rescued at birth, she sues to gain custody of the little girl she once tried to murder.

Defense attorney Danial Solomon is drawn into both cases. Sparks and attraction fly as he and Franks clash both inside and outside of the courtroom. Solomon's crusade for the truth catapults him headlong into a lethal labyrinth of conspiracy and corruption that could cost him his life.

This fast-paced, faith-based legal thriller races from the life-and-death decisions of the operating room to the tension-packed fireworks of a murder trial with the unique mix of intrigue and page-turning suspense that catapulted John Grisham to the bestseller list.

Racism. Romance. Revenge. In *Lethal Ambition*, a crusading congressional candidate, Marcus Blanchard, is framed for an election-night murder. Three powerful foes - his entrenched opponent, a drug lord, and a racist political boss – all want him dead. Accused of killing the woman ordered to kill him, Marcus turns to the only man he can trust.

Edward Mead, 77, still brilliant but struggling with the ravages of age, reluctantly takes the case. Clinging to the twilight of a once-distinguished career while nursing his wife of 52 years through Stage 4 breast cancer, Mead is thrust headlong into the gritty underbelly of the inner city. He collides with drug dealers and thugs, race riots and protests, and an all-pervasive political corruption that enslaves its citizens in poverty while sowing the seeds of division and hatred.

Ripped from today's headlines, this fast-paced murder mystery wrapped in a legal thriller grapples with the complicated urban issues and unrest in African American communities across the country. This book will leave you exhilarated and entertained, breathless and shaken, but most of all it will make you think.

In *Lethal Objection*, an arrogant and abusive Judge Samuel Chesterfield is murdered in his chambers during a sensational wrongful-death suit brought against a prominent abortionist. Only the four trial lawyers had access.

Edward Mead, a 77-year-old distinguished law professor, acts as special prosecutor. Still brilliant but struggling with the ravages of age and the recent death of his wife, Mead is thrust headlong into a lethal maelstrom of crime and corruption that threatens to submerge his mind and body, with the slightest misstep costing his life.

Special Agent Sarah Riehl sees the case as her one chance to shatter the glass ceiling that has suffocated her career at the FBI. Her impetuous drive to succeed recklessly propels her on a deadly gambit where the hunter becomes the prey.

This fast-paced legal thriller ripped from today's headlines combines the action and suspense of John Grisham with the classic twists and turns of an Agatha Christie locked room murder mystery.

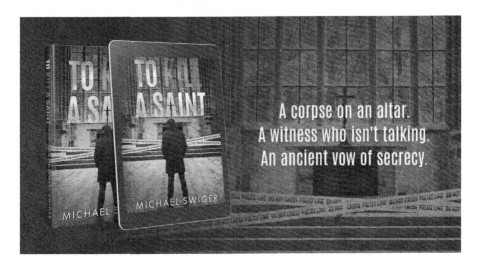

In the book *To Kill A Saint*, it's 2 a.m. when County Prosecutor Peter Saul arrives at the scene of a grisly murder at St. Andrew's Church in an affluent suburb of Cleveland, Ohio. Pastor Howard Jamison is covered with the victim's blood, and there's a Satanic Bible on his desk.

Attorney Hunter St. James has spent a lifetime fighting his father's disgraceful legacy. With his career in shambles and his socialite girlfriend pregnant, St. James is assigned a pro bono case he knows he can't win. His atheist beliefs have not prepared him for a Bible-believing client and a subsequent crusade for truth that hurls him headlong into the dark, supernatural world of the occult.

Psychologist Faith McGuire, recently divorced with a special-needs son, longs for a second chance at romance. A confluence of deadly events thrust her into the epicenter of this whirlwind thriller, threatening everything she loves.

The physical and spiritual worlds collide in this high-suspense thriller that pierces the veil of secret societies and conspiracy theories and will leave you struggling to put it down.

ACKNOWLEDGEMENT

A special thanks:

... to Dr. James Dobson, whose 20 years of influence on my life has profoundly impacted the contents of these pages;

... to my editor, proofreader and copy editor, Mike Jackoboice, whose penetrating insights and impeccable sensibilities have smoothed off some of the rougher edges of my prose, and whose tireless efforts, keen eye, and quest for perfection have resulted in a book that I am very proud of;

... to my son, James Edward, and my daughter, Audrey, for making my life complete;

... to my wife, Susan, whose sharp eye and keen mind are indispensable to everything I write; and

... to my Lord and Savior Jesus Christ, in whom I live and move and have my being.

Made in United States
North Haven, CT
23 June 2025

70063687R00163